Praise for

FOR HONOUR'S SAKE

"A vibrant picture of the war's major battles on land and at sea.... Highly recommended, *For Honour's Sake* is a must-read."

—*Esprit de Corps*

"Zuehlke presents a clear, thorough account of both the conflict and the peace negotiations that influenced and warped its outcome, and does so without bias. You couldn't ask for a clearer account of events."

—*The Vancouver Sun*

"An authoritative, convincing work."

—*The Globe and Mail*

"*For Honour's Sake* does more than fill in a gap in our collective memory; it uncomfortably foreshadows the wars of the twenty-first century . . . We're often chided for not knowing our own history, and it's too true. This book is a good place to start learning it."

—*Tyee Books*

"Zuehlke deftly wades through the complexity of early nineteenth-century politics, identifying key moments in history without excessive or convoluted details. . . . [His] extensive research will not only appeal to academics, but his readable style and the well-paced flow will also intrigue lay historians with an interest in early nineteenth-century Canada."

—*Winnipeg Free Press*

FOR HONOUR'S SAKE

THE **WAR** OF

1812

BROKERING

– OF AN –

U N E A S Y   P E A C E

MARK·ZUEHLKE

VINTAGE CANADA

VINTAGE CANADA EDITION, 2007

Published in Canada by Vintage Canada, a division of Random House of Canada Limited, Toronto, in 2007. Originally published in hardcover in Canada by Alfred A. Knopf Canada, a division of Random House of Canada Limited, Toronto, in 2006. Distributed by Random House of Canada Limited, Toronto.

Vintage Canada and colophon are registered trademarks of Random House of Canada Limited.

www.randomhouse.ca

Library and Archives Canada Cataloguing in Publication

Zuehlke, Mark
For honour's sake : the War of 1812 and the brokering of an uneasy peace /
Mark Zuehlke.

ISBN 978-0-676-97706-6

1. Canada—History—War of 1812. 2. United States—History—War of 1812.
3. Canada—History—War of 1812—Participation, Indian. 4. Canada—History—War of 1812—Peace. 5. Clay, Henry, 1777–1852. 6. Great Britain. Treaties, etc. United States, 1814 Dec. 24. 7. Tecumseh, 1768?–1813. I. Title.

FC442.Z83 2007   971.03'4   C2007-900758-9

Text design by Leah Springate
Printed and bound in the United States of America

2 4 6 8 9 7 5 3 1

CONTENTS

ACKNOWLEDGMENTS

———

Knopf Canada's Michael Schellenberg originally approached me with
the idea of a book about the War of 1812, spotlighting the negotiations in
Ghent. From the moment he proposed the idea, I started seeing the pos-
sibilities for a contemporary examination of a war that all sides claimed
to not want and, when it ended, all declared to have emerged from triumphant. There were so many parallels with events unfolding today on
the international scene. Consider this: a superpower grossly underesti-
mating an adversary whose motivations for fighting it seems impossible
to comprehend and whose ability to fight is dangerously underestimated.
A rising power that claims to be motivated in going to war to pursue one
just cause, but is bent simultaneously on prosecuting the war out of territorial ambitions. Caught between are two peoples—the Canadians,
who are only just beginning to define themselves in any way as a nation,
and North America's Indians, who are desperately trying to hang on to
their traditional homelands and preserve themselves from genocide.

I am distinctly grateful to Michael for asking me to write this book.
And working with him on it has been an enjoyable experience. In fact,
everyone at Knopf Canada has been excellent to work with. Among
these are managing editor Deirdre Molina and copyeditor Shaun Oakey.
The latter saved me from many sins of commission and omission in
the text. Executive publisher Louise Dennys was also an enthusiastic
supporter of this book, as was evidenced by her many questions and
reflections during a lovely lunch here in Victoria.

Much of the research for this book was conducted at Library and
Archives Canada in Ottawa and the staff there as always did their best
to smooth the way for the search through endless documents. I was

fortunate, too, that the University of Victoria's McPherson Library proved a treasure trove of historical documents, books, and articles on the War of 1812 and the American and British negotiators at Ghent.

I am fortunate to have Carolyn Swayze for my literary agent. Her tireless work enables me to concentrate on writing. C. Stuart Daniel, as always, did a fine job with the maps. Finally, and most important, I am blessed to have the companionship and support of Frances Backhouse, who has come to know more about the art and practice of war over the ages than she probably ever could have imagined possible.

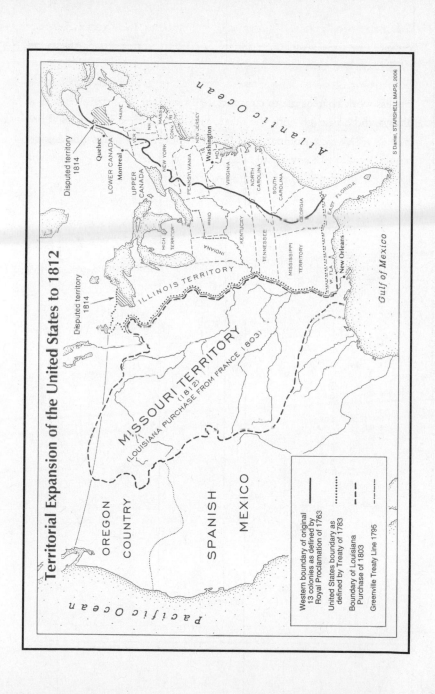

Territorial Expansion of the United States to 1812

S Daniel, STARSHELL MAPS, 2006

Pacific Ocean

Atlantic Ocean

Gulf of Mexico

OREGON COUNTRY

SPANISH MEXICO

MISSOURI TERRITORY
(1812)
(LOUISIANA PURCHASE FROM FRANCE 1803)

ILLINOIS TERRITORY

MICH. TERRITORY

INDIANA

Disputed territory 1814

Disputed territory 1814

LOWER CANADA
Montreal

UPPER CANADA

Quebec

MAINE

VER. N.H. MASS. CONN. R.I.

NEW YORK

NEW JERSEY

PENNSYLVANIA

Washington
MD. DEL.

VIRGINIA

OHIO

KENTUCKY

TENNESSEE

NORTH CAROLINA

SOUTH CAROLINA

GEORGIA

MISSISSIPPI TERRITORY

W. FLA. EAST FLORIDA

New Orleans

Western boundary of original 13 colonies as defined by Royal Proclamation of 1763

United States boundary as defined by Treaty of 1783

Boundary of Louisiana Purchase of 1803

Greenville Treaty Line 1795

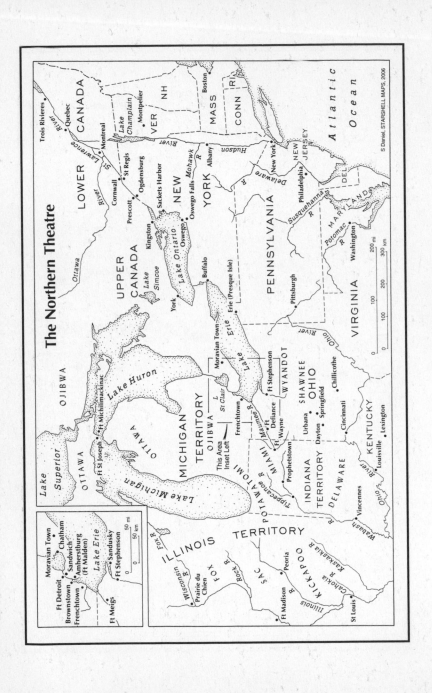

The Northern Theatre

S Daniel, STARSHELL MAPS, 2006

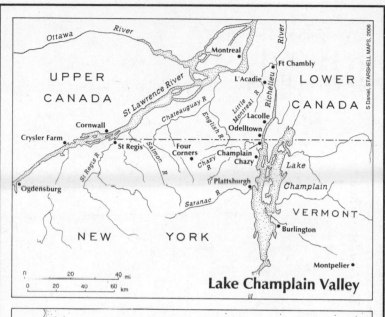

Lake Champlain Valley

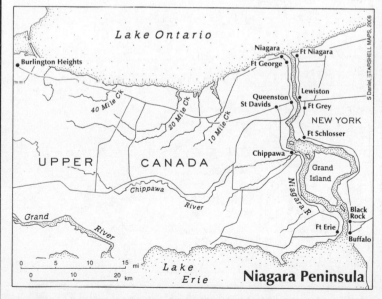

Niagara Peninsula

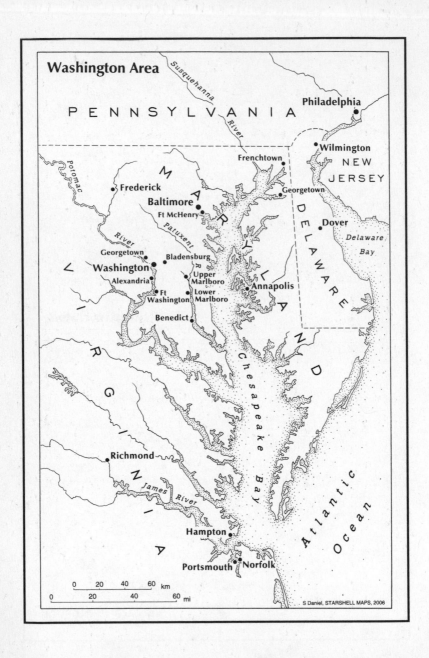

Washington Area

PENNSYLVANIA

Susquehanna River

Philadelphia

Frenchtown

Wilmington

NEW JERSEY

Georgetown

Potomac

Frederick

MARYLAND

Baltimore
Ft McHenry

Dover

Delaware Bay

River

Patuxent

DELAWARE

Georgetown

Bladensburg

Washington
Alexandria

Upper Marlboro

Ft Washington

Lower Marlboro

Annapolis

VIRGINIA

Benedict

Chesapeake Bay

Richmond

James River

Atlantic Ocean

Hampton

Portsmouth   Norfolk

0   20   40   60   km
0   20   40   60   mi

S Daniel, STARSHELL MAPS, 2006

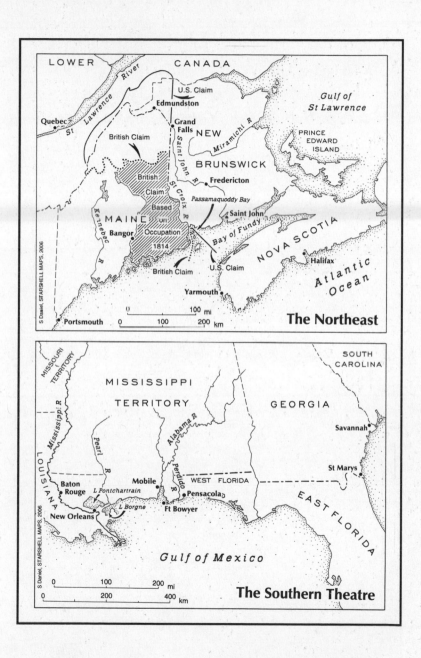

The Northeast

The Southern Theatre

―

To Meet with Frankness and Conciliation

*I*n August 1814, eight men travelled to the ancient Flemish city of Ghent to negotiate the end of a war being fought on a far-away continent. They numbered three Britons and five Americans, for these were the two belligerent nations. The conflict had started on June 18, 1812, when President James Madison signed a war proclamation against Great Britain. Two years later, neither side could claim that the war went well.

The British had never wanted this war. Early summer of 1812 had been a period of great crisis for the nation, and war with America only worsened matters. Since 1805 Britain had been locked in a titanic struggle of empires for mastery of Europe. So far it had been unable to stop France's Emperor Napoleon Bonaparte from turning most of the continent into his personal fiefdom. For the past four years Viscount Wellington's army had been engaged in a bloody campaign to prevent France's conquest of the entire Iberian Peninsula. In June of 1812, as the United States sent troops marching toward Canada, the British finally prevailed in Portugal. Pushing into the heart of Spain, they drove the French before them.

That, however, was about the only good news Lord Liverpool's government could savour, for France's setbacks could be attributed directly to Napoleon's failure to reinforce his Iberian army. While Wellington besieged one French bastion after another in Spain, Napoleon assembled the 530,000-strong Grande Armée, eyes turned east toward Russia. Once the French boot heel rested on Russia, the little Corsican would wheel about and send Wellington, a general he considered timidly cautious, reeling right off the continent. British spies had reported the existence of Napoleon's massive juggernaut and its purpose. Odds that Tsar Alexander's antiquated army could stave off the French were considered poor. If Russia fell, Britain would face Napoleon alone.

The grinding war had reduced Britain's economy to a shambles. Loss of European trade and the war's ever-escalating costs had plunged the nation into a depression and imposed severe food shortages. Starvation had threatened during the past winter, and there was unrest in the streets. Ireland remained a festering sore—conditions there were worse than elsewhere in the British Isles. The cost of sustaining Wellington's Peninsular Army placed enormous strain on the government's coffers. At the same time, the Admiralty was demanding more resources to ensure the world's largest fleet continued to master the seas that not only were so essential to retaining the empire but also served as Britain's lifeline for food and other vital imports.

On May 11, an added crisis had arisen when Prime Minister Spencer Perceval was assassinated. On June 8, a reluctant Lord Liverpool, then secretary for war and the colonies, accepted the Prince Regent's pleas to lead the government. The Prince had become de facto sovereign on February 5, 1811, when his father, King George III, was declared unfit to rule because of insanity. Faced with a glut of foreign and domestic crises and frantically trying to ensure a stable government to effectively deal with them, Liverpool had focused for the rest of the month on forming a workable cabinet. Most pressing were matters foreign, and to address these Liverpool decided not only to retain Viscount Castlereagh as foreign secretary but also to make him leader of the House of Commons, a position that Perceval had previously held. Believing it imperative that this wartime government have the support of the country and not just of the House of Commons, Liverpool announced that he would dissolve Parliament at the end of September and hold a general election. With all these events swirling about Liverpool and his cabinet, Britain's government needed nothing less in the summer of 1812 than another war, on the other side of the Atlantic. But they had also been so distracted by matters domestic and European that attempts to head off such a war were half-hearted and badly bungled.

Britain had defended British North America during that summer and fall with sufficient zeal to thwart America's attempts at conquest. Somewhat to the surprise of British colonial officials there and to the consternation of the Americans, almost all Canadians remained loyal to the Crown. In both Upper and Lower Canada the militia stepped forward to strengthen the thin ranks of the British redcoats. Local knowledge of battlegrounds and the ability of these farmers, fur traders, small businessmen, and shopkeepers turned soldiers to wage irregular war gave the defenders of British North America a much-needed edge over the numerically superior American forces.

The Americans had assumed that the colonists would welcome the chance to throw off the British yoke—particularly the French-Canadian majority in Lower Canada, themselves conquered by Britain less than forty-five years previously. In Upper Canada they had thought the many recent immigrants from the United States would welcome the opportunity to raise the American flag over their new homeland. But neither French Canadians nor American immigrants had heeded their calls to rise against the British. That refusal ultimately doomed all the attempted invasions.

Not only Canadian loyalty to the Crown dashed the American dream of an easy conquest of British North America. Most Indian nations, too, cast their lot in with Britain. Led by the charismatic warrior chief Tecumseh, the leaders of the powerful Indian confederacy on the western frontiers believed the best way to preserve their nations, their lands, and their way of life from the avarice of American settlers determined to expand the boundaries of the United States ever westward was through military alliance with Britain.

By the summer of 1814, the darkest days of the North American war appeared to have passed for British North America. Although supremacy on the Great Lakes had been forfeited, Britain's armies in Canada had moved from defence to the offence—taking the war for the first time in strength onto American soil. Along the U.S. coastline, amphibious forces carried out major landings, and the naval blockade of the ports had crippled America's economy.

Heartening as this news was, it paled when compared to the great events unfolding in Europe. On April 11, Napoleon had abdicated and accepted exile to Elba. This after Paris surrendered on March 31, following a string of decisive battles that crushed the French army and delivered a vast Allied army before the city's gates. With an armistice in Europe, the large British army serving there was freed for deployment to North America. By early summer, about ten thousand reinforcements—a flood compared with the paltry trickles of earlier years—had sailed from Europe to North America. It was the influx of these troops that made it possible for Britain to seize the initiative. But even as these reinforcements had disembarked in Halifax, Britain's government was loath to continue what clearly promised to be a long, harsh campaign to defeat the United States. Lord Liverpool and his cabinet were as weary of war as were His Majesty's lesser subjects. And although the European war was at an end, the pressing business of dividing the spoils amongst the victors remained. Empires and nations had to be reformed or created on the spot to fill power vacuums left by the French dismemberment of the old order; new boundaries needed to be drawn. Measures also had to be taken to permanently hobble France. This was the task that required the full attention of Liverpool and Castlereagh.

In Vienna, the European statesmen were gathering for the congress that would settle these matters and impose the terms of surrender on France. The continuing conflict in North America was but an unfortunate distraction, a pointless war fought over issues rendered moot by the developments in Europe—accepting, of course, that the causes America claimed had driven it to arms had ever been genuine and not mere pretexts to mask less honourable ambitions. Whatever might be the truth on that front, a negotiated peace that concluded the war quickly was desired. So long, that is, as the terms of the treaty guaranteed the security of Canada and the frontier Indians against future American aggression.

With this intent in mind, a long process of invitation and discussion finally resulted in three British commissioners proceeding across the English Channel to Ghent. They were His Lordship Vice-Admiral James Gambier, Undersecretary to the Secretary for War and the Colonies Henry Goulburn, and William Adams, a lawyer expert in maritime and naval law. In their diplomatic pouch they carried extensive instructions as to the treaty terms to be proposed to their American counterparts that strictly limited their ability to make independent decisions.

For their part, the American commissioners had trickled into Ghent by ones and twos and by various circuitous routes of travel, for they came not only from the United States but also from Russia and other parts of Europe. They were U.S. Minister to Russia John Quincy Adams; Albert Gallatin, who until recently had been Madison's secretary of the treasury; Speaker of the House of Representatives and Kentucky Republican Henry Clay; Federalist senator from Delaware James Asheton Bayard; and Jonathan Russell, the former chargé d'affaires in London and newly appointed U.S. minister to Sweden. Although these men fancied themselves as tethered to a longer leash than their British counterparts and consequently able to negotiate more independently, their instructions were as extensive and precisely stated as the British briefs. The Americans were to arrange an amity that retained American honour and required no surrender of either land or the right to continued expansion without threat of interference from Great Britain. In effect, the American government sought a treaty that returned North America to the status quo that had existed before 1812 and would accept no penalty for its resort to arms.

Each side distrusted the other. The British suspected that the American government was insincere and would treat for peace only if it could win by diplomacy what it had failed to gain through war. Among the Americans there was lurking suspicion that Britain sought to impose terms that would unravel the Union and re-establish dominance of king and crown over North America. Both believed that they were the aggrieved party, the one forced into this war by the other.

A major problem that the commissioners had to resolve was the actual manner of negotiation. Little precedent existed in European diplomacy to end a war where neither combatant had vanquished the other or was on the verge of inevitably doing so. Nor were the belligerents prepared to declare an armistice until the negotiations either failed or culminated in an acceptable treaty. While the commissioners talked, blood would continue to flow in North America. This fact added urgency to matters, but also rendered the discussions more uncertain.

It was entirely possible that battles yet to be fought could decide the war before the commissioners reached acceptable terms.

Normally European treaties were negotiated—often with mediation provided by a neutral third-party nation—merely to determine the penalties an already defeated nation must accept to end hostilities. A province or two would be carved away as spoils to the victor, indemnities paid for the costs of prosecuting the war. Surrender of a colony might assuage the thirst of the winner for further gain, and the exile of a ruler sometimes made way for a more acceptable sovereign. Neither the British nor the American commissioners were coming to the other with cap in hand, so they would have to steer a course through largely uncharted diplomatic waters.

For all these reasons, and despite a fervent desire by both the United States and Great Britain to bring this unpopular war to an end, their commissioners arrived in Ghent little expecting success. Yet the prospect of failure dismayed them and proved a source of great anxiety for both themselves and their respective governments. Should the negotiations fail, the war would surely drag on for years, its eventual outcome impossible to predict.

Castlereagh, in a letter given to the British commissioners close to their departure from London, urged them "to assure the American commissioners that the British Government, whatever sense it may entertain of the causes of the rupture, is sincerely desirous of a permanent adjustment of all differences, and that this desire is not abated by the successful termination of the war in Europe; and that, with this view, you are authorized to meet with frankness and conciliation whatever propositions the American negotiators may be prepared to offer, for terminating the war which has been declared by their Government."[1]

The American government was less inclined to have its commissioners extend olive branches. Meeting with President Madison in his office in early August, Secretary of State James Monroe insisted that the British must accept certain conditions or there would be no peace. The room was like an oven, both men sweating heavily in the humid Washington heat. Were it not for the direness of the war and the urgent need for a negotiated peace, neither man would have still been in the capital. Instead they would have sought the refuge of their respective Virginian country estates, and the business of government would have languished until the cooler fall temperatures rendered the city again habitable. Monroe's desire to end the war almost matched that of his master, but he counselled a firm stance. Ultimately, no matter the just causes that had driven them to the declaration, the war was of America's making. To come away at the end with nothing gained would spell political ruin for both men, be disastrous for the Republican Party, and dishonour the nation. There was no reason, Monroe insisted, that although America could not prevail on the battlefield it could not win an honourable peace through negotiation. The dream of annexing British North America might even still be achieved if the British could be persuaded that it was in their ultimate interest to be rid of this costly-to-maintain colony. Madison thought Monroe's optimism misplaced, but he recognized how an honourable peace—one that yielded America a secure base for future westward expansion—was essential. The five men in Ghent must win this.

Accordingly, on August 11, Monroe penned detailed instructions to the negotiators. "If Great Britain, does not terminate the war on the conditions you are authorized to adopt," the war must continue. "The conflict may be severe, but it will be borne with firmness, and as we confidently believe, be attended with success." After setting out several minor compromises that he was willing to offer the British, Monroe declared: "This government can go no farther, because it will make no sacrifice of the rights or honour of the nation."[2]

Part One

—

CLAY'S WAR

ONE

A Republican of the First Fire

NOVEMBER 1811

*A*mong the commissioners gathered in Ghent that August of 1814 was a man who, more than any other, could claim responsibility for leading America into war. Had Henry Clay not been elected to the Twelfth Congress of the House of Representatives, there were many who believed that its 142 members would have failed to muster the collective resolve to pass the war bill. And had Clay not been there to privately stiffen the president's backbone, Madison might not have affixed his signature to it.

On the day America went to war, Clay was just thirty-five, yet he was undeniably the nation's most powerful congressman. When the House went into session on November 4, 1811, the young Kentuckian was immediately elected as its Speaker in a two-to-one first-ballot vote. Selection of a speaker on the first day was unprecedented.[1] It was not unusual for a month or more to pass between various factions advancing their preferred candidates and the election. The interim was a time of long speeches by supporters who extolled a candidate's virtues and talents while detractors responded with equally lengthy bouts of rhetoric, redolent of politely veiled criticism, that chipped blocks out from under the candidate's feet. In stuffy, overheated rooms powerful men gathered for dinners, drinks, cigars, and hands of cards. It was here that negotiations were conducted, deals made. Outstanding debts were called in, new credits extended.

This time there had been none of that, which was surprising on the surface, for the Twelfth Congress marked Clay's House debut. But Clay was no political neophyte. At the age of twenty-six, just six years after arriving in Kentucky from Virginia to practise law, he had thrown himself onto that state's brawling political stage. In 1803, after demonstrating both masterful oration and, on at least one occasion, keen marksmanship with a long Kentucky rifle, he was elected to the state legislature.[2]

Although the son of a Baptist minister, he was neither conservative nor outwardly religious. He loved cards, drinking, and women equally, and the latter usually considered him both attractive and blessed with a fine wit. The fifth of nine children, Clay was only four when his father died. Young Henry's formal education consisted of three years in Hanover's one-room school, which stood near the courthouse in front of which local orators gathered on the green to hold forth on local and national politics. Early on the boy developed a passion for what was commonly referred to as declamation. At best an indifferent student, he proved a keen reader, eagerly reciting the text aloud to hone his public-speaking skills.

That Clay might have a future in the law and even politics was recognized early by his stepfather, who introduced the lad to Hanover's Virginia Assembly delegate, Col. Thomas Tinsley. Suitably impressed, the politician persuaded his brother, Peter Tinsley, the clerk of the Virginia High Court of the Chancery, in Richmond, to accept Clay as an assistant. Clay was now fourteen, and his parents, infected by western fever, had sold up and headed for Kentucky.

The adolescent Clay demonstrated a shrewd aptitude for gaining the patronage of powerful men. Besides Thomas and Peter Tinsley, Chancellor George Wythe and Virginia's attorney general, Robert Brooke, both took him under wing and advanced the lad along a course that concluded with his being called to the Virginia bar at age twenty.

But Clay never practised in that state. Instead, he saddled up and rode to the new frontier in Kentucky. As a boy, Clay had been lean and gangly, with overly long arms. Now, he was roughly handsome, with tousled hair so blond it was almost white and blue eyes that could, by turns of light, appear either pale and grey or as vividly blue as a robin's egg. He stood six feet tall, and across his wide, craggy face emotions were always writ large. Some described his face as "a compromise put together by a committee," particularly because of the width of his mouth, which others claimed gave him unfair advantage in that he could "completely . . . rest one side of it while the other was on active duty."[3]

A dandy, Clay took great care about his appearance and dress. His linen cravat was always carefully knotted, cloth breeches fashionably cut, yellow-top boots polished to a shine, high-collared, eagle-buttoned blue cutaway coat freshly brushed.[4] On March 20, 1798, he was appointed to Lexington's bar and within a few months established his social position by marrying Lucretia Hart, daughter of a wealthy Lexington business-man. While the marriage was opportune, he was by all accounts devoted.

Clay pursued a legal career out of financial necessity, but politics was his passion. The local press soon acclaimed his Lexington Green speeches. He declaimed for abolition of slavery and carved out his ground as a Radical Republican. Clay criticized President John Adams for treading on state and individual rights, for pandering to Britain, and for seeking to build a standing army when everyone knew militias were all the defence America needed. He praised revolutionary France and, when Napoleon gained power, lauded him as well for taking on the tyrant King George III and the aristocratic hegemony of Britain's government.

In 1803 he was elected to the state legislature, and three years later the Kentucky legislature sent him to serve out the remaining year of the term of a federal senator who had resigned. Despite being four months younger than the thirty years required by the Constitution for holding such a seat, Clay was sworn in on December 29.[5] Although most of the other thirty-three statesmen representing the Union's seventeen states were so-called Fathers of the Revolution, Clay showed them no deference. He quickly shifted focus from the parochial matters of Kentucky to those of national interest, even as he was disenchanted to find that the Senate was a forum where "solemn stillness" rather than energetic debate reigned.[6]

Outwardly the Senate itself was a rather grand place, with a semi-circular chamber elegantly appointed with lush carpeted floors, scarlet leather-cushioned chairs for the senators' backsides, various wall maps to help them locate places that arose in debates, and a small portrait of George Washington dwarfed by the full-length portraits of Marie Antoinette and Louis XVI that inexplicably dominated the room. However, the Senate roof leaked, so the place had about it a lingering cellar-like dampness. With a high, rotting ceiling overhead and equally deteriorating walls directly behind the senators, some displayed a "state of fear & uneasiness, least the wall, which is thick & high, should fall on them & either maim or kill them."[7]

Clay waded into what passed for debate with a vigour quickly noted by his fellow senators. Most of the older members were nonplussed that this youth, "in the plenitude of puppyism," as Connecticut's venerable Uriah Tracy mockingly depicted him during one of many debates where the two men crossed swords, dared show such temerity in their august midst. A few were quietly impressed.

Clay, the upstart young Republican, was soon debating in a more congenial manner than in his duels with Tracy with James Asheton Bayard, the distinguished Federalist senator from Delaware who would eventually become the Kentuckian's fellow negotiator in Ghent. Politically the two men were diametrically opposed, particularly with regard to relations between America and Great Britain. Whereas Clay proposed war at the first offence, the Delaware senator preferred to turn the other cheek while simultaneously seeking a negotiated accommodation. But for all their political differences, Clay and Bayard had similar backgrounds. Both had lost their fathers at the age of four, both were lawyers by training and fiercely political by inclination, both were tall and handsome. Had it not been for their divergent political views, they might have been friends. Instead, they treated each other with respect.

Born on July 28, 1767, and raised in the privileged family of an uncle, Bayard had graduated from Princeton in 1784. Four years later he was admitted to the bar, briefly practising in Philadelphia before establishing a practice in Wilmington, Delaware. On February 11, 1795, Bayard married Ann Basset, the daughter of the state's chief justice. Two years later he was elected to the House of Representatives and held a seat there until March 1803. In January 1805 he took a seat in the U.S. Senate.[8]

By the time of his Senate appointment Bayard was undisputed leader of the southern Federalists, who trod a more conservative path than their New England counterparts. Bayard was a moderate, always willing to work toward compromise to ensure a stable federal government. One observer described his attitude as that "of a man who, believing his own party to be possessed of superior political wisdom, is nevertheless willing to do whatever lies in his power for the country as a whole, even though it must be done through the opposing party."[9] Where many congressmen and senators were notoriously partisan, susceptible to influence and outright graft, Bayard was rigorously ethical and moral.

Not that Bayard was a man of pure reason and little passion. On May 5, 1800, a heated debate on the Senate floor erupted between Bayard and Christopher Champlin, the representative for Rhode Island, when the latter moved to redraft a bill setting commissions paid to port collectors so that the percentages allowed collectors in Wilmington and New London could be reduced. Bayard saw the move as a personal swipe at those particular port collectors—the one in Wilmington was a friend. Two days after the exchange, the two senators met in Philadelphia to settle the matter with pistols. It was a grim day, raining heavily, so the duel occurred in an abandoned shed next to a stone bridge. Champlin and Bayard paced off the agreed distance, turned and fired. Bayard's ball ripped open Champlin's cheek while his opponent's struck his thigh.

Duelling being illegal in Pennsylvania, both men and their seconds were forced to flee the state's jurisdiction or face charges. Bayard wrote his cousin, Andrew Bayard, a couple of weeks later to say that the "escape I made from the city was quite lucky, but I do not like the idea of perpetual banishment which the affair is likely to occasion." He asked the cousin to enquire of the state governor whether it would be possible for him to grant everyone involved clemency from prosecution.[10]

Perhaps this incident served even more to incline Bayard toward caution, for by the time Clay took his seat in the Senate his debating style was noted as the exact opposite of the young senator's. New Hampshire Federalist William Plumer considered Clay more emotional and enthusiastic while Bayard's style was that of the "precise reasoner."[11]

Clay's first foray into Washington politics was short; the senatorial term he filled expired after just one session.

Back in Kentucky, Clay was re-elected to its legislature and appointed Speaker. Rather than adhering to tradition by confining himself to maintaining order and ensuring that legislative procedure was upheld,

Clay never hesitated to step down from the chair in order to wade into the midst of debates—a practice he would continue as Speaker of the House of Representatives. During one such foray, an observer wrote that "every muscle of [Clay's] face was in motion; his whole body seemed agitated, as if every part were instinct with a separate life; and his small, white hand, with its blue veins apparently distended, almost to bursting, moved gracefully, but with all the energy of rapid and vehement gesture. The appearance of the speaker seemed that of a pure intellect, wrought up to its mightiest energies, and brightly glowing through the thin and transparent veil of flesh that enrobed it."[12]

In December 1808, Clay brought before the legislature a series of resolutions intended to support President Thomas Jefferson's responses to maritime measures taken by Great Britain to bar America and other neutral nations from conducting trade with France. Under these measures the Royal Navy had been authorized by House of Commons orders-in-council to seize neutral merchant ships apprehended while attempting to enter any French Empire port. Increasingly outraged by Britain's apparent disregard for America's sovereignty, Clay sought legislative approval of Jefferson's embargo, whereby the United States would voluntarily cease conducting any trade with either Britain or France. He also called upon it to condemn Britain's orders-in-council and to pledge that Kentucky would back the U.S. government in any measure considered necessary to uphold its rights.

Humphrey Marshall was the only legislator to oppose the resolutions. On January 4, 1809, the two locked in a heated verbal joust that ended with Marshall calling Clay a liar. A fistfight would have ensued had others not intervened to restrain the two. When Clay calmed down, he apologized to the House and then poured more coals on the fire by stating he would never have resorted to blows if Marshall had been a man of honour. Marshall snapped back that Clay's apology was that of "a poltroon!" He then issued a challenge, accepted by Clay in a formal note that same evening.[13]

On the early morning of January 19, the two men, their seconds, and appointed surgeons gathered on a meadow covered in frost-hardened Kentucky bluegrass next to the Ohio River near Louisville. Clay and

Marshall faced each other from a distance of ten paces with pistols hanging down by their sides. One of the seconds called out, "Attention! Fire!" Two pistols cracked, and Marshall was staggered when Clay's ball grazed his stomach. Both took aim again, but Clay's pistol failed to fire and Marshall missed again. Marshall reloaded more quickly and snapped off a slug that tore a gash out of Clay's thigh. Unbalanced as he was by the ball's impact, Clay's third round went wild. Although Clay demanded that the duel continue, the seconds hastily announced that his wound meant that the men now fought an unequal contest and that honour had been served.[14]

The duel only furthered Clay's reputation throughout Kentucky, so it was hardly a surprise when he was once again selected to serve out the term of a federal senator upon completion of his sixth term in the state's legislature. Clay rode toward Washington in January 1810 preoccupied with one overriding concern. The time had come, he believed, when the United States must make war on Great Britain.

When Clay's tired mount plodded up the muddy streets, past the many half-built houses that had stood abandoned since the collapse of Washington's building boom three years previous, there was little about the capital to inspire a man into believing this was the seat of power of a nation capable of challenging one or both of the world's most powerful empires. Although still growing rapidly, Washington's population was just 5,650. Large stretches of farmland and small woods separated tiny clusters of buildings. The capital of the United States was no more akin to London, the world's most populous and powerful commercial centre, or Paris in all its elegant opulence than was America's economy a challenge to that of Britain and France. Except in its slightly larger size and the presence of a handful of modest government buildings, Washington more closely resembled Clay's Lexington than the great European cities.

This was true for all of America's burgeoning cities. Boston, Baltimore, and Philadelphia were older and larger than Washington and presented a more orderly form, with cobblestone streets running between rows of stone and brick buildings. But Boston and Philadelphia were suffering decline brought on by harbours clogged with silt and a resultant loss of commerce to the new shipping capital of New York City. With its deep harbour surrounding three sides of Manhattan Island, this was the new boomtown where the real estate speculators, shipping magnates, trading houses, and financial firms concentrated.

But in 1810 even New York City was only just beginning a process of growth that would in the near future transform it from village to large city. Together, the four most populous American cities—Boston, New York, Philadelphia, and Baltimore—claimed no more than a combined population of 175,000 out of a national population of 5.3 million. Two million white males in the land were enfranchised, and 85 percent of these were farmers. The United States was an agrarian nation. Its economy was almost entirely dependent on, in the words of President Jefferson, what its "yeoman farmers" produced. These farmers, Jefferson had declared, were the backbone of the nation, and it was to them that the Republican Party pandered.[15]

That suited Clay, for he was a man of the new west, where most men held modest land holdings. They tilled fields with ploughs either dragged by a mule or propelled forward by nothing but the brute strength of a man's shoulders and back. Food was what could be raised or grown. Wives spun the family's clothing from cotton or wool either produced on the farm or bartered for, and it was easy to place a man's social position by whether he wore homespun or imported British broadcloth. Cash was of little importance to such men, for during an entire lifetime of toil few would ever see a hundred dollars pass through their hands.[16] In recent years, as anti-British sentiment rose to fever pitch in Kentucky, a wise politician like Clay had stored most of his broadcloth fineries and donned the rough homespun of his neighbours. But that would not do in Washington. His luggage contained the clothes that had given him the reputation of a dandy in earlier years.

Clay rode into a Washington in turmoil. Jefferson was gone, President James Madison just eleven months into his term after taking the oath of office on March 4, 1809. The government was in crisis, beset by how to respond with any effect to what many Americans called the British outrages. Clearly Jefferson's embargo, brought into effect on

December 22, 1807, was a failure. Described as "a self-blockade of the purest water," the Embargo Act had prohibited departure of all vessels, American or foreign, from U.S. harbours for any foreign port. Stranded foreign ships could leave American waters only in ballast and with empty holds. This exception had been added to the act at the insistence of the always pragmatic secretary of the treasury, Albert Gallatin, who feared that holding the few non-American ships would encourage other countries—particularly Britain and France—to retaliate in kind.[17]

Although the embargo was the brainchild of Jefferson and then Secretary of State Madison, enforcing the act had fallen on Gallatin's shoulders. By cutting Europe and European colonies off from the vast quantities of agricultural products they imported from America, Jefferson believed France and Britain could be brought to their knees without recourse to war. Madison asserted that "the power of this great weapon, the embargo," would force the two countries to negotiate terms that would end the trade restrictions that had wreaked havoc on America's maritime trade.[18]

The fact that the two European powers had imposed the restrictions in order to wage economic war on each other rather than to harm the United States offered cold comfort to America's government and maritime traders. Although Britain had fired the first volley, it was Napoleon's retaliatory response that collaterally struck American shipping. On May 16, 1806, the House of Commons enacted its first order-in-council that proclaimed the coast of continental Europe from the Elbe River to Brest under a state of blockade. While this effectively closed all French ports, it did not curtail America's ability to trade with Europe, as all Iberian, Mediterranean, and Baltic ports remained open to shipping. Although inconvenienced, it was still possible for France to receive American imports through these routes.

France had not been quiescent before the blockade. Ever since 1793, the French had done their best to keep British goods out of the areas of Europe they controlled. During the Republic, the French Republic Directory had seized any ship known to have put into a British port and then sailed into French waters. The French Republic Directory believed it possible to defeat Britain—so reliant on trade for its survival—by cutting off its exports, thereby forcing a reduction in its gold stock and ultimately bankrupting the government. Soon after Napoleon seized power, he introduced the continental system, whereby Britain was to be barred from any commercial activity with the rest of Europe and ultimately isolated from any world trade outside its own colonies. With his naval power greatly limited after the destruction of most of France's naval fleet at Trafalgar, Napoleon sought to conquer the oceans that he could not control through a war fought on European soil. The defeat of Prussia in the Battle of Jena gave him possession of much of the Baltic coast and provided the opportunity to put his economic strategy into force. On November 21, 1806, Napoleon's Berlin Decree imposed a blockade on the British Isles; any ships coming into French ports from either Britain or its colonies would be seized. Russia, demoralized by the defeat of the Prussians, agreed to adhere to the decree, and when Spain and Portugal fell to France in 1808 virtually all European ports were slammed shut to British ships and those from neutral nations that had entered her ports.

The British retaliated with another order-in-council, on January 7, 1807, forbidding ships from carrying out coastwise trade with France or her allies or from entering ports closed to her. Napoleon struck back with the Fontainebleau and Milan decrees of the same year that declared that any neutral ships conforming to the British orders-in-council would be subject to seizure. Britain's final retort came on November 11, 1807, with a proclamation that all French ports and those of her allies, and of all countries closed to British trade, were now blockaded. Further, all trade in goods from blockaded countries was forbidden, and any ships carrying such goods would be subject to capture and condemnation of both goods and ships. Any ship carrying a certificate of origin issued by France could also be taken by the Royal Navy as a prize. In an attempt to offset the economic losses sure to result from its inability to trade with Europe, the British government also declared that neutral ships entering its ports were to be considered under its direction and must purchase licences. This, it was hoped, would provide funds for the hard-pressed treasury.[19]

For Britain, the effect of the French measures was significant. In 1807, almost 44 percent of trade passing through British ports was aboard neutral ships, and many decided not to risk Napoleon's wrath or lose all possibility of trade with continental Europe—including Russia—in order to have access to British ports and markets. Able to trade with only a few nearby countries, such as Sweden (until it fell within France's sphere of influence in 1811), Britain's exports fell by 10 percent within the year.

The American Embargo Act was more devastating. No sooner had it come into effect than nationwide shortages of timber, grain, and cotton caused inflation. Before the embargo the United States exported about 46 million pounds of cotton per year, with 80 percent of that going to Britain. The embargo slashed that source of cotton to nothing, and alternative markets for supply had yet to be developed. Across the country textile mills were forced to cut back or shut down, causing a surge of unemployment, which was only slowly alleviated by increasing cotton imports from Brazil.[20] Meanwhile, the Royal Navy was hard hit by the timber shortage, as it was virtually dependent on Scandinavian and North American lumber and spars for shipbuilding.

The embargo also sharply reduced British exports because America had become one of its primary trade partners. In 1806 more than half of cotton and wool products—$41 million worth—had been shipped to the United States. Almost a quarter of all British exports were to America. Loss of this market threatened the country with an economic depression.[21]

France also faced shortages because of the embargo, particularly of tobacco and cotton, but with all Europe under its heel and Russia opting for continental trade rather than backing Britain—its traditional ally—imports and exports remained relatively strong. And with each passing month Napoleon added more territory to the empire's reach. That Napoleon's continental system might prove a viable economic strategy seemed increasingly likely.

Although Napoleon's decrees equally threatened U.S. trade and freedom of the seas, politicians, the newspapers, and most Americans railed against Britain's orders-in-council and seldom seemed aware of the French role. Many was the Republican, particularly those from the new western states, who believed against all logic that the emperor somehow still embodied the revolutionary spirit of France and was the "agent chosen to spread its great benefits and reforms to Europe's oppressed peoples." Among these true believers was Henry Clay, who thought

Napoleon a healthy foil to Britain and "rejoiced at the continued blows he struck" at the Crown.[22]

Not all Americans held Bonaparte in such regard. Jefferson considered him a tyrant who had hijacked a revolution that had promised to sow liberty in Europe. But even the best-informed Republican thought a war between France and Britain would be advantageous to the United States. Like most Republicans, Jefferson and Madison believed that, were it not for the European war that absorbed Britain's attention and military might, the Union would be in jeopardy. While not wanting to see France conquer Britain, Jefferson would happily see her humbled at Napoleon's hands. Federalists, on the other hand, generally looked fondly on Britain, thinking her the "world's last hope" and fearing that if France prevailed then it would not be long before America was added to her conquests. Though they would welcome Napoleon's downfall, most feared the consequences to the balance of power in Europe and the world that might come from a complete French defeat.[23]

Balance of power was something that the president, his administration, the Senate, and the House of Representatives all gave much thought to and generally agreed upon. So long as France and Britain remained equal—the Royal Navy mastering the sea, the Grande Armée the soil of Europe—America was unlikely to be directly threatened by either and would be free to prosper by trading with both great empires. Only a few cranks on either side of the political spectrum advocated the United States' aligning itself with either Britain or France; the prevailing view was that America should instead keep isolated from European affairs. Since Independence, isolationism had dominated the country's approach to foreign policy and affairs. Jefferson summed up American feeling when he wrote that the country was "kindly separated by nature and a wide ocean from the exterminating havoc of one quarter of the globe; too high-minded to endure the degradation of the others; possessing a chosen country."[24]

Most Americans considered it an inarguable fact that the United States was a country chosen by God and hence morally superior to all others. Why else had the Union managed to prevail during the revolution against a vastly more powerful foe? That moral purity remained possible only so long as the country maintained a strictly neutral stance. "The moment we enlist ourselves by sliding even imperceptibly into European politics, intrigue and warfare, we must abandon our peaceful, commercial, and hitherto prosperous system," warned the General Republican Committee of the City and County of New York in the midst of the embargo crisis.[25]

Pure isolationism, of course, was impossible. No matter how much it might want to, America could not simply withdraw into itself and ignore the outside world, because of a need for imported manufactured goods and an inability to sell all of its own production entirely within the United States. This made it necessary to foray out into the dangerous world across the sea to engage in the international commerce essential to ensuring prosperity. And with the implementation of Britain's orders-in-council and Napoleon's various decrees, those seas had become very dangerous indeed for American merchantmen.

Until Napoleon's attack on neutrals trading with Britain and the introduction of the orders-in-council, American traders had developed a system that enabled them to profit hugely from France's lack of either a powerful navy or a significant merchant fleet. By importing large quantities of such products as coffee, cotton, and sugar from the colonies of France and Spain to the United States, American traders were then able to re-export to ports in continental Europe without Britain being able to claim that the ships carried products that originated directly from the colonies of its enemies. By this means, in 1806 alone U.S. merchants moved 146 million pounds of sugar, 47 million pounds of coffee, and 2 million pounds of cotton into the country and out again to France. Effectively the American merchantmen were using their neutrality to provide supplies that France desperately needed and could acquire by no other means.

The U.S. government not only condoned this circumvention of the Royal Navy's efforts to cut off the flow of goods from the colonies of its enemies but actively encouraged the practice. Both the government and the merchants prospered mightily from the war. Between 1802 and 1810 the American maritime service grew from 558,000 tons to 981,000. Before the war, imported and exported goods were never worth more than $30 million in a single year. At the high-water mark, in 1807, exports totalled $108 million and imports $138.5 million. While Britain's military spending ballooned its national debt, Jefferson and Madison were steadily able to reduce America's indebtedness—which, in 1801, had stood at $82 million.[26] While France and Britain had been at war, Secretary Treasurer Albert Gallatin had steadily paid down this debt with intent to eliminate it entirely over sixteen years. In 1808, for example, he was able to apply $8 million to debt reduction. The source of funds for this aggressive assault on the public debt was largely customs duties, about $9.5 million a year before the invocation of the embargo.[27]

Well aware of what the Americans were doing, the British government repeatedly accused the U.S. government and its merchants and ship owners of being allied with Napoleon. For his part, Napoleon was happy to receive trade goods from his colonies by means of American ships, but he did not consider those exports vital to the maintenance of France's economy and he had only scant interest in sustaining the overseas colonies. What he wanted was to ruin Britain's economy, and to that end he sought to force America to cease all trade with her.

No sooner were his decrees issued than France struck hard at American shipping. Despite Napoleon's meagre navy, he was able to seize a great number of U.S. ships, mostly by detaining those that entered French ports unaware that these were no longer safe havens. Between 1807 and 1812, a report prepared by Secretary of State James Monroe disclosed, France and her allies seized 479 American ships compared with 389 detained by Britain.[28] Yet the anti-British sentiment prevailing in the popular press and on the House floor was so implacable that French seizures went largely unmentioned. Instead, most Americans, particularly the likes of Henry Clay, singled out Britain for condemnation, for Britain's seizures of shipping were inextricably linked with another, graver marine depredation that the British lion imposed upon the American eagle.

———

TWO

Insult to the Flag

*W*hen Henry Clay rose in the United States Senate on February 22, 1810, to denounce the depredations visited upon America by Britain, it was not the orders-in-council that fired his righteous indignation into hot fury.

While conceding that France and Britain were each guilty "of mercantile spoliations, inflicted and menaced" that provided "just cause of war with both," Clay believed that if "we are forced into a selection of our enemy, then am I for war with Britain; because I believe her prior in aggression, and her injuries and insults to us were atrocious in character.

"Britain," he declared, "stands pre-eminent, in her outrage on us, by her violation of the sacred personal rights of American freemen, in the arbitrary and lawless impressment of our seamen."[1]

The Royal Navy's impressment practice had been authorized during every war fought over the course of the seventeenth and eighteenth centuries. Despite her mastery of the seas, when not at war Britain mothballed most of her fleet and discharged the bulk of her sailors. This saved vast sums of money, but also ensured that with each new war Britain must scramble to refloat the powerful navy vital to defence of an island nation dependent on a global empire. First, a bounty was offered for volunteers. Naval service being a grim duty frequented by death, maiming, or debilitating sickness, the volunteer call inevitably fell short of requirement. The Admiralty then authorized a "hot press." Press gangs comprising trusted naval ratings roamed port-town streets to round up merchant sailors and fishermen as they stumbled out of bars or appeared on the quays and docks to rejoin their vessels. Without recourse to formal protest or complaint, the men suddenly found themselves serving before the mast—a fate that had likely befallen many during earlier wars. Land-based press gangs were common, but the majority operated from boats that lurked off the entrances to the empire's harbours to scoop crews off merchant and fishing vessels entering port.[2]

Although hugely unpopular with those Britons who made a living by going down to the sea, impressment was enshrined in legal precedent. A 1743 court ruling upheld subsequently by repeated courts declared the "right of impressing mariners for the public service . . . a prerogative inherent in the crown, founded upon common law and recognized by many acts of Parliament."[3]

Until the first Franco-British war, in 1793, impressment had met the Royal Navy's wartime needs. But this time it was soon clear that the mariner pool available for impressment was too small to meet the navy's insatiable appetite while also keeping Britain's merchant and fishing fleets at sea. In 1795 the government voted to bolster the naval ranks to 100,000 men, but where were such numbers to be found?

Beggars, pickpockets, thieves, and other criminals, known or suspected, were dragooned, prisoners-of-war were forced into service against their homeland, and foreign mariners were rounded up. No longer was impressment limited to British ports. Press gangs rowed ashore from ships anchored in foreign ports to troll dockyards and streets for potential victims. When the frigate HMS *Macedonian* put into Lisbon it sent ashore a "press-gang . . . made up of [the] most loyal men armed to the teeth." They captured several deserters who had fled other Royal Navy ships in the harbour, yanked in some crewmen from British merchantmen conducting trade ashore, and detained any foreign sailors who had the misfortune to cross their path. "Among them were a few Americans," noted one of *Macedonian*'s crew. "They were taken without respect to their protections, which were often taken from them and destroyed. Some were released through the influence of the American consul: others, less fortunate, were carried to sea to their no small chagrin. To prevent recovery of these men by their consul, the press-gang usually went ashore in the night previous to our going to sea so that, before they were missed, they were beyond his protection."[4]

The U.S. government denounced impressment of Americans to no effect. Britain argued that there was no cause for complaint because merchant shipping was not sovereign territory. Therefore it could be boarded, searched, and any British subjects aboard impressed. Not so, countered the Americans, who consented only to the Royal Navy's having a right of search during wartime for contraband trade and "persons . . . in the military service of the enemy."[5] Accordingly, French sailors aboard an American ship could be removed, but no Britons or Americans.

But who was a legitimate American and how was one to tell? America held to a doctrine of voluntary expatriation, whereby a man could freely apply for American citizenship and renounce loyalty or obligation to the land of his birth, but this practice had no basis in international law. Great Britain considered all Britons subjects of the Crown and bound by "indelible allegiance." They could not, without consent of the state, change nationality or escape the obligations of subjects to the state. There was no middle ground between these two views of the rights of man relative to the rights of the state.

Through revolution America had gained independence from British rule only scant years before. Every American over thirty years of age had initially been a subject of the Crown, indeed a subject of King George III, who, although increasingly mentally incapable and having been unofficially superseded by his son, the Prince of Wales, George Augustus Frederick, still wore the crown. Before coming to think of themselves as Americans, there were hardly any who had not previously been English, Scottish, Irish, or Welsh. Indeed, many still held fiercely to their national roots even as they maintained they were now first and foremost American. They generally thought of America as a British nation in its traditions, laws, and values. In America, however, the state served the needs of the individual rather than the other way around.

America naturally looked first for British citizens to help populate the vast, unpopulated territories to the west. To foster such immigration, qualification for American citizenship was made a simple matter of residency, which after 1802 had been dramatically reduced to a mere five years.

Whether native-born or naturalized, no American was issued proof of citizenship. Hoping to avoid impressment, the wise seaman had a notary public or justice of the peace draft a sworn certification, called a protection. On July 12, 1790, a justice of the peace named Thomas Veale swore such a document on behalf of one Henry Lunt. It read: "I, Henry Lunt, do solemnly swear on the holy Evangelist of Allmighty God that I was born in Portsmouth in the County of Rockingham, State of New Hampshire and have ever been a subject of said State."[6] Such a document was easily forged by British seamen, so Royal Navy captains often dismissed their authenticity and just impressed anyone they wanted off American ships.

Had the American merchant marine not welcomed thousands of British seamen into its ranks without regard to whether some were Royal Navy deserters, the impressment problem might not have been so volatile. Wages on American ships were double that of British merchantmen and more than twice that again of the Royal Navy. Besides the great financial incentive, there was also the hope that it would prove easier to escape impressment if one served on a foreign ship. Estimates of how many seamen were impressed varied wildly in reports of both nations.

Whatever the real numbers—whether they were as high as 50,000 as one 1801 British report held or as few as 10,000 as some American reports stated—the fact that the Royal Navy considered itself lawfully empowered to board American merchantmen for the purpose of impressment was, in the eyes of many Americans, a clear act of war. Each boarding for impressment, Henry Clay argued in the Senate in 1810, formed but another part of "the long catalogue of our wrongs and disgraces, which has been repeated until the sensibility of the nation is benumbed by the dishonourable detail."[7]

Not only impressment figured into Clay's catalogue of grievances. Also gnawing at his soul was the clear violation of sovereignty imposed on June 27, 1807, against an American naval ship.

American harbouring of Royal Navy deserters had long been a thorn in the side of the British Admiralty. In early 1807 the matter came to a head when a Royal Navy squadron blockaded two French ships of war sheltered in

Annapolis, about a hundred miles inside Chesapeake Bay. For several weeks the squadron lurked a little distance from Hampton Roads, ready to pounce the moment the French attempted to flee their safe harbour. Buffeted by storms and other calamities, a few British ships lay up in the anchorage at Hampton Roads or the navy yard at nearby Gosport for repairs or to take on supplies. Also anchored in Hampton Roads was the American frigate *Chesapeake*, flagship of Commodore James Barron, which was being outfitted for a two-year term of sea duty in the Mediterranean.[8]

Within easy distance of American soil, several sailors risked either execution or at best a severe flogging by fleeing their posts to take refuge ashore. In late February, three men crept down ropes from the decks of the squadron's flagship, *Melampus*, stole the captain's gig, and rowed it to shore.[9] On March 7, an entire crew manning a jolly boat from the gun sloop *Halifax* deserted.[10]

The three men who deserted *Melampus* were all impressed Americans— William Ware, an Indian from Pipe Creek, Maryland; Daniel Martin, a Negro from Westport, Massachusetts; and a white Marylander, John Strachan. All three had been impressed about two years earlier onto *Melampus*.[11] In each of these group desertions the captains of the ships involved shortly learned that some or all of the men had volunteered for and been accepted as seamen aboard *Chesapeake* while the others were granted protection by local authorities. Among those who deserted *Halifax* was a stocky former London tailor named Jenkin Ratford, who enlisted on *Chesapeake* under the alias John Wilson.[12]

Soon after the *Halifax* desertions, the sloop's captain encountered Ratford and another of the men ashore and asked them to return to service. Ratford berated the officer with "abuse and oaths," adding "that he was in the land of liberty and would do as he liked." Formal complaints were filed with the local authorities, and the British consul in Washington, also duly alerted to the incident, lodged a protest that resulted in the secretary of the navy ordering an inquiry into whether *Chesapeake*'s captain was knowingly recruiting deserters. The inquiry ruled that the three men off *Melampus* were Americans and so not subject to reclamation by the British. The presence of Ratford or other British deserters aboard the ship went unmentioned.[13] As for the deserters who had not signed on with *Chesapeake*, they were allowed to head off to new lives in America.

While the inquiry was under way, the desertions were duly reported to Vice-Admiral George Cranfield Berkeley in Halifax, Nova Scotia. In charge of "His Majesty's Ships and Vessels employed & to be employed in the River St. Lawrence, along the coast of Nova-Scotia, the Islands of Prince Edward and Cape Breton, in the bay of Fundy & the islands of Bermuda," Berkeley was one of the most powerful figures in British North America.[14] He also owed his position less to ability than to political influence he and his brother wielded in Britain. Since arriving in Halifax in the spring of 1806, Berkeley had distinguished himself mostly by way of authoring "a steady stream of complaints against the Admiralty, against Jefferson, against the United States," which, with scant regard for normal channels, he forwarded directly to Lord William Grenville, the leader of the opposition party responsible for his appointment to the command.[15]

The fifty-two-year-old vice-admiral was incensed that any of the deserters should have been taken on the roster of an American ship of war. Deciding the affront to King and Crown was too much to be left to diplomats to resolve, Berkeley determined to settle the matter by force of arms if necessary. On June 1, 1807, he issued orders to all ships under his command that in a long preamble argued that deserters off at least six Royal Navy ships were aboard *Chesapeake*. Included in this list of ships was *Halifax*, but not *Melampus*. These same deserters, he wrote, had "openly paraded the streets of Norfolk, in sight of their officers, under the American flag, protected by the magistrates of the town and the recruiting officer belonging to the above-mentioned frigate, which magistrates and naval officer refused giving them up, although demanded by his Britannic Majesty's consul, as well as the captains of the ships from which the said men had deserted."

The "captains and commanders of his Majesty's ships and vessels under my command are therefore hereby required and directed, in case of meeting with American frigate *Chesapeake* at sea, to show to the captain of her this order, and to require to search his ship for deserters."[16]

To ensure that the squadron standing off Hampton Roads brought *Chesapeake* to heel, Berkeley ordered his flagship, *Leopard*, to deliver the order and then remain on station there in hopes the American frigate would venture out to sea. Although an aging 50-gun fourth-rater whose career as a fighting ship was nearing an end, *Leopard* was more than a match for the 36-gun frigate. Capt. Salusbury P. Humphreys dropped anchor in the bay on June 21. The very next morning *Chesapeake* put up sails and departed Hampton Roads on a fair breeze. Humphreys quickly weighed anchor and headed seaward, keeping well ahead of the American vessel in order to present the illusion that he was engaged on a routine reconnaissance mission and had no interest in *Chesapeake*. Six and a half hours later, the two ships were about 10 miles southeast by east of Cape Henry and beyond the 3-mile territorial limit.

Suddenly *Leopard* came about and rode down the wind to come alongside *Chesapeake*. Shouting into a brass speaking trumpet, an officer aboard *Leopard* reported that he bore dispatches for Commodore Barron. The commodore ordered Capt. Charles Gordon, who while in nominal command of *Chesapeake* deferred to the senior officer in every decision, to heave to and prepare to receive a boat from the British ship. At 3:45 a young lieutenant named Meade clambered up from a rowboat onto the frigate's deck, was escorted to Barron's cabin, and delivered a copy of Berkeley's order with a short covering note from Humphreys stating that he hoped Berkeley's instructions could be respected "in a manner that the harmony subsisting between the two countries may remain undisturbed."[17]

While reading Berkeley's order, Barron noted that *Melampus* was not on the list of ships reported to have lost deserters to *Chesapeake*. While Barron knew that the three sailors from this ship were aboard, he was unaware of any from the ships that Berkeley cited. Taking up his quill, Barron penned a reply. "I know of no such men as you describe," he wrote. The commodore stated that the ship's recruiters were under standing instructions "not to enter any deserters from his Britannic Majesty's ships, nor do I know of any being here. I am also instructed never to permit the crew of any ship that I command to be mustered by any other but their own officers."[18]

As Meade scrambled back into the rowboat and the oarsmen started rowing back to *Leopard* at 4:15, Barron told Gordon to clear the gun deck for possible action. *Chesapeake*'s poorly trained 340-man crew set to in a desultory manner, with Gordon and his officers little hurrying the pace.

Meade, meanwhile, had rejoined *Leopard*. Seeing *Chesapeake*'s crew preparing for action and having read Barron's note, Humphreys fetched up his speaking trumpet and shouted, "Commodore Barron, you must be aware of the necessity I am under of complying with the order of my commander-in-chief."

Knowing *Chesapeake* could not be ready for battle in less than thirty minutes, Barron played for time. "I do not hear what you say," he replied.

Not intending to give Barron the time needed, Humphreys ordered a shot fired across the American frigate's bow and, when this failed to elicit a response, fired another after a delay of only one minute. Then, at precisely 4:30, and just two minutes after the second warning shot, *Leopard* unleashed a full broadside. Eleven 24-pound guns on *Leopard*'s lower deck and a matching number of 12-pound guns on the upper deck roared, and a deadly barrage of solid shot and canister fired point-blank at a range of about 150 feet crashed into *Chesapeake*. Round shot tore through the hull, ripped holes in the sails, and battered the ship's three masts. Spars and rigging crashed down upon the decks, joining a deadly rain of grapeshot. Without pause, *Leopard* followed its first broadside with two more.

With *Chesapeake*'s guns still covered, the American crew huddled behind whatever cover presented itself. Three men died, eight were severely wounded, and ten less so. Barron was among those lightly wounded. Fifteen minutes after *Leopard*'s first broadside, Barron ordered *Chesapeake*'s colours struck. As the flag dropped, a single gun on the American ship fired a ball into the British hull.

A British boarding party mustered the Americans and detained the three deserters from *Melampus*. Although between twelve and fifteen other alleged deserters were pointed out by members of the boarding party, the officers in charge were uncertain enough of their identity to decline to take them into custody. A thorough search of the ship turned up Jenkin Ratford hiding in a hold loaded with coal. After Ratford was dragged onto the deck, the British boarding party returned to *Leopard*.

They carried with them a note to Humphreys from Barron conceding that *Chesapeake* was the British captain's prize. Humphreys declined his right of battle and offered instead whatever assistance the commodore might need to see to the safety of his ship. "I ... do most sincerely deplore that any lives have been lost in the execution of a service which might have been adjusted more amicably, not only with respect to ourselves but the nations to which we respectively belong."[19]

Leopard returned with its four prisoners to the squadron off Hampton Roads while *Chesapeake* limped slowly back to the port itself. The four men lifted off the American vessel were taken to Halifax, where the three Americans were imprisoned. Tried for mutiny, desertion, and contempt, Ratford was convicted and hanged. One of the Americans died in custody while the other two were released only in 1812, just before war broke out between the United States and Britain.[20]

THREE

—

The Search for Satisfaction

SUMMER 1807

*I*n the aftermath of *Leopard*'s attack on *Chesapeake* it seemed reasonable to assume that war would come five years earlier than it eventually did. Along the Virginian side of Chesapeake Bay, the militia, acting under orders from their governor, barred British ships from taking on supplies. A young lance corporal named Winfield Scott took prisoner a party of Royal Navy sailors who had rowed ashore to take on water. Ever prone to riot, a New York mob vandalized an English ship that lay alongside a dock, while the city's British consul had to be placed under police protection. Elsewhere public meetings were held and Great Britain resoundingly condemned. Even in staunchly pro-British Boston more than two thousand people gathered to demand action.[1]

David Erskine, Britain's youthful ambassador, cautioned his superior two weeks after the incident that even the "most temperate people and those most attracted to England say that they are bound as a nation and that they must assert their honour of the first attack upon it, or subject themselves to an imputation which it may be difficult to remove." While war over the orders-in-council was unlikely, Erskine feared the *Chesapeake* incident could inflame "the passions of the people" to such a point that the Jefferson administration would be forced to act.[2]

President Jefferson recognized that the country "has never been in such a state of excitement since the battle of Lexington" and that, if he sought it, Congress would approve a declaration of war. But neither Jefferson nor his secretary of state, James Madison, wished to take that fateful step.[3]

As in so many things, the two most powerful men in America were of like mind. These Virginians of the old landed gentry were the closest of friends, enjoying an intimacy many observers described as like that of a father and son. Having been born in 1743, Jefferson played father to Madison, eight years younger. Where Jefferson was tall and patrician in manner, Madison was short and painfully shy. Always outgoing, Jefferson revelled in large dinner parties followed by long discussions over Madeira. Madison preferred small gatherings and an early bed. Both men shared an appetite for good wine and expensive books, but Jefferson acquired both without concern for the costs. He was subsequently a president shouldering a crushing debt that his $25,000 annual salary did little to relieve. Both men, in terms of land and slaves owned, appeared wealthy, but the cash value of these was far less than either imagined. More realistic, Madison chose to moderate his desire for wine and books, but found it impossible to curb his wife Dolley's appetite for luxury. New gowns were a constant, a carriage to whisk her about Washington absolutely essential, and the pursuit endless for all considered fashionable and necessary to maintain their proper station in the ranks of America's elite. This placed serious strain on Madison's meagre $5,000 salary as secretary of state that was little augmented by income from the plantation.[4]

It was not only their lifestyles and background that bound Madison and Jefferson. They were both men of the Revolution who shared its ideals and desired to build a nation anchored on the principles of liberty and individualism that had led America to revolt against king and country. The America they sought was one where the power of government was limited, taxes were minimal, and Congress represented and expressed the will of the people.

Jefferson and Madison were grateful that Congress was not in session, and the president astutely resisted recalling it for an emergency sitting that would certainly result in rapid drafting and passage of a war bill.[5]

Jefferson urged the Virginia governor to restrain his militiamen to avoid any clash with the British. Showing restraint now, he argued, would leave Congress the freedom later to decide "whether, having taught so many other useful lessons to Europe, we may not add that of showing them that there are peaceable means of repressing injustice, by making it the interest of the aggressor to do what is just."[6]

When the French minister to America, Gen. Louis Marie Turreau, sounded Jefferson out about whether war was imminent—something France desired—the president declared, "If the English do not give us the satisfaction we demand we will take Canada, which wants to enter the Union." A shrewd man, Turreau recognized bluster. He reported that "the President does not want war and that Mr. Madison dreads it now still more."[7]

In a series of meetings in rooms steaming under Washington summer heat, Madison urged Jefferson's cabinet to react cautiously. *Leopard*, he said, had executed an order issued by Vice-Admiral Berkeley without the British government's authorization. An immediate war declaration would be a tactical blunder because of the numerous British warships already concentrated in American waters. These ships could easily close the nation's ports and seize its merchant ships as they returned home. Better to wait until the majority of the American merchant fleet came home in the late summer and early fall.[8]

Madison's moderate line met strong opposition from an unexpected corner, Secretary of the Treasury Albert Gallatin. Being neither native born nor of British stock, the forty-six-year-old Gallatin was an American political rarity. Born to wealthy parents in Geneva, he had emigrated to the United States in 1780, at the age of twenty, with the desire to "drink in a love for independence in the freest country of the universe."[9] More pragmatically, Gallatin also knew there was more opportunity to make his fortune in a new country than in Geneva, where a financial clique controlled the economy.

Gallatin ventured into the still-opening expanses of western Virginia and purchased a thousand acres on the bank of the Ohio River for 100 Virginian pounds. In partnership with a friend, Gallatin also bought warrants for 120,000 acres between the Great and Little Kanawha rivers in Virginia's Monongalia County. Selling off some of this land left the two men comfortably prosperous. Within five years of arriving in America, Gallatin owned a farm that he named Friendship Hill, on a bluff overlooking the Monongahela River across the boundary from Virginia in western Pennsylvania. Having just attained his age of majority at twenty-five, Gallatin received a large infusion of capital from his family back in Geneva that cemented his position as one of the county's wealthiest and most educated citizens. He also married, without the permission of her mother, a woman much younger than himself. She died just a few months later.

As a palliative to his grief, Gallatin threw himself into politics. He was elected to the Pennsylvanian state legislature in 1790 and three years later to the United States Senate. In 1793, Gallatin married Hannah Nicholson less than a month before taking his seat in the Senate that December. Unlike his first wife, Hannah was no beauty, but, raised in a family tightly linked to the navy (her father was a retired commodore with close ties to Washington), she possessed a keen political mind. His twenty-seven-year-old bride, Gallatin confided to a friend, was "far less attractive than either her mind or her heart. . . . Her understanding is good, she is as well informed as most young ladies . . . and she is a pretty good democrat (and so, by the bye, are all her relations)."[10] Two years later, on December 7, 1795, Gallatin was elected to Congress and hooked his wagon to Thomas Jefferson's rising star. When Jefferson won the presidency in March 1801, he appointed Gallatin federal secretary of the treasury. It was a position Gallatin had held ever since.

In charge of the federal finances, Gallatin clearly understood how ill prepared the nation was for war. As the men behind Jefferson gathered for another sweaty meeting to discuss how the government should react to the *Chesapeake* incident, Gallatin's face was sallower than normal. His hair, sharply receding from a high, sloping forehead, was a tangled, dark mass. His long nose thrust like a sword out from between dark eyes. Gallatin was a hardened survivor, a politician who had held the reins of the treasury for six years despite many House and Senate attempts to get rid of this foreigner, this fiscal rationalist who so opposed incurring national debt that many capital projects that would benefit political colleagues and adversaries alike died for lack of federal funding.

In his cold and ever-rational manner, Gallatin argued for a war he acknowledged would be "calamitous."[11] But this was a war forced on America by the *Chesapeake* incident and the ever-tightening economic screws of the orders-in-council. Gallatin feared economic chaos and depression, but he feared more that turning the other cheek would be a humiliation the nation would never rise above because its moral supremacy in relation to the corruption of Europe would be forever lost. America's essence required it to stand up for independence and act against violations of the rights of man. When *Leopard* tore into *Chesapeake* with its broadsides, killing three sailors and maiming many others, Gallatin considered a line had been crossed and war was the ultimate and only redress available to the aggrieved nation.

"We will be poorer, both as a nation and as a government, our debt and taxes will increase, and our progress in every respect be interrupted. But all those evils are . . . not to be put in competition with the independence and honor of the nation; they are, moreover, temporary, and very few years of peace will obliterate their effects. Nor do I know whether the awakening of nobler feelings and habits than avarice and luxury might not be necessary to prevent our degenerating, like the Hollanders, into a nation of mere calculators."[12]

Gallatin not only advocated war but he had much considered the means by which it could be waged. America's navy, severely reduced by his own conservative national fiscal policies, could not best the Royal Navy. From a treasury point of view, Gallatin held that "it would be an economical measure for every naval nation to burn their navy at the end of a war and to build a new one when again at war, if it was not that time was necessary to build ships of war."[13] The best the navy could do was to huddle inside the safety of the few well-fortified American ports or act individually as privateers by preying on helpless British merchantmen. Defending America's coastline would be a daunting challenge, Gallatin concluded, but not insurmountable if preparations began immediately.

Gallatin recognized that a purely defensive war could not be fought effectively. The initiative always lay with the enemy to choose where and when to fight. He therefore proposed a multi-pronged invasion, conducted in stages over several months, of British North America and the seizure of New Providence and Bermuda by amphibious assault. Only Newfoundland, too far away and too heavily garrisoned, was to be left alone. Upper Canada, Lower Canada, New Brunswick, Nova Scotia, all were to be invaded in turn. Halifax, with its great port, was the most difficult objective to capture but also the most vital. So "long as the British hold Halifax they will be able, by the superiority of their naval force, to blockade, during the greater part of the year, all our principal seaports. ... If we take it, the difficulty to refit and obtain refreshments will greatly diminish that evil, and enable us to draw some advantage from our small navy on our own coast." Taking Upper Canada was also critical "in order to cover our northern frontier and to ruin the British fur-trade."

Gallatin placed the cost of the proposed operation at about $18 million and requiring deployment of around 30,000 men. The war could be financed by drawing down the present surplus by $8 million, dedicating $2.5 million in taxes and duties, selling $500,000 of federal land, and borrowing $7 million.[14] Gallatin sat and awaited the response of the rest of the executive.

Madison was aghast and Jefferson in no mood to act so intemperately. No, president and secretary of state argued, diplomacy and economic retribution would be the first response. War was unthinkable before those avenues of winning redress were exhausted. Reluctantly Gallatin acceded to Jefferson and Madison's arguments. He knew both men well and was first and foremost a loyal servant of the president. But he doubted the efficacy of Jefferson's proposed course.

On July 2, Jefferson issued a written proclamation denying the Royal Navy access to American ports. The president hoped this measure would satisfy public calls for action while ensuring there would be no further attacks on British ships and crew by mobs or militia. Good, traditional Republicans, Jefferson and Madison were also anxious that the administration not ignite hostilities between Great Britain and America. Authority to make war lay with Congress, Jefferson argued, and the president and his executive "should do no act committing them to war, when it is very probable that they may prefer a non-intercourse to war."[15]

Madison sent a dispatch on July 6 to James Monroe, then the U.S. minister in London, demanding that the British government formally disavow the attack on *Chesapeake* and return the four seamen. That the entire incident had been the misguided inspiration of one man was increasingly clear, and there was every reason to believe that the British would agree to this demand, but Jefferson and Madison were not content to limit discussions to the incident that had brought the nation to the brink of war. Jefferson, Madison later explained, had decided to convert "a particular incident into an occasion for removing another and more extensive source of danger to the harmony of the two countries."[16] Monroe was to wrest from the British a far greater concession than an admission that America's national sovereignty had been violated by the attack. "As a security for the future," Madison wrote, "an entire abolition of impressment from vessels under the flag of the United States . . . is also to make an indispensable part of the satisfaction."[17]

Gallatin realized that Monroe was being sent on a fool's errand. "Great Britain will not, I am confident, give either satisfaction or security," he commented.[18] Jefferson, too, doubted the wisdom of the ultimatum. He confided to a friend: "Although we demand of England what is merely of right, reparation for the past, security for the future, yet as their pride will possibly, nay probably, prevent their yielding them to the extent we shall require."[19] The only recourse when the British refused his demands would be war. More administration meetings followed through July in rooms so scorching hot that clarity of thought was almost impossible. Gallatin's plans to attack Canada were reviewed in detail and his plans for funding the war discussed.

All this time, nearly three weeks, the dispatch to Monroe rested on Madison's desk as if there was no urgency in sending it. Finally Madison passed it to a courier, who boarded the USS *Revenge* on July 28 for the cross-Atlantic journey. Four days later, with nothing decided about how to, when to, or even whether to declare war if the demands were not met, Jefferson fled the steam bath of the capital for his beloved plantation, Monticello. Decisions about how to prepare for war could, it seemed, be left to the cooler days of fall.

Three days before *Revenge* sailed, the British secretary for foreign affairs, George Canning, had told Monroe the basic facts of the *Leopard* and *Chesapeake* incident. Shocked by the affair, Canning expressed regret and assured the American minister that if British officers were found in the wrong, his government would offer a "most prompt and effectual reparation." Thinking Canning's comments a sign of weakness, Monroe demanded that Britain admit the incident had been an attempt "to assert and enforce the unfounded and most unjustifiable pretension to search for deserters." The British government must, he said, immediately renounce the principle that the Royal Navy had used to justify the search and agree to punish the officers responsible.[20]

Although not yet having received Madison's instructions to tie the *Chesapeake* incident inextricably to the issue of impressment, Monroe had seized on precisely the same strategy. Irritated by Monroe's strident language, Canning snapped back that Great Britain would make reparations only when all the facts were known. Somewhat more calmly he assured the American that His Majesty's government did not assume any right to search ships of war for deserters. If an investigation revealed that this had in fact taken place, Great Britain would disavow the act and discipline the responsible officers.

Word of Jefferson's proclamation barring British ships from American ports reached Britain well before *Revenge* brought Monroe his instructions. A powerful lobby of ship owners, Royal Navy officers, East and West India Company merchants, and leading politicians clamoured for immediate declaration of war on the United States. The president's actions, Canning advised Monroe, "without requiring or waiting for any explanation" were unwarranted and dangerous.[21]

There matters lay until Monroe, now with Madison's terms in hand, sent Canning a note on September 7. America demanded by way of reparations that Britain restore the seamen taken, punish the officer who ordered the attack, abandon all impressment from merchant vessels, and send a special mission to Washington to announce its compliance with these demands. Knowing Britain would not readily accept tying impressment to the *Chesapeake* incident, Monroe argued that whether the act was carried out on a ship of war or a merchant ship was irrelevant. The simple fact was that impressment, in either case, was a violation of the individual rights of seamen and that a citizen of America was justly entitled to his country's protection from it.[22]

Canning fired back that the *Chesapeake* incident and the matter of impressment from merchant vessels were "wholly unconnected." Impressment was a right exercised by Great Britain since it first built a navy and the practice was legally legitimized. Monroe offered the faint compromise that he was willing to discuss impressment informally while settling the *Chesapeake* matter formally. Canning declined, saying that there would be no discussions of impressment until after the *Chesapeake* issue was settled. With Canning refusing to tie the two matters together and Monroe equally adamant that they could not be separated, the negotiations came to an abrupt end.[23]

Fitful attempts were made by both the American and British governments to get negotiations going again in either London or Washington, but all met the same result. Each side remained adamant about the terms and so neither budged. In America, the initial fervour for war had begun to decline by the fall of 1807. Although the slight that Americans declared had been inflicted upon their national honour by *Leopard*'s attack on *Chesapeake* remained a festering sore, nobody but the most diehard pro-war advocates, like Henry Clay, were ready to resort to violence by way of cure.

As the orders-in-council and decrees by Napoleon made it ever more difficult for American merchantmen and traders to operate freely wherever they chose, Jefferson moved from barring British ships access to U.S. ports to a full-scale embargo. This in turn was weakened by the House and the Senate into a Non-intercourse Act that was only fitfully and ineffectually applied. By 1810, it was clear that these measures had failed and neither the French nor the British, locked as they were in a death struggle, were about to accommodate America's desire to trade with each and thus profit from its neutrality.

That the orders-in-council and the *Chesapeake* affair seemed insufficient cause to justify war posed a major hurdle to the loose coalition of politicians that constituted the pro-war lobby. Still, by the winter of 1810, when Henry Clay rode into Washington to assume his seat in the Senate, this group remained undaunted. If maritime issues were insufficient to rally public outcry and force the government's hand, then additional reasons must be found. And for Clay and the other westerners among their number there was a need to look no further than the wilderness beyond their own doorsteps. In those dense woods lurked Indians, who, rumour had it, were being incited by British agents operating out of Upper Canada to rise up and slaughter American settlers.

FOUR

Imperious Necessities

1794–1795

*I*ndependence had freed America to concentrate on expanding its frontiers, and one result was a long, brutal struggle between whites and Indians over supremacy in the Ohio River country. Every time the frontier settlers pushed into fresh Indian territory they met stiff resistance, particularly from the Shawnee, who considered this their native land. The fighting was vicious, with atrocities ruthlessly committed by each side. Warriors and soldiers both took scalps, butchered women and children, burned settlements down upon their inhabitants, and hunted down and killed any enemy that happened across their path. This was war without quarter, each side bent upon purging the land of the other.

The pioneers leading the western expansion had an insatiable thirst for new territory. They were part of "an agricultural society without skill or resources," noted one observer, who "committed all those sins which characterize a wasteful and ignorant husbandry." Working with crude tools and even less agricultural knowledge, they cleared only the land in their parcel essential to growing food to meet personal needs or to trade with neighbours. The rest was left in timber through which farm animals roamed in search of forage. Not realizing that soil required rebuilding with compost or manure, these pioneers, whom contemporary American folklore hailed as the advance guard bringing civilization to the wilderness, soon exhausted their fields. Faced with sudden crop failures and looming starvation, they could think of no other option but to move farther west, where virgin country could be had. This explained, the same observer reflected, "why the American frontier settler was on the move continually. It was not his fear of a too close contact with the comforts and restraints of a civilized society that stirred him into a ceaseless activity, nor merely the chance of selling out at a profit to the coming wave of settlers; it was his wasting land that drove him on. Hunger was the goad. . . . He could succeed only with a virgin soil."[1]

A second wave of far different pioneers followed close on the heels of these frontier settlers. As often as not, these were European immigrants with farming experience in their old countries, who understood the benefits of crop rotation and the need for adequate holdings. From the land speculators, who had happily bought up the depleted plots abandoned by the first settlers, these new farmers assembled parcels from what previously constituted a half-dozen or more crude homesteads. They planted orchards, vegetables, hemp, and other crops that could yield commercial value. And they set about building a society that resembled that to be found in the eastern United States. Roads, even though often rough, connected farms and the small villages and towns that cropped up to provide the stores, banks, offices for doctors and lawyers, churches, courthouses, and other services necessary to the conduct of a relatively civilized agrarian society.

This process of frontier settlement, soon followed by settler displacement and reclamation by a true agrarian class, fuelled America's rapid territorial expansion. Inevitably, each westward push brought the frontiersman up hard against those peoples already dwelling within the forests that lay just over the hill or across the river from the recently settled territory. Disease and war had decimated the Indian peoples of the eastern seaboard. When the expansion inland reached the Appalachians, white settlers faced a better-organized and more determined foe—the many Indian nations who lived there and had formed a series of loosely organized confederacies. Most had been heavily involved in the French–Indian wars, had gone on to fight for one side or the other during the wars fought by France and Britain on North American soil, and had engaged in a series of conflicts with the Americans from the moment the first shots of the revolution of 1776 were fired.

Between 1784 and 1789, American representatives attempted to legitimize the pioneer incursions into the Ohio by imposing four treaties on the Indians who were being forcibly displaced. None of these documents were signed by Shawnee chiefs. Instead, chiefs from other native tribes, such as the Iroquois, who lacked historic claim to the land, accepted cash and guarantees of the security of their own territories in exchange for great swaths of the Ohio. The Shawnee denounced these treaties even as the white pioneers quickly moved beyond the boundary that each had set as the limit of American expansion. As the ink was drying on the parchment of these worthless documents, the fighting continued. Treaties or not, slowly and inexorably the Shawnee and other Indian nations living west of the Appalachians were forced to cede more ground to the settlers' relentless advance.

Among their number the Shawnee counted a warrior with a reputation for courage and wisdom that increased with each passing year. Tecumseh, which in his own language meant "Shooting Star," stood five-foot-ten at a time when most whites rarely exceeded five-six. The straightness of his bearing added to the impression that here stood a man of great height. Powerfully and athletically built, uncommonly handsome, articulate, and keenly intelligent, Tecumseh engendered both respect and fear in the hearts of the Americans he met. Likely born in March 1768 at Old Piqua on the banks of western Ohio's Mad River, he was the fifth child in a family that would eventually number nine, including triplets. Although one of the triplets died soon after birth, the rest of the family survived infanthood.

Tecumseh and his siblings enjoyed no idyllic upbringing in an Edenic wilderness. When Tecumseh was six, his father was mortally wounded during an attack on a Virginian stockade at Point Pleasant on the Ohio River. The family's eldest son, Chiksika, although only fourteen, assumed responsibility for feeding the other children. In 1779, after a particularly ruthless band of Kentuckians commanded by Col. John Bowman attacked one of the Mad River settlements and was only narrowly driven off by the Shawnee warriors, one thousand men, women, and children fled down the Ohio Valley to take refuge in southeastern Missouri. Among the refugees was Tecumseh's mother, taking only her second daughter with her. Aided by the eldest sister, who was now married, Chiksika assumed full responsibility for raising the others. In 1788, however, he died leading a raid on the outpost of Buchanan's Station in east Tennessee. The twenty-year-old Tecumseh was close by, for he had taken up the warrior's way in 1782—at the same age that Chiksika had sat at the side of his dying father and sworn to care for his siblings. Tecumseh had revered both his elder brother and the greatly embellished memory of his father passed down to him by Chiksika. There could be no peace between the Shawnee and the whites, Chiksika had counselled the young man, until the Ohio was scourged of the invaders.[2] Tecumseh held that counsel close in his heart after his brother's death, committing himself to the path of war. But the Shawnee hold on the Ohio was being pried loose with each pioneer advance, inevitably supported by the American Long Knives, as the Indians called the cavalry. Tecumseh was twenty-six when the decisive battle at the rapids of the Miami River on August 20, 1794, ended Indian hopes of preserving control over any of the Ohio.[3]

"The proximity of the [Shawnee] towns to the Ohio River—the great highway of emigration to the west—and the facility with which the infant settlements in Kentucky could be reached, rendered this warlike tribe an annoying and dangerous neighbour," complained one American contemporary.[4] In 1794, the American government decided to end that threat forever and dispatched an army under command of Maj. Gen. "Mad Anthony" Wayne to gain control of the area.

Previously, the Americans had conducted only raiding parties that savagely fell upon one or two Shawnee villages, burned them to the ground, and slaughtered as many inhabitants as they could before withdrawing in the confident assumption that this would warn the Indians off the advancing pioneer settlements. The strategy had proven less than successful, for often the Shawnee stubbornly refused to flee. Instead, they withdrew, regrouped, and then filtered back to continue the struggle.

This time Wayne was going to secure the Ohio once and for all. Leading an army of 3,500, grandly named the Legion of the United States, Wayne marched into the Ohio country that spring. His force consisted of 1,500 notoriously ruthless mounted Kentucky volunteers, a large contingent of infantry, and several artillery pieces. The advance proceeded slowly, Wayne pausing regularly to construct another in a string of forts that by August had pierced ninety miles into the heart of the Ohio from Fort Washington (Cincinnati) to Fort Recovery (in present-day Mercer County, Ohio). Badly outnumbered, the Shawnee grudgingly withdrew before the lumbering American force. They abandoned one village after another, until finally falling back to the British-held Fort Miami, named after the adjacent river. Here the warriors turned to face the enemy, sending their women and children to Swan Creek, where they were confident that the British would protect and supply them while the warriors engaged the Americans. Until recently Fort Miami had been virtually abandoned and falling into decay, but having learned that Wayne was assembling an army for a summer campaign into the Ohio, the governor of Canada, Lord Dorchester (previously Gen. Guy Carleton), had sent a party of engineers protected by a small force of regular infantry to reconstruct and garrison the post to assert Britain's territorial rights.[5]

The Shawnee had assembled one of the largest war parties in recent history, about 1,500 strong and composed not only of their own but also of warriors from the Ottawa, Ojibwa, Potawatomi, and Wyandot nations. In command was the Shawnee war chief, Blue Jacket, who had been leading his people into combat for decades.

Although the British declared themselves neutral, several coureur de bois traders and fifty-two English-Canadian volunteers from Upper Canada working on the fort decided to join the warrior ranks, for sentiments were strong among the Canadians living on the frontiers that America was about to align itself with France and invade both Canada and the frontier Indian country. Tensions between Canada and the United States were at their highest point since the failed American invasions of the Revolutionary War. Matters had been further worsened when, in a "bellicose speech" at Quebec on February 10, 1794, Lord Dorchester told an Indian gathering that war between Great Britain and the United States was imminent and they should revive the old confederacies to enable them to resist American aggression.[6]

The Shawnee needed no encouragement on this front, for it was obvious they could resist Wayne's army only by mustering an alliance such as they rallied at the Miami River. For his part, the newly arrived lieutenant governor of Upper Canada, Gen. John Graves Simcoe, considered the Legion of the United States an invasion force engaged in an act of war against his Indian allies. He sought authorization from Dorchester to lead a small force of British regulars to cut Wayne's supply lines back to Fort Washington in order to force the American general to either surrender or starve in the wilderness.[7] It was a bold plan conceived too late, so that the troops had not yet even begun to gather before Wayne met the Indians on the Miami River.

After some initial skirmishes on August 18 and 19, Blue Jacket ordered his warriors to establish a defensive position four miles up the Miami from the British fort on the river's northwestern bank. Believing American resolve weak and that Wayne was not yet near the battleground, no haste was made to get into position on the morning of August 20. Many warriors were still visiting the civilian encampment at Swan Creek or the small Indian settlement adjacent to the British fort when Wayne's troops attacked. No more than five hundred warriors, including the Canadian volunteers, faced them. The Canadians took up a position on the right alongside a force of Wyandot while an equal number of Shawnee, including Tecumseh, met the Americans on the left. Outnumbered, the Indian force was quickly driven back from the riverbank and routed to the fort. Here they sought shelter inside the stockade. The British commander, Maj. William Campbell, refused to open the gate, fearing that Wayne would retaliate by overrunning his small garrison and spark an international incident. "I cannot let you in! You are painted too much, my children!" he cried down from the stockade ramparts.[8]

The warriors managed to escape anyway when Wayne diverted his attention to Fort Miami and demanded Campbell surrender the fort. The major steadfastly refused; outnumbered or not, he would fight if forced. Wayne's men circled the fort menacingly for a while before withdrawing to the other side of the river.[9] In the brief melee upstream and the ensuing pursuit, his army had lost 44 killed and another 89 wounded in exchange for 40 dead Indians.[10] This casualty rate was sufficient to give him pause. He was also wary of the potential for trouble between America and Britain if he attempted to bypass or capture Fort Miami.

That the fort on the Miami River, 60 miles below Detroit, was clearly not on ground that Great Britain had legitimate claim to was lost on neither the Americans nor the British. But it fit within a series of forts manned by the British at the end of the Revolutionary War that stood either on American soil or in territory that neither country had legitimate claim to. Fort Miami fell within the latter category, but its being regarrisoned by the British and its role in frustrating Wayne's intent to deliver a punishing defeat to the Indians sparked an immediate crisis between the two countries. Chief Justice John Jay was dispatched from Washington to London and there, on November 19, 1794, Jay's Treaty was signed. It called for Britain to surrender the disputed western posts by June 1, 1796, and also relaxed some outstanding issues regarding restrictions the British had imposed on American trade with the West and East Indies. The treaty had the effect of temporarily lessening tensions between the two countries, but it also satisfied neither side. From Upper Canada, Simcoe and his officers anxiously monitored the American expansion westward but could offer the Indians nothing beyond moral encouragement.

Disheartened by their defeat at what became known as Fallen Timbers, and realizing the redcoats would not resist further American advances, Shawnee resistance crumbled. On August 3, 1795, most of the nation's chiefs, led by a dispirited Blue Jacket, accepted the terms of the Treaty of Greenville as offered to them by a stone-faced Wayne. The American demanded, and the Shawnee duly surrendered, the southern, central, and eastern sections of Ohio, approximately two-thirds of the present state, and several strategically important positions within their territory such as Fort Wayne and Fort Defiance. Tellingly, Tecumseh, now a minor chieftain, refused to attend the peace talks at Fort Greenville and politely rebuffed Blue Jacket when the chieftain tracked him down at a summer hunting camp to explain why he had accepted the American terms.[11] The fifty-year resistance to American expansion was at an end, Blue Jacket said, and all the battles and the deaths had been for nothing. Tecumseh did not agree with the old warrior. This treaty would not likely last longer than those before, he said. Tecumseh knew the American thirst for land was insatiable, and soon the frontier settlers would again bay for access to more Indian territory.

Although the terms of the Treaty of Greenville prevailed for several years, Tecumseh divined that American expansionism would be little restrained by its terms. True enough, a stampede descended on Ohio, and by 1800 this territory was on the way to statehood. That same year the United States government declared the country beyond the western border of Ohio over to the Mississippi River to be Indiana Territory. Already this area was home to about six thousand whites, concentrated at Vincennes and nearby farms straggling along the shores of the Wabash, Kaskaskia, and Cahokia rivers. Twenty-seven-year-old Virginian William Henry Harrison became Indiana's first governor. Closely aligned to western land speculators and their powerful lobby group in Washington, Harrison was eager to open the area to white settlement and help his supporters line their pockets. Having fought beside Wayne at Fallen Timbers, he believed that Indians and whites could not live side by side unless the former abandoned their way of life and adopted that of the pioneers. Alternatively the Indians must sell their lands in Indiana and move west of the Mississippi. There they could live as they wished until America expanded to that side of the river.

Through seven treaties of dubious legality negotiated between 1802 and 1805, Harrison coerced eleven tribes, including the Shawnee, into surrendering title to all of present-day southern Indiana, much of what would eventually become Wisconsin and Missouri, and the majority of Illinois. In exchange Harrison agreed that the United States Treasury would ante up on average two cents an acre. On the surface Harrison portrayed himself as a mild-mannered, congenial fellow. But in his dealings with the chiefs, he never hesitated to resort to bribery or threats. Often, if a chief refused to sign the new treaty Harrison presented, he withheld previously guaranteed annuities. Should one tribe have greater claim to the land in question but be unwilling to treat with him, Harrison simply found a chief from another nation willing to exchange land that was not his own for the governor's coin. Before discussions began, Harrison was always careful to offer the chiefs good amounts of liquor to get them feeling sufficiently "mellow."[12]

While Governor Harrison was brokering his deals, the federal government was pulling off a coup that would double America's size, extending its dominion to the eastern flanks of the Rocky Mountains with one grand stroke of a pen. President Thomas Jefferson had clearly articulated the hope in 1801 that the United States must eventually encompass the continent or even the entire hemisphere. It "is impossible," he said, "not to look forward to distant times, when our rapid multiplication will expand itself beyond those limits and cover the whole northern, if not the southern, continent with a people speaking the same language, governed in similar forms and by similar laws."[13]

But Jefferson never believed he would live to see this. He envisioned America instead as remaining a "medium-sized agrarian republic" that would grow only by the kinds of leaps and bounds the likes of Harrison were masterminding on the frontier.[14] By 1801, however, those fitful expansions had brought the leading wave of American settlers hard up against the wilderness of the Louisiana Territory, which was the rightful possession of the Spanish Empire. This vast territory extended finger-width-wide from the Gulf of Mexico at New Orleans north along the western bank of the Mississippi until, breaking free of the boundary of the part of Spanish Mexico Americans would come to call Texas, it thrust northward in a rapidly ballooning bulge to the headwaters of the Missouri and Yellowstone rivers high in the Rockies, and eastward almost to the southwestern border of Upper Canada.

Despite Spain's complete neglect of these holdings, colonial authorities in New Orleans were gravely concerned by reports that American pioneers were beginning to illegally cross the Mississippi into their territory. But, given neither the will nor the military means to contest this undeclared invasion, the Spanish could do little to stem the tide. Their only real recourse, and the one that most concerned President Jefferson, was to threaten to cancel the 1795 Treaty of San Lorenzo, which permitted commercial traffic out of the western states to pass through New Orleans.

The Americans had been squeezing out the Spanish and the French in Louisiana and Florida, and Clay was affronted by Great Britain's resistance to the continuance of this strategy. For the northern states and the adjoining western states and territories the situation was less advantageous for expansion. Here the frontier Indians posed a continued threat to attempts by settlers to secure large tracts of land they claimed as their own. Farther north, the British, widely believed to be fomenting anti-American sentiment among the Indians, clearly had no intention of surrendering the Canadas to American expansionist interests. To the likes of Henry Clay, this situation was not only extremely galling but it posed a direct threat to the nation's security that must be addressed with the same determination and resolve that the federal government had directed toward southern expansion.

FIVE

British Intrigue

When the United States Senate convened in the late winter of 1810 one of the first orders of business was a congressional bill calling on President Thomas Jefferson to scrap his controversial 1807 embargo in favour of the softer non-intercourse policy. Whereas Jefferson's embargo had curtailed all international trade, including that with Canada and the Spanish Empire to the south, non-intercourse excluded only British and French ships from American ports and prohibited importation of goods from either country.

Non-intercourse had previously proven a weak, ineffectual tool, Henry Clay argued before the Senate on February 10. It was incapable of prying from Great Britain the concessions required. Impressment, the orders-in-council, and the continued inciting of frontier Indians would continue unchecked. In the absence of the embargo, the only alternative was war, and he passionately advocated its declaration.

"No man in the nation desires peace more than I. . . . But I prefer the troubled ocean of war, demanded by the honor and independence of the country, with all its calamities, and desolations, to the tranquil, putrescent pool of ignominious peace." Harkening back to Albert Gallatin's earlier remonstrance that war would delineate Americans from money-grubbing Hollanders, Clay asked: "Are we to be governed by the low, groveling parsimony of the counting room, and to cast up the actual pence in the drawer before we assert our inestimable rights?" Clay disparaged the claim by anti-war advocates that nothing of value could be won from Britain. "The conquest of Canada is in your power. I trust I shall not be deemed presumptuous when I state, what I verily believe, that the militia of Kentucky are alone competent to place Montreal and Upper Canada at your feet. Is it nothing to the British nation—is it nothing to the pride of her monarch to have the last of the immense North American possessions held by him in the commencement of his reign, wrested from his dominion? Is it nothing to extinguish the torch that lights up savage warfare? Is it nothing to acquire the entire fur trade connected with that country?" Either reject the congressional bill and hold the course of non-intercourse, he advised, or plunge into war with Britain.

Clay's impassioned admonition failed to sway the senators to either take the path that led to war or to hold to the embargo course. Instead, non-intercourse was adopted. Disgusted, Clay condemned the decision in the *Kentucky Gazette*. All "our commercial restrictions having in view the coercion of foreign governments to abrogate their edicts, will be abandoned; and our commerce once more left to its fate."

Failing to prevail in the Senate, Clay chafed through the rest of the session—convinced that the time had come to move to where real national decisions were made. Next time he came to Washington it would be as a congressman. And with him would be sufficient young men of like mind to force the nation into war. There was growing consensus throughout the western states that an Indian uprising masterminded by British agents was imminent. Clay envisioned little problem in finding the support he needed.

Since Maj. Gen. "Mad Anthony" Wayne's victory at Fallen Timbers in 1794 and the ensuing series of land-grabbing treaties that Indiana governor William Henry Harrison inveigled the Indians into accepting, the plight of the Shawnee and other Ohio country nations had steadily worsened. Hunting grounds lost to the pioneer axe and plough forced tribes to disperse into shrinking groups in order to seek out pockets of territory sufficient to provide for their needs. Starvation was common, influenza ran rampant through the villages, and American whisky traders plying their goods only worsened an already desperate situation.

Non-intercourse unwittingly exacerbated matters by shutting off Indians' access to the British traders they largely depended on, for provisions from American sources were always insufficient. A great number of Indians were forced to seek assistance directly from the British holding Fort Malden and Fort St. Joseph. They came to the posts starving, destitute, increasingly discontented with their treatment by the United States.[3]

Meanwhile in Ohio, Indiana, and the other northwestern territories, many Indians had turned to a new hope that promised to improve their lot: returning to the way that they had lived before the white man came. In 1808, Tecumseh and his younger brother, Lalawéthika (one of the two surviving triplets), created a Shawnee settlement in northern Indiana on the Wabash River, about three miles below the mouth of the Tippecanoe River and one hundred miles east of Fort Wayne. Here Lalawéthika changed his name to Tenskwatawa, meaning "Open Door." More commonly called the Prophet, Tenskwatawa believed he spoke directly for the Great Spirit.

On the outside, the Prophet little resembled his handsome brother. Slim, of average height, he was sallow-faced with a down-turned mouth that lent his expression a doleful air, furthered by an old injury that had permanently closed his right eye. Until his thirtieth birthday, Lalawéthika had eked out a living as a minor healer and been noted as a lazy, often drunken, fellow. But the winter of 1805 brought particularly cold temperatures and an influenza epidemic that none of his potions or knowledge of bleeding could prevent taking lives. Then, in a life-transforming vision, the Great Spirit revealed that the Indians must repent their sinful life or be denied entry to heaven.

Overnight Lalawéthika repented his ways and demonstrated remarkable ability to capture the hearts and minds of all who heard his preaching. Sitting with eyes closed, face masked in reverence, he spoke eloquently and with hands in constant motion. Set aside whisky, he counselled, cast off evil medicines provided by the whites, cease murdering each other, "never think of war again," turn no cruel hand against either women or children, take only one wife and to her be true, be never dishonest or commit slander against another.

In a stunning attack on tradition, the Prophet also demanded that each Indian must destroy the medicine bags in which each person kept fetishes that aided connection to personal guardian spirits. Medicine bags, he said, were agents of witchcraft. Henceforth he was the only spiritual guide anyone should look to.

Traditional ceremonies, however, must be revived. Most tellingly, the ways of the white man adopted out of convenience and because of the insistence of the traders were to be rejected. Clothes worn by the whites were to be shunned, muskets, flints, and steel abandoned in favour of the bow and arrow. All animals introduced by whites, save the horse, were to be slaughtered. No more would Indians eat alien food such as pork, chicken, and wheat. They should completely return to the limited horticultural ways of the past and embrace the essential hunting life. All the white man's efforts to transform Indians into tillers of soil were to be rejected.

White culture, the Prophet said, was the root evil that had caused the Indian slide from grace toward damnation. An apocalyptic reckoning was coming when supernatural means would overthrow the whites and bury all of them alongside those Indians who still sinned. Then the land would be returned and the people would again live in Eden.[4]

The Prophet's message inspired the Shawnee and many of their allies. And while his younger brother became the people's spiritual leader, Tecumseh was their most powerful chief. The two men led their followers to the banks of the Wabash near Tippecanoe in 1808 to found a new home. Called Prophetstown by the whites, the community soon numbered 200. Neatly ordered, bark-sided houses overlooked the river from a height of ground. A prominent council house and medicine lodge stood to the west of this residential area, facing out on a wide expanse of prairie. By the river, in the adjacent bottomland, a hundred-acre plot had been cleared for cultivation. Ranks of canoes were beached alongside the river. Those living in the village were required to adhere to the standards and behaviour that the Prophet decreed.[5]

By October, the village had a population of about four hundred. But the winter of 1808–09 proved as hard for the Indians there as elsewhere. The cultivated fields failed to yield a fall harvest, the unusually heavy snowpack hampered hunting efforts. Starvation threatened.

Tecumseh was unaware of the troubles plaguing the settlement. He spent the winter in Ohio recruiting more followers among disaffected young warriors of the Wyandot and Seneca. While the Prophet prayed and preached, Tecumseh tirelessly built a new confederacy.[6] Yet even though Tecumseh avowed repeatedly that he sought only peace, and that he also generally abided by the tenets preached by his brother, the warrior never set aside the musket. He was also disinclined to await some supernaturally inspired apocalypse that would rid the land of whites. Peace would come, he believed, only through strength. To build this strength, he tracked relentlessly across the northwest—pushing, prodding, cajoling, threatening when necessary, to win the other chiefs over to the cause.

Despite his diplomatic skills, Tecumseh's efforts yielded only limited results until Harrison advanced his most ambitious land grab with the Treaty of Fort Wayne, concluded on September 30, 1809. Assembling a group of friendly chiefs cultivated among the Miami, Potawatomi, and Delaware, Harrison had them sign over three million acres to the United States in exchange for a greater annuity and more trade goods. That the Potawatomi had never resided in the land in question and the other tribal chiefs had only dubious authority to agree to such a deal bothered Harrison not a jot. Harrison used the fact that President James Madison had only just been inaugurated that March to present this treaty as distinct from the string of earlier treaties he had masterminded. "This is the first request that your new Father has ever made of you and it will be the last, he wants no more of your land."[7]

The treaty enraged Tecumseh. With the Prophet at his side, he threatened to execute the chiefs as traitors, but there was nothing either preacher or warrior could do to reverse the treaty. Tecumseh, however, warned that any whites attempting to survey or settle the new land—comprising as it did all the lower Wabash River territory and being where many of those people earlier driven out of the Ohio now dwelt—would do so at risk of their lives.

Outrage spread through the tribes, and with the coming of the first spring grasses that provided feed for their horses, warriors by the hundreds rode into Prophetstown. Potawatomi, Kickapoo, Delaware, and Miami—mostly disenchanted young warriors—arrived. In late May about 240 men from the Sac and Fox nations offered their support before carrying on to Upper Canada, where they hoped to receive provisions from the British. Tecumseh believed they would, for the only thing that had enabled the people of Prophetstown to survive the winter had been several pack trains of food that British officials had sent south to assist them.[8]

When Harrison learned of these supply shipments and the growing Indian anger over the Fort Wayne treaty, he saw sure evidence of a British conspiracy. On July 4, 1810, he wrote a long letter to Madison's secretary of war, William Eustis. "The treaties made by me last fall, were concluded upon principles as liberal toward the Indians as my knowledge of the views and opinions of the government would allow. . . . But, sir, the President may rest assured, that the complaints of injury, with regard to the sale of lands, is a mere pretense, suggested to the prophet by British partisans and emissaries."

He claimed on good authority that "a Miami chief" returning from a visit to a British trade post, "after having received the accustomed donation of goods, was thus addressed by Elliott, the British agent: 'My son, keep your eyes fixed on me—my tomahawk is now up—be you ready, but do not strike till I give the signal.'"[9]

Harrison was not alone in this belief. Until 1810 most Kentuckians paid only scant attention to the reported interactions between British and Canadian authorities and the Indians. But as Tecumseh's confederacy grew toward fruition, whites living near the frontier felt increasingly uneasy, and even those who, like Clay, lived in secure western communities like Lexington believed they faced a "serious Indian menace." The *Kentucky Gazette* opined on September 11, 1810: "We have always been of opinion that the confederacy which has been formed by the Prophet, was the effect of British intrigue; and we have never doubted that the secret agents of that power, which are known to exist in every part of America, but particularly in the Indian country, gave it all the confidence in their power."[10]

Two months earlier, citizens from Knox County had descended on Vincennes, Indiana, to deliver a resolution to Harrison that demanded the destruction of Prophetstown. As the village was only 150 miles up the Wabash from the territorial capital, they claimed it constituted a

clear and present danger to the settlers. Prophetstown and the confeder-
acy it embodied, they said, "is a British scheme, and . . . the agents of that
power are constantly exciting the Indians to hostilities against the
United States." Another resolution, forwarded by residents of St. Clair,
Illinois, called "the seditious village . . . the great nursery of hostile
Indians and traitorous British Indian traders."

The *Kentucky Gazette* railed: "From the friendly course pursued by
Mr. Jefferson, towards our red neighbors, and which has been followed
by Mr. Madison, we had supposed the Indians would never more treat
us otherwise than as brethren. But we have been mistaken—British
intrigue and British gold, it seems, has greater influence with them of
late than American justice and benevolence. . . . We have in our possession information which proves beyond doubt, the late disturbances
to be owing to the too successful intrigues of British emissaries."[11]
Tellingly, the evidence of British intriguing was never produced.

All this fervour suited Harrison well, for he planned a military operation to wipe out the village the whites were beginning to call Tippecanoe.
The possibility that such an attack might provoke war with Britain was
even welcome. "The people of this Territory and Kentucky are extremely
pressing in offers of their service for an expedition into the Indian
Country. Any number of men might be obtained for this purpose or
for a march into Canada." Harrison declared that vast numbers of
Indians were returning from British trading posts laden with rifles,
fuses, powder, and lead. "And that the language and measures of the
Indians indicate nothing but war."[12]

In reality, Tecumseh was keeping his people in check, for the time
was not yet ripe for military action. The confederacy could not act
alone. But the warrior chief believed war between Great Britain and
America was inevitable and that then the confederacy could act and
possibly succeed. Until then he urged the warriors to bide their time
and chastened those who carried out small running raids against frontier settlers during the summer of 1811. Tecumseh knew the actions of
these renegades could well provide the excuse that Harrison needed.

Not that Harrison needed the excuses of others. He manufactured
his own quite capably. As the Twelfth Congress started assembling that

November in Washington for a new session and its members openly talked of war, Harrison closed upon Tippecanoe with a force of about one thousand regulars and militia. From intelligence reports, Harrison knew that Tecumseh had recently departed on a winter-long tour to build support for the confederacy among the Creek to the south. "I hope," Harrison wrote to Eustis on the eve of his march, "before his return that that part of the fabrick, which he considered complete will be demolished and even its foundation rooted up."[13] Harrison intended to destroy Tippecanoe and kill or scatter its residents.

On November 6, the Americans cut through a series of swamps and dense thickets to reach a plateau overlooking the village from a distance of about a mile. Harrison sent a message to the Prophet that he was willing to talk, but a deserter from the American camp warned that this was a deception; the plan was to attack Tippecanoe in the morning. The warriors with the Prophet decided that they had no recourse but to try to seize the advantage by assaulting Harrison's camp that night. Only about 500 strong, they could never hope to fend off the Americans if they were allowed to move against the village in full battle order. The Prophet sought the counsel of the spirits and reported not only that the Americans would be surprised but that their gunpowder would turn to sand. For added measure, the Indians would be rendered bulletproof.

Heavy cloud cover cloaked the warrior advance on the camp in inky darkness, but just as the order for the attack was imminent a sentry fired a shot in alarm. With a scream of defiance the warriors rushed the camp, sending the sentries reeling toward its centre, where the Americans formed a defensive line. Although the American formation buckled several times, forcing a short withdrawal to regroup, the Indians were unable to break it completely. Finally, as the first glimmer of dawn tinged the eastern skyline, Harrison saw that he outnumbered the Indians and ordered a counterattack on both flanks. Caught in the open, the warriors were quickly routed, falling back to the village. After two and a half hours Harrison's men had won the field. The butcher's bill was staggering for the Americans. Harrison counted 68 of his men dead and 120 wounded—almost one-fifth of his entire force. Although defeated, the Indians had fared better. Estimates ranged from 20 to 50 killed.

Having taken such a hard battering, the Americans failed to assault the village. Fearing a renewed attack, they threw up fortifications and hunkered in their shelter for the next two days except for brief sorties out onto the field to scalp the Indian corpses left behind. Some fixed these grisly trophies to their gun muzzles. As darkness fell on November 8, a patrol probed the village and found it deserted save a wounded warrior and an old woman both accidentally left behind during the withdrawal. Harrison ordered the village plundered of anything useful to the Indians such as pots and utensils, seized what corn stocks could be used by his men, and then burned the village to the ground. He made sure that the granary, vital to winter survival, was torched. The next day, the Americans loaded their many wounded on wagons and trailed slowly away from the blackened, smouldering ruins of Prophetstown.[14]

When Tecumseh returned to the village in the early spring of 1812, he later recalled, standing "upon the ashes of my own home . . . there I summoned the spirits of the braves who had fallen in their vain attempts to protect their homes from the grasping invader, and as I snuffed up the smell of their blood from the ground I swore once more eternal hatred—the hatred of an avenger."[15]

Even though Harrison had marched against Prophetstown with the clear intent to annihilate it, Americans in the west and many congressmen in Washington were quick to declare the night attack on his camp clear evidence of Indian treachery. Maj. Gen. Andrew Jackson, commander of the Tennessee militia and a man who never hesitated to slaughter an Indian whenever possible, wrote to congratulate Harrison on the action. But, he said, the "blood of our murdered countrymen must be avenged. I do hope that Government will see that it is necessary to act efficiently and that this hostile band which must be excited to war by the secret agents of Great Britain must be destroyed."[16]

The Battle of Tippecanoe became a rallying cry for the pro-war movement. Preposterous accounts were published in newspapers and pamphlets that elevated each fallen soldier or militaman into a heroic martyr who surrendered life in order to protect innocent American settlers from being murdered in their homes by savage Indians. In Kentucky, the legislature passed a resolution blaming Great Britain for "inciting the savages . . . to murder the inhabitants of our defenceless frontiers—furnishing them with arms and ammunition . . . to attack our forces; to the loss of a number of our brave men."[17] In the House, Tennessee's Felix Grundy declared that America must "drive the British from our Continent." Doing so would ensure that "they will no longer have an opportunity of intriguing with our Indian neighbors, and setting on the ruthless savage to tomahawk our women and children. That nation will lose her Canadian trade, and, by having no resting place in this country, her means of annoying us will be diminished."[18]

There was little truth to these accusations against the British. As Tecumseh, the Prophet, and their followers had shown increasing hostility toward America, the British representatives with whom they had contact counselled caution and moderation. Maj. Gen. Isaac Brock, Upper Canada's military commander, enunciated British policy clearly in instructions issued in the spring of 1811 to his officers stationed on the frontier. "I am decidedly of opinion that upon every principle of policy our interest should lead us to use all our endeavours to prevent a rupture between the Indians and the subjects of the United States." His officers and those of the Indian Department were "to use all their influence to dissuade the Indians from their projected plan of hostility, given them clearly to understand that they must not expect any assistance from us. The officers, however, must be extremely cautious in pointing out to them, that it is for their good only that this advice is given to them, and not from any dereliction of that regard with which we always view their interests."[19]

These were not just empty words. Throughout 1811, British agents stationed at frontier trading posts reduced the amounts of gunpowder and lead normally issued to the Indians so they would have sufficient supply to enable hunting but no surplus for military use. In past years, one report stated, the Indians coming to Amherstburg had been issued almost 3,200 pounds of powder; this was cut to 1,211 pounds.[20]

The British effort to avert war on the American frontier had little to do with altruism toward either the Indians or the settlers. Unlike the politicians in London, Brock fully expected that Canada could face attack from the United States at any moment. He hoped that by constraining the Indians to keep the peace, their military potential could be retained until the Americans declared war outright. Then he would rally the Indians to the British cause and deploy them effectively in concert with his own regulars and Canadian militiamen. If the Indians acted independently, Brock feared they would be slaughtered by the American troops, resulting in the confederacy being scattered and its members so demoralized they would be of no use in the future defence of Canada.

Brock's pragmatic approach was typical of British North American dealings with Indians, which largely continued the policies of New France. For the 150 years of its duration New France's European settler population had always been grossly outnumbered by the Indians. To secure their power in North America, the French had entered into alliances with various Indian nations that established military and commercial interdependencies. Fur-trade camps, missionary outposts, and military garrisons were scattered thinly through the frontier beyond the St. Lawrence River's banks where most of the *habitant* settlers lived. New France's influence over the Indian nations was cemented by the mutual benefits realized through the fur trade more than military dominance. Indeed, without these military alliances, New France could not have survived.

New France was almost perpetually at war with the British colonies south of it. On the northern frontier of these colonies the British authorities established similar trade and military alliances with Indian nations that were pitted against those allied to the French. When New France was vanquished in 1769, the British conquerors not only undertook to quell discontent among the *habitants* but also sought to develop peaceful relationships with the majority of the Indian nations, for, like the French had been, they were grossly outnumbered. Also like the French, the British commercial interest in the newly acquired colonies was based on the fur trade rather than agricultural expansion. This was no longer the case in the older southern colonies that would form the United States.

The fur trade simply could not exist without a wilderness peopled by Indians who could trap and skin animals and then deliver their pelts to the traders in exchange for European goods. This coexistent relationship meant that the Europeans living in British North America did not see the Indians as savage enemies impeding the march of progress. While Indian nations were displaced by settlement within Upper and Lower Canada, the pace of this agrarian expansion was sufficiently slow that the advance was not preceded by bloody territorial warfare.

Heavily influenced by the church, the British administration also looked upon the Indian nations with a paternalistic eye. The French missionaries had sought to convert the Indians in order to save their souls and gradually wean them from a hunting-and-gathering life considered at odds with the influence of Christianity. But missionary zeal after Britain conquered New France became less vigorous as the power of the Roman Catholic Church was reduced. Instead the British governors made little effort to undermine the traditional Indian way of life so long as the natives kept the peace and continued to work in the fur trade. And, knowing the thin line of redcoats and Canadian militia could not alone repel any determined American invasion, the British continued to foster a web of military alliances with the Indians on the frontier and to husband their power so that they could be unleashed against any invading force.

—

SIX

War Hawks

*S*outh of the Canadian border the pro-war rhetoric mounted, becoming increasingly hysterical and fanciful. Nowhere was this more the case than on the debating floor of the Twelfth Congress. From the Speaker's chair, Henry Clay orchestrated the select team of young westerners who had come to Washington in the fall of 1811 with clear intention to force the issue. They were called the War Hawks. Although each was a man of hot temper and independent spirit, Clay provided leadership. Upon arriving in Washington, Clay and six of the most prominent War Hawks together rented several cramped rooms over a tavern. Given Washington's critical shortage of lodging for senators and congressmen, such arrangements were common. Often two or more congressmen shared a single room.

John C. Calhoun, William Lowndes, Felix Grundy, Langdon Cheves, and George M. Bibb joined Clay in the tavern. Grundy and Cheves were thirty-five, Clay thirty-four, Calhoun and Lowndes just twenty-nine. All believed President Madison lacked the mettle to lead Congress into war and so it fell on their shoulders to exert "some controlling or at least some concentrating influence." Dubbing their quarters the War Mess, on November 3 they set to work in these dingy environs hammering out a strategy to win their colleagues over. Absolutely essential was the need to have one of their own elected Speaker. Lowndes of South Carolina argued that the man with the requisite talent and experience "to urge and drive, to conciliate and persuade," was Henry Clay, that "clever man whom they call the Western Star."[1] The others concurred and the following day pulled off the unprecedented coup of having Clay elected on the first ballot.

Despite the War Hawks' fears that Madison lacked the fortitude to take the necessary, bold, and decisive step, the president expressed reluctant support for their position in his annual address to the opening of Congress. While sharply rebuking France for its imposition of maritime trade restrictions, Madison laid greatest blame for America's predicament on Great Britain's doorstep. The actions of the British, both on the seas and on the western frontier, he said, were forcing America to strengthen its navy and army to meet these dual threats. All efforts at reconciliation had been rebuffed and Britain's cabinet was imposing on "the threshold of our territory . . . measures which under existing circumstances have the character as well as the effect of war on our lawful commerce. With this evidence of hostile inflexibility in trampling on rights which no independent nation can relinquish . . . Congress will feel the duty of putting the United States into an armor and an attitude demanded by the crisis, and corresponding with the national spirit and expectations."[2]

The president sought laws to expand the army to full strength, mobilize the militia as needed, develop military academies, enlarge military supply stocks, and stockpile materials for naval construction. Although the national treasury had collected more than $13.5 million in the past year, enabling $5 million in debt reduction, Madison sought authority to take out loans to meet potential defence expenditures. He came very close, but not quite, to recommending Congress declare war.

Madison's message outlined the government's economic, military, and foreign policies for the forthcoming year. It fell to Congress to study the various parts of this plan and accept, modify, or reject each component while also deciding whether to cross that line in the sand beyond which war must follow. As Speaker, Clay moved immediately to ensure that the War Hawks dictated Congress's reaction by dividing Madison's message into nine parts, referred to seven select and two standing committees. Ignoring seniority, Clay assigned the three vital subjects of foreign relations and military and naval affairs to committees where the War Hawks held the chair and comprised most of the membership.

Those congressmen opposed to Madison's presidency and reputed to be either pro-British or anti-war were shut out of these committees or granted only minority standing. This fate befell veteran Congressmen John Randolph and Josiah Quincy. This was Randolph's seventh congressional session. From Roanoke, Virginia, Randolph had broken with Jefferson years earlier to become the "mad genius of discord" around whom rallied a group of southern congressmen opposed to Republican policies and equally despising the Federalists. Shrill of voice and almost freakishly emaciated, Randolph was a quick-tongued, fast-fisted bully who played the role of congressional bad boy by dressing carelessly and casually tossing his legs over his desk while slouching low in his chair when bored. Continually courted by the Federalists, he shunned them, sitting instead as an independent. Randolph was determined to challenge this "horde of upstart patriots" led by Clay, who, he wrote, had "strided from the door of the Hall as soon as he entered it to the Speaker's Chair."[3]

Quincy, a Massachusetts Federalist returning for his fourth term to Congress, believed that Madison and the War Hawks conspired to bring the nation to war purely to advance the desires of those "wild men on the Missouri" for more land. He thought everyone living west of the protective wall of the Appalachians was "foreign, uncouth, abhorrent and menacing to the divine right of Eastern conservatives to dominate society and politics." Quincy argued that Jefferson and Madison's western policies, particularly the Louisiana Purchase and those that had created new states there, violated the Constitution and threatened to tear the Union apart.[4]

The House was a notoriously rowdy forum described by various newspapers as akin to "a turbulent cock-pit." The Speakers of the two previous sessions had each proven incapable of maintaining order and decorum, particularly when Quincy or Randolph held forth.[5] Three days into the Tenth Congress, Randolph had tromped into the House with his favourite female hound dog in tow, a clear violation of protocol. Hesitant to confront a man who spoke often of his love of pistols and duelling, Speaker Joseph B. Varnum failed to order the animal ejected. By urging the dog to bark threateningly and lunge at any congressmen Randolph disliked who dared to take the floor, the Virginian not only disrupted proceedings but virtually hijacked control of the House.

When Congressman Willis Alton complained that the dog had tripped him, Randolph battered the man with his cane.

Having cowed Congress in the past, it surprised nobody that within days of the Twelfth Congress convening Randolph sauntered into the House with the dog on his heels to challenge Clay's authority. No sooner had the dog passed through the door, however, than Clay ordered the doorkeeper "to take her out," as no females were allowed into the House. The dog was summarily removed without protest from Randolph and it never reappeared. Congressman John A. Harper, a New Hampshire War Hawk, thought Clay's quick thinking greatly increased his stock while devaluing Randolph's.[6]

Clay carefully orchestrated the debates and never hesitated to relinquish the Speaker's chair to personally argue for war. When the House split over a bill amendment that would increase enlistment of new soldiers from 15,000 to 25,000, Clay declared that simply investing Quebec's fortifications would require the greater total proposed. While giving lip service to the value of volunteer militia, Clay said only regulars were capable of carrying out such a "siege" and of also building and manning the garrisons necessary to secure other strategically vital positions during an invasion of Canada. He then proposed the following scenario for the conquest of all British North America: "Canada is invaded; the upper part falls, and you proceed to Quebec. It is true there would be no European enemy behind to be apprehended; but the people of that country might rise. . . . Therefore . . . a portion of the invading army would be distributed in the upper country, after its conquest, amongst the places susceptible of military strength and defence. The army, considerably reduced, sets itself down before Quebec. Suppose it falls. Here again will be requisite a number of men to hold and defend it. And if the war is prosecuted still farther, and the lower country and Halifax are assailed . . . it [is] obvious that the whole force of 25,000 men would not be too great."[7]

A standing army was generally anathema to Republican philosophy, so at issue was not only the size of the force to be raised but its very creation. Many a Republican feared that if the regular army was too large a rogue president might employ it to impose a dictatorship.

Alternatively, the army might also rise of its own accord to establish military rule. Clay assured the House that this army would be "enlisted for a limited time, raised for the sole purpose of war, and . . . disbanded on the return of peace." Even "supposing it to be corrupted and its arms turned by the ambition of its leaders against the freedom of the country," the people, "consisting of upwards of seven millions, affording a physical power of about a million of men capable of bearing arms, and ardently devoted to liberty, could not be subdued by an army of 25,000 men." In Massachusetts, Clay declared, every militiaman was being armed "and he trusted in God that that great object would be persevered in until every man in the nation could proudly shoulder the musket which was to defend his country and himself. . . . Such a people has nothing to fear from a petty, contemptible force of 25,000 regulars."[8]

The object for such an army, Clay said, was "distinctly to be war, and war with Great Britain." He then used the debate on the amendment to advance the case for declaring war. In its campaign against France, "England is said to be fighting for the world, and shall we . . . attempt to weaken her exertions?" This, of course, was the prime argument of New England Federalists opposing war. Clay scorned the idea that Britain acted for the world. Were that the case, would not Britain scrupulously observe the rights of others and abide by international laws? Instead, he said, America was "called upon to submit to debasement, dishonour and disgrace—to bow the neck to royal insolence." The "real cause of British aggression [against the United States] was not to distress an enemy [France], but to destroy a rival. . . . She sickens at your prosperity, and beholds in your growth—your sails spread on every ocean, and your numerous seamen, the foundations of a power which, at no very distant day, is to make her tremble for naval superiority."[9]

The amended bill passed by ninety votes to thirty-five against on December 31, 1811. Madison had authorization to add 25,000 men to the regular army. A contented Clay wrote to William Worsley, editor of Lexington's *Reporter:* "I consider it as the strongest war measure that could be adopted, short of an actual declaration of war, which I have no doubt will be made before we rise, unless England ceases her aggressions."[10]

As the congressional session ground on through the winter of 1811–12, the War Hawks clamoured ever more loudly. Increasingly their speeches addressed less the supposed outrages Britain had visited upon the nation than the right of America to conquer Canada in order to expel the British from North America. Grundy set the tone on December 9, during debate on the report of the foreign relations committee. "This war, if carried successfully," he said, "will have its advantages. We shall drive the British from our Continent. . . . I therefore feel anxious not only to add the Floridas to the South, but the Canadas to the North of this empire." War Hawk Richard Johnson of Kentucky invoked God in support of American domination of Canada: "I shall never die contented until I see her expulsion from North America and her territories incorporated with the United States. . . . In point of territorial limit the map will prove [conquering Canada's] importance. The waters of the St. Lawrence and the Mississippi interlock in a number of places and the Great Disposer of Human Events intended those two rivers should belong to the same people."[11]

Others voiced even grander designs. An ardent supporter of the War Hawks from Tennessee asked where it was "written in the book of fate that the American republic shall not stretch her limits from the capes of Chesapeake to Nootka sound, from the isthmus of Panama to Hudson bay?"[12] Although the term manifest destiny had yet to be coined—that would wait upon John L. O'Sullivan in 1845—the Republican War Hawks expressed essentially the same philosophy. There was little to differentiate their position from O'Sullivan's claim that it was America's mission to fulfill its "manifest destiny to overspread the continent allotted by Providence."[13] And as would prove true in the 1840s, the vision of a United States whose wings spread wide and unchallenged over the entire continent enticed the imagination of many Americans.

The eternal pioneer thirst for fresh land made Canada a tempting target for conquest. Indeed, many Americans had already settled there. Because of the barrier presented by the Appalachians to westward movement, a common migration route popularized in about 1800 drew thousands of pioneers from the United States into Upper Canada at Niagara. They then moved down the Niagara Peninsula to cross back into America at Detroit on their way to the Ohio and upper Mississippi valleys. Many of these Americans passing through Canada decided to stay. Land was cheap, the result of the government of Upper Canada's generous land grant system that allowed a settler to claim 200 acres for little more than payment of modest administrative fees and swearing allegiance to the British Crown. The soil was fertile, and the Indians in Upper Canada, as opposed to those on America's western frontier, were not hostile.[14]

By 1812, three out of every five Upper Canadian settlers were American. Despite their pledge of allegiance, few thought themselves British subjects or even Canadians—that distinction they left to the French Canadians. The oath was an insignificant matter of convenience.[15] After all, many had earlier forsaken allegiance to the Crown by fighting for American independence or had parents who had done so. Most continued to consider themselves Americans. The War Hawks so blithely believed Upper Canada would easily fall partly because these settlers would surely welcome their liberators with open arms or at least offer no resistance.

While Canada was considered ripe for picking, the main argument for its invasion was more strategic than imperialistic. Neither the War Hawks nor Madison's administration could conceive of any other means of effectively making war on Britain. Conquering Canada would drive the British out of North America. And, if Halifax could be taken, the Royal Navy's ability to enforce the orders-in-council upon American shipping would be greatly reduced for lack of one of its two key harbours on the western side of the Atlantic. Even if the invasion did not go as well as Clay imagined it must and only the Canadas or just Upper Canada fell into American hands, what was conquered could be used as a bargaining chip to force Britain to repeal the orders-in-council and impressment.

In the House, it fell to one of Randolph's allies to summarize the lack of strategic options open to the United States. During the debate over raising the size of the regular army, Virginian Republican Hugh Nelson put it simply. All the War Hawks could advance to gain recognition of America's neutral rights, he said, was the invasion of Canada. Nelson refuted the idea that Canada could be conquered. And even if it could, would that somehow enforce America's rights? "Certainly not. The way to enforce these rights [is] by way of a great maritime force, which the nation [is] incompetent to raise and support."[16]

"Ever since the report of the committee on foreign relations came into the house," Randolph cried, "we have heard but one word—like the whip-poor-will, but one eternal monotonous tone—Canada! Canada! Canada! If you go to war it will not be for the protection of, or defense of your maritime rights. Gentlemen from the North have been taken up to some high mountain and shown all the kingdoms of the earth; and Canada seems tempting in their sight. That rich vein of Genesee land, which is said to be even better on the other side of the lake than on this. Agrarian cupidity, not maritime right, urges the war. . . . Not a syllable about Halifax, which unquestionably should be our great object in a war for maritime security. . . . Are there no limits to the territory over which a republican government may be extended?"[17]

Randolph had missed the point that Clay, at least, had Halifax clearly in his sights. He just intended to get there by land rather than by sea, which showed little more than that the Kentuckian had a poor sense of British North America's geography. Marching a large army from Upper Canada to Nova Scotia was not a proposition deserving serious consideration.

But Clay was a man of ideas rather than details, and that ultimately was the problem that stymied the House. All but a handful of congressmen agreed that the nation had just cause for initiating hostilities, but how to prosecute a war without unduly discomfiting the average citizen or the country's vital business interests? There was also the issue of how to conduct a war without repudiating any of the human liberties enshrined in the Constitution.

On December 17, 1811, Langdon Cheves, chairman of the select committee studying naval matters, presented Congress with a bill to build ten additional frigates to add to the navy's current strength of five and repair five out-of-service frigates that were slowly rotting away. This was a compromise on Secretary of the Navy Paul Hamilton's request for construction of twelve 74-gun ships of the line and twenty frigates to be added to the existing ten.

An immediate furor erupted, with congressmen expounding loudly that the bill violated the long-standing policy that America should not have a permanent navy. Cheves found himself under fire from most of his fellow War Hawks, who feared that construction of a navy would draw money and resources away from any land war. The Federalists inclined to endorse the bill because it would require federal expenditures sure to be unpopular and might consequently erode public support for Madison's government.

No sooner had this bill been advanced than Secretary of the Treasury Albert Gallatin tabled a long-delayed report on the projected costs of the war. Although he had earlier tried to convince Jefferson and his administration that war was necessary, Gallatin had begun to have second thoughts when Madison showed him an advance copy of his intended address to the opening of Congress. In essence it sought congressional authority to declare war on Britain. Deeply alarmed, Gallatin had cautioned the president against issuing "an outright recommendation of war" and quietly counselled him to follow a more cautious course. "Is it more eligible to resort to war than to rely on the effect of non-importation?" he asked. And if so, is "it proper and consistent with policy to recommend it?"

Gallatin answered no to the first proposition, not out of any belief that non-importation could succeed but more out of "the uncertainty in every respect of the effect of a war." Gallatin's estimates for the cost of war and the resources required to win were alarming, and more than he believed the nation could afford.

Not only were the costs worrisome, Gallatin feared that "the measures necessary to carry on the war must be unpopular and by producing a change of men may lead to a disgraceful peace, to absolute subserviency hereafter to Great Britain and even to substantial alterations in our institutions." Correctly anticipating that the Federalists in both the Senate and Congress might support measures guaranteed to heighten federal spending in order to spawn such unpopularity that the government fell, Gallatin believed that a Federalist president would immediately negotiate a peace on British terms. Madison, he suggested, should leave it to "the body with whom our Constitution has exclusively vested the power of making war" rather than present it as a presidential recommendation.

Such an approach ensured that final responsibility for war would rest with the House and the Senate rather than the president. As a consequence of Gallatin's counsel, Madison had struck from his speech any reference to what he believed America should do in response to the evidence of Britain's "war on our lawful commerce" that he cited at length. Instead he said only that "the period has arrived" without clearly stating what the import of this moment necessitated. Had it not been for Gallatin's intervention, Madison's message to Congress would have directly called for a declaration of war.

In advancing an argument for moderation, Gallatin was not outright attempting to prevent the war. Although haunted by concerns about how it would be funded and prosecuted, he believed that a recommendation by Madison for war would cost the United States any element of surprise over the British and might well precipitate a pre-emptory strike. "If war is certainly to ensue it is better," he said, "as soon as we are sufficiently ready, to make it at once instead of announcing beforehand that determination and thereby enabling the enemy to strike at once, to sweep our commerce, to send a fleet and reinforcements on our coast and vicinity."

Gallatin's intervention had persuaded Madison to tone down the rhetoric in his message, but when it was delivered the treasurer still thought the president had advocated war over any other options. Non-intercourse or renewed attempts at negotiation were not mentioned and neither option was considered by Congress. Disappointed, Gallatin confided to William Lowndes in a rare moment of candour that "he was dissentient from the President's message at the opening of Congress because he was averse to war."[18]

When Gallatin presented his financial news about its cost he offered no position either for or against war. He merely stated its price—$50 million. The United States would have to borrow heavily while introducing new taxes and raising those already in place to foot the bill. Gallatin also made public the sobering news that America had produced almost $45.3 million in domestic products the previous year, and, in the absence of the embargo, had exported $38.5 million of this to Great Britain and her allies Spain and Portugal while only $1.194 million had gone to France and Italy. The unasked question was whether it made sense to make war on one's major trading partner.

Gallatin's report panicked Congress. Even though the estimate of the cost of the war was ridiculously lower than what Gallatin believed was likely, the pro-war lobby declared the figures inflated. The War Hawks also called the treasurer to task for suggesting that taxes would be necessary to fund a war.[19]

Senator James Asheton Bayard, who staunchly opposed war, noted on January 25, 1812, in a letter to his cousin, Andrew Bayard, that nothing "has depressed the war spirit here more than the frightful exhibition made by Gallatin of War taxes. Many who voted for the army will not vote for the taxes and I much doubt whether any one proposed by the Secretary can be carried [through] both Houses of Congress. They are not such fools at the same time as not to know that war cannot be carried on without money. And when they have arrived at the point—no money no war—even they who are now panting after war if they can't have it without taxing the people and of course ruining their popularity will abandon the object.

"I shall consider the taxes as the test, and when a majority agree to the proposed taxes, I shall believe them in earnest and determined upon war, but till then I shall consider the whole as a game of juggling in which the presidency and the loaves and fishes belonging to it are the objects they are contending for."[20] The following day, in another letter, Bayard sarcastically referred to a colleague who had approached him to say "he had no objection to going to war, but did not want it to cost anything."[21]

Federalists such as Bayard fell upon Gallatin's grim estimates with glee. Massachusetts congressman Samuel L. Taggart thought it must surely "cool the war fever and disabuse the public that it would be easy to take Quebec." Some Republicans, meanwhile, accused Gallatin of having done nothing to discourage the war movement in the House until it had advanced so far that to step back now from war would disgrace them all. Outside the House, Gallatin faced slanderous attacks in the pro-war newspapers. One headline described him as "The Rat—in the Treasury."[22]

Brushing aside criticism, Gallatin pressed home the fact that it was impossible to make war without paying the piper of higher taxes and increased duties to cover the costs. Nor would it be possible to avoid incurring public debt. War was expensive, and Congress would have to wake up to that fact or the entire adventure would necessarily fail. Not above pressing his case through back channels, Gallatin enlisted the assistance of one of the elder War Hawks, forty-year-old Jonathan Roberts of Pennsylvania. A bachelor, Roberts was happy to accept Gallatin's frequent invitations to dinner and was soon converted to the necessity of the treasurer's prescription. Carrying this message repeatedly back to the War Mess over the tavern, he slowly won over some of the young westerners. Most important, he convinced Clay that Gallatin's recommendations were correct.[23]

By early 1812, Gallatin no longer believed war could be avoided, which made it all the more important that Congress adopt the taxation, borrowing, and duty-raising measures. Were they to fail, the treasurer was convinced America would lose this war that it seemed hell-bent on starting.

Meanwhile Congress was determined to keep its head buried in the sand. Although it passed the bill to increase the size of the army, that was about the only concrete preparatory step it authorized. Even Clay's powerful rhetoric failed to save the navy bill. In a series of motions, Congress whittled down the number of new frigates from ten to six, then to five, four, three, and finally to none at all by a vote of sixty-two to fifty-nine. Stockpiling building materials was narrowly approved, but the Senate then scuttled fully repairing the decommissioned frigates by slashing the number to be rehabilitated by a third. Not to be outdone, Congress rejected a bill to arm and to classify the militia as subject to federal control and deployment to wherever the administration so desired—it being a long-standing policy that state militias could not be required to serve outside U.S. boundaries and, in some cases, not even outside the state in which they were raised.

Congress's unwillingness to prepare for war infuriated Madison, even as his failure to recommend war exasperated many congressmen. Federalist Senator Nicholas Gilman blamed Madison's "want of manliness and candor" for destroying "the confidence that ought always to subsist between the different branches of government."

Madison had clung to the slender hope that Britain might indicate willingness to repeal its orders-in-council when the Prince Regent took over from mad King George III. But the Prince had made it clear in a speech delivered in London that resumption of normal trade with America would occur only when practicable. He went on to tell Parliament that any attempt at conciliation with America must be consistent "with the due maintenance of the maritime and commercial rights and interests of the British Empire." Madison complained to his old friend Thomas Jefferson on February 7: "All that we see from Great Britain indicates an adherence to her mad policy towards the United States." Gloomily, he added of Congress: "With a view to enable the Executive to step at once into Canada they have provided, after two months delay, for a regular force requiring twelve [months] to raise it, and after three months for a volunteer force, on terms not likely to raise it at all for that object."[24]

By February's end, Madison and his administration were committed to war. It was agreed, however, that no declaration would be made until the return of the American sloop-of-war *Hornet* from Europe. *Hornet* had sailed to Europe in late 1811 and had been held there pending the outcome of negotiations with France over a possible commercial treaty. An accommodation with France would strengthen America's international position and the British might be pressured to cancel the orders-in-council.

That was a faint hope, however, and having decided that war was almost inevitable, Madison implemented a bizarre scheme intended to whip up popular support throughout the nation for such an enterprise. On March 9, he set before Congress documents purported as proof that in 1808 Canadian governor Sir John Craig had hired a spy named John Henry to recruit a force of traitors, particularly among the Federalists, to mastermind a rebellion in New England to secede from the Union. Madison and his secretary of state, James Monroe, had been enticed into buying these reputedly seditious documents by a French-Canadian con man posing as a French count. Eager for what they hoped would be evidence not only of British intrigue but also of Federalist disloyalty, Madison and Monroe had forked over $50,000 (the entire annual secret service fund) in February and then waited until the timing was right to release them.

It seems unlikely either bothered to read the documents before the purchase or after. They proved worthless. No conspirators were named, no specifics of rebellious plots revealed. Henry was quickly exposed as a sleazy opportunist. Several American journalists noted that the papers contained nothing that could not be learned by reading any Boston newspaper.[25] After an initial flurry of outrage in both the popular press and on the Congress floor, the matter largely fizzled out.

Meantime the tone of debate in both Senate and Congress reflected growing support for war and some recognition that the administration needed the means to prosecute it. On March 14, Congress authorized an $11-million loan but refused to impose taxes on the American people or on business transactions conducted within the boundaries of the country. That left Gallatin increasingly dependent on declining customs duties and export taxes for government revenue.[26]

Clay and Monroe met the morning after Congress approved the war loan and agreed that matters had to be brought to a head. Their idea was that America should again impose an embargo upon itself for thirty days and that upon its termination war would automatically follow. In a note Clay sent Monroe that afternoon, he argued that an embargo would "above all powerfully accelerate preparations for the War. By the expiration of the Embargo the *Hornet* will have returned with good or bad news, and of course the question of War may then be fairly decided."

In the margin of the note, he scribbled, "Altho' the power of declaring War belongs to Congress, I do not see that it less falls within the scope of the President's constitutional duty to recommend such measures as he shall judge necessary and expedient than any other which, being suggested by him, they alone can adopt."[27]

On March 31, Monroe huddled with the House Committee on Foreign Affairs in what were supposed to be secret proceedings. John Randolph, however, refused to be bound by secrecy and read to Congress some of the notes he took during the meeting. Monroe, he revealed, opened the meeting by saying that "without an accommodation with Great Britain Congress ought to declare war before adjourning." The only reason for not issuing an immediate declaration, Monroe had continued, was that the country was unprepared. He therefore proposed an embargo not exceeding sixty days "as preparatory to war." There was also the need to await the return of *Hornet*. Monroe added: "Without war, public expectations would be defeated and our character destroyed abroad."[28]

Two days later Congress passed an embargo bill by a vote of seventy to forty-one. The following day, April 3, Senate approval was given but the embargo's length extended to ninety days. Madison signed the bill into law three days later.

The pace of events now quickened, and all eyes in Washington turned toward the Atlantic in anticipation of *Hornet's* imminent arrival. But by early May she still had not appeared, and Madison stuck to his guns that no war declaration could occur until she arrived. A Kentucky newspaper editor vented his frustration that a single ship should take on such prominence. "Ever since her sailing the cant word has been, the *Hornet*, the *Hornet*. What sting she will bring on her return."[29]

On May 18, Madison was nominated Republican candidate for the next presidential race and five days later a bag of dispatches from the just-arrived *Hornet* was rushed to Washington. The news was disappointing. Joel Barlow, the minister to France, reported that no commercial treaty seemed imminent. The French were also unwilling to release the American ships they had impounded. For his part, Jonathan Russell, chargé d'affaires in London, reported that the orders-in-council were being strongly contested by British manufacturers but there was scant hope of their repeal. No instructions had been sent to the British minister to the United States to offer any olive branches.[30]

Finding France's policy "puzzling," Madison and his administration became suddenly hesitant. Gallatin was again vacillating away from war, and Monroe was falling into bouts of depression over its prospect. Had Madison thought back to a letter that Russell had sent to Monroe in July of 1811, while he was legation secretary to America's French mission, France's purpose might have been understood. "The great object" of Napoleon's policy, Russell had written, was "to entangle us in a war with England."[31]

Shortly after *Hornet's* return, Clay led a deputation of congressional Republicans into a private meeting with Madison. Clay told the president that the time had come for decisive action and "that a majority of Congressmen would support war if the President recommended it."[32]

On June 1, Madison did precisely that, and three days later the House voted for war by a margin of seventy-nine to forty-nine. The vote, however, was taken in secrecy and not announced, pending its adoption by the Senate. There the matter was more closely contested. Various senators presented motions to modify the effect of war or to limit its dimensions. One called for the Senate to approve only a maritime war, as it was on the seas that America's rights had been violated. The motion was defeated on June 15 by a vote of eighteen to fourteen.

The following day, Bayard, who still believed that the British would rescind the orders-in-council, introduced a motion to "postpone the further consideration of the bill to the thirty-first day of October." Now, he said, "was not a time at which war ought to be declared. . . . It is not enough that we have cause of war; we must see that we are prepared, and in a condition to make war. You do not go to war for the benefit of your enemy, but your own advantage; not to give proofs of a vain and heedless courage, but to assert your rights and redress your wrongs." He pleaded for time to bring home American ships to save them from seizure, time to raise a proper army and to build a strong navy. "Was any nation ever less prepared for war?" Bayard asked. The senator warned that war would cause economic chaos because of the loss of trade that could not be elsewhere replaced. "The laws of war will operate still more extensively than the Orders-in-Council; and though no doubt we shall gratify the Emperor of France, we shall enjoy little commerce with his dominions. As it regards, therefore, our interest, it is found in protracting the present state of affairs." The motion was defeated twenty-three to nine.[33]

On June 17, the Senate voted nineteen to thirteen in favour of immediate and unrestricted war. The next day, the House accepted a few minor Senate amendments to the war bill and then Madison fixed his signature to it. Then, noted government comptroller Richard Rush, the president personally visited the offices of War and Navy "in a manner worthy of a little commander in chief with his little round hat and huge cockade."[34]

"We shall have war," Clay wrote ecstatically. "Every patriot bosom must throb with anxious solicitude for the result. Every patriot arm will assist in making that result conducive to the glory of our beloved country."[35] Henry Clay had his war.

Part Two

—

RELUCTANTLY TO WAR

———

SEVEN

While Disunion Prevails

"*A*t the moment of the declaration of war," James Monroe later wrote, "the President, regretting the necessity which produced it, looked to its termination." The secretary of state and the majority of James Madison's administration were similarly minded. Monroe, however, was more ardent than the others in this desire. As a result, he indulged in the fanciful delusion that declaration of war alone would bring about the downfall of Secretary of Foreign Affairs Viscount Castlereagh, a hard-line supporter of the orders-in-council. Nobody in Washington, however, was aware that Britain's government had been cast into disarray by Prime Minister Spencer Perceval's assassination on May 11.

Perceval was gunned down by a deranged man named John Bellingham, who while imprisoned in Russia had sought assistance in securing his release from the British representative, Leveson Gower, but was refused any help. Upon serving out his sentence, Bellingham returned to Britain bankrupt and intent on revenge. Unable to locate Gower, he decided that Perceval—whom he had never met—would suffice. Bellingham was hanged for the murder.

Having only returned to the cabinet earlier that year to head the Foreign Affairs Department, Castlereagh handily survived the ensuing month-long cabinet reorganization, not only retaining that position but also being appointed leader of the House of Commons. Save for Prime Minister Lord Liverpool, this made him the cabinet's most powerful member.

Ignorant of these events, Monroe considered that the continuing war with France was surely so calamitous that the British would prefer to treat rather than deny themselves all trade with America. Such were the growing shortages in Britain, Monroe believed, that the government must "afford vast facilities to our trade," so that the United States could perhaps prosecute a war against that nation while simultaneously trading with it until peace was agreed. America should, he confided to John Taylor of Carolina, "open our ports & trade & fight & fight & trade." If there was war, Monroe assured his friend, none of it would be fought on American soil and there would be no more loss of commercial trade than had been the case under the embargo or non-importation act.¹

This rosy scenario, where the United States was spared any loss or inconvenience, was glaringly at odds with events already unfolding in Washington and elsewhere. The day after the declaration's signing, Madison received Augustus Foster, the British minister to America. Foster, having assumed the post in the summer of 1811, had issued a stream of reports home detailing the many divisions present in American society and among its politicians regarding any discussion of war. The tenor of these notes had lulled Castlereagh into complacently believing no true crisis brewed and consequently no reconsideration of the orders-in-council was warranted. Now Foster belatedly attempted to limit the consequence of the war declaration by proposing that both sides avoid hostile acts until he could personally carry the declaration back to Britain. He would, of course, welcomely also take along any proposal Madison wished to send that might resolve the matter peacefully.

Hobbled by the necessity to offer no fodder to the many critics who accused him of lacking sufficient martial fire, Madison reluctantly declined this offer. Diplomatic relations between the two countries, the president said, must cease immediately. He would, however, leave chargé d'affaires Jonathan Russell in London to oversee treatment of prisoners, and Foster's legation secretary, Anthony St. John Baker, could do the same in Washington. Desperate to offer some olive branch, no matter how meagre, Foster said Baker's first duty would be to see to the repatriation of two of the seamen seized from *Chesapeake* five years earlier. They were, he reported, already aboard HMS *Bramble* en route from Halifax to American waters.

Madison received this news without comment, no doubt because those unfortunate sailors had long since been martyred to the cause of war and their release was of no consequence. Instead, he assured Foster that British packet ships could pass freely under flag of truce between North America and Britain to sustain a limited channel for diplomatic communication through the offices of Baker and Russell.

Foster was still packing when a pouch of British newspapers borne by such a ship was delivered to Madison on June 22. The press reported that the British government might be on the verge of rescinding the orders-in-council. Realizing Liverpool's government could have no knowledge yet that America had declared war and so must be responding purely to domestic opposition, Madison sensed an opportunity to secure peace and hurriedly invited Foster for a farewell visit. With Baker in tow, Foster reported to Madison's office, where the president made it plain that he desired to eliminate the causes of the war in order to restore peace.

"If the Orders-in-Council were revoked," Foster asked, "would peace be restored?"

Their revocation, Madison replied, and a "promise of negotiation given on the question of impressment . . . would suffice." Great Britain, he added, "could not perhaps do more on the latter at present than offer to negotiate." Foster pressed whether such a move by the British government would result in an immediate armistice, but Madison demurred that such a decision was the responsibility of Congress and could not be made until its next sitting. If the president unilaterally announced cessation of all military operations pending negotiations, Foster said he could guarantee that Vice-Admiral Herbert Sawyer, commanding the British fleet at Halifax, would reciprocate. Madison responded coldly that the war declaration granted the presidency a specific mandate that must be carried out without compromise or modification.

Frustrated by Madison's alternating passive and aggressive tactics, Foster observed that the orders-in-council had been rendered pointless by the fact that now that America was at war scarcely a neutral nation remained; every country was pretty much aligned either with Britain or with France. Foster feared that the United States would now see fit to formally align with Bonaparte.

Madison countered this concern by asking whether Portugal and Spain were not bound by treaties to fight alongside Britain. "Not against the United States," Foster replied, but did America plan to invade Florida? Foster wrote of Madison's reply: "The President observed the Executive could not well be justified in stopping any expeditions which might have been undertaken at a time when perhaps alone they could be successful. It seemed indeed evident that he was decided to take Florida if he could, and for purposes of defense that something else might be done, probably Fort Malden taken." That the Americans intended to clear the British out of Fort Malden, near Detroit, was worrisome because that was the first natural step toward an invasion of Upper Canada.

The meeting ended coolly. Outside the president's office, Foster was taken aside by Monroe. The secretary of state promised he would meet informally with Baker and receive any communications from Foster through him. Thus, a thin line of formal communication was preserved, but with Atlantic crossing time averaging five to six weeks it was a tortuously slow path.[2]

Madison and his administration were classically caught on the horns of a dilemma of their own making. While seeking to avoid hostilities that might render peaceful settlement impossible, there was the at least equally pressing need to initiate operations intended to win victory. Yet, while rushing toward war, neither Congress nor the president had done much to enable the nation to wage one effectively.

The 35,603-man army Congress had approved existed only on paper. On June 6, War Secretary Dr. William Eustis had reported to Congress that the regular army numbered just 6,744 officers and men, with another 5,000 having been raised under the authorization to increase the army by 25,000 soldiers. Most of these troops were poorly trained and their officers either equally inexperienced or elderly veterans of the Revolutionary War.[3] Theoretically the various state militias could supplement this total, but Congress had refused Madison the power to force militiamen to serve beyond American borders.[4]

Congress's gutting of the navy bill left that service in even more parlous straits. Five frigates were in service and another five listing in harbours awaiting repairs. Additionally the navy could boast a mere three sloops, seven brigs, and sixty-two coastal gunboats. The latter were useless for anything beyond limited harbour defence. The navy mustered 4,000 seamen and 1,800 marines.

Given the paucity of ships and sailors, Secretary of the Navy Paul Hamilton's inclination had been to preserve what he had by laying up all the ships in safe harbours. But Madison scotched that idea. He told Hamilton "not to despair of our navy; that though its numbers were small . . . it would do its duty."[5] That said, no naval strategy was agreed upon before war was declared.

When Madison donned his little military hat on June 18 and visited the Navy Office, he told Hamilton to grant Commodore John Rodgers and Capt. Stephen Decatur "every belligerent right." These orders were rushed to New York City, where the thirty-nine-year-old Rodgers, who was the senior officer, "ten minutes after the receipt of . . . instructions . . . put to sea" intent on pursuing a British convoy out of Jamaica reportedly consisting of 100 merchantmen protected by a thin screen of warships. Rodgers had five ships: the frigates *President*, *United States*, and *Congress*, the sloop *Hornet*, and the brig *Argus*. Departing with such haste, the commodore was well out to sea when a more detailed set of orders arrived instructing him to sail northward with *President* and *Hornet* from the Virginia capes while Decatur headed southward from New York with the other three ships. Their joint purpose was to protect from Royal Navy seizure American merchantmen bound for U.S. ports.[6]

This revised order had emanated on Sunday, June 21, from Secretary of the Treasury Albert Gallatin, who knew that a great number of vessels bearing between one and one and a half million dollars of imports were to arrive over the next four weeks. The navy's primary mission, he argued, must be to protect these ships, orders that "ought to have been sent yesterday . . . at all events, not one day longer ought to be lost."[7] Madison listened, issuing orders early Monday morning to "afford to our returning commerce all possible protection—nationally and individually."[8] But

Rodgers and the fleet were long gone, so there was nothing Madison could do until he decided to return to port. Failure to agree on a naval strategy prior to hostilities had given Rodgers opportunity to do as he pleased, which perfectly suited the impetuous and daring sailor.

Planning for land operations had proceeded little better. Although congressmen like Henry Clay had boasted that Canada could be quickly and easily conquered, nobody had bothered to draft a real invasion strategy. No team of staff officers was assigned to the War Office to undertake such planning. Eustis, with only a dozen civilian staff, held a dizzying array of responsibilities that included being quartermaster general, commissary general, Indian commissioner, and commissioner of public lands.[9] A civilian, Eustis's only military experience was as a surgeon during the Revolutionary War.

The senior military officer was sixty-one-year-old Maj. Gen. Henry Dearborn, who had seen no action since the Revolution. Although his appointment to command of the Northern Department on January 27, 1812, was more due to political connections than past military record, responsibility for conducting land operations fell on his shoulders. With more verve than an eye for tactics, intelligence, or logistics, Dearborn envisioned a three-pronged invasion of Canada. In April, he submitted a formal plan to Madison and Eustis. A main column would advance on Montreal by way of Lake Champlain, while another struck along the Niagara River and the third swept out of Fort Detroit across Upper Canada. The latter force would be commanded by Brig. Gen. William Hull, governor of Michigan Territory, who had been persuaded by Madison to take a regular army commission for this purpose. No timetable coordinating the three offensives was developed, so it was assured that each would be launched independently of the others.

Hull had accepted his appointment on April 9 and received immediate instructions from Madison to "repair with as little delay as possible to Detroit."[10] He responded that the many American inhabitants of Upper Canada would welcome his army as liberators. All agreed that the conquest of Canada would more than offset any gains the British might win with their supremacy at sea.[11] Former president Thomas Jefferson offered regular counsel to his friend and successor Madison.

"The acquisition of Canada this year as far as the neighbourhood of Quebec," he said, "will be a mere matter of marching."[12]

In truth, nobody knew what American forces would face once they crossed the border into Canada. The lack of intelligence was such that estimates of British troop strength were grossly understated while the naval presence on the North American station was equally inflated. Although Britain had almost 700 warships at sea, including 260 ships of the line and frigates, in North American waters there were only 3 ships of the line, 23 frigates, and 53 sloops, brigs, and schooners. These were spread out across the seas from the West Indies to Halifax to Newfoundland.[13]

For the defence of Canada, Lt. Gen. and Governor in Chief Sir George Prevost had roughly 5,600 regulars. Only about 1,200 of these were stationed in Upper Canada and they were scattered across a string of small garrisons. While on paper the militia in Lower Canada numbered an impressive 60,000, Prevost considered them "a mere posse, ill armed and without discipline." In Upper Canada, there was potential to call up 10,000 militiamen, but Prevost believed only 4,000 trustworthy enough to consider arming. The rest might as likely desert to the Americans and turn their guns against the redcoats.[14]

The British could also depend on some support from native tribes, but to what extent was hard to predict. Before returning to Britain in October of 1811 to attend to urgent personal business, Upper Canada's lieutenant governor Francis Gore reported on the strengths and allegiances of the various tribes that might be brought to the battlefield. Gore's report illustrated that the British could expect limited support from the tribes remaining in Lower Canada, while the existence of Tecumseh's confederacy on the western frontier could provide a significant number of warriors.

In Lower Canada, the once great Iroquois presence had largely been expunged by wars and disease. Just three villages remained. Two of these were dependent on "Presents and Supplies from the Government Stores at Montreal." Gore believed the warriors there, about half the total available, would stand by the Crown. The Iroquois at St. Regis were more dubious, as that village was "placed immediately on the frontier line, which divides Lower Canada, from the United States of America, and receiving from the American Government, an Annual Pension for Lands conceded, which they probably would not wish to forfeit. Some of them are known to be disaffected; we might however rely on half of them. These three Villages can muster 500 Warriors brave and active. They are all Christians, and have a Church in each of their Villages." Although several other tribes were scattered in small numbers elsewhere in Lower Canada, Gore discounted them as being Christians who had lost their warlike ways.

Things looked much better in Upper Canada. Clustered near York and Niagara were mostly Mohawk and Mississauga that he considered "at the Governor's devotion." They had also fought well and hard against the Americans in the Revolutionary War and could provide about 350 warriors for this fight. On the frontier dwelt a great confederacy of peoples including Miami, Wyandot, Shawnee, Potomac, and Delaware that drew "their Annual Presents at the Garrison of Amherstburg despite living on the American side of the border. They have no attachment to the Americans." This, Gore said, was because of Indiana governor William Harrison's attack on Tippecanoe. He estimated that the confederacy painstakingly built by Tecumseh could deliver about 3,000 warriors. Added to this were 700 Ottawa warriors—"a very warlike tribe"—living near Lake Huron and Lake Michigan and the Fox and Sac peoples living between Lake Michigan and the Mississippi River. The Fox and Sac could raise about 500 warriors. These three tribes all drew supplies and presents from the British at Fort St. Joseph and were judged loyal.

Gore estimated all the warriors in Lower Canada, Upper Canada, and out on the frontier at about 5,300. He also thought it possible to lure the Sioux, who controlled the lands lying between the Mississippi and Missouri rivers, into joining the British in a war against the United States. Their lands, after all, would be next up for occupation by the American pioneers once the Ohio was overrun. The Sioux were "well trained under their War Chiefs," and could easily provide 3,000 warriors—a potent force indeed.[15] Whether they would march so far to make war, however, was uncertain.

While Gore had found comfort in the idea of anywhere up to 8,300 warriors rallying to fight the Americans, Prevost showed no inclination to include them in his plans. The governor intended no offensive operations against the Americans and saw no defensive role for these warriors. Prevost fervently desired to avoid a fight altogether. Having assumed responsibility for governing all British colonies and territories on the western side of the Atlantic on September 13, 1811, Prevost brought to the job a distinguished military record and a reputation as an able administrator. But he was one for conciliation wherever possible and could countenance nothing as rash as America invading Canada for such trivial reasons as Madison had cited in his war declaration. War promised calamity and cost for both belligerents and was to be averted until diplomatic negotiations resolved the current dispute.

Prevost's parents were Swiss Protestants who came by their British citizenship because of his father's service as one of the many Swiss officers enlisted for service in the Royal American Regiment of Foot. Born in New Jersey on May 19, 1767, Prevost was raised in a household where French was spoken more than English. Educated at schools in England and on the continent, the already worldly young man took a commission in 1783. War with France brought rapid advancement. Twice wounded in the campaign to repel French invaders from the West Indies island of St. Vincent, then Lieutenant Colonel Prevost was promoted to a colonelcy and granted a wartime appointment to brigadier general. Facility in French contributed to Prevost's assignment as governor of St. Lucia after its conquest. Adopting a conciliatory manner, Prevost proved a popular governor who ran the island ably until its return to the French with the 1802 Treaty of Amiens. With war's renewal in 1805, Prevost successfully defended Dominica from French invasion and was promoted to major general and granted a baronetcy. The *Chesapeake* affair brought his transfer to Nova Scotia in the spring of 1808 to assume command of the troops there and also to take over as the lieutenant governor. From there it was a natural step up the career ladder to his new responsibilities in 1811.[16]

When war with America threatened the following spring, Prevost thoroughly evaluated his military capability in Canada and was dismayed by what he saw. In a report to newly appointed Secretary of War and the Colonies Henry Bathurst, Prevost struck a sober tone beneath which a note of panic lurked. "If the Americans are determined to attack Canada it would be in vain the General should flatter himself with the hopes of making an effectual defence of the open Country, unless powerfully assisted from Home." Virtually all the settlements and forts in Upper Canada were imperilled. If the Americans seized Kingston— an event Prevost feared likely—the province would be cut off from Lower Canada and the British would lose contact with their naval forces on the lakes. Things were not much better in Lower Canada. The vital fur-trade centre of Montreal could be defended only by maintaining "an impenetrable line on the South Shore, extending from La Prairie to Chambly, with a sufficient Flotilla to command" the St. Lawrence and Richelieu rivers. His hope for defending Lower Canada was to bleed the Americans slowly to a standstill by forcing them to overcome one fortified position after another when they attempted to break through to Quebec.

Prevost speculated that his army might repel the Americans if they launched an invasion "undertaken presumptuously and without sufficient means." But even then he was unwilling to risk depleting the 2,500-strong garrison with which he intended to hold Quebec. Ensuring possession of this rundown bastion with almost half of his entire regular army strength was paramount, Prevost argued, for Quebec was "the only Post that can be considered tenable at the moment, the preservation of it being of the utmost consequence to the Canadas, as the door of entry for that Force The King's Government might find it expedient to send for the recovery of both, or either of these provinces." Prevost envisioned the Quebec garrison besieged by the Americans until reinforcements from Britain could arrive to save the day and retake the rest of Canada.[17]

Prevost thought the best hope for defending Canada lay in doing nothing to start a fight with the Americans. This led him to worry mightily about his subordinate commanding Upper Canada. Maj. Gen. Isaac Brock had a reputation for tempestuous, even reckless behaviour. "Nothing should be impossible to a soldier; the word impossible should not be found in a soldier's dictionary," he once declared.[18] As a young officer in Barbados, he had ridden up the steep eastern flank of Mount Hillaby to its 1,115-foot summit, a feat considered impossible by the other horsemen in the garrison.[19]

Born in St. Peter Port, Guernsey, on October 6, 1769, Brock shared his birth year with Arthur Wellesley and Napoleon Bonaparte.

Whereas Wellesley—Viscount Wellington—had gained glory and advancement on the battlefields of India and of late against the French as commander of British forces in Iberia, Brock's military career had languished in Canada. Entering the service as an ensign in 1785, he managed to purchase a lieutenant colonelcy in 1797. The following year, commanding the 49th Regiment of Foot, Brock was slightly wounded during the battle of Egmont-op-Zee in Holland by a bullet that failed to penetrate a thick black silk cravat and cotton handkerchief he had wrapped around his neck before going into battle. He gained more honour in 1801 when the regiment participated in Lord Nelson's assault on Copenhagen. But in the spring of 1802, the 49th was ordered to Canada, and there, except for a short leave to Britain in 1805, Brock had been ever since, chafing for a posting where battle and the possibility of winning fame and promotion could be had. "I must see service," he wrote his brothers, "or I may as well, and indeed much better, quit the army at once, for no one advantage can I reasonably look to hereafter if I remain buried in this inactive, remote corner, without the slightest mention being made of me."[20]

Although he liked and respected Brock, Prevost knew restraining a man desperately seeking battle honours was going to be extremely difficult. Particularly at such a distance, for Brock was headquartered at Fort George, which lay a good week away by horse-mounted courier and over a month by regular post. He therefore issued strict instructions in early 1812 designed to deny Brock the ability to act independently. The best way to rein Brock in, Prevost decided, was to leave him woefully short of manpower. To the 1,200 men stationed in Upper Canada, therefore, he added only another 500, and with them came orders that nothing the Americans did was to "justify offensive operations being undertaken, unless they were solely calculated to strengthen a defensive attitude." He cautioned against "committing any act which may even by construction tend to unite the Eastern and Southern states."[21]

Drawing on intelligence reports from Augustus Foster in Washington, Prevost believed that America was anything but united in seeking war with Britain. He therefore thought it "prudent and politic to avoid any measure which can in its effect have a tendency to unite the people in the

American States .... Whilst disunion prevails among them, their attempts on these provinces will be feeble."[22]

On June 24, Prevost learned from two Montreal fur traders that the American president had declared war. The following day, Brock received like news at Fort George from an American source. His first thought was to immediately attack Fort Niagara and other American forts near the border. But he was too faithful and responsible a soldier to flagrantly disobey Prevost's orders. On July 3, Brock sent a note to his superior confessing his natural offensive inclinations but adding that, upon reflection, "I relinquished my original intention, and attended only to defensive measures."[23] This consisted of ordering a hastening of efforts by Lt. Col. Thomas Blight St. George to improve the defensive works at Fort Malden, next to Amherstburg, which he believed would most likely face attack when Hull's column crossed into Canada. Tecumseh, whom Brock had yet to meet, was already at the fort and had brought with him some 300 warriors. St. George had an equal number of regulars, and some 850 militiamen had responded to a call-up.[24] "Every exertion is made by us all," St. George reported on July 8, and as a consequence the fort was ready as could be to withstand the expected American onslaught.[25]

South of the border, the Americans muddled forward. Although back in April Madison had urged that Brigadier General Hull make haste to Detroit and ready his army for an immediate crossing of the narrow neck of the Detroit River into Upper Canada at war's outbreak, the reluctant Hull had dallied for weeks in Ohio. Only on June 15 did he finally muster out from Urbana, about 185 miles south of Fort Detroit, at the head of a powerful army numbering 2,000 men. The march soon resembled more a retreat as the soldiers and their long pack train and cattle herd wallowed through unceasing rain that clogged the rough tracks with thick mud. On June 26, just short of the aptly named fifty-mile-wide morass of Black Swamp, Hull received a message from Secretary of War Eustis that urged him to greater speed but failed to mention that America was now at war. Five days later his bedraggled troops straggled out of the worst of the swamp and regrouped on the banks of the Maumee River near where Maj. Gen. "Mad Anthony"

Wayne had defeated the Shawnee at Fallen Timbers in 1794. A little farther on, at Frenchtown on the River Raisin, Hull chanced upon the captain of the American schooner *Cuyahoga* and arranged to load his sick, his exhausted young bandsmen, and all the baggage of his officers and his own personal papers aboard the vessel to be carried up Lake Erie to Fort Detroit. With his column lightened of this extra weight and the prospect of easier going ahead, Hull expected to complete the journey quickly. He was spurred to increase the pace when a follow-up letter from Eustis arrived on July 2 informing him that the nation was at war.[26]

Unfortunately for the ill-starred brigadier general, this was the same day that *Cuyahoga* was overtaken by Provincial Marine Lt. Charles Frédéric Rolette aboard a longboat being rowed by "a dozen sailors armed with sabers and pickaxes." The schooner captain surrendered without a fight and Rolette "ran up the British flag," ordered the bandsmen to play "God Save the King," and then directed the ship into captivity at Fort Malden. St. George was soon happily sorting through Hull's papers, which contained his entire invasion plan and details on the strength and composition of his army.[27]

Three days later Hull's column trailed into Fort Detroit and he learned of *Cuyahoga*'s capture. Realizing the disaster that capture of his personal papers entailed, Hull attempted to salvage the situation by sending an envoy under flag of truce to Fort Malden with a politely worded note asking St. George as a matter of gentlemanly honour to return all officer baggage and papers. The implication was that a gentleman would not stoop to reading another's private documents. Responding with equal politeness, St. George advised that he could not comply without authorization from higher command.

Not that the capture of his plans provided the British anything they had not already surmised. Hull's strategic options were restricted. On July 12, he duly conformed to them by crossing the Detroit River and occupying Sandwich, a pleasant French-Canadian village of houses each surrounded by a small orchard. First ashore was Col. Lewis Cass, commander of one of Hull's three Ohio militia regiments, who unfurled the Stars and Stripes from around his waist and ran it up the tallest available pole.[28] The landing was unopposed, Brock wisely deciding it was impossible to defend the village with Fort Detroit's guns looming just across the river.

Having attained a toehold in Upper Canada, Hull selected Sandwich's finest Georgian-style red-brick home for his headquarters and ordered no advance beyond its outskirts. Although Hull had embarked upon the crossing, he was still badly shaken by the difficulties encountered during the march to Detroit and events that had unfolded in the days after the column arrived there.

First there had been his failure at a conference convened at Brownstown, near the mouth of the Detroit River, to persuade the tribes in the area to come over to the American side or at least adopt a stance of neutrality. Tecumseh was noteworthy by his absence, but word of the fiery denunciation he gave to the deputation of warriors who had asked him to attend overshadowed Hull's efforts at conciliation. "Here is a chance presented to us—yes, a chance such as will never occur again— for us Indians of North America to form ourselves into one great combination and cast our lot with the British in this war. . . . I have taken sides with the King, my father, and I will suffer my bones to bleach upon this shore before I will recross that stream to join in any council of neutrality."[29] Some of the chiefs and their warriors opted to straddle the fence, committing neither to neutrality nor to one of the belligerent sides. But others filtered away, obviously heading for the British lines. None threw in his lot with Hull.

While occupying Sandwich, Hull kept a wary eye open over his shoulder in fearful expectation of an Indian attack on Fort Detroit or his more than 200-mile-long supply line. The crossing was stalled, however, for nearly two days, during which Hull was forced to badger, hector, and plead with many of the Ohio militiamen who invoked their right to not serve outside the United States. Cass and the other militia commanders finally managed to bully sufficient troops into submission to enable the attack to proceed, but Hull could no longer depend on their cooperation. Before launching his boats to cross the border, Hull registered his anxiety in a note to Eustis: "The British command the water and the savages. I do not think the force here equal to the reduction of Amherstburg. You therefore must not be too sanguine."[30]

Yet he still firmly believed that most Canadians would welcome the American invaders with open arms. Discovering that the Roman Catholic priest at Detroit had an antiquated printing press, Hull drafted a bombastic proclamation that was then crudely printed and distributed as far afield as possible. "INHABITANTS OF CANADA!" it began, then plunged into a long diatribe regarding the "Tyranny" under which Canadians had suffered so long as British subjects and offered American protection. "The United States are sufficiently powerful to afford you every security consistent with their rights and your expectations. I tender you the invaluable blessings of Civil, Political, & Religious Liberty." Hull urged everyone to remain at home and not to rise up in resistance. The "arrival of an army of Friends must be hailed by you with a cordial welcome. You will be emancipated from Tyranny and oppression and restored to the dignified status of freemen." Anyone who opposed the Americans, he warned, would "be considered and treated as enemies and the horrors, and calamities of war will Stalk before you." And, should the "barbarous and Savage policy of Great Britain be pursued, and the savages are let loose to murder our Citizens and butcher our women and children, this war, will be a war of extermination. Scalping Knife will be the Signal for one indiscriminate scene of desolation. *No white man found fighting by the Side of an Indian will be taken prisoner.* Instant destruction will be his Lot." He then called for volunteers to join his army. The Canadians must choose, he said in closing, "but choose wisely; and may he who knows the justice of our cause, and who holds in his hand the fate of Nations, guide you to a result the most compatible, with your rights and interests, your peace and prosperity."[31]

Hull hoped to force the British to either neutralize the Indians or to frighten the militia into refusing to take up arms to avoid being summarily executed if captured fighting alongside them. At first it worked, and Brock reported to Prevost with dismay that "the disaffected [militiamen] became more audacious, and the wavering more intimidated." Over a three-day period, half his recruits melted away. But the rest remained, and many expressed outrage at Hull's threat to show them no quarter if it came to a fight. Because one thing was clear: whether the British or Canadian militiamen liked it or not, Tecumseh's warriors were committed to the fight. So, too, were Brock's redcoats, few as they might be. In the end, the proclamation rankled as many Canadian settlers as it cowed.

The relationship between Canadians and the native tribes differed dramatically from the American pattern, where frontiersmen relentlessly sought to displace them from traditional lands. Between the arrival of Samuel de Champlain in 1609 and New France's conquest by the British in 1763 there had been a state of almost perpetual war, with the Indian nations aligning either with one side or the other. The fur trade added economic ties to these military alliances, and the unceasing efforts, particularly by the French clergy, to convert the tribes to Christianity led to their being further interwoven into the fabric of Canada. Yet the colony's need to have the natives out in the forests trapping and hunting for the furs that formed the basis of its economy resulted in the mostly church-driven efforts to transform the tribes into mock Europeans, who tilled the soil and dragged the plough, being more half-heartedly pursued than was true in the United States. Intermarriage was also common, particularly with regard to the French traders, resulting in the development of the Métis, who provided a bridge between white and native cultures. The competition between natives and whites for land was also less fierce than in the United States. The far smaller white population tended to settle along the banks of the St. Lawrence and other major rivers because these served as the highways running between communities and to the ports through which furs, timber, and agricultural products were exported back to Europe. When settlers moved into Upper Canada this pattern continued, with farms and villages generally being situated along the shores of the Great Lakes and any major rivers flowing into them. Although the native tribes were displaced from some of the best sites for villages, particularly in Upper Canada, by 1812 they were still not competing for use of much of their traditional territories. Consequently, few Canadians saw the tribesmen in their midst or out in the woods beyond as posing any particular threat to their survival. And they correctly realized the potent force that the warriors could bring to the battlefield during times of conflict.

Upper Canada was also not a place where British tyranny was in evidence. There were no taxes, no heavy-handed troops terrorizing or repressing a helpless populace. Furthermore, it was not the slightest bit like the American frontier with which men like Hull were familiar. "This is a pioneer society," one writer observes, "not a frontier society. No Daniel Boones stalk the Canadian forests, ready to knock off an Injun with a Kentucky rifle or do battle over an imagined slight. The Methodist circuit riders keep the people law abiding and temperate; prosperity keeps them content. The Sabbath is looked upon with reverence; card playing and horse racing are considered sinful diversions; the demon rum has yet to become a problem. There is little theft, less violence. Simple pastimes tied to the land—barn raisings, corn huskings, threshing bees—serve as an outlet for the spirited."[32]

The Americans did not confine themselves to just marching about the surrounding countryside distributing Hull's proclamation. Hull, who tended to fret inordinately about being insufficiently supplied, ordered a foraging party under Ohio Militia commander Lt. Col. Duncan McArthur to raid area farms for food, equipment, and fodder for the army's animals. Ranging over an area of about sixty miles, McArthur's men pillaged the small farms they encountered. There was little resistance, as most of the farmers had gathered up their families and fled before the Americans arrived. Those who didn't stood by helplessly as McArthur looted anything of value. The American commander dismissively assured any who complained that the U.S. government would eventually compensate them once its hold on Upper Canada was consolidated. A few skirmishes were fought as British regulars, Canadian militia, and allied native warriors brushed up against the American foraging parties. After one such encounter, the Ranger commander Capt. William McCullough was the first American to collect an Indian scalp. He wrote a letter to his wife describing the act of using his teeth to tear the scalp from the dead warrior's head. Several Americans were also killed in these exchanges that were too often punctuated with the savagery of scalping. After five days, McArthur returned to Sandwich dragging wagons loaded with two hundred barrels of flour, stocks of whisky, cloth, ammunition, guns, salt, and hundreds of blankets. In their wake his men left burned grain fields, wrecked homes, cut-down orchards, and broken fences.[33]

Any chance of Hull's proclamation winning the hearts and minds of the local populace was undone by McArthur's work. Afterward, most settlers still hoped to avoid a fight with Americans that they were ill trained or armed to carry out, but many were willing to do their duty to defend Upper Canada from further depredations. Even the recent American immigrants failed to rally to Hull, and sufficient numbers stood beside the other Canadian militiamen to make a difference. In doing so they inevitably dashed the misguided American expectation that Canada would prove an easy conquest, providing that vital bargaining chip Madison's administration and Congress had expected was theirs for the taking to then trade for maritime concessions from Britain in order to secure its return.

———

EIGHT

Failures of Communication

SUMMER 1812

*T*he failure of his proclamation to either rally the American immigrants or frighten the Canadian militia into deserting the British thoroughly demoralized Brig. Gen. William Hull. Although skirmishers sent toward Fort Malden reported the British few in numbers, Hull still refused to act. At every turn the American commander found reason to delay, and with each passing day his inactivity encouraged the growing enemy to probe the Americans for weakness. A large supply column was supposedly headed his way, but none of his scouts had been able to contact it. Hull worried that it might be massacred en route by the Indians he imagined lurked everywhere in the surrounding forests. While his men huddled behind breastworks in Sandwich, Hull returned to Detroit on July 21 and contented himself with writing fatuous letters to Eustis.

His cannon were useless, he reported, requiring new gun carriages. Replacing them would take at least two weeks. Despite this setback, he wrote, it "is in the power of this army to take Malden by storm, but it would be attended in my opinion with too great a sacrifice under present circumstance . . . if Malden was in our possession, I could march this army to Niagara or York in a very short time." After pleading for another 1,500 men and a great deal more supplies, Hull continued his vigil in Detroit, growing ever more despondent. About July 30, he received unconfirmed reports that the British, rather than sensibly remaining on the defensive, had sallied forth with a small force from the fort on St. Joseph's Island and seized the small garrison at Fort Mackinac, at

Michilimackinac in the northwestern corner of Lake Huron, almost three hundred miles by boat from Fort Detroit. The loss of this small fur trade outpost was irrelevant to Hull's operation. But his spirits sagged and he found in the fort's loss explanation for why the Wyandot tribe living near Detroit suddenly abandoned their camps and crossed into the British lines. Hull's fear of the Indians now became so magnified that he feared Detroit would be overrun and its inhabitants all slaughtered. He contemplated retreating from Sandwich to enable his army to better defend Detroit from the safety of its fort.

On July 30, across the Atlantic, Prime Minister Lord Liverpool and his cabinet had just learned that the United States had declared war.[2] The news rocked them, particularly Viscount Castlereagh. The secretary of foreign affairs had been confident that steps taken in recent weeks to appease American discontent would avert hostilities. A ship had sailed in mid-June with news that should have prompted President James Madison to step back from the abyss of war. That ship, of course, would just now be entering American waters. The Americans, impatient as children, had acted with impetuous haste.

Castlereagh knew the Americans believed themselves aggrieved by the orders-in-council and impressment, but he had not divined from reports by his minister in Washington or discussions with the American chargé Jonathan Russell that war was at hand. Frankly, he had thought America so ill organized and divided that it was incapable of embarking on a war. Most everyone sitting in the House of Commons and the House of Lords had agreed with this assessment.

Russell had correctly interpreted the British mood. Reporting to James Monroe on March 20, 1812, he wrote, "I cannot perceive the slightest indication of an apprehension of a rupture with the United States—or any measures of preparation to meet such an event. Indeed such is the conviction here of our total inability to make war that the five or six thousand troops now in Canada are considered to be amply sufficient to protect that province against our mightiest efforts."[3]

Castlereagh, a master of complex international diplomacy, had been caught flat-footed by the American action. When the orders-in-council were first introduced in 1807 he had been secretary for war and the colonies and had realized they posed a source of trouble between the two nations. He had wondered then if war might result. If the United States managed to organize its military along European lines and invaded Canada, it was likely that all of British North America save Newfoundland could be lost. After examining America's military organization, however, he had considered it unlikely that they could muster sufficient unanimity to field a large army. So long as the Royal Navy remained "alert and proper defensive exertions are made [in Canada] the Americans are not likely to attack in force, more especially in view of the fact that the northern States of the Union . . . are those which are least disposed to a contest with us." Still, he had thought that "while relying mainly upon the local Canadian militia to defend themselves, it might be well to reinforce it by a regular corps of 10,000–12,000 men."[4]

The Peninsular campaign in Portugal the following year rendered this deployment to Canada impracticable. When each passing year brought little from the Americans but diatribes and ineffectual attempts to cut the flow of trade between the two countries, Castlereagh was lulled into a complacency interrupted only by Madison's war declaration.

Augustus Foster's reports on the debates during the unusually prolonged sitting of the Twelfth Congress had caused Castlereagh a slight inkling of concern. But he had expected more bluster and perhaps some new version of the Non-intercourse Act or a return to the curiously self-defeating embargo. Still, it had seemed wise to avoid incidents that might provide fuel for the War Hawks. Accordingly, in May, the British Admiralty had instructed its commanders operating in American waters to "take especial care" to avoid clashes with U.S. warships and to show "all possible forbearance towards the Citizens of the United States." These orders were shortly followed by ones directing all British warships to withdraw to a boundary fifteen leagues off the American coast.[5] Asked on June 8 whether he thought continuation of the orders might incite the United States to war, Castlereagh had emphatically rejected the possibility.[6]

At the same time, despite his ardent support for the orders-incouncil, Castlereagh was facing increasing political pressure to consent to their repeal. Perceval was dead and the new government struggling to demonstrate its legitimacy. Lord Liverpool was less convinced of their necessity and sympathetic to the manufacturing and merchant lobby's claims that the orders were ruining them. Robert Banks Jenkinson might be a lord, but he was not one of those noblemen who disdained the man who turned his hand to commerce. Liverpool had "been bred up in a school where he had been taught highly to value the commercial interest."[7]

The prime minister was also given to compromise. At forty-two he was young for the office, but such had been the nature of his career since election to the House of Commons in 1790. A handsome, slender, tall young man noted as a graceful, engaging conversationalist, he had given an impressive maiden speech. Then prime minister William Pitt "the Younger" declared it "not only a more able first speech than had ever been heard from a young member, but one so full of philosophy and science, and strong and perspicuous language, and sound and convincing arguments, that it would have done credit to the most practised debater and the most experienced statesman that ever existed."[8]

Pitt marked him for rapid advancement, and in 1792 he became a member of the Board of Control for India. From there his career advanced in strides encompassing three years of service at a time in the positions of master of the mint, foreign secretary, two terms as home secretary, and by 1812, secretary for war and the colonies.

But Liverpool's appointment as prime minister came as a surprise and was generally considered the result of more suitable candidates, who believed the government would be short-lived, turning the position down. Given the crisis brought on by Perceval's death, an almost immediate non-confidence vote in the House of Commons, and the ensuing resignation of the entire cabinet, the Prince Regent had initially sought Whig and Tory coalition, but the two parties were irreconcilable. The Tories supported the Peninsular War and opposed Catholic emancipation while the Whigs opposed the former and supported the latter. Finally, in what seemed a fit of pique more than reasoned decision, the Prince declared Liverpool prime minister. On June 8, Liverpool accepted the position. Two days later, he commented in a letter that with "respect to myself I feel placed in a most arduous and difficult situation from which I should have been most happy on many accounts to have been relieved; but could not have shrunk from it with honour, and I owe it now to the Prince to use my best endeavours for carrying on his government."[9]

Liverpool asked Castlereagh to return as foreign secretary and to assume the duty of house leader. He also sought to include George Canning despite the bad blood that lingered between Castlereagh and this veteran Tory. In the late summer of 1809 the two had respectively held the posts of secretary for war and the colonies and foreign secretary in the Duke of Portland's government. With the duke on his deathbed, Canning had been at the centre of a web of cabinet ministers conspiring to eject Castlereagh from cabinet in such a public manner that it would necessarily besmirch his honour. Learning of the plot in mid-September, Castlereagh resigned. Then, on September 19, he wrote a three-page letter that set out with cold precision his understanding of Canning's hand in the matter. That Canning had every right to seek his dismissal, Castlereagh acknowledged, but he asserted that this should not have been pursued "at the expense of my honour and reputation."[10] Given the manner in which Canning had proceeded, Castlereagh wrote, "I must require that satisfaction from you to which I feel entitled to lay claim." When Canning opened the letter the following evening, he declared, "I had rather fight than read it, by God." He quickly dashed off a response. "The tone and purport of your Lordship's letter (which I have this moment received) of course precludes any other answer, on my part, to the misapprehensions and misrepresentations, with which it abounds, than that I will cheerfully give to your Lordship the satisfaction that you require."[11]

The two met at six on the morning of September 21 at Lord Yarmouth's cottage on Putney Heath. En route Castlereagh had calmly talked with Yarmouth, who was acting as his second, about Catalinia, a currently fashionable opera singer, and hummed several bits of an aria she had popularized. As their carriage crossed over a bridge to gain the cottage, the river below had looked grey and murky, the water matching the sky overhead. Although Castlereagh had not fired a pistol since leaving Ireland to enter the British House of Commons, he had always been a good shot. Canning, however, had never before fired one. Standing several paces apart and sideways to each other, the two men exchanged a first round in which both missed their target. Castlereagh said he remained unsatisfied as Canning had not yet apologized. The guns were reloaded. Canning fired and the ball nicked a button free from Castlereagh's coat. Aiming deliberately, Castlereagh shot his opponent in the leg. The seconds rushed to where Canning had collapsed in a huddle to the ground. The wound proved nasty but not life-threatening.

"We each fired two pistols," Castlereagh wrote his father, "my second shot took effect, but happily only passed through the fleshy part of his thigh. Mr. Canning's conduct was very proper on the ground."[12] That two cabinet ministers would duel caused a great stir in the British press, and Canning was forced to follow up Castlereagh's resignation with his own. For Castlereagh the exile from cabinet lasted two and a half years, until he returned in March 1812 as Perceval's foreign secretary.

Liverpool had always walked a fine line between these two men, seeking the friendship of each and to moderate their sharp differences because he admired and respected both. Summoned to a meeting, both acknowledged the other with formal politeness. Castlereagh, knowing how much Liverpool wanted Canning, offered to relinquish the post of foreign secretary but retain management of the House of Commons. Canning said he wanted both positions, as he could not in conscience serve under Castlereagh in the House. Downcast, Liverpool refused to dismiss Castlereagh and the meeting broke up. Castlereagh retained the two positions Liverpool had originally assigned him.

Canning remained a sharp critic speaking from the Tory back-benches. If Liverpool resented this, he typically gave no sign. His was a moderate, always reasonable, self-effacing character. The many years spent at the forefront of the nation's public service had taken their toll on the once lanky young man. One observer noted that "the cares of office stamped their marks upon his face, but though his expression had hardened, his broad brow and thoughtful gaze showed his calm and even character."[13] Another considered Liverpool "kind by temperament," possessing "an instinctive tact in dealing with others. His conciliatory manner smoothed away innumerable personal difficulties. He was a man whom it was almost impossible to dislike."[14]

Despite his having held nearly every senior cabinet post and demonstrated ability and efficiency in them all, even Liverpool's friends did not believe him marked with "genius or even brilliance."[15] Wellington wrote from Iberia, "You have undertaken a most gigantic task and I don't know how you will get through it."[16]

The Tories were desperately short of talent sufficient to build a solid government and could easily fall to a non-confidence motion if the Whigs and independents voted together. Liverpool drew in a few old Tories, including the 3rd Earl of Bathurst, Henry Bathurst, who became secretary for war and the colonies. But with Canning and other veterans remaining on the sidelines, Liverpool was forced to rely on junior colleagues. With his usual careful consideration, he chose them well. Lord Palmerston, Robert Peel, and Frederick Robinson—future prime ministers all—numbered among the recruits.

"I have no recourse but to bring forward the most promising of the young men . . . I should be happy to see another Pitt amongst them. I would willingly resign the government into his hands for I am fully aware of the importance of the minister being if possible in the House of Commons."[17] This was his most ardent hope, to serve only so long as it took to find or train some yet to be determined brilliant successor. Liverpool's administration seemed a caretaker government that would survive only so long as it took the Whigs and a suitable number of independents to agree upon how to divide the spoils after bringing the government down.

Yet despite all the meetings carried out behind closed doors, such agreement was not to be found. A June 11 non-confidence motion fell short by 125 votes. There would not be time for another such motion before the summer recess, and Liverpool had promised an election for September, so his government was assured survival until the voters went to the polls.

Compromises would be necessary. Accordingly, on June 18, Castlereagh rose in the House and haltingly, obviously stinging with embarrassment and biting back personal anger at having to make the concession, announced that the government would repeal the orders-in-council insofar as they affected the United States. The repeal would go into effect on August 1 to allow time for instructions to be distributed throughout the Royal Navy. This revocation, he stressed, was conditional on America agreeing to remove all restrictions on British ships entering American ports.[18]

Formal repeal of the orders-in-council was ratified by both houses on June 23, and word was immediately dispatched by ship to Minister to America Augustus Foster, still believed to be in Washington. Confident that once Madison and Congress knew of the repeal they would abandon war, Castlereagh had not given the Americans further thought until learning on July 30 of the declaration of June 18—coincidentally his forty-third birthday.

Born to a prominent Anglo-Irish Dublin family, Robert Stewart had attained the courtesy title of Viscount Castlereagh when his father became an earl in 1796. Educated at Cambridge, he was just shy of his twenty-first birthday when he won election to the Irish Parliament in 1790, sitting as an independent representing County Down. Coming to London in early 1794 to attend upon a dying grandfather he deeply admired, Castlereagh was soon smitten by the twenty-two-year-old daughter of the Earl of Buckinghamshire. Grey-eyed and fair-haired, Lady Amelia Hobart, commonly known as Lady Emily, was slim, gay, and vivacious, but she also had a reputation for eccentricity that revealed itself through a predilection to be "petulant, capricious, and indiscreet."[19] Castlereagh saw only her beauty and a playful, spirited personality. After a brief courtship the two engaged to marry that June. In April, Castlereagh's grandfather passed away. Grief stricken, he turned to Lady Emily for comfort. "Your heart," he wrote, "is too much alive not to feel for me at this moment; you have left me, as far as I am myself concerned, nothing to wish for: you have given repose to all my disquietude and opened prospects of happiness which give me a new interest in life ... for God's sake, dearest Lady Emily, continue to love me, and let me some day or other have gratification to think that since you knew me your happiness has not diminished."[20]

Castlereagh's devotion to his wife only grew stronger with each passing year. In a society where nobles often strayed and kept mistresses or dallied with prostitutes, particularly when a marriage proved childless as did this one, there was never a rumour that Castlereagh even considered unfaithfulness. When away from home, his letters were regular, and occasionally he sent plaited strands of his hair to go inside a locket he had given her. The locket contained a portrait of Castlereagh at twenty-five as painted by the Regency's leading miniaturist, Richard Cosway.[21]

Such depth of attachment was typical of the man. Intensely loyal to friends, he expected loyalty in return. Once resolved on a course of action, Castlereagh unflinchingly committed to its implementation. This was what had made repeal of the orders-in-council so personally galling.

Throughout his political career, he had demonstrated this characteristic. Appointed chief secretary of Ireland by his relative and then lord lieutenant of Ireland Earl Camden in 1798, Castlereagh was at the forefront in quelling the revolt of that same year. The severe measures taken to crush the rebellion were not his work alone, but they were to place a lifelong stain on Castlereagh's reputation. Yet overlooked by his critics was the fact that once the rebellion was suppressed he called for a general amnesty for all but those who had incited the uprising. "It would be unwise," he wrote, "to drive the wretched people, who are mere instruments in the hands of the more wicked, to despair."[22]

The rebellion, which could easily have brought the excesses of a French-style revolution to Ireland, convinced Castlereagh that only formal union with Britain could avert an eventual slide into anarchy. Almost single-handedly he rammed passage of the Union Act through the Irish Parliament despite bitter Protestant resistance to a related bill that would emancipate Roman Catholics, who constituted 80 percent of Ireland's population. When the Union vote passed on June 7, 1800, Castlereagh claimed a personal triumph that left him proud to feel less Irish than English.

Despite his support for Catholic emancipation and a tendency to favour comparatively liberal economic and financial policies in relation to other leading Tories, Castlereagh's role in the rebellion dogged him. He was often derided as a man with "limited understanding and no knowledge," who demonstrated "a cold-blooded contempt of every honest public principle."[23] His manner in the House only served to accentuate the perception that he was a hard man. Lacking oratorical skill, Castlereagh came at opponents ruthlessly, ferreting out their weaknesses. His style was that of the plodding pugilist who won by bludgeoning an opponent while shrugging off the effects of every punch thrown his way, no matter how well delivered. There was a brutish quality about Castlereagh that stood at odds with the polite posturing and delicate mannerisms of the British upper classes.

"He had a natural slowness of constitution of which he was quite aware," Lady Harriet Arbuthnot—the wife of Tory MP Charles Arbuthnot, a confidant of Wellington, and a woman who revelled in careful observation of the men at the centre of power in London—confided to her journal. He "has often told me he required the goading and violence of the House of Commons to rouse him, and that he was determined never to go into the House of Lords as they were too quiet and sleepy for him. The consequences of this temperament, and of his not having a classical education, which rendered his language involved and often incorrect, were that, when he had to make a statement or an opening speech, he was generally flat and dull and scarcely commanded the attention of the House." Although she thought him clumsy, Lady Arbuthnot also believed he was so "gentlemanlike and so high minded" that he was one of the nation's finest leaders.[24]

—

NINE

The Demons of War Unchained

*P*arliament had recessed when the American declaration of war became known in London, and Castlereagh was dividing his time between the city and a forty-acre farm in Kent he had leased in 1810. Fourteen miles from Westminster Bridge, the farm had a small, secluded farmhouse with extensive grounds cut through by a trout stream. Following in King George III's footsteps, Castlereagh had purchased a herd of Spanish merino sheep that he bred according to the best scientific principles of the day. Lady Emily, meanwhile, established an exotic zoo to amuse her friends. A zebra was the centrepiece of a curious collection of wildlife imported from distant parts of the empire.

Once Castlereagh turned to farming he could remember his duties in London only with difficulty. Whenever he reluctantly returned to the city another crisis in Liverpool's continuing attempts to consolidate a strong cabinet always needed attention. So it was not until August 24 that he made time to receive Jonathan Russell, who came seeking an armistice. The forty-one-year-old diplomat from Rhode Island had trained as a lawyer but never practised, instead entering into a European trade venture soon after his graduation in 1791. His business often took him to Europe, and this background had prompted Madison to appoint him chargé d'affaires to Paris in 1810 and then to London the following year. The London posting had been one of frustration for Russell, instilling a deep distrust of the British, whom he believed capable of the most nefarious stratagems.

While waiting on Castlereagh, he had noted various alarming government responses to the declaration of war. "The government," he wrote

James Monroe on August 4, "has laid an embargo on all our vessels in port and given orders to detain & bring in such as may be encountered at sea—excepting those which have licences [from Britain]. Reinforcements in troops are likewise ordered for Canada & the West Indies and an additional squadron under the command of Sir John B Wairen"—actually Admiral Sir John Borlase Warren, who was made commander-in-chief of the North American and West Indies stations—"for the American seas. These measures are professed here to be merely of a defensive & precautionary character & to enable this government to treat more advantageously for an adjustment with us. The vessels embargoed or detained will not be proceeded against for condemnation until it is certain that we persist in hostilities on our part after a knowledge of the revocation of the orders in council. I feel my situation here to be delicate & have thought it to be my duty to suspend the formal exercise of my functions but without asking for any passports to depart."[2]

About the time he wrote Monroe, Russell received detailed instructions from the secretary of state proposing an armistice only if the orders were repealed, they were not replaced by any other form of blockade, impressment immediately ceased, and those sailors already pressed were returned. Russell was to "assure Britain that Congress would pass a law barring British seamen from serving aboard either the public or commercial vessels of the United States."

That was the carrot. The stick Russell was to wield was that a protracted war would cause Britain irreversible losses in North America. Prosecution "of the War for one year, or even a few months," Monroe wrote, "will present very serious obstacles on the part of the United States to an accommodation, which do not now exist. . . . Should our troops enter Canada you will perceive the effect which that measure cannot fail to have . . . on the public mind here, making it difficult to relinquish Territory which had been conquered."[3] The threat was implicit. Either Liverpool's government agreed to immediate armistice or the Americans would conquer and keep Canada.

Castlereagh received the American diplomat with glacial formality and the meeting devolved into Russell presenting ultimatums that the foreign secretary roundly rejected. For a man ostensibly seeking an armistice,

Russell seemed intent on making enacting one all but impossible. First, he insisted, the declaration of war nullified revocation of the orders-in-council by the House of Commons. A new revoking motion would be required. Castlereagh dismissed this notion out of hand. Letting the matter slide, Russell demanded that impressment cease. Britain would never, Castlereagh retorted, "consent to suspend the exercise of a right upon which the naval strength of the empire mainly depends." Russell failed to understand the "great sensibility and jealousy of the people of England on this subject . . . no administration could expect to remain in power that should consent to renounce the right of impressment, or to suspend the practice, without the certainty of an arrangement which should obviously be calculated most unequivocally to secure its objects."[4] Castlereagh abruptly ended the meeting, asserting that the chargé d'affaires had no authority from Madison to legitimately negotiate on behalf of the American government.[5]

Shortly after this rebuff, Russell received fresh instructions from Monroe that softened the American position but still tied an armistice to ending impressment. He exchanged a flurry of notes with Castlereagh, who roundly rejected this link. Declaring the matter hopeless, Russell bitterly quit London in early September and sailed for America.[6]

Again the inability of diplomats to conduct discussions that reflected realistic appraisals of events on the other side of the Atlantic frustrated any chance of an armistice. Russell had acted on the basis of instructions written before three American armies marched sluggishly toward Canada and well before Brig. Gen. William Hull crossed from Fort Detroit and occupied Sandwich. The declaration was only days old when Monroe set his instructions to paper, and he had been confident that the summer would yield a string of victories that would only strengthen the hand of the United States at the negotiating table. Revoking the orders-in-council and ceasing impressment would be the price Britain paid to regain its chunks of Canada. And perhaps those lands would not have to be returned at all. Perhaps Canada, or at least Upper Canada, could be retained in exchange for not kicking the British right off the continent.

Such had been the heady temper in Washington in those early days of the war, but by the time Russell acted on Monroe's instructions it was painfully evident that the summer had brought the Americans nothing but disaster on the Canadian frontier.

By August, Hull had frittered away the initiative that had been his for the taking. Realizing the superior American force in Sandwich was not—after sitting still for almost a month—likely to march on Fort Malden, Col. Henry Procter, the garrison commander, launched offensive operations against the American side of the Detroit River. From native scouts, he knew that a relief column was carrying badly needed supplies from Urbana to Hull and that the American general had dispatched 150 Ohio militia and a few cavalrymen to help secure it from Indian attack. Procter sent 100 regulars from the 41st Regiment of Foot, a handful of Canadian militia, and two dozen warriors led by Tecumseh across to intercept Hull's men. On August 5, as the Ohio horsemen forded Brownstown Creek, Tecumseh ordered his warriors to open fire. The cavalry broke and fled back to Detroit, leaving the infantry to their fate. Scattering into the woods, most of the terrified militiamen managed to escape. But seventeen were killed. Another two were captured and tomahawked by Tecumseh's men in revenge for the death of one of their braves—the only casualty suffered by the British force.

This drubbing was the last straw for Hull. On the morning of August 8 he ordered Sandwich abandoned and withdrew his entire army behind the walls of Fort Detroit. The supply column commander, Capt. Henry Brush, meanwhile, had gone to ground about thirty-five miles from Detroit on the banks of the Raisin River and sent word that he could not get past the British at Brownstown without support. Brush had three hundred cattle and seventy packhorses each carrying two hundred pounds of flour, but too few men to both control these animals and fight through to Detroit.[7]

Convinced that the woods between Detroit and the Raisin River thronged with Indians and British soldiers, on August 9 Hull ordered Lt. Col. James Miller to take six hundred men—almost half of his effective troops—and break through to Brush. Miller's men blundered noisily into the woods, with no scouts probing ahead of their advance, and were quickly detected by Indian patrols who reported their presence to Procter at Fort Malden. Procter sent 150 regulars and militia supported by a small group of warriors led by Tecumseh to ambush the Americans. On the way to the ambush site, the force gathered in an ever-growing number of warriors, so that the British commander, Capt. Adam Muir, had no idea how many were with him. Marching in the British ranks was a sixteen-year-old Canadian volunteer from Amherstburg, John Richardson.

"No other sound than the measured step of the troops interrupted the solitude of the scene," he later wrote, "rendered more imposing by the wild appearance of the warriors, whose bodies, stained and painted in the most frightful manner for the occasion, glided by us with almost noiseless velocity . . . some painted white, some black, others half black, half red; half black, half white; all with their hair plastered in such a way as to resemble the bristling quills of the porcupine, with no other covering than a cloth around their loins, yet armed to the teeth with rifles, tomahawks, war-clubs, spears, bows, arrows and scalping knives. Uttering no sound, intent only on reaching the enemy unperceived, they might have passed for the spectres of those wilds, the ruthless demons which war had unchained for the punishment and oppression of man."[8]

Sixteen miles from Detroit, Muir's force took cover behind a low rise facing a narrow river and hid until the Americans came within range. Then the British rose to form a fighting line that the militia attempted to mimic while Tecumseh's warriors sallied forth on either flank of Miller's advancing troops. Having never fought alongside Indians, Muir and the redcoats had no idea how to use their numbers to advantage. The battle quickly degenerated into chaos, with the Americans, British regulars, and militia exchanging volleys at point-blank range while the Indians poured fire in from behind the cover of trees. When one party of warriors was pushed back by an American charge, the British mistook them for enemy and ripped off a fusillade of musketry. Tecumseh's men replied in kind. The Americans meanwhile had broken out into a battle line and were able to use their superior numbers to bull across the river. Muir, who had taken a ball in the shoulder and another in the leg, ordered a retreat. The British were spared the deadly consequence of a full-scale rout, however, when Miller failed to attempt a pursuit.

The British took to their boats and paddled to safety. Muir counted 6 dead and 21 wounded with another 2 lost as prisoners. Tecumseh's losses were uncertain because, rather than returning to Fort Malden, many warriors scattered into the woods. The Americans claimed about one hundred Indians had been killed, but this was more than the number of warriors the British believed Tecumseh had brought to the field. Miller's losses were 18 killed and 64 wounded.

Although the way lay open for the Americans to join Brush at the Raisin River, Miller could not even persuade his troops to go back into the woods to retrieve their knapsacks. They huddled in the middle of a small clearing, spending a "tentless and foodless night in pouring rain." With the dawn, Miller trailed back to Detroit.

Desperate for Brush's supplies, Hull sent another escort column of four hundred men under command of the militia officers, Colonels Lewis Cass and Duncan McArthur, toward the Raisin River. Fed up with his timidity, these two men had been conspiring to arrest Hull and take over command, so he was glad to temporarily remove them from the fort. Cass and McArthur reached the Raisin River without incident, but discovered that Brush had decamped back to Urbana, destroying whatever supplies he had not taken with him. After briefly considering following Brush's example, the two men decided to rejoin the Detroit garrison. Leading their men back at a leisurely pace, neither bothered sending a messenger to inform Hull of what had transpired.[9]

Hull, meanwhile, was panicked by news that on August 13 Maj. Gen. Isaac Brock had arrived at Fort Malden with 50 regulars, 250 Canadian militia, and a six-pound cannon. The balance was beginning to tilt toward the British. Brock's arrival was greeted by Tecumseh's warriors firing off several musket volleys. After being introduced to Tecumseh, Brock quietly commented that the musket salutes were "really an unnecessary waste of ammunition when Detroit had to be captured." Tecumseh turned to his warriors and said, "This is a man." Of Tecumseh, Brock wrote, "a more sagacious or a more gallant Warrior does not I believe exist."[10]

Three days later Brock crossed the Detroit River to the south of Fort Detroit with a force of 300 regulars and 400 militia supported by

30 artillerymen manning three six-pound and two three-pound cannon. Tecumseh brought to the field 600 warriors, ostensibly under the direction of Lt. Col. Matthew Elliott of the Indian Department. Brock realized that if these braves managed to get inside Fort Detroit a massacre was inevitable, for the British had scant control over them. Brock also was able to draw the brigs *Queen Charlotte* and *General Hunter* up the river so that the fort was within range of their eighteen-pound cannon. He then called upon Hull to surrender, playing on the old general's fear that, if Detroit was taken by storm, Brock could not restrain the Indians. Hull refused.

That evening the British shelled the fort and the next morning Brock's troops and Tecumseh's warriors advanced toward its walls. Before battle was joined, Hull hoisted a flag of truce. Terms were quickly arranged, whereby Hull surrendered not just the garrison but also the men out in the field with Cass and McArthur. Some 1,600 Ohio militiamen were paroled home and escorted by British regulars beyond range of Tecumseh's warriors, who had greeted the surrender amicably and posed no threat to the fort's inhabitants. Hull and 582 regular troops were marched off to prisoner-of-war camps near Quebec City. Brock was pleased to capture thirty-three cannon and 2,500 muskets, as his own armament supply was limited and these would help arm more Canadian militia. It was a bloodless victory that put the British in undisputed control of the frontier country.

The only two remaining American forts, Fort Dearborn and Fort Wayne, soon fell. At Fort Dearborn the garrison attempted to withdraw and were fallen upon by 400 local Potawatomi warriors, who now rose against the Americans, and about two-thirds of the fleeing men, women, and children were massacred. Fort Wayne was thereafter overrun by an Indian assault. By summer's end no significant American presence remained in the disputed frontier. Hull's army had not only been defeated, it had been annihilated.

As the grim news from the northern boundaries of the United States filtered in by messengers riding fast horses and was added to the discouraging reports from Jonathan Russell regarding attempts to arrange an armistice through the offices of Viscount Castlereagh in London, disillusionment with the war had grown within President James Madison's administration. Personally shaken by the revelation that the very day he had signed the declaration of war Castlereagh had revoked the orders-in-council, Madison later lamented that if this news had been received promptly he would have either recalled the document or sought an immediate armistice.

Yet Madison also thought the revocation strengthened his hand, persuading himself that Castlereagh had taken the step because of a combination of the firm American position and domestic pressure to normalize commerce between the two countries. "I think it not improbable," he wrote Jefferson, "that the sudden change in relation to the Orders in Council . . . was the effect of apprehensions in the Cabinet that the deliberation of Cong[res]s would have upon that issue, and that the Ministry could not stand [against], the popular torrent [against] the Orders in Council, swelled as it would be by the addition of a war with the U.S."[11]

Despite the diplomatic victory implicit in cancellation of the orders, Madison was convinced that it was too late to use this as a pretext to back away from war and unilaterally declare an armistice. He and Secretary of State James Monroe brushed off attempts by the remaining British representative in Washington, Anthony St. John Baker, to renew negotiations because they preferred to pursue discussions through Russell in London. They continued to foster the belief that this channel for negotiation remained open for several weeks after the chargé d'affaires had actually departed England.

In August the president and Monroe decided that peace would be possible only if the British ceased impressment. Monroe later defended this hardening of the American position in a letter to his former mentor Col. John Taylor. "Impressment having long been a ground of complaint, and a principal cause of the war, the British claim would have been confirmed, as it was thought, if the war was terminated without some adequate provision for it. I was satisfied, that, had we caught, at the modified repeal of the orders in council, made afterwards without an arrangement of other questions particularly that of impressment, the British government would have concluded that it had gained a victory, and maintained the whole system in full vigor, even the principles of the orders in council in the form of blockades, against the United States. Having gone to war, it seemed to be our duty, not to withdraw from it, till the rights of our country were placed on a more secure basis."[12]

This decision to insist that any peace agreement depended on Britain's discarding impressment coincided with several British representatives approaching the Americans almost simultaneously with varying proposals for a negotiated settlement. In Canada, Sir George Prevost had been trying to limit the fighting even as Brock mustered troops to drive Hull out of Upper Canada and seize Detroit. Having learned that the orders were cancelled, he thought it reasonable the Americans would welcome a return to the negotiating table. On August 5 he dashed off a dispatch to Lord Liverpool reporting that despite the failure of his earlier attempts at conciliation, the prime minister "may rest assured that unless the safety of the Provinces entrusted to my charge should require them, no measures shall be adopted by me to impede a speedy return to those accustomed relations of amity and goodwill which it is the mutual interest of both countries to cherish and preserve."[13]

Within days Prevost's aide, Lt. Col. Edward Baynes, met under a flag of truce with Maj. Gen. Henry Dearborn at the American commanders' Greenbush headquarters, across the river from Albany, New York. The sixty-one-year-old general responsible for the prosecution of the invasion of Canada was "a ponderous, flabby figure, weighing two hundred and fifty pounds."[14] Called Granny by his men, this veteran of the Revolution had fought at Bunker Hill and followed Benedict Arnold on his ill-fated march through the winter wilderness to Quebec only to be captured and exchanged. He had been living the comfortable life of a successful Massachusetts politician until Madison called him back to the flag.

Since assuming command Dearborn had focused his attention on a largely futile recruiting campaign in the New England states, not returning to Greenbush until July 26 to find only 1,200 men had reported. These men were ill equipped and untrained. As Dearborn took no measures to prevent Baynes sizing up the encampment and its occupants, the British officer gathered a great deal of intelligence on his opponents. He reported that Dearborn did "not appear to possess the energy of mind or activity of body requisite for the important station he fills." The American general basically confirmed this, advising Baynes that "the burden of command at this time of life was not a desirable charge." The soldiers under Dearborn's command impressed the professional soldier not a bit. They were "independent in their habits and principles, their officers ignorant and totally uninformed in every thing relating to the possession of arms and possess no influence over the militia but in proportion as they court it by popular and familiar intercourse."[15]

Dearborn received Prevost's armistice offer with the relief of a drowning man grabbing hold of a safety line, although he allowed that it was impossible for the matter to be formal. Unauthorized to enter into such an agreement, he would carry out only defensive actions. Lacking direct authority over Hull, he could do no more than advise the general to cease offensive operations. The two officers agreed that reinforcements and supply convoys could continue moving west without threat of attack by either side.

On August 9, hands were shaken and each man's honour staked on the guarantee that their side would fairly apply the informal terms. Baynes was happy. He had secured a much-needed breathing space for the British and the right to continue moving men and materiel out to Brock without the worry of American interference. And there was always the slight possibility that the armistice would last long enough to allow the governments to actually negotiate a formal truce. Certainly that process would be helped if meantime not too much blood was shed. Dearborn was equally content, assured that he now had time to amass the 5,000 to 6,000 men he considered necessary for the main invasion of Canada. He sent a dispatch to Hull asking him to consider withdrawing from Canada, but by the time it arrived Detroit was in Brock's hands and Hull a captive travelling toward Quebec.

It took six days for Dearborn's letter reporting the informal armistice with Prevost to reach Washington. Madison was infuriated, and War Secretary Dr. William Eustis immediately ordered the general to give Prevost notice that the agreement was repudiated and to "proceed with the utmost vigor in your operations." Having also received communiqués from Hull about how dire his situation was, Eustis advised Dearborn that "the President thinks it proper that not a moment should be lost in gaining possession of the British posts at Niagara and Kingston, or at least the former." On August 25, Dearborn sent a message to Prevost that the armistice should be considered terminated. He then informed Eustis that shifting headquarters to the Niagara front in time to have any effect during the campaigning season was impossible, so he would continue gathering his forces at Albany and "push towards Montreal at the same time that our troops on the western frontier of this state strike at Upper Canada." The advance on all fronts would begin in October.[16]

Believing no more could be done to chivvy his generals into pressing the campaign, Madison left Washington for Montpelier on August 28. He and his wife were in a carriage dragging slowly along a rain-soaked road when a hard-riding horseman dispatched by Eustis intercepted them with the news that General Hull had surrendered his army. Furious, Madison ordered the carriage turned about and hastened back to the capital. "Do you not tremble with resentment at this treacherous act?" Dolley Madison tersely asked. "Yet we must not judge the man until we are in possession of his reasons."[17] There was no question of Hull's escaping a court martial once he was exchanged by the British and returned to Washington.

Until receiving this awful news, Madison had nurtured a scenario unfolding whereby Hull's "triumphant army would have seized Upper Canada." Lake Erie would be an American pond. "The Indians would have been neutral or submissive to our will." Thousands of Americans, inspired by this great victory, would rush to enlist. Most important of all "the intrigues of the disaffected would have been smothered."[18]

Instead, the president railed, Hull "sunk before obstacles at which not an officer near him would have paused, and threw away an entire army." The surrender, he feared, must certainly turn "the people of Canada, not indisposed to favour us . . . against us" and persuade the Indians to ally themselves with the British. Madison gloomily noted that "a general damp spread over our Affairs."[19]

The president needed victories, successes to justify the war and convince an increasingly dubious public that the adventure was warranted. But it was hard to conceive that any of the remaining armies were capable of bringing such an event about before the weather turned, and Madison also entered a bid for presidential re-election in the late fall that failure on the battlefield might just cause him to lose. Indisposed to journey 300 miles west to take personal charge of the army gathered at Lewiston, New York, facing Niagara, Dearborn sent Virginian Gen. Alexander Smyth in his stead with vague instructions to share command responsibility with New York Gen. Stephen Van Rensselaer. Dearborn provided Smyth with 1,650 regulars to bring this central army up to about 5,000 troops—what he considered necessary for it to cross the Niagara River and enter Upper Canada. The old general, however, failed to dictate which general was superior to the other.

No soldier, Van Rensselaer had been appointed by New York governor Daniel D. Tompkins. Perversely, this was not an act of patronage on the governor's part but rather a clever stratagem to dispose of his most likely opponent in the 1813 spring gubernatorial race. The forty-five-year-old Van Rensselaer hailed from one of New York's first families and had inherited a 12,000-square-mile estate named Rensselaerswyck near Albany. Rather than sell the property off in sections to sustain the family wealth, he opted to lease parcels and soon had more than 3,000 tenants working the land for him. A Federalist, Van Rensselaer was assured the party's candidacy for governor. Popular, wealthy, politically well connected, and considered somewhat of a reformer, Van Rensselaer promised Tompkins a hard run. When Tompkins offered him command of the central army because of his being a militia officer, Van Rensselaer could hardly refuse. To do so would seem unpatriotic, but if he accepted then it would be impossible for him to stand for election. And should he fail as a commander, his reputation would suffer. Realizing there was no way to escape Tompkins's trap, Van Rensselaer had insisted on one stipulation, that his cousin Solomon Van Rensselaer be his aide-de-camp. Where Van Rensselaer's expression and bearing exuded refinement and gentleness, his cousin looked every bit the soldier. "The handsomest officer I ever beheld," one contemporary commented. His father had been a general in the Revolution and he had entered the military as soon as possible. As a seventeen-year-old ensign Solomon had distinguished himself fighting alongside Maj. Gen. "Mad Anthony" Wayne at Fallen Timbers, where he had been seriously wounded. Ten years junior to Stephen Van Rensselaer, he had served the past twelve years as New York's adjutant general before accepting the rank of lieutenant colonel and joining the Army of the Center.[20]

Van Rensselaer was not enthusiastic about the war, and his appointment caused discontent, even amazement in the ranks of New York's Republicans. When the call to arms had been issued it had been mostly Republicans who rallied to the flag and volunteered. But Van Rensselaer quickly surrounded himself with Federalist officers, such as his cousin, so that the commanders bore one political stripe and the troops another. When confronted by New York Republican leader John Canfield Spencer in early September over his lack of enthusiasm for the war, Van Rensselaer stated his position plainly. The general, Spencer wrote Tompkins, "is openly declaring against the war, represents it as undertaken from base, selfish, motives." Solomon Van Rensselaer and the other Federalist officers were no better. They "whisper the same thing and worse," Spencer declared. The result of this open criticism of the war's purpose by their commander caused many a soldier to lose "confidence in the justice of their cause and that zeal in its support . . . necessary to the successful termination of the war." This was not an army that Spencer thought would ever "go to Canada under [its] present officers."[21]

As the tragedy of Hull's surrender became known, Van Rensselaer became convinced that he was being set up by his political rivals for a similar fate. He and his cousin privately hoped that Madison or Eustis would relieve them in favour of some Republican officers of equivalent rank and status. Tompkins certainly could take command as his privilege as governor. That no such order was issued from Washington infuriated Van Rensselaer, who portrayed the administration as "weak and despicable." Nor could he request dismissal, for to do so would be to expose himself to accusations of cowardice. He was trapped, likely destined, he believed, to being "Hulled," forced to serve as a scapegoat for Republican incompetence.[22]

General Smyth's arrival on September 29 at Buffalo, south of Lewiston, only furthered Van Rensselaer's increasing paranoia that a Republican conspiracy swirled around him. Born in Ireland, Smyth had come to America when he was ten years old and settled in Virginia. Trained as a lawyer, he had served multiple terms as a Republican in the Virginia House of Delegates. In 1808, he entered the army and when the war broke out was Eustis's acting war secretary. Having reached Buffalo, Smyth announced his arrival and then refused to proceed to Lewiston or to meet with Van Rensselaer.

By letter, the two bickered over where to cross the river and who would lead the attack. Having had weeks to reconnoitre the British positions, Van Rensselaer and his cousin had concluded that the most likely crossing point was at Queenston Heights, where the defences were weak because of the natural obstacle presented by a section of rapids. Lacking in guile, Van Rensselaer had consequently brought his army up to Lewiston, which faced the heights from the opposite side of the river. But he had then been unable to muster sufficient strength to make the attack. Smyth disdained Van Rensselaer's strategy, claiming instead that the best crossing was where he was headquartered. Next to Buffalo the Niagara River was more easily crossed, but the British recognized this and so had the opposite shore more heavily defended than at Queenston Heights. With both generals refusing to compromise or conform to the other's opinion, an entirely American-made stalemate set in on the Niagara front.

Although the rift between the two officers dismayed Madison, the president chose to do nothing about the matter. Instead he left it to Dearborn to sort out, who typically confined himself to gently reminding the generals that such behaviour was "regrettable."[23] Finally, Van Rensselaer decided to carry out the invasion with the 3,000 men under his command. Solomon Van Rensselaer and the other Federalist officers urged the general to use his command authority to coerce Smyth into cooperating with the attack, but Van Rensselaer refused. If the crossing succeeded then he would have upstaged the Virginian Republican, a result that would silence his critics in New York and Washington. Consequently, on October 10, he mustered the troops in Lewiston and ordered them to prepare to cross the turbulent waters in boats after nightfall.

TEN

The Valiant Have Bled

OCTOBER 1812

By the time Gen. Stephen Van Rensselaer finally decided to attack Queenston Heights, Maj. Gen. Isaac Brock was on the scene organizing the defence. The informal armistice and the Army of the Center's inherent lethargy had provided critical time to enable him to journey from Detroit to Niagara to personally meet the new threat. Had Hull and Van Rensselaer coordinated their assaults on Upper Canada, the British position would have been precarious, with Brock's command desperately overextended and caught between two mighty pincers. Brock was still concerned. The Niagara front was thirty-six miles long, running across the narrow neck of land separating Lake Erie and Lake Ontario. Almost directly in the centre, the great thundering falls prevented boats using the river to pass between the two lakes. To defend this peninsula Brock had 400 regulars, 800 militiamen, and about 200 Indian warriors. The militia had just returned to service after the fall harvest and were weary to the bone. Morale amongst the redcoats, who had been standing guard over the frontier for two long, largely inactive months, was dangerously low. The small garrison from the 49th Foot at Queenston were fed up to the point of near mutiny. Brock realized his forces were stretched dangerously thin, a situation exacerbated by his inability to gauge accurately where the Americans would try to force a crossing, because they were formed into two large bodies—one at Lewiston, the other at Buffalo. The two logical crossing points were both upstream of the falls, so he divided most of his men between Chippawa and Fort Erie to meet these threats. Below the falls a narrow gorge made crossing more difficult all the way to where Lewiston and Queenston glared across at each other. Here the river was only 250 yards wide and could be crossed in ten minutes by rowboat or mere seconds by a musket ball fired from one shore to the other.

Despite the presence of Van Rensselaer's force in Lewiston, a crossing here seemed less likely than upstream. Brock assumed the Americans gathered here because of the convenience offered by the village rather than for strategic reasons. So he positioned only two companies and about the same number of militia in and around Queenston. The little village of a hundred houses was overshadowed by the towering heights. Near the village the defenders had dug in a tiny, ineffectual three-pound gun. About halfway up the long, gradual slope to the summit, an eighteen-pound cannon was emplaced, while a mile downriver, at Vrooman's Point, a twenty-four-pound gun covered the river. Brock knew that the Americans in Lewiston were bristling with about 200 to 300 cannon, so every effort was taken to conceal the location of the three small artillery pieces the British had deployed to protect them from counter-battery fire.

Rather than assume the defensive, Brock would have preferred to undertake his own offensive against Lewiston. Deserters had reported the American militia's poor morale, and Brock believed a sharp attack would bring this rabble of "enraged democrats . . . who . . . die very fast" to its knees. An attack would also enable him to hit the Americans with all his strength. But Governor Sir George Prevost would countenance no offensive actions, still believing that the Americans must soon come to their senses and formalize an armistice pending negotiation of a treaty. Fortunately Detroit, which he regretted Brock's having taken, had been a bloodless victory. But a battle in which much American blood spilled could jeopardize chances of peace, so Brock was to remain on his side of the river and not molest the Americans. Prevost hoped that the Americans would do the same until winter set in and that by the spring this unfortunate war would be an unhappy memory.

Brock thought Prevost plain wrong, but could not openly say as much. "I have implicitly followed Your Excellency's instructions, and abstained, under great temptation and provocation from every act of hostility," he said in reply to Prevost's admonishments. But in a private letter he vented his frustrations. "I am really placed in a most awkward predicament.... My instructions oblige me to adopt defensive measures, and I have evinced greater forbearance than was ever practised on any former occasion. It is thought that, without the aid of the sword, the American people maybe brought to a full sense of their own interests. I firmly believe that I could at this moment sweep everything before me from Fort Niagara to Buffalo.

"It is certainly something singular that we should be upwards of two months in a state of warfare, and that along this widely extended frontier not a single death, either natural or by the sword, should have occurred among the troops under my command, and we have not been together idle, nor has a single desertion taken place."

Across the river the Americans were obviously gathering strength and likely shuffling toward some offensive act. When they did, Brock intended to meet it head on and either win a decisive victory or go down in bloody defeat. The battle for Upper Canada would be decided here on the banks of the Niagara. He would not willingly surrender ground. To his brother he wrote, "I say decisive, because if I should be beaten, the province is inevitably gone; and should I be victorious, I do not imagine the gentry from the other side will be anxious to return to the charge."[1]

That the Americans were coming was confirmed beyond question in his mind by a small party of sailors under command of Lt. Jesse D. Elliott, who had been sent to Lake Erie to organize a naval force capable of disputing British mastery of its waters. On the night of October 8–9, rowing quietly in among the cluster of British vessels tied up under the protective guns of Fort Erie, the sailors scrambled aboard two brigs, *Caledonia* and *Detroit*, cut them loose, took them under tow, and started dragging them toward Buffalo. Although they managed to get the two-gun *Caledonia* away, the larger brig ran aground and had to be burned. This audacious act boosted American morale. It also served warning that the U.S. Navy might in time seriously contest British control of the lakes. As the lakes provided the most efficient means for moving men and supplies around Upper Canada, both sides knew that the initiative lay with whoever mastered their waters.[2]

Two nights after Elliott's raid, sentries on Queenston Heights heard a great ruckus across the river at Lewiston. It was a dirty night, thick clouds blocking any star or moonlight, and a cold rain quickly soaked wool uniforms. Across the river yelling and many splashes suggested men were taking to boats for a crossing, but nothing could be seen in the stygian blackness. After about two hours the racket ceased and all fell quiet.

In Lewiston, 600 sodden, dispirited Americans trudged back to their billets. The attempted crossing had played out like some comic opera. Trudging through heavy mud, Lt. Col. Solomon Van Rensselaer and Capt. John Machesney had led an evenly constituted body of regular and militia troops to the ferry landing where they were to board large boats and row across to the Canadian shore. To their consternation the officers discovered that the boat officer had somehow been swept off in one of the biggest bateaux, on which all the oars for the others had been stored. It took a couple of hours to discover that the bateau had run aground downstream and that the boat officer had wandered into the darkness. Van Rensselaer ordered the attack set back forty-eight hours.[3]

It was a calamitous start to what he had hoped would be the victorious battle that would salvage his reputation. At three in the morning on Tuesday, October 13, the 600 troops of the first assault wave again returned to the Lewiston ferry landing. This time thirteen boats, all equipped with oars, waited, and the men crowded aboard. Under the cover of an intense artillery bombardment, the soldiers frantically paddled out into the rushing current. The three leading boats, over-loaded for the number of oarsmen, were swept helplessly downstream by the swirling waters. Almost 200 men were lost before the fight began. Cannonballs whistling overhead, the others hunkered down in the remaining ten boats as the facing shoreline erupted with the flash of musketry and shot hammered with sharp, splintering cracks into wood or the sickening moist-sounding thud of lead piercing flesh.

A mere forty-six regulars with a handful of militiamen under Capt. James Dennis waited for them on the Canadian shore, but the rate of fire poured out by the British infantrymen was withering. No army in the world could match the British soldier's rate of musketry. Thick cartridge paper ripped open with powder-blackened teeth, Brown Bess musket primed, frizzen snapped closed, musket upended and butted onto the ground, the powder poured into the barrel, followed by the ball, both rammed home with the thin rod quickly returned to the barrel rings that held it, musket shouldered, doghead pulled back to full cock. The men aimed into the obscuring smoke lingering from earlier shots, remembered to aim low and to wait for the order—conforming to the endless routine drilled into them by hundreds of hours of practice. Then Dennis shouted and the muskets slammed into bruised shoulders and as if by instinct the men began to reload. Each man loosed two rounds a minute.

As Solomon Van Rensselaer leapt ashore with sword brandished, a bullet struck him in the right thigh. In rapid succession, five more balls struck the lieutenant colonel in the legs before he abandoned the attempt to overwhelm the defenders and hobbled with his surviving troops back to the shelter of the steep riverbank. Despite rapid blood loss, Van Rensselaer still looked for some way to turn the tide of battle. The plan for the assault was in tatters; the waves of troops that were supposed to follow the first landing group failed to come across. From halfway up the slope leading to the summit, the eighteen-pound cannon sprayed the helpless troops with canister. Continuing the frontal assault would be suicide. The heights appeared unscalable, making it impossible to flank the British.

Suddenly Capt. John E. Wool, a twenty-three-year-old U.S. 13th Infantry officer, crawled up to where Van Rensselaer lay bleeding. There was a rumour, the young officer said, that fishermen had developed a path down the cliff from the summit. If he could gain the heights then Wool could overrun the gun on the slope. Van Rensselaer agreed he should try, and taking sixty men, Wool set off, hugging the shoreline.[4]

Meanwhile Maj. Gen. Isaac Brock had been awakened at four by the sound of cannon to the north and immediately realized that the Americans were crossing at Queenston. Before going to bed Brock had written a gloomy report to Prevost that uncharacteristically predicted failure. Lacking "willing, well-disposed characters," he said, to fill out the ranks of the militia to the 2,000 necessary to ensure Upper Canada's defence, Brock was forced to take in American immigrants. He distrusted their loyalty and motivation. Consequently, he wrote, "I fear I shall not be able to effect my object [to] defy all their efforts against this part of the Province."[5]

Within minutes of waking, Brock and his aide, Lt. Col. John Macdonell, were galloping toward Queenston. Behind them the regulars and militia at the fort were roused and set marching at the double toward the battle about seven miles to their south. Along the way the two officers passed two companies of York Volunteers and shouted for them to follow at the run to Queenston. Arriving with the dawn, Brock saw another wave of American troops crossing by boat and realized the attack was in earnest. Deciding that the light company that was up the slope defending the eighteen-pound cannon was needed to repel this new assault, Brock rode to the gun emplacement. Just as he reached it, Wool and his men emerged from the woods on the summit and descended toward the position. Outnumbered by the better-positioned Americans, Brock ordered the gun spiked and abandoned. The British on the slope retreated quickly to the village below.

With the American second wave beginning to reinforce the remnants of troops still with Van Rensselaer, and Wool in possession of the heights, Brock saw he was badly outnumbered and that the reinforcements coming from Fort George would arrive too late to prevent the British garrison being overrun. The safest thing to do would be to retreat, something Brock would not do. Brock had often declared that he would never send men "where I do not lead them."[6] And he had no intention of doing so now. Jumping off his horse, Brock formed his 100 regulars and an equal number of "tired and dazed" militia into line and ordered the advance. With sword held high he led them up the slope toward Wool's men. His cocked hat, shining gold epaulettes, dazzling red coat with two rows of gilt buttons on front, sword, and decorative scarf that Tecumseh had given him after the capture of Detroit wound around the waist marked him. But Brock never hesitated, even when a musket ball tore open his wrist. When the regulars suddenly hesitated and several men turned, he shouted, "This is the first time I have ever seen the 49th turn their backs!"[7] The soldiers rallied, cheered, pressed on into the fire that scythed men down like hay. Up the steep slope they went, slipping and sliding on the wet grass, cursing, a few pausing to fire up at where the Americans had taken cover behind fallen logs and trees before pressing onward. More Americans clambered up Wool's path to add to the weight of the fire directed toward the British and Canadians following Brock.

When Brock was about 165 feet from the American line, he shouted for the men to fix bayonets and charge. As he rushed on, just ahead of the advancing line, an American scout rose from behind a bush and took careful aim with his long rifle. The musket cracked and a ball tore into Brock's chest just above the heart. Fifteen-year-old George Jarvis, a Canadian volunteer serving in the 49th, rushed to his side. "Are you much hurt, Sir?" he asked, before realizing Brock was dead. The moment Brock fell, the charge foundered. Some troops of the 49th quickly gathered up the body of their fallen commander and joined the general retreat.

As the men fell back they were intercepted by Lieutenant Colonel John Macdonell, who had a small number of York Volunteers in tow. A brilliant lawyer who in peacetime was Upper Canada's attorney general, he revered Brock and determined to renew the advance. Macdonell found a willing partner in the 49th's Capt. John Williams. "Charge them home and they cannot stand you!" Williams bellowed. "Revenge the General," shouted the 49th's survivors. Seventy strong, the mixed British and Canadian force headed up the slope behind the mounted Macdonell. Facing them were several hundred Americans. A ball slammed into Macdonell's horse, causing it to rear and wheel about. A second shot slapped into the officer's back. Mortally wounded, Macdonell toppled to the ground. Williams was also down, a bloody gouge torn out of his scalp. The attack collapsed.[8]

Also wounded, Capt. James Dennis gathered the survivors of the two badly reduced 49th companies and militiamen, abandoned Queenston at 10 a.m. and fell back on Vrooman's Point, where the long twenty-four-pounder still blazed away at the Americans crossing the river. Here they awaited the arrival of Maj. Gen. Roger Sheaffe and the main force from Fort George. Word of Brock's death spread quickly. Their morale unde-flating, the British and Canadian troops vowed to avenge their fallen commander. Shortly thereafter Sheaffe marched in with 300 men of the 41st Regiment of Foot, 250 militiamen—including Capt. Robert

Runchey's Company of Coloured Men from the Niagara Light Dragoons—and an artillery battery drawn by draught horses of local farmers, only to receive the news that he now commanded. Before Brock's move from Detroit to Niagara, Sheaffe, a forty-nine-year-old Boston-born Loyalist, had been in overall command of the region. A regular army officer with nineteen years of service on the Canadian front, he was Brock's opposite—a cautious officer, given to deliberate, methodical action. Unlike Prevost, he was not one to shy from a fight.

Taking a good long, hard look at the situation, Sheaffe decided a frontal attack would be doomed. Instead he marched inland, following the grain of the escarpment. He would join battle from the flank and in his own time. Meanwhile, the Vrooman's Point battery continued to smash American boats plying back and forth across the river. During the march, Sheaffe continued receiving reinforcements. From Chippawa to the south, the garrison of the 41st came in, as did about 300 Mohawks from the Grand River Reserve. Sheaffe now had more than 400 regulars, about as many militia, and the Mohawks. But he knew the Americans holding the high ground were probably more numerous and should now be dug into a highly defensible position. Poor odds, but he was determined to root them out.[9]

Sheaffe was unaware of how badly disorganized and demoralized the Americans clinging to the heights were. Hundreds of militia at Lewiston still awaited boats to carry them across, but almost half had sunk or been carried off downstream. While some militiamen were anxious to support the men already across, far more refused to budge—the New Yorkers asserting their right to not serve beyond the nation's borders. No amount of encouragement or disparagement could shift them. Thousands simply sat on the river's edge to watch the battle like so many spectators.

Across the river, some militiamen had also taken shelter in Queenston, fearing that to go up the heights would cut them off from the boats in the event of a retreat. Captain Wool had been badly wounded during Macdonell's attack, Solomon Van Rensselaer evacuated in an unconscious state. Brig. Gen. Stephen Van Rensselaer sent Lt. Col. Winfield Scott, the young Virginian officer who in a fit of patriotic fervour had taken a party of British sailors prisoner after the

Chesapeake incident, to assume command. With Scott was a party of engineers to fortify the position on the heights, but their entrenching tools were left behind so there was little that could be done to prepare the position. Ammunition, water, and food were in short supply. After deducting casualties, the New Yorkers refusing to come out of the village, and pickets necessary to protect his flanks, Scott had 350 regulars and 250 militiamen to defend the heights.

He was still sizing up his defences when, at about three in the afternoon, Mohawk skirmishers struck the Americans from the west. Moments later an extended line of British and Canadian troops advanced out of the woods toward Scott's left flank. Completely surprised, backs to the river, the Americans had no time to wheel about before Sheaffe halted his men. With brisk efficiency the soldiers shouldered their muskets, loosed a shattering volley, and then at Sheaffe's command charged with fixed bayonets. Within seconds the Americans broke. Although Scott jumped up on a log to rally them with a dramatic harangue to turn about and redeem the honour lost by Hull's surrender, he was ignored. Some fled the hill, hoping to reach the river and escape. A few hurled themselves off the cliffs, choosing to die that way rather than be scalped. Others huddled in a mass at the cliff edge, terrified that the Mohawks would murder them, until Scott signalled surrender by waving a white cravat.[10]

What should have been an easy American victory had turned into another disastrous defeat. Sheaffe's troops rounded up 958 prisoners. More than 300 Americans were killed or wounded. British losses were only 14 killed, 77 wounded, and 21 missing for the entire one-day battle.[11] But among the dead was Brock, and with his loss the British lost the man who could most effectively defend Canada.

When Van Rensselaer proposed a three-day armistice to allow for exchange of prisoners and burial of the dead, Sheaffe agreed because the prisoners taken outnumbered his regular troops. He resolved the problem by paroling the New York militiamen and keeping only regular officers and soldiers as prisoners. These were marched off to join Hull's contingent in a camp near Quebec. Sheaffe would be awarded a baronetcy, while Brock had recently been raised to Knight of the Bath for the capture of Detroit—an honour he died unaware of.

Brock's body was taken back to Government House in Niagara (now Niagara-on-the-Lake), a small village just north of Fort George, where it lay in state for three days. There then followed a funeral described by one attendee as "the grandest and most solemn that I have ever witnessed or that has been seen in Upper Canada."[12] The funeral was actually for two fallen commanders—Brock and Macdonell. Pallbearers carried their caskets between a double line of militia and Indians. The 5,000 militiamen stood solemnly with muskets reversed while several cannon fired a salute every minute during the course of the procession. Across the river, the batteries at both Fort Niagara and Lewiston thundered salvoes in honour of the fallen general. After the funeral, the two caskets were interred in a bastion deep inside Fort George.

The next day, the October 17 issue of the Kingston *Gazette* carried a fanciful account of Brock's death that began the process that would transform soldier into mythical Canadian icon forever twinned with another myth born at Queenston Heights—that of the pre-eminent role played by the militia in repelling the invasion. Here was Brock in the midst of militiamen who were "ever obedient to his call, and whom [he] loved with the adoration of a father." A Brock who fell in the midst of their ranks, his last dying words, "*Push on brave York Volunteers.*"[13] Throughout Upper Canada the story was told, the legend recast and embellished until everyone—save perhaps the British regulars who fought at Queenston and buried their dead there—believed the militia carried the day. That Brock had considered them at best barely competent and had distrusted their loyalty was forgotten. Brock, an Englishman who desired nothing more than to quit North American service to seek glory on the European battlefields where careers were made, was quickly anointed a hero whom all Canadians, whether English, French, or American Loyalists, could claim as their own.

Previously English Canadians had esteemed Gen. James Wolfe, whose death on the Plains of Abraham during the pivotal battle that decided the outcome of the battle for Quebec in 1759 had elevated him to near-martyrdom both in English Canada and at home in Great Britain. But that same battle had claimed the life of Marquis Louis Joseph de Montcalm, commander of French forces in Canada, and signalled the end of New France. So Wolfe's stature in Canada remained ambiguous, a hero only half of the colony could claim. Such was not the case for Brock.

His death and the Queenston Heights victory had another immediate outcome as the defeatist talk that had pervaded Upper Canada and the low turnout of volunteer militia dissipated. Sheaffe soon reported to Prevost that he was no longer plagued by militiamen leaving the field at the slightest excuse. Further, the militia serving in the Niagara area were "very alert at their several posts and continue generally to evince the best disposition."[14]

This contrasted starkly with the situation south of the border, where the New York militia was almost in open rebellion. Predictably the outcome of the Battle of Queenston Heights had brought disgrace rather than accolades to the officers involved. At first Stephen Van Rensselaer attempted to shift the blame to others, including Smyth, who he maintained should have come to his aid. But the real culprits, the general reported to Secretary of War Dr. William Eustis, were the New York militiamen who refused to cross the river and cost Van Rensselaer the battle. "I can only add that the victory was really won, but lost for the want of a small reinforcement: one-third part of the idle men might have saved all."[15]

His excuses mattered not; it was obvious the man's military career was washed up. Realizing this, Van Rensselaer bowed to the inevitable and requested retirement rather than waiting to be relieved. General Dearborn readily accepted and then wrote a letter to the president placing responsibility for the failure squarely on the Dutchman's shoulders. He then gave Gen. Alexander Smyth command of the Army of the Center. Smyth quickly purged the Federalist officers from the ranks and made a clumsy attempt to escape being subordinate to Dearborn. "Give me here *a clear stage*, men, and *money*, and I will retrieve your affairs or perish," Smyth advised War Secretary Eustis. Recognizing Smyth's intention in contacting him directly, Eustis icily replied: "You are too well acquainted with service to require to be informed that all communications respecting your command should be directed to that officer."[16]

Despite the bluster, the defeat had shaken Smyth, and he faced the same problems Van Rensselaer had—the lack of enthusiasm that permeated the ranks of the New Yorkers. Smyth tried to bolster morale by issuing a proclamation that blamed the defeat on Van Rensselaer and the officers he had disposed of and assured that within days regular troops under his command would "plant the American standard in Canada." But, he acknowledged, success would depend on the militiamen pitching in. "The present is the hour of renown," Smyth declared. "Have you not a wish for fame? . . . Then seize the present moment; if you do not you will regret it and say: 'The valiant have bled in vain, the friends of my country fell and I was not there.'

"Advance, then, to our aid. I will wait for a few days. I cannot give you the day of my departure, but come on. Come in companies, half companies, pairs or singly. I will organize you for a short tour."[17]

The New Yorkers were in no mood to credit Smyth's bluster. All about the Army of the Center was cracking at the seams. Having not been paid for weeks, two regular regiments mutinied. Hundreds of militiamen refused to obey orders until their barrack conditions were improved. Dysentery and pneumonia were rampant in the ranks. There was a desperate shortage of meat rations, and winter clothing was entirely lacking while temperatures were dropping rapidly. Many—militia and regulars both—were barefoot. A group of barrack lawyers declared themselves spokesmen for the Men of New York and responded to Smyth's appeal in writing. "Go, General, if you will. Should you ever reach the walls of Quebec . . . and when you fall, the men of New York will lament that folly has found new victims."[18]

Realizing he could not take the offensive immediately, Smyth agreed to an indefinite extension of the armistice with the understanding that it could be cancelled by either party on thirty hours' notice. The American general then settled into writing more reports full of fiery pronouncements and drafting bold plans for definitive actions while Sheaffe turned his more practically inclined mind toward calling up more militia and strengthening the defences running across the breadth of the peninsula.[19] It was a strange way to carry on a war, but the armistice suited each man's purpose, and, as Smyth did not report its existence to Washington, President Madison remained unaware that the war on the Canadian front was effectively at a standstill.

ELEVEN

Opportunities for Usefulness

*T*he British government was even less aware of events in North America, for the most recent communiqué from Governor Sir George Prevost had reported only Hull's surrender. Late summer had been a period of reorganization as Sir Henry Bathurst took the reins of secretary for war and the colonies, but by mid-September the man responsible for prosecution of both the war against France and this undesired conflict with America, in addition to most matters of colonial administration, had taken his desk at the War and Colonial Office. Despite being one of the world's two most powerful nations and undisputed master of a far-flung empire, Britain had a distinctly small bureaucracy. Most offices directly serving the cabinet were clustered in cramped quarters between St. James's Park and the Thames, making them convenient to the Houses of Parliament. The War and Colonial Office occupied a humble seventeenth-century house at No. 14 Downing Street, close to St. James's Park and just a few doors from the prime minister's No. 10 residence. Although prestigiously situated, the house was shabbily constructed, not only dark and drafty but usually damp because of a leaking basement that had to be regularly pumped dry. The offices were cramped and dreary.[1]

Scattered through the small, dank rooms was a modest staff that consisted of two undersecretaries, a chief clerk, nineteen clerks, a private secretary, a précis writer, a librarian, and several translators.[2] In 1801, the war and colonial bureaucracies had been amalgamated because the two inextricably overlapped. Although the theory seemed sound, execution resulted in an office constantly bursting at the seams with files and paperwork while being inevitably short-staffed.

Tradition held that responsibility for ensuring each ministry operated efficiently rested with the minister. This meant that the minister was expected to personally handle all important matters. Furthermore, there was a clear division of function between the political men, such as Bathurst, and the permanent officials in the office, such as the undersecretaries. It fell to the minister to decide policy, which was modified only "in response to the criticism of colleagues in the Cabinet."³ The permanent officials then implemented the policy, but generally played no major part in its development or in orchestrating modifications once policy met the test of reality.

Lord Liverpool's cabinet was much inclined toward this traditional bureaucratic model because the prime minister was noted for "his assiduity as a man of business."⁴ Liverpool was never given to standing back and letting others manage things. Rather, he was deeply involved in all important matters of state. Viscount Castlereagh was so similarly inclined that most dispatches emanating from Foreign Affairs were not only drafted by him but a product of his own hand.

Such exercise of control came at a price: a ministry's effectiveness was limited by the ability of the minister to process its regular business while also developing sound policy in response to critically important issues or developments. The workload for ministers holding major portfolios was crushingly heavy, and this was particularly the case in 1812 for Castlereagh and Bathurst, for they were jointly responsible for the war with France and now the one with America. A workhorse, Castlereagh prided himself on mastery of every detail, so was as well suited for such great responsibility as anybody could have been. Bathurst's abilities were less clear.

His early political appointments resulted from close friendship with William Pitt "the Younger" and his family's record of government service dating back to the Restoration. His distinguished grandfather had served in the House of Lords after gaining a peerage in 1712, becoming privy councillor in 1742. His father, the 2nd Earl Bathurst, who bestowed his first given name on his eldest son at his birth on May 22, 1762, followed a legal path that resulted in his appointment as a judge of the Court of

Common Pleas in 1754. From 1771 to 1778 he was Lord Chancellor. The younger Bathurst succeeded to the earldom when his father died in 1794. He was fifty when Lord Liverpool asked him on June 10, 1812, to become secretary for war and the colonies.

Contemporaries saw Bathurst's appointment as a sign that the Liverpool administration was scraping the barrel for talent. His previous posts had been of an inconspicuous nature, requiring only pedestrian administrative skill. The ever-watchful Lady Harriet Arbuthnot thought him "a very bad minister for present times, he likes everything to go in the old way, likes a job for the sake of a job, not to get money into his own pocket for there cannot be a more disinterested man, but he hates all innovations."[5]

While Bathurst figured among the true Tories, who disdained the emerging liberal economic theories, and was a devout High Church Anglican, he was more open to innovation than Lady Arbuthnot credited. Bathurst's manner was his enemy, for he was self-effacing to a fault and too shy to be a competent public speaker. Like many shy men, Bathurst deflected attention with affable good humour, a light-hearted wit, endless anecdotes cast together in a seeming jumble, and a lack of apparent seriousness that left the impression of shallowness.

Bathurst's true nature was exposed in his writing. Quill in hand, he scratched out words quickly and without hesitation. Thoughts were put down with assurance, almost never corrected. He seldom bothered writing a first draft. As his penmanship was easily read, Bathurst saw little point in giving his correspondence to a private secretary to transcribe. Also, awkward at formulating thoughts verbally, he avoided dictation.

On June 11, the day after his appointment, Bathurst threw himself with typical vigour into running No. 14 Downing Street. But it was in how he came at the job that Bathurst demonstrated an innovative trait. Quickly accepting that the vast responsibilities of the ministry were beyond the ability of any single person to competently master, Bathurst carefully delegated duties and responsibility to his staff—particularly the two undersecretaries.

In 1810, Castlereagh, then secretary for war and the colonies, had decided that although the ministry had been combined originally because of the interrelation of military and colonial issues, there should be some measure of specialization within the staff. He therefore created a War Department and a Colonial Department, each overseen by an undersecretary with his own staff. Bathurst refined matters, not just using the undersecretaries to implement his instructions but entrusting these men with responsibility in developing policy and determining the best response to immediate problems.

The War Department undersecretary was Maj. Gen. Sir Henry Bunbury, who had been undersecretary for the entire office from the time of his appointment in 1809 until Castlereagh's reorganization. At that time Castlereagh brought in young Robert Peel to become Colonial Department undersecretary. Although this was Peel's first political office, his needing only to focus on colonial matters rather than also juggling the prosecution of the war with France led to his performance being noted. When Liverpool formed his government, he appointed Peel chief secretary for Ireland, creating an opening in the Colonial Department.

His replacement, Henry Goulburn, reported for duty on August 4. In two years time this young man, who was expected to be more intimately involved in details of the war's prosecution than any other person in the British government, would be in Ghent treating with the Americans. Goulburn was tall and slim, with a mop of dark hair beginning to recede from the forehead, and his slender face was often set in a serious expression. As an infant, Goulburn had been the victim of a bizarre accident when his nurse sat on his head, leaving a permanent indentation in his skull and equally lasting vision damage to his right eye that rendered him slightly "cock-eyed." This affliction, combined with his dour demeanour, led some to believe that he looked upon them with condescension and more than a touch of arrogance.

The young man's grimly serious manner resulted from a life where the pleasures of a normal British upper-class childhood had been lost early. Goulburn had been but nine and the eldest of three children when his father, Munbee, died at age thirty-five. Born in Jamaica, Munbee Goulburn had been the only child of a sugar-plantation owner who had died six months after the boy's birth. Sent to Eton for his education, Munbee had remained in England after graduation and married

Susannah Chetwynd. Although Susannah's family was of noble lineage, its link to landed property had been lost two generations earlier and her prospects for marriage were such that a young man boasting unencumbered title to an estate in Jamaica yielding an annual income of never less than £5,000 made an attractive match.

Munbee soon succumbed to the common temptation of absentee colonial estate holders by living far beyond his means. To cover the growing debts, he mortgaged the estate several times over. Young Henry was oblivious to the brewing calamity of this financial recklessness, revelling in the idyllic environment of Prinknash Park, a Cotswold country manor four miles from Gloucester that Munbee rented. Here he frolicked through a small beech forest, doing his best to escape attempts by Munbee and the local curate to instill the beginnings of an education—a process complicated by the fact that the Goulburns followed the fashion of the times for nobility of speaking French at home, so that the boy was more conversant in this language than in English. He was also given to tantrums, resulting in long periods of incarceration in his room that interrupted his education. When Henry turned seven he was packed off to Dr. Moore's School in Sunbury and surprisingly discovered that his English and Latin equalled that of the other students. But his "passionate" temper remained, marked by impetuosity and rebelliousness that got him into constant trouble.

Then his father died, and Susannah's comfortable life collapsed as Munbee's many debts were called in and she was forced to sell his personal property and cast the family's affairs to the Court of Chancery for disposition. At the same time her health, always frail, began to decline. While waiting for the grindingly slow court determination on what, if any, of the estate in Jamaica would remain hers, Susannah was by stages forced to find more modest residences. Years dragged by and circumstances only worsened, while the court was closed more often than engaged in deliberations over the many such cases lying before it. Eventually, through the intervention of family friend Matthew Montagu, Spencer Perceval—then a prominent lawyer—helped negotiate their case through the court. Seeing much potential in the young lad, Montagu also took an interest in Henry's future.

At sixteen, Henry began studying for the entrance exams to Trinity College, Cambridge. Upon his father's death, he had undergone a distinct character change. As his mother's health worsened, the bouts of sickness becoming more extended, Henry had quietly assumed the role of head of the household, to the point of even supervising the business management of the Jamaican estate. In Matthew Montagu the teenager found a father figure, the man showing uncommon integrity that Goulburn sought to emulate.

By the end of 1801, Goulburn matriculated and was admitted to Trinity. He studied hard, but was handicapped by having had no consistent tutoring or schooling during his childhood. There was also the problem of poverty relative to his peers. While there was sufficient money to cover tuition, Goulburn carefully concealed the fact that there was no butler to clean his clothes or servant to prepare the family breakfast. Not long before graduating with an MA in 1808, Henry had to sell his mother's dinnerware to raise sufficient money to provide her with an allowance capable of covering the cost of a small house in Phillimore Place, Kensington, where she could live out the last of her life in relative comfort.

Goulburn left Cambridge with an unremarkable academic record, a belief in evangelical Anglicanism that suited his deeply conservative world outlook, and vital links with men holding positions of power in the government that Montagu knew would serve the young man well in the future. Disinclined to enter into commerce or to return to Jamaica to directly oversee the plantation that now yielded an annual return after expenses of £2,000, Goulburn was drawn to public service. He naturally inclined this way, his religion and tutelage by Montagu having instilled in him the belief that this was a higher calling for a man of good character.

In 1807, he gained election to the House of Commons. "Opportunities for usefulness which were open to a politician seemed unlimited," he wrote.[6] Perceval was chancellor of the exchequer in Lord Palmerston's government and held all the conservative values that Goulburn admired. Despite the erratic behaviour and moral dissolution of King George III, Goulburn believed in an unfaltering loyalty to the Crown and that the constitution was inviolable. The concessions to Roman Catholics, that benchmark of Castlereagh's Irish policy, were anathema to the young man, nothing more than an invitation to growing radicalism that might plunge the country into the chaos of revolution that had befallen France in 1789. Goulburn's evangelical Anglicanism was anti-libertarian. He believed that the individual cast adrift from the need to be obedient to traditional authority ultimately became distanced from God. Social order, after all, was God's work. In entering politics, Goulburn sought "to maintain the established institutions of the Country, to advance the cause of Religion and Learning, and to uphold, as essential to both, the interests of the University and of the Established Church."[7]

Goulburn's initial performance in the House of Commons little marked him for advancement into offices of government service. It was two years before he gathered the nerve to speak, and his declamation failed to impress. But in 1809 he travelled to Spain and Portugal to witness first-hand the difficulties facing the campaign there. He returned with a distinct appreciation for the army's difficulties and a disdain for the Spanish and Portuguese that served to confirm in his mind the superiority of the British over all others. Shortly after his return that winter, Goulburn was offered a position as Home Office undersecretary, which he accepted enthusiastically. While serving with distinction in this post, the young bachelor briefly lost his head over Lady Selina Stewart. Having never learned the suave ways of his university fellows, he tried clumsily to court her, without success. "I am always afraid of marriages that arise out of excited feeling or sudden impulse," he later stated and made no further mistake in that regard. Instead, considering his debt to the Montagus beyond repayment, he sought the hand of their third daughter, eighteen-year-old Jane, hailed by friends as such "a captivating little soul" that she resembled a "wren." It was widely predicted that the marriage would prove a grand success, with each bringing out the best in the other. Goulburn commented that it was her "strength of intellect, her warmth of affection, her strong religious feeling" that attracted him. They were married on December 20, 1811, and Spencer Perceval turned over his house to them for a brief Christmas honeymoon.[8]

Perceval's assassination five months later stunned the young couple, who heard the news while on a late-afternoon carriage drive in St. James's Park. They hurried home, and once Goulburn was sure that his wife had recovered from her initial attack of near-debilitating grief, he rushed to his office, only to find the home secretary personally interrogating the crazed murderer. Goulburn noted Bellingham's "haggard countenance, his glaring eye, quivering lip and considered how short a time was to elapse before he would be called upon to answer before God for the crime which he had committed." Later, Goulburn considered the fact that Bellingham was "taken, committed, tried, condemned, executed, dissected, all within one week from the time that he fired the shot" an overly hasty application of the King's justice.[9]

With Perceval's death, Goulburn's future became uncertain. The Home Office received a new minister, Lord Sidmouth, who rewarded a member of his family with the undersecretary position. Goulburn was rescued from having to leave public service by Liverpool, who personally appointed him to replace Peel as the Colonial Department undersecretary. It was an attractive position that paid a handsome annual salary of £2,000, assuring financial security for as long as he held the post.[10] Goulburn was immediately impressed by Bathurst. As had been his inclination with Montagu, with the outgoing home secretary Richard Ryder, and with Perceval, Goulburn found in Bathurst a new father figure. That both men were staunch conservatives, who believed there was little chance for the improvement of the human race and that only institutions of social order suppressed its baser instincts, helped strengthen this almost immediate bond. Bathurst took a kindly interest in Goulburn and the younger man responded with intense loyalty.

Goulburn and Peel worked briefly together to ensure a smooth transition within the department, and Peel was greatly impressed. "He approaches the nearest to perfection," Peel later observed.[11]

The distinct division of authority Castlereagh had instituted and which Bathurst reinforced was such that Goulburn soon "knew no more of what was going on in the War branch than any stranger unless during the absence of my Colleague [Henry Bunbury]."[12] This was often enough the case as Bunbury's health was poor, requiring frequent convalescing. Also, as Bathurst sat in the House of Lords it fell to Goulburn to be the spokesman for the ministry in the House of Commons, so he had to keep abreast of its entire operation. Consequently Goulburn became rather an odd man out in the operational structure of the ministry, for he somewhat unwittingly was more fully informed and involved in its running than his superior likely intended.

Bathurst's preoccupation was the war with France, so he expected Goulburn to oversee most colonial affairs while he exercised only "the most general form of supervision."[13] As such the twenty-eight-year-old was de facto head of the empire. And the most pressing colonial matter was the war with America.

Goulburn gave scant credence to American justifications for the war. After examining President Madison's war message and the causes cited in it, Goulburn dismissed them as mere camouflage. He believed Madison conspired with Napoleon Bonaparte—the two men, or at least their governments, having a secret understanding where each would work assiduously to bring about Britain's defeat. The seizure of parts of Spanish West Florida and the massing of troops on the Canadian border preparatory to an invasion there confirmed that the true American intent was conquest and expansion of territory at the cost of Britain and her Spanish ally. Like many Britons, Goulburn considered the American declaration of war a "stab in the back" at a time when Britain was locked in a life-and-death struggle to prevent world domination by Napoleonic France. Taking advantage of Britain's desperate straits, America sought to conquer all British North America. That was "the real object of the war on the part of the United States."[14]

Initially the situation in Canada looked grim. Sir George Prevost complained in one report after another about the general air of defeatism pervading Upper Canada and the low militia turnouts. He also fretted about the French Canadians in Lower Canada and how they might turn against the British at any moment. Goulburn read all these reports closely. As was his custom with most of the vast volume of documents arriving from all points of the empire, his replies were concisely written on a turned-up corner. Occasionally he jotted "Put-by" in the corner and set it aside so he could take time to reflect upon its contents. Rarely did he pass reports up to Bathurst for input, fulfilling to the letter his minister's expectation that he should on his own initiative handle matters responsibly and efficiently. Like

Bathurst, he seldom used departmental clerks to write responses, preferring instead to draft all dispatches in his own careful hand.

Prevost's pessimism grated on Goulburn and he worried about the man's competency while doing what he could to bolster the ability of the army in Canada to defend itself. In August he managed to gather up clothing and equipment to send to Canada sufficient to meet the needs of 800 men and diverted one of two heavily laden supply ships bound for Iberia instead to North America. He also authorized Prevost to offer 100 acres of land to each colonist who enlisted in the army. At the same time he fretted that the obvious need to use Indian warriors to meet the American threat would lead to wanton and unnecessary bloodshed that might hamper attempts to negotiate a peace settlement. The solution, Goulburn thought, was "to prevent the commission of those excesses which are so much to be apprehended from their Employment" by having the warriors serve only under the immediate direction of experienced Indian Department officers.[15]

That the help he could send to Prevost was terribly scant was not lost on the young bureaucrat and, given that British forces in Canada were badly outnumbered by the Americans, Goulburn was not optimistic they could hold out. Then, on October 7, a special messenger banged on the door of his residence in the middle of the night. An anxious Goulburn clambered out of bed and hastily read the report so urgently delivered. With relief the undersecretary saw that rather than news of disaster the note announced the surrender of the U.S. western army and Detroit to Brock. His spirits were momentarily buoyed but almost as quickly deflated by the grim news that the Americans had handed the Royal Navy a string of stinging defeats. On the streets the news of Brock's victory was received with joy, but Goulburn noted that the "feeling in the British public in favour of the Navy rendered in their eyes the military triumph no compensation for the naval disaster."[16]

A maritime nation possessed of the largest navy in European history, Britain took great pride in her naval prowess, accepting as cant that she could never be bested on the seas. Throughout October and November of 1812, however, the Admiralty received one report of defeat or failure after another that threatened to shatter this myth of invincibility.

The first calamity had befallen the frigate HMS *Guerrière* on August 19 about 400 miles south of Newfoundland, when she was intercepted by the 55-gun *Constitution*, crewed by 460 sailors commanded by Capt. Isaac Hull, whose uncle was in the process of surrendering Detroit. Aboard *Guerrière*, Capt. James R. Dacres considered the two ships evenly matched despite his being undermanned with a crew of only about 280 men and mounting just forty-nine cannon. For an hour the two ships jockeyed for advantage, with *Guerrière* firing two ineffective broadsides while Hull concentrated on closing the range so he could fire with effect. When *Constitution* was 50 to 60 yards from the British ship, Hull, who had drilled his gunners to an unusually high state of competency, opened with a broadside that flung more than 700 pounds of iron out of the guns per volley. The British return fire hurled back 550 pounds but was far less accurate. Few hits were scored, while the American broadsides hammered home.

A punishing duel ensued that left *Guerrière*'s hull holed in many places and her sails and rigging badly ripped. Fifteen minutes into the cannon exchange, the British mizzenmast suddenly collapsed, falling off the starboard quarter to hang into the sea. Hull immediately took advantage of Dacres's inability to manoeuvre by swinging *Constitution* broadside to the British bow, from which only a few guns could be fired at the American ship, and raked *Guerrière* with heavy shot. Soon the fore and mainmasts crashed over the side and the ship rolled in the troughs so badly that seawater mixed together with the blood of the dead and wounded washed about on the main deck. With 15 crewmen dead and another 63 wounded, Dacres realized further resistance was suicidal and ordered the colours struck. The action had lasted two hours. *Constitution* lost only 7 sailors killed and 7 injured. *Guerrière*, however, would be no prize for Hull to parade into an American port. Her damage was so severe he had to take the surviving British sailors aboard and then burn the hulk.

News of this defeat reached London on the same day as word of the surrender of Detroit, but *The Times* gave prominence to the naval story. The "loss of the *Guerrière* spread a degree of gloom through the town, which it was painful to observe," declared an editorial. *The Times* returned repeatedly to the defeat and with each setback on the seas asserted that Royal Navy captains who surrendered their ships were a disgrace to their service and that in the past they would have gone down with colours flying rather than strike. Although the paper continued to maintain that British sailors were the best in the world, it allowed that those from America were obviously next in superiority and worried that United States frigates were, in comparison to their British counterparts, "larger, finer, [and] better built."[17]

Soon thereafter, Commodore John Rodgers returned to America with the fleet he had taken to sea without authorization on the day of the declaration of war. Although his seventy-day voyage had taken him within a day's sail of the coast of England, Rodgers had failed to sight a single British warship except for early in the venture when he unsuccessfully attempted to capture the frigate *Belvidera*. He had, however, seized seven British merchant ships as prizes.

More bad news followed as the result of a contest between the British brig *Frolic* and the American sloop *Wasp* near the West Indies reached London. Although the two ships were evenly matched with thirty guns each and a difference in crew size of 130 Americans to 120 British, *Frolic* was punished into surrendering after an action of only fifty minutes. British losses were 17 killed and 23 wounded while the American dead numbered 5 with another 5 wounded. That *Wasp* was captured in turn later that day and *Frolic* recovered by the British ship of the line *Poictiers* provided scant comfort to either the Admiralty or the public. The realization that the nation's merchantmen were vulnerable to capture and her naval ships not invincible depressed British morale.[18]

In America the small victories at sea seemed weak tonic, deemed too little and too late in coming to enable President Madison to easily win re-election. After a mere four months of war fought with little enthusiasm, the nation was weary of the conflict. The growing anti-war movement blamed the entire affair on Madison and his administration, conveniently forgetting Congress's role in forcing its declaration. Even those who believed the war just and necessary tended to lay responsibility for its poor prosecution on the steps of the White House.

TWELVE

Failures of Command

*I*n the fall of 1812 President James Madison faced the curious situation of having a fellow Republican running against him for presidential office. DeWitt Clinton, the forty-three-year-old mayor of New York City, had ardently opposed President Thomas Jefferson's policies and considered Madison a Jeffersonian pawn put into office merely to continue the "Virginian dynasty." Once considered by many party insiders a strong presidential contender, Clinton's vitriolic criticism of two successive Republican presidents had by 1812 reduced him to an outcast. He advanced himself for the party's presidential nomination anyway, and the 1812 Republican caucus rejected him in an 82–0 vote that endorsed Madison for a second term. Undeterred, Clinton used his influence in New York to persuade Republicans in that state's legislature to endorse his presidential candidacy in May with equal unanimity.

Clinton knew he could win only by crafting an alliance between antiwar Republicans and Federalists. Consequently, the election devolved into a contest between northern and southern states, with Clinton's support concentrated in New England. It was soon evident that his anti-administration campaign was causing the most hotly contested presidential election in the nation's short history. While Clinton spent the autumn stumping with frenzied haste throughout the northern states to drum up support from Federalists, disgruntled Republicans, and merchants suffering reduced trade because of the war, Madison adhered to the custom of the time by pretending that playing politics was beneath the dignity of his office. He made no speeches, released no campaign pamphlets, and was noticeably absent from public events where he could have shaken hands and solicited votes.[1]

Not that Madison was sanguine about being re-elected. By November, gatherings in the White House drawing room were notably "dismal and dark" and the ranks of supporters attending were "thin and solemn," as many a Republican congressman and senator kept his distance for fear of the taint that might touch him from too close an association with a man soon to be voted from office. One observer noted that the month was punctuated by negative news of military and electoral setbacks "day after day, like the tidings of Job's disasters."[2]

Efforts to renew offensives against Canada in November had proved farcical. Finally rousing himself on November 28, Gen. Alexander Smyth crossed the Niagara River above the falls under cover of darkness and established two small bridgeheads on the Canadian shore near Fort Erie. But when he failed to reinforce the advance troops quickly enough they were thrown back. With 1,200 men in boats waiting to renew the attack, Smyth convened his senior officers for a council of war. Such councils generally resulted in cautious decisions. Predictably, Smyth was advised that this first wave of embarked troops was too small to carry Fort Erie by assault, so he cancelled the attack.

Two days later he loaded 1,500 men in boats and then convened another council of war, which drew the same conclusion as previously. Smyth defended these decisions, claiming that many of the regular troops embarked were so ill they could hardly have stood a day's march and the militiamen could not be trusted to perform their duty. The militia, he wrote, tended to "look on a battle as on a theatrical exhibition; who if they are disappointed of the sights, break their muskets; or if they are without rations for a day desert." After this debacle, Smyth applied to Maj. Gen. Henry Dearborn for leave to visit his family. The old general cheerfully agreed. Smyth went off, keeping quiet the fact that he had no intention of returning to duty.[3]

For his part, although plagued by frequent, almost debilitating bouts of rheumatism, Dearborn had by mid-November assembled 3,000 regulars and an equal number of militia at Plattsburgh on Lake Champlain, from where he marched on Montreal. The American force was quickly detected, and Maj. Charles-Michel d'Irumberry de Salaberry of the mostly French-Canadian Provincial Corps of Light Infantry moved to meet it with a mere two companies of Voltigeurs and 300 Indian warriors. Marching through swamps, the Canadians established a blocking position at Burtonville. On November 19, Dearborn's army occupied Champlain on the western bank of the Richelieu River only to discover the Canadians on the opposite shore. Shortly before dawn, the Americans forced a crossing against scattered resistance from a thin screen of Voltigeurs and Indians. In the confused first minutes of this engagement a number of American troops fired upon each other. Several men were killed and a number of others wounded, prompting the rest of the invaders to retreat back across the river.

That was enough for Dearborn. He immediately led his troops back to Plattsburgh and wrote to Secretary of War William Eustis, "I had anticipated disappointment and misfortune in the commencement of the war, but I did by no means apprehend such a deficiency of regular troops and such a series of disasters as we have witnessed." Dearborn asked Madison to allow him "to retire to the shades of private life, and remain a mere interested spectator of passing events."[4]

The only good news from the Canadian front stemmed not from land-based operations but rather from the efforts of America's small navy. Madison had always appreciated that whoever controlled the Great Lakes was free to move men and supplies with virtual impunity. American control of any of the lakes would jeopardize British ability to defend their communities and forts standing on the shoreline. Lying as it did at the nexus of Lower and Upper Canada, with York and Kingston on its shores, Lake Ontario was the most strategically important lake. Madison had ordered the navy to gain control of it, a duty that had fallen on September 3, 1812, to Commodore Isaac Chauncey. Establishing his headquarters at Sackets Harbor on the southeastern shore, Chauncey discovered his only war vessel was the brig *Oneida*. But several lake schooners had been commandeered and were being converted into fighting ships.

On November 10, Chauncey sallied forth with *Oneida* and six armed schooners. Overtaking the corvette *Royal George*, Chauncey chased it into

Kingston harbour. Unable to press his advantage because of cannon fire coming from the town's forts, the American commodore retired after exchanging cannonades with the British for two hours. Only one man on either side was killed and none of the ships suffered notable damage. But Chauncey could correctly assert that he now controlled Lake Ontario, for the British naval officers on the lake proved unwilling to venture out from Kingston harbour for fear of being intercepted. Their timidity was such that even Sir George Prevost reported that the "officers of the Marine appear to be destitute of all energy and spirit," though he conceded this resulted partly from a lack of sailors. *Royal George*, for example, had just seventeen men fit for duty and *Earl of Moira* ten.[5]

The fact remained, however, that after Brock's death, Prevost had assumed a purely defensive strategy. Clinging to the notion that the United States would agree to an armistice, the Canadian governor steadfastly refused to sanction any violation of American territory. While along the Upper and Lower Canadian fronts his forces were too weak to conduct major operations across the border, the potential existed on the western frontier for British troops to advance from Detroit in support of Tecumseh's confederacy, which in September had launched a major offensive aimed at driving the Americans out of the territory north of the Ohio River.

On August 29, Brock had briefly outlined Tecumseh's forthcoming strategy in a letter to Lord Liverpool. Explaining that Tecumseh "for the last two years has carried on, contrary to our remonstrances, an active warfare against the United States," Brock wrote that the Shawnee chief now appeared "determined to continue the contest until they obtain the Ohio for a boundary. The United States government is accused, and I believe justly, of having corrupted a few dissolute characters whom they pretended to consider as chiefs, and with whom they contracted agreements and concluded treaties, which they have attempted to impose on the whole Indian race."[6] He also made the case, subsequently endorsed by Prevost, that any peace treaty with the Americans must include provisions for the Indians, particularly the return of "an extensive tract of country, fraudulently usurped from them."[7] In effect, the intent was to undo all the treaties negotiated by then Indiana governor William Henry Harrison. While the British hoped to achieve this through negotiation, Tecumseh determined to win the land back through military action.

Brock's success at Detroit had emboldened many of the tribes that had earlier bowed to Harrison's threats and entered into treaties. Shortly after Hull's surrender the Potawatomi at Tippecanoe and Fort St. Joseph rebelled, laid siege to Fort Wayne, and sent an urgent message to Amherstburg for help from the warriors and British there. Tecumseh was soon on the march, while Lt. Col. Henry Procter, commanding the British forces after Brock hurried off to the Niagara front, first dithered, then reluctantly sent about 500 troops and a matching number of Indians under command of Maj. Adam Muir to establish a firm position on the Maumee River southwest of the dilapidated ruin of Fort Defiance in order to cut the easiest route by which Fort Wayne could be reinforced. Reliant on boats to carry supplies and several small artillery pieces, Muir's force crawled slowly forward, hampered by typically low late-summer river levels. The boats were dragged more often than floated.[8] It was soon evident that the Indian confederacy's campaign would be over before the British were in position.

While Tecumseh's forces were formidable, they were also widely scattered and too short of gunpowder and shot for sustained operations. Tecumseh's intelligence network also failed, for even as he led the tribes in an all-or-nothing uprising his old nemesis Harrison entered the Ohio Valley at the head of a vastly superior army of Kentucky militia and regular troops. Harrison, who had resigned the Indiana governorship to return to Kentucky and raise a militia army, had his sights set on command of a reconstituted Army of the West. Congressional Speaker and fellow Kentuckian Henry Clay supported this ambition, making it plain to the White House that Harrison should get the command.

Patriotic war fever burned more fiercely in Kentucky than elsewhere in the Union. While few other states were able to fill militia quotas, recruiting officers in Kentucky were overwhelmed with volunteers. When 2,000 men had mustered on a parade ground at Georgetown in August, Clay had been there to address them. "Kentucky was famed for her bravery" and so "they had the double character of Americans and Kentuckians to support," he declared.[9] The Kentucky militia had then expected to march north to reinforce Hull and join in the conquest of Canada. And it was widely believed that their leader would be the hero of Tippecanoe, William Henry Harrison. "If you will carry your recollection back to the age of the Crusades," Clay wrote James Monroe, "and of some of the most distinguished leaders of those expeditions, you will have a picture of the enthusiasm existing in this country for the expedition to Canada, and for Harrison as the commander."[10]

But Eustis had already given command of the Army of the West to Brig. Gen. James Winchester, another tired veteran of the Revolution and a former North Carolinian Indian fighter turned plantation owner in Tennessee. In late August, Winchester had camped at Cincinnati and was still preparing to march to the aid of Fort Wayne when Harrison rode in and announced that he was taking command of the Kentucky militiamen there while Winchester could lead the regular troops. He also insisted that overall command was his. Through an exchange of tightly worded notes the two men bickered until at last Winchester acquiesced.

Content for the moment, Harrison ordered Winchester to take 2,500 men and establish a position at the rapids of the Maumee River that could serve as the army's forward base for the winter. Harrison, meanwhile, would move across country with 2,000 men to relieve Fort Wayne. Consequently Winchester was groping his way through the forests toward the Maumee at the same time as Muir approached it from the north. On September 25 some Indian scouts captured several Americans, interrogated them, and then killed the men before carrying back the news that a far superior force approached. Muir sought to ambush the Americans but was foiled when the bodies were discovered and Winchester ordered his men to cease the advance, throw up a stout wooden breastwork, and await an attack. Realizing he could never carry the field against a prepared enemy, Muir withdrew. As the Americans were now between him and Fort Wayne, the entire object of his mission was frustrated, so Muir and his men manhandled their boats back to Amherstburg.[11]

Although Harrison broke the siege of Fort Wayne, the western frontier ignited in the kind of vicious war that American settlers and Indians had fought so often before. Tecumseh's warriors enjoyed limited success in attacks on various forts and settlements, especially against Fort Harrison, where they succeeded in burning most of the supplies stored there—including barrels containing 25,316 rations of whisky. Able bush-fighters, the warriors were tactically baffled as to how to breach the stout fortress walls behind which the Americans took shelter. Each attack was ultimately repulsed or brought to an end when reinforcements arrived to break the siege. Yet rather than drawing upon their fighting strengths by merely harassing the forts and blockhouses in which the Americans had taken shelter to keep them pinned uselessly inside and deploying their main strength to ambush Harrison's badly extended supply lines, the warriors continued futilely trying to overrun these strongpoints. Tecumseh was too astute a tactician to not recognize where Harrison was most vulnerable, but just as his campaign was set into motion the warrior chief's iron constitution failed him. Incapacitated by illness, he lay stranded in a small camp on the Wabash River unable to direct operations. So there was little cohesion in the offensive and almost no coordination of effort. By November, it was clear that Tecumseh's all-or-nothing campaign had failed.

The vulnerability of his supply lines had haunted Harrison, for there was little he could do to protect the creaking, overloaded wagons, the strings of weary packhorses, defenceless flatboats, and large herds of cattle and hogs required to provision his army.[12] When the Indians failed to strike these columns, Harrison thanked his good fortune and retaliated with a search-and-destroy mission. Regular cavalry and the ruthless mounted Kentucky volunteers rode hard through the forests, burning villages, destroying crops, slaughtering any Indian who crossed their path. No distinction was made between friend and foe. The Potawatomi and Miami—many of the latter having remained loyal to the United States—fled to Brownstown and Amherstburg and claimed British protection. Dependent on the British for food, these and other tribes switched their allegiances accordingly.

Raids and ambushes carried out by both sides raged on as the snows fell and the rivers and lakes froze hard, but it was clear that the winter would pass in a bloody contest where neither side could prevail.

In Washington, a gloomy pall pervaded. Madison, Monroe, Secretary of the Treasury Albert Gallatin, and War Secretary William Eustis faced constant criticism for a mismanaged war. Even some War Hawks had turned against them, most noticeably Congressional Speaker Henry Clay. Eustis was under siege, constantly assailed by congressmen and senators demanding his resignation. Madison, ever faithful to those who served him, refused, even though such loyalty must surely cost him votes.

Hoping to bolster support for the war, as part of his annual address to the opening of Congress on November 4, Madison released the diplomatic documents exchanged between Britain and the United States during the summer. Here, he said, was proof that America had sought an honourable peace only to be spurned. He implored Congress to enact laws to increase the army, revise laws governing the state militias so they would be obliged to serve wherever they were sent, enlarge the navy and provide for strong squadrons on the Great Lakes, and prohibit American businessmen from continuing to trade with the British. By carefully avoiding any blockades of New England ports or seizure of ships from the northern states, Britain had been able to supply its armies in Canada and Iberia and its colonies in the West Indies with American agricultural products—a fact that infuriated Madison. In his mind, New England's continuing trade with Britain was nothing less than treason. He sought reinstatement of an embargo to deprive the British of the goods they desperately needed.

Congress responded to the last request with customary horror and overwhelmingly voted against any form of embargo, rightly realizing that their constituents would not respond kindly to losing any source of income from the sales of agricultural products. The Senate also refused any attempt to confine trade so that the war against Britain could be waged on an economic front. That left Madison and his administration no alternative path to forcing Britain to seek terms with the United States but to conquer Canada.

Not that Congress had any intention of enabling the president to raise an army that would meet Dearborn's estimates of what was required for this purpose. Thirty thousand men, Dearborn said, but as the end of the year drew close the entire army numbered barely 19,000. The committee studying the recommendations for reforming the army made repeated demands for ever more information and continued to express its lack of confidence in the war secretary.[13]

While Congress dithered the nation voted, and on December 3 the Electoral College revealed returns that gave Madison a sweeping victory, with 128 presidential electors to Clinton's 89. The results, however, revealed a deep national rift that directly resulted from the war. Clinton had won every seaboard state from New Hampshire through to Delaware and a goodly chunk of Maryland. Madison swept the rest of the country.[14]

But the president's re-election failed to quell the criticism being heaped on his administration by the House and the Senate. No sooner were the election results in than a strong lobby of Republican congressmen demanded Eustis's removal. Before Madison could decide what to do, Eustis resigned. He left Washington in disgust and retired to Boston. Madison offered the position to Monroe, who agreed to assume it only temporarily, until a permanent replacement could be found. Consequently, for a little more than a month Monroe was both secretary of state and secretary of war, but his attention focused on attempting to manoeuvre a series of bills through the House and the Senate that would prepare the army and navy for operations in 1813.[15]

Two days before the end of the year, in a letter to a friend in Delaware, Henry Clay enumerated the errors of the campaigns of 1812. "Mr. Madison is wholly unfit for the storms of War. Nature has cast him in too benevolent a mould. Admirably adapted to the tranquil scenes of peace—blending all the mild & amiable virtues, he is not fit for the rough and rude blasts which the conflicts of Nations generate. Our hope then for the future conduct of the War must be placed upon the vigor which he may bring into the administration by the organization of his new Cabinet. And here again he is so hesitating, so tardy, so far behind the National sentiment."

If Madison was unfit, Clay advised his friend, the same could not be said of Congress. Never "was there a body assembled more disposed to adopt any and every measure calculated to give effect and vigor to the operations of the War than are the members of the 12th Congress."

The nation, too, was strong and determined. Clay dismissed Clinton's sweep of New England as resulting from the incompetence with which the war had been prosecuted in 1812. Given some successes, the north would rally to the war that the south and west unshakeably supported. "The justness of our cause . . . the spirit & patriotism of the Country . . . will at last I think bring us honourably out."[16]

The House and the Senate were hardly as keen to support the war as Clay made out, a fact quickly made evident when Monroe and Secretary of the Treasury Albert Gallatin tabled a series of urgent proposals. Gallatin's dilemma was how to finance a war from a nearly empty treasury chest. Expenses in 1813 would total $32 million, of which $17 million would go to the army and $5 million to the navy. Yet he forecast only $12 million in revenues, meaning a shortfall of $20 million. Where was the money to come from? The nation's banks had already loaned as much as could be expected, and an 1812 float of various war bonds had netted only $3.2 million from individual investors. Scouring the federal troves, Gallatin found what he thought was a perfect source of the needed funding. During the confusion that followed British cancellation of the orders-in-council, and as New England traders flagrantly carried on trade with the enemy, the government had collected about $23 million in bonds and duties levied on goods imported from Britain. Normally most of this money would be returned to the importers, but Gallatin proposed a bill allowing the government to retain half of it on the basis that the importers had realized huge profits from this questionable trade.

Ways and Means Committee Chairman Langdon Cheves led the moral outcry against the proposal. "I would rather see the objects of the war fail," declared this stalwart War Hawk. "I would rather see the seamen of the country impressed on the ocean and our commerce swept away from its bosom, than see the long arm of the Treasury indirectly thrust into the pocket of the citizen through the medium of a penal law." Henry Clay stepped away from the Speaker's chair to shout, "Let us not pollute our hands with this weltgild!"[17] The motion was roundly defeated.

At the same time, Clay would brook no criticism of Madison and his administration that opposed the war. Josiah Quincy, the Boston Federalist, had, along with Virginian John Randolph, been a constant thorn in the side of Madison and Jefferson for five congressional terms. Although Randolph had lost a bid for re-election, Quincy had been handily returned and came to the House determined to defend the nation from a perceived secret agenda that threatened the very roots of its freedom. The president's cabinet, he announced, was "little less than despotic, composed, to all efficient purposes of two Virginians and a foreigner." This triad of Madison, Monroe, and Gallatin—always suspect because he was foreign born—Quincy alleged was bent on subjugating Americans with "a King or an Emperor, dukedoms, and earldoms and baronies." James the First, of course, would be succeeded by James the Second, a pact already made between Madison and Monroe to bring this to effect.

When Quincy's diatribe ended, Clay responded with a two-day-long harangue. Standing in the congressional hall, which was so cold and damp that his breath clouded around him like smoke, Clay reiterated all the causes of the war, detailed Madison's peace overtures during its opening months, and scathingly pointed out the baseless nature of Quincy's allegations of presidential conspiracies to corrupt the nation's democratic foundations.

The "Speaker opened all his portholes upon poor Quincy," New Hampshire's John A. Harper commented. "He brought his artillery to play well—the fire on board *Constitution*, the *Wasp* or the *United States* could not have been better directed."[18]

Although most Federalists agreed that Quincy had stepped across the line of decorum, they also saw enough truth in his allegations to cause a serious congressional split that resulted in the majority of the northern congressmen stoutly opposing almost every bill that the administration presented. Any attempt, whether real or not, to give the White House a free hand in prosecuting the war was suspect.

In this atmosphere Gallatin's proposals for financing the war stood no chance of endorsement. Instead he was given authority only to issue more treasury notes and to borrow another $16 million on whatever terms could be negotiated so long as repayment was guaranteed to take place within twelve years. That the $11 million loan authorized by Congress the previous year was still unfulfilled because Gallatin had been unable to find a lender for $5 million of it made no impression on the legislators. There was also the fact that a stack of treasury notes remained from the 1812 issue, so a new issue was unlikely to succeed.

Yet it was clear that if the United States was to make a better showing on the field of battle than it had in 1812, the army must be greatly enlarged and a navy built that could master the Great Lakes. It was equally clear that the British were unlikely to retain the passive, defensive stance of the previous year in light of the failure to negotiate a lasting armistice. The most obvious threat was that the Royal Navy would blockade American ports and raid its coastal cities. They might also land an army in Florida to threaten the United States from the south and force a war on two fronts.

To meet the coastal threat Gallatin suggested that Monroe divide the country into military districts defended by a contingent of regular troops under command of a permanent commander who could also draw upon local state militias in the event of an attack. Ten thousand men would be required for this duty from a total authorization of 35,000. The immediacy of the threat to America's coast was made apparent in January, when two Royal Navy ships of the line and several frigates out of Halifax sailed into Chesapeake Bay and established a blockade that the American navy dared not contest.[19]

Monroe fretted that the remaining 25,000 men available for offensive operations would be insufficient. He really wanted 35,000 men to carry out an ambitious campaign that included invading all of British North America before the end of the year and the seizure of East Florida, and another 10,000 in reserves—a total army of 55,000. Debates raged on the House and Senate floors, and when the voices stilled, authorization was granted to raise only 20,000 more men to bring the army up to 35,000. The term of service, however, was reduced from a mandatory five years to just twelve months.[20] It was a desperate scheme, designed to achieve nothing more than to enable the army to take the field in the spring. If the war was not won by the end of the year, the government would have to cobble together sufficient forces to carry on the fight by returning to the next congressional sitting with cap in hand.

As for seizing East Florida, Monroe argued that when the war on the Iberian Peninsula was settled Spain would be an appendage either of Great Britain or of France. In either case the United States would be threatened from the south if the territory was not annexed. The majority of its population were Americans anyway, he maintained, and would welcome annexation. A bill to enable the president to order occupation of both Floridas and to govern until the seizure of the country east of the Perdido River might be legitimized by "future negotiation" with Spain was presented to the Senate.

The division in the Senate between north and south was immediately made plain when Maryland senator Samuel Smith moved an amendment that effectively gutted the bill's intent by having the second part—that which authorized the occupation of Florida east of the Perdido—struck. On February 2, the Senate voted on the amendment. Only two southern senators voted for the amendment while all northerners but four diehard Republicans supported it. The amendment carried nineteen to sixteen.[21]

While the Senate might have scuttled Monroe's ambitions to annex East Florida, the president did not wholly abandon the project. Rather, he and Monroe decided that the transfer of this Spanish colony to the United States might well be made a condition of peace negotiations to end the war—assuming that Spain would soon be nothing more than a British puppet. In the meantime, they decided that the heavily fortified town of Mobile, the only Spanish presence remaining west of the Perdido, would be taken by force before the spring was out.[22]

Gallatin never shared his colleagues' enthusiasm for the Florida adventure, believing that it satisfied little but a southern ambition to open new territory for settlement and risked a war with Spain that could turn the European powers against America. He also believed that securing East Florida would necessitate commitment of a major military force—indeed, even as the Senate amended the bill, Gen. Andrew Jackson was marching from Tennessee to New Orleans with 2,000 volunteers to carry out the expected conquest—that would bleed money from the treasury badly needed to fund the war with Britain. Raising an army in the south to march against a Spanish colony made no sense to Gallatin when the shortage of manpower in the north was such that it was improbable that the British could be expelled from North America. So Gallatin breathed a sigh of relief when orders went out for Jackson to turn about and come home.[23]

For the forthcoming operations against Canada, Gallatin believed it improbable that more than 15,000 men would be available. This meant that the most America could do was occupy that part of the Canadas between Lake Erie and Montreal. Achieving even this modest ambition, he told Madison, would depend on gaining control of the Great Lakes.[24]

In January, the president appointed John Armstrong his new secretary of war. Armstrong was not the president's first choice, but both William H. Crawford of Georgia and Henry Dearborn had refused the position. So he had turned to the fifty-four-year-old veteran of the Revolution and renowned New York political intriguer with powerful ties to the state's leading Republicans. Armstrong was a controversial choice because he was the author of a series of papers known as the Newburgh letters that had incited the U.S. Continental army to mutiny in 1784. Having as secretary of war a man who had sought to turn the army against the administration seemed risky to many senators, who approved his appointment by a vote of only eighteen to fifteen.[25]

Madison, who often seemed perplexed that anyone would engage in political manoeuvring while the nation was at war, hoped Armstrong's reputation for being the country's most noted authority on the art of war would offset his less desirable traits. In August 1812, Armstrong had published a treatise entitled *Hints to Young Generals from an Old Soldier* that cemented his status as a military expert. But the "Old Soldier" was a certain wild card. He harboured presidential ambitions, held Monroe in low esteem, and was renowned for a bad temper exacerbated by regular attacks of rheumatism and gout. There were also rumours that Armstrong was notoriously lazy.

Arriving in Washington on February 4, Armstrong dispelled this last criticism by diving into his duties with apparent energy and enthusiasm. Armstrong actually had many reservations about the job he had undertaken, not the least of them being that he was to serve in an executive dominated by Virginians. Like many New Yorkers, he believed the time had come to end the Virginian dynasty in favour of one based on their own state. Assuming his duties after Congress and the administration had largely determined how the War Department was to operate through 1813 also meant he was tied to a course not of his choosing.

Armstrong had also consulted with Dearborn in Albany, who had stated that the major thrust against Canada would be made from New York rather than New England, which would have been Armstrong's preference. To his friend and fellow New York intriguer Ambrose Spencer, Armstrong confided that he was "to execute other men's plans and fight with other men's weapons."[26] Fearing political disaster if the army should fail, the New York Republicans launched two new journals—the *National Advocate* and the *Albany Argus*—to promote the administration's war program in the state and boost recruitment. Not coincidentally, Spencer made sure that the editors of both publications routinely presented Armstrong as a military genius and offered with mock secrecy that before May 1 the "Old Soldier" would oversee a "brilliant campaign" in Canada.[27]

Madison would have settled for any semblance of military competency in the early months of 1813. February brought news of another disaster on the Detroit frontier, where Brigadier General Harrison had made assurances that despite the frigid winter conditions he could take the field to recover Detroit and capture Fort Malden. With 6,300 men, his army vastly outnumbered Lieutenant Colonel Procter's meagre force. Harrison sent Brig. Gen. James Winchester with an advance guard of about 1,000 men to clear the approaches to Detroit. Eager to prove himself superior to Harrison, whom he considered merely a political appointee, Winchester determined to take Detroit on his own.[28]

On January 18, his leading elements swept down upon the outpost of Frenchtown at the mouth of the Raisin River and easily drove off the fifty Canadians from the Essex militia and about a hundred Indians after a protracted skirmish. Detroit lay just 26 miles away, but it took two days for Winchester to bring the rest of his troops up. Believing that he owned the field, the American commander issued no orders to erect defensive positions around the small settlement and sent no patrols out to scout the area.

It was a fatal error and a demonstration of clear incompetence. Just before dawn on the morning of January 22, the Americans awoke to an attack by about 600 redcoats and militia and the same number of Indian warriors who had all crossed the ice on the lake from Fort Malden during the night. Procter bungled the attack, however, by pausing to deploy artillery carried across the ice on sleighs rather than taking advantage of the complete surprise won by charging the Americans, who were just awakening and rolling out of their bedding to take up position. A fierce firefight ensued, during which 185 of the attackers were killed, but when Prevost sent a message to Winchester that he feared being unable to constrain the Indians if the Americans were overwhelmed, the American commander ordered his entire force to surrender. By this time the Americans had suffered heavily, with almost 400 having been killed. Barely 100 Americans managed to escape, slipping off into the woods by one and twos. Among the captured was Henry Clay's brother-in-law Capt. Nathaniel Hart and, of course, Winchester.

Lacking sufficient soldiers to guard all the prisoners, Procter left about thirty of the most seriously wounded at Frenchtown under the care of an Indian guard while he withdrew his force and the other prisoners to Brownstown. Many of the Indians were drunk on captured stores of liquor, but this failed to alarm the British officer. Soon after the redcoats and Canadian militia departed, a group of drunken Indians pushed the guards aside and scalped the American prisoners.[29]

It was a clear atrocity and one that rocked Washington when word of the murders reached it. "Remember the River Raisin" became a political slogan and battle cry. But the fact remained that Harrison's winter offensive to regain Detroit had been defeated.[30]

Again it fell to the United States Navy to bolster the spirits of the American people, and a new secretary was at the helm. Paul Hamilton had shown less military acumen than had Eustis in the War Department. A drunk and spendthrift, he depended on the office for an income and clung tenaciously to the position even after repeated congressional delegations begged him to resign. The North Carolinian failed to grasp the significance of mastery of the Great Lakes and so had presented a naval bill seeking only a large increase in the ocean fleet that panicked the Republicans over its costs. The Senate slashed his designs down to an addition of only four 74-gun ships and six 44-gun ships and gave the department $2.5 million funding. That bill only barely passed Congress when a minority of Republicans voted alongside the Federalists (always keen to strengthen the navy that protected New England shipping) to carry it against the opposition of most Republicans, who thought the price tag too rich. Hamilton's performance during the bill debates, where he was often clearly inebriated, proved the final straw for Madison, who pointedly advised the man to resign. He went noisily, publicly accusing Madison of personal betrayal.

His successor was easily decided—William Jones, a Pennsylvania Republican with some familiarity, via business connections, with maritime issues. Jones reported that Hamilton had left the department in chaos that could be rectified only by radical reform. He also thought that such reform would save the government about $1 million annually in wasteful administrative costs. But he also aspired to greatly increase the number of seventy-fours to ensure the navy's ability to protect American merchant mariners, while Gallatin continued to argue that the costs of building even the ships approved by Congress would drain the treasury.[31]

Despite ineffectual leadership from the top, however, the naval officers taking ships out to sea continued to wreak havoc on the Royal Navy—much to the joy of the president and public. On February 22, a delighted Madison sent a message to Congress reporting that the 49-gun *Java* had been engaged and sunk by *Constitution* off Brazil.

But the navy could not alone bring Great Britain to its knees. America simply had too few ships to gain mastery of the seas or even to break any blockades. Madison recognized this and also realized that the conquest of Canada, which was to have provided a decisive bargaining chip to gain concessions from the British government necessary to enable the United States to negotiate its return in exchange for an honourable peace, was equally unlikely in 1813. A protracted war that the nation could ill afford loomed. So it was with great relief that Madison took hold of a possible lifeline cast his direction during a celebratory banquet hosted at the Russian minister to America's house two days after he took the oath of office for his second term as president on March 4. During what Dolley Madison described as a "brilliant & pleasant" affair, André Daschkoff handed the president a note from

Tsar Alexander I in which the Russian emperor offered to act as a peacemaker between Great Britain and the United States.

Madison quickly accepted this "humane and enlightened" offer. Russia, he said, was "the only power in Europe which can command respect from both France and England."[32] Peace, and more importantly an honourable peace by which America might achieve all its objects, seemed within grasp.

Part Three

—

THE FORTUNES OF WAR

THIRTEEN

Peace Sincerely Desired

SPRING 1813

*I*n September 1812, Tsar Alexander I had taken the fancy that he might arbitrate a peace agreement between the United States and Great Britain. While partly motivated by a wish to open both countries to Russian commerce, he also thought playing peacemaker would enhance his influence in world affairs even as his reign stood endangered. On the cold, clear Monday of September 7, more than 250,000 soldiers had met on a field of battle near the town of Borodino. When the smoke drifted away from the stark ridges and wide farm fields, 38,000 French lay dead and wounded while the Russian Army barely escaped destruction at the cost of more than 45,000 casualties. Victory at Borodino opened the road to Moscow for Napoleon, and like a rising tide the Grande Armée moved relentlessly into Russia's heartland, posing the threat that the French might soon parade through the streets of St. Petersburg.

Yet two weeks after the great slaughter, the Russian foreign minister, Count Nikolai Rumyantsev, acting on Alexander's instructions, summoned America's minister to Russia, John Quincy Adams, to an evening meeting. With rumours swirling through the emperor's court that Moscow, the heart of Russia, had fallen to Napoleon just that day, Adams could scarcely imagine the cause of the unexpected summons as he entered Rumyantsev's drawing room at seven o'clock. Tall and courtly but also virtually deaf since suffering a stroke upon hearing the news that France had invaded Russia, the count was the chancellor Adams most often had dealings with. In the three years he had been posted to Russia,

Rumyantsev had also become a valued friend. Theirs was a relationship of comfortable confidants, who valued each other's opinion and discretion. This night Rumyantsev was unusually formal, stating that he saw Adams "by the Emperor's command." The war between America and Great Britain, Rumyantsev said, adversely affected Russia's commerce with both combatants and so Alexander proposed to mediate indirect negotiations. Would the Americans agree to such a course?

Adams quickly became intrigued. He believed that President Madison had been forced into the war by Britain's insistence that America accept intrusions to its sovereignty that would require "a dishonourable abandonment of all the unquestionable rights . . . and even the essential characteristics of an independent nation. The blame of the war was therefore entirely on the English side." But at the same time he "so deeply lamented the very existence of the war, that I should welcome any facility for bringing it to a just and honourable termination." Adams believed his government would welcome any attempt to negotiate a settlement, but he reminded Rumyantsev that there was "a third party to be consulted as to the proposal—the British Government."

The count assured Adams the idea had already been presented to the new British ambassador, Lord Cathcart, who had sent it on to London for consideration. Adams agreed to advance the idea to his own government while the count would instruct André Daschkoff, his minister in Washington, to also raise the proposition with President Madison. As the meeting was ending, a messenger delivered a note from Cathcart that Rumyantsev read to Adams. Wellington, the message said, had taken Madrid. The war on the Iberian Peninsula had turned decisively in Britain's favour.[1]

Adams had yet to get the measure of the new British ambassador. On the one hand, Cathcart professed sympathy for the United States because his wife had been born there. But he had also commanded the irregular British Legion during the inconclusive 1778 Battle of Monmouth and afterward served as the quartermaster general for the British army fighting to put down the American Revolution. "The English talk much about their honor and national morality—sometimes without meaning, but generally with a mixture of hypocrisy and self-delusion in about equal portions,"

Adams wrote after meeting Cathcart.[2] He suspected the ambassador fitted the normal English mould.

When Cathcart proposed the two men meet, however, Adams agreed even though they represented nations at war. Surprised that Cathcart would make the offer, he justified accepting on the grounds that he had not yet received a copy of the declaration of war from Washington. Cathcart reiterated, as he was prone to do whenever he and Adams crossed paths, his "particular attachment to America, and to cherish a wish that the political differences between that country and England might yet be settled amicably."[3] Adams could only echo the last desire. If the British would just be reasonable, he believed peace could be easily agreed.

To John Quincy Adams reasonableness was a virtue, one of many that he aspired to while at the same time fearing the incapacity of their attainment. Eldest son of America's second president, from his birth on July 11, 1767, in Braintree, Massachusetts, Adams had been set on a course that his father believed would lead to greatness, not for personal aggrandizement, but rather to fully serve the United States and the greater good of humanity. Although he was formally educated at private schools abroad and at Harvard, his fuller education came direct from John Adams—an education relentlessly tended to whether the father was at home, on a diplomatic mission abroad (with young Johnny at his side), or sitting in the Senate and later the president's chair. Conversation more resembled that between tutor and student than father and son. Wherever young Adams went, his father's presence remained subliminally close to his shoulder, urging him to excel.

Not that John Quincy Adams became a mirror reflection of his father. Soon after his acceptance to the bar, Adams established a reputation for independence of mind. Where his father was a stout Federalist, Adams flirted with Republican views. But he remained too much of an individualist to be comfortable with warping personal beliefs to conform to any party line.

Of one thing there could be no doubt. Like his father, he was an unhesitating patriot, a loyal American to the core. In 1797, while in London en route to a posting in Berlin, Adams had married Louisa Catherine

Johnson, daughter of the United States consul to Great Britain, whom he had fallen in love with three years earlier. His devotion to Louisa was total. When apart he wrote great streams of letters, each running on for many pages—not love letters, for that would have been disgracefully self-indulgent, but rather lengthy reports full of thoughts and observations.

Writing was his true passion. Never did he take to bed of an evening without first recording the events of the day just passed and many other observations. Only his deepest emotions were absent from the pages of the massive journals amassed. He rose before six each morning, often beating the dawn, to ensure five hours of unbroken time for self-improvement. Adams devoured books and reflected deeply on all he read, commented in his journal about their worth, occasionally published pamphlets refuting an author's thesis. The classics, science, philosophy, history, the Bible, all methodically analyzed. While trying to work his way through Milton's *Paradise Lost*—a favourite of his father's and thus mandatory reading—for a second unsuccessful time, Adams had taken up smoking in hopes of focusing his concentration so as to get beyond the first half. His pipe was now always close by, the habit impossible to give up. That failing was chalked up alongside the other character lapses for which Adams privately berated himself. A man who stood in such harsh self-judgment found it difficult not to be deeply critical of others.

While in Russia, where initially there was little for an American diplomat to do in the emperor's court, he had undertaken a study of weights and measures. Adams recorded his height as "five feet seven inches," his stride covered "two feet six inches and eighty-eight one-hundredths of an inch at a rate of thirteen hundred and sixty-six paces" every eleven minutes. He reported to Louisa the precise distance that lay between St. Petersburg's various bridges.[4] It was a matter of pride that he could name and locate all the stars of the heavens. One evening he saw a constellation that seemed new, and upon carefully looking it up in Joseph-Jérôme Lalande's *Bibliographie astronomique*, which listed the positions of 47,000 stars, was mortified to discover he had observed common Orion.[5]

This obvious lapse of memory only further fuelled his pessimism about the ability of humankind to improve. With each passing year Adams became increasingly pessimistic, his outward countenance emanating a joyless, cold personality. At forty-six, Adams had become stout. His hair had receded beyond his pate and what remained hung thin and lank down the back of his neck. Arched eyebrows furthered the impression of a judgmental, unforgiving nature. Always awkward in society, Adams compensated by being domineeringly intense. He seldom participated in the witty repartee so common to the parlour-room discussion of society's upper crust and could be sharply impatient with its irrelevance. Afterward, Adams would berate himself for his lack of manners and pray to find a patience and understanding seemingly beyond his grasp.

At home Adams was another man; a sensitive and reflective husband, a caring father. One of his great pleasures during the long years in St. Petersburg was to take long walks in the parks with Louisa and their children. Occasionally on such outings they encountered a young, tall Russian. Alexander I cheerfully offered advice on the upbringing of the children.[6] These encounters helped cement a friendship uncommon in the Russian court.

While personally doubting the emperor's mediation offer would bear fruit, Adams thought if anyone could bring the British to the table it was Alexander. He longed to have the discussions begin, but until instructions arrived from Washington he could do nothing.

So Adams busied himself meeting various representatives of the Russian government and the ministers to the court from other countries, always seeking what various attitudes each held toward the United States. There was also the invasion of Russia, the "dreadful accounts of the burning of Moscow since the French entered it." Rather than being dispirited by the worsening news, Adams noticed that Alexander's "spirit stiffens with adversity."[7] When Napoleon sought an armistice, Alexander sharply declared "that he would not make peace while an armed enemy should remain on the Russian territory."[8] The emperor's resolve was soon rewarded, for on October 19 Napoleon ordered Moscow abandoned and turned his army homeward in a futile race against winter. Pursued by the Russians, ill clothed for the plunging winter temperatures, famished, running out of ammunition and powder, the Grande Armée straggled west. On December 13 the last French troops crossed the frozen Niemen River. Half a million men had followed

Napoleon into Russia; only 20,000 staggered out. The Russians counted more than 200,000 of their own soldiers dead. Yet by enduring, by refusing to negotiate or bend to Napoleon's will, by conducting a scorched-earth policy that denied the conqueror any resort to local food sources, the Russians handed France a stunning defeat—one from which Napoleon could not recover. The Grande Armée could not be rebuilt to its former glory, and Adams thought the sun was perhaps setting on Napoleon's great empire. If France were defeated, Britain would be free to turn its full might against America.

During a long discussion with Count Rumyantsev on February 1, Adams expressed this gloomy outlook. He feared the war was "too popular with all parties" in Britain, while in the United States opinion was divided. The only outstanding reason for the war was impressment of American sailors, but on "this point the whole English nation, or at least all the political parties, were unreasonable." The losses the Royal Navy had suffered at the hands of the U.S. Navy "had mortified their national pride, and touched their point of honor in its tenderest part . . . and would make them think they must now fight not only for their honor, but for revenge."

Rumyantsev wondered about the potential for American successes in the forthcoming campaign against Canada. "I [expect] for the present little or nothing from it," Adams answered. "We [are] all too raw and unskilled in war to make much progress in Canada." He believed that Lord Liverpool's government was stronger now than when first consti-tuted the previous summer, so its ministers would be even more intran-sigent in any peace negotiations.[9]

His minister to Russia's pessimism would have disturbed President James Madison, who informed the Russian minister to America, André Daschkoff, that Adams would be one of a special delegation to conduct the forthcoming negotiation. The speed of the president's acceptance of the offer surprised Daschkoff, for in the past Madison had been cool and his sympathies seemed to lie more with France and Napoleon even after the Grande Armée invaded Russia. In January, the two had lingered one evening at Madison's dinner table after the other guests had departed. Daschkoff had suggested that it might be time for the United States to make peace with Britain and floated the idea that the emperor might mediate. "I acknowledge your offer is very liberal and the moment very favourable," Madison replied, "but will you or can you guarantee to us all the rights we claim?" When Daschkoff replied that obviously the outcome of such negotiations could not be foreseen, Madison seemed to lose interest in the subject.[10]

But by March international circumstances had changed dramatically as it became increasingly clear that France would inevitably be defeated by the growing coalition of nations taking arms against it. Any subjugation of France would leave Russia as the most powerful nation on the European continent.

It was also inescapable that Madison had gone to war with Britain expecting France to either triumph or at least remain strong enough to ensure the war in Europe continued to be waged fiercely. War in Europe meant the British could never direct their full military attention against the United States. If the war in Europe ended, American prospects for victory dimmed dramatically. He had to acknowledge that to date the army had demonstrated no capacity to achieve victories against British forces they outnumbered, so there would be no likelihood of success if Britain transferred a significant portion of its standing army from Europe to Canada. And eventually the British would go over to the offensive, carrying the war into the United States.

Ironically, if Britain's war with France ended before its war with the United States, the only remaining *casus belli* of the conflict would be lost, for impressment of American sailors would cease. Peace always brought a reduction in British warships and a resultant discharge of surplus sailors.

There was also the grave financial cost of the war. The day after his inauguration on March 4, Secretary of the Treasury Albert Gallatin had informed the president, "We have hardly enough money to last till the end of the month." Gallatin advised "cutting by the root militia expenses, and . . . reducing the Western expenditure to what is necessary for defensive operations, relying exclusively on the possession of the Lakes for anything of an offensive nature."[11] Although by month's end he had managed through a series of frantic meetings with bankers—word of the Russian mediation offer slightly lifting the spirits of the financiers—to raise sufficient capital through loans repayable at 7.5 percent interest, the treasury was by no means on solid footing.

Considering all these factors, Madison was anxious to end the war as expediently as possible. The president informed Daschkoff that he would send other envoys to join Adams in St. Petersburg without first waiting to see if Britain accepted the emperor's offer.[12] To demonstrate the mission's importance, Madison wanted to send one of his senior cabinet members—Albert Gallatin—even though this would cost him the administration's most able financial manager. Gallatin, Madison recognized, was his most diplomatic minister. He retained the sophisticated European mannerisms and would be comfortable dealing with the tsar and whomever the British assigned to the negotiation. On March 14, when asked by the president if he would serve, Gallatin immediately agreed. To his sixteen-year-old son, James, Gallatin explained he did so out of duty. "Father rarely talks to anybody now, his mind seems fully occupied with the grave situation. I think I am the only person he confides in," James recorded in his diary. When his father decided to take him along as his private secretary, the young man jumped at the opportunity to see the world. Three days after Gallatin accepted the president's request, Madison told him "that there was nobody compared to him as a negotiator." To James, Gallatin admitted the compliment "pleased him greatly."[13]

But the president would not send Gallatin alone. He was reviled by too large a segment of Americans. Even having John Quincy Adams at the table would fail to silence the critics. In a gesture intended to rob the thunder from those who would seize any opportunity to rail against the administration, Madison approached the Federalist senator from Delaware James Bayard. By this sleight of hand, Madison was able to demonstrate that his administration's policies were not driven to further narrow party ambitions.[14] For the good of the country he would send one of the nation's most respected opposition politicians to Russia and the man who was the rock upon which the foundation of his presidency rested.

Gallatin thought the treasury would be able to operate for the rest of the year without his supervision. He fervently wanted to end this mad adventure, which he believed beyond America's capacity to win. "I have made up my mind," he wrote his brother-in-law, "that I could in no other manner be more usefully employed for the present than on the negotiation of a peace. Peace is at all times desirable. England must be desirous at this critical moment to have it in her power to apply her whole force on the continent of Europe, and the mediation of Russia saves her pride."[15] Gallatin acknowledged that the Russian mediation would also allow the United States to retain its pride.

"Provided we can obtain security with respect to impressment," he explained to Madison, "peace will give us everything we want. Taught by experience, we will apply a part of our resources to such naval preparations and organizations of the public force as will within less than five years, place us in a commanding situation."[16] Gallatin sought peace, but he also wanted America to never again be so defenceless that it could not protect its merchant mariners. There would be a standing, viable navy, and a regular army capable of defending the country's borders. Gallatin had come to a crossroads and departed from his normally fiscally conservative, anti-federal spending course. He was willing to venture down the road of expanding the role of the federal government in the affairs of Americans.

But he was quite happy to leave the difficult battle to win approval for permanent taxation to be fought by others. Gallatin admitted to being "well aware that my going to Russia will probably terminate in the appointment of another Secretary of the Treasury and in my returning to private life."[17] That was a small personal price to pay for peace. The long years in the administration, the constant heckling and bitter attacks on his reputation, the fact that he distrusted and disliked the newly appointed Armstrong had disenchanted Gallatin with political life. Being an arbiter of peace would serve as a fitting finale to his public career.

Monroe extended the invitation to Bayard on April 5. Bayard received the note at his Wilmington home two days later. His response was immediate. "The proposition . . . was entirely unexpected," he wrote. "I do not allow myself however to hesitate in my determination on the subject.

"If the President considers that it is within the means of my abilities to render any service to our common country, it is for him to command the full exertion of them. The occasion is of that nature that I do not allow myself to enquire what is my private interest or convenience.

"I beg you Sir to make known to the President that I am highly flattered by this mark of his confidence which certainly shall be met by a correspondent fidelity and I will also beg you at the same time to assure Him that I can promise every thing which belongs to an unbiased devotion to the interests of the Country."[18]

The announcement that Bayard and Gallatin were to be the envoys brought immediate response in the press. The anti-war newspapers saw a conspiracy by Madison to pretend to desire peace and engage in negotiations that the administration would then ensure failed so as to create new impetus for banging the drum of war. On the other hand the War Hawk lobby noted that both Gallatin and Bayard opposed the war. Did their joint appointment not suggest that the administration sought peace too eagerly and would agree to any conditions that the British might insist upon? Not surprisingly Bayard faced some sharp rebukes from Federalist colleagues for deigning to serve as an agent of Madison's administration. Killiam K. Van Rensselaer, Solomon Van Rensselaer's uncle and a veteran New York State senator, expressed the fear that Madison was "disposed to sacrifice you in the apparent attempt to make a peace, when no one here has the least idea that the Administration is sincere."[19]

Bayard refused to credit claims that the mission was some kind of administration plot to build American support for the war. "If any Sinister views be entertained," he replied, "they are unknown to me, but if that be the case I should think it very wonderful, that they should select a political adversary to trust with the Secret. I can well imagine without the exercise of either confidence or charity that peace may be sincerely desired by the Administration."

That the Americans going to St. Petersburg were to eagerly seek peace at any cost was an equally ridiculous charge. Monroe's April 15 instructions to Bayard and Gallatin jeopardized the likelihood of a successful negotiation from the outset. If Great Britain gave "satisfactory assurance that she would abandon her claim with respect to impressment of seamen and 'illegal blockades,' " warfare on the part of the United States would cease.[20] Also the article contained in Jay's Treaty of 1794 that allowed British traders from Canada to trade with Indians within the boundaries of the United States was not to be renewed. "The pernicious effects of this privilege have been most sensibly felt in the present war, by the influence which it gave to the traders over the Indians, whose whole force has been wielded by means thereof against the inhabitants of our Western States and Territories." There would also be no restrictions on America's right to deploy any size navy it wished on the Great Lakes and to use that navy to exclude British traders from navigating the lakes and rivers exclusively under American jurisdiction. Both Britain and the U.S. must return any territory seized during the war.[21]

If these conditions were not enough to scuttle things, Monroe added another on April 27. Britain must understand that the Floridas were irrevocably going to come under American control. West Florida had been legally ceded to the United States by France, and Congress had authorized the president to seize East Florida if any foreign power attempted its occupation. The message was to be made clear that Britain must not consider establishing a presence there.[22]

Gallatin and Bayard were both in Philadelphia preparing to embark for Russia when the Florida letter reached them on May 2. Each man thought bringing Florida up at all a bad idea. In a letter to Monroe, Gallatin confided that this idea had prompted Bayard to express "his apprehensions that we would fail, and his regret that we had not more discretion on the subject of impressments." Bayard wanted to enter into an informal understanding with the British rather than forcing them to sign "a solemn article." This approach, he believed, would succeed because it saved "the pride of Great Britain."[23]

Monroe's reply was quick. On May 5, he left to their discretion how the treaty was worded regarding the end of impressment, but that "leaving it in silence and trusting to a mere understanding liable to doubts and different explanations, would not be that security which the United States have a right to expect." The next day he wrote again, setting out a long list of grievances against Britain and defending raising

Florida in the negotiations. Possession of both East and West Florida, he argued, "would facilitate your negotiations in favour of impressment and every other object, especially if it was distinctly seen by the British ministers or minister that, instead of yielding them or any part of either, we would push our fortunes in that direction and in Canada if they do not hasten to accommodate. Satisfied I am that the more we endeavor to tranquilize their fears and to conciliate their esteem by any species of concession . . . which may be imputed to timidity or a desire to get out of the war, by the tone assumed in the negotiation, the more certain its failure, and the longer will be the continuance of the war afterwards."[24]

Gallatin starkly warned Monroe on May 8 against recklessly proceeding with outright occupation of East Florida and investing the heavily fortified West Florida town of Mobile, which remained a Spanish island in the American sea there. Such action, he believed, would cause a war with Spain that would "disgust every man north of Washington" because it was motivated purely by southern desire for more land. Gallatin reassured Monroe that he agreed that no informal arrangement regarding impressment would be acceptable. There would have to be a *sine qua non* treaty clause.[25]

The next day Gallatin and Bayard boarded the 300-ton *Neptune* at Newcastle and sailed down the Delaware River to gain the Atlantic. James Gallatin was also aboard, as was Madison's twenty-one-year-old stepson, John Payne Todd. He and George Dallas, the twenty-year-old son of Philadelphia senator and stout Madison supporter Alexander J. Dallas, had been assigned by the president to serve as Gallatin's secretaries—a chance for the two young men to gain diplomatic experience that would help prepare them for political careers. Bayard's secretary was Col. George B. Milligan.

As it was customary for those attending the Russian court to wear uniforms, Todd, Dallas, and James Gallatin had been commissioned as third lieutenants of cavalry without pay so that they could be appropriately turned out. Colonel Milligan had packed his standard utility and dress uniforms, while Gallatin and Bayard were provided with individually tailored uniforms not associated with any military rank or service.

Monroe had expressed particular pleasure with Gallatin's uniform, an embroidered "blue coat, lined with buff, with a buff waistcoat and small cloaths, yellow buttons." The secretary of state thought it "a handsome uniform, national and economical."[26]

Because of the British blockades *Neptune* could not avoid interception, so the Russians had formally requested a pass for the envoys from Admiral John Warren in Halifax. As Warren issued the necessary documents, he asked the Russian consular officer if the United States might be disposed to an immediate armistice to remain in effect until negotiations were concluded. Madison refused, unless the British first removed their blockades and withdrew all troops from American territory—something he knew they would not do.[27]

Whether the pass would be honoured was of great concern. Just after dawn on May 11, Bayard stood on the main deck looking toward the capes that flanked the mouth of the Delaware and noted that square in the middle of river stood a British ship that *Neptune*'s captain, Lloyd Jones, identified as the 38-gun frigate *Spartan*. There was virtually no wind, *Neptune* drifting on the ebb tide at a painfully slow pace toward the river's mouth. It took four hours for the ship to come alongside *Spartan*. When the British captain, Edward Brenton, was advised of the ship's mission and the identity of the two envoys, he invited Gallatin and Bayard aboard his ship. The two men declined the invitation, sending Jones and secretaries Dallas and Milligan instead. "They were at first received coldly," Bayard noted in his diary, because Brenton believed the ship a merchant vessel and was bent on searching it for contraband goods. Jones quickly produced papers certifying *Neptune* as a U.S. naval ship and the guarantee of safe passage provided by Admiral Warren. Brenton's "manners . . . changed and he behaved with marked civility." When Jones and the secretaries returned to *Neptune*, the ship was "allowed to drift to sea with the tide."[28] The American commissioners were on their way to Europe.

FOURTEEN

An Expanded War

SPRING 1813

*W*hile President Madison hastened to send envoys to Russia to take advantage of Tsar Alexander's mediation offer, the war intensified. In Great Britain, the government's attitude toward America had hardened during the winter of 1812–13 as news of Royal Navy losses to the U.S. frigates filtered in. When the presidential election swept Madison back to power, Lord Liverpool's cabinet decided it must commit more resources to the war or risk losing British North America.

On January 9, the Prince Regent issued a declaration that for the first time officially acknowledged that there was no end in sight to the war between the two nations. The message was carefully crafted to further foster the general public feeling that Madison had started this war in collusion with Napoleon Bonaparte and was in fact little more than a puppet dancing on the end of the emperor's strings.[1] Speaking from the House of Commons backbenches, George Canning decried Madison as "the arch enemy of this country."[2]

In London, *The Times* demanded an end to negotiation with "these blustering democrats; for surely no person in his senses could ever have believed that Mr. Madison would accede to any terms consistent with the honour or safety of this country." The editors spurned Madison's persistent denials that the United States was in any way aligned with France.[3]

At No. 14 Downing Street, Lord Bathurst and Undersecretary Henry Goulburn worked feverishly to drum up reinforcements for Canada. It was a painfully complicated business, requiring gleaning a battalion of infantry in one corner of the empire, a company of artillery in another. As each unit was confirmed a letter was dashed off to Sir George Prevost bearing the news. Finally Bathurst provided Prevost with a complete accounting and the promise that when the ice melted on the St. Lawrence River sufficient to permit navigation, the 19th Light Dragoons regiment, a company of Royal Artillery as well as reinforcements to bring the existing four artillery companies in Canada up to strength, detachments of drivers, sappers, and miners, battalions from seven infantry regiments, and two regiments of Swiss troops would arrive. Bathurst could not, however, promise that many of these troops would reach Canada in time for the 1813 campaign season because they were coming from great distances. One of the Swiss regiments, for example, was being released from the Iberian campaign, where the tide had so turned in Britain's favour that Wellington's army could be slightly reduced.[4] It was entirely possible that Prevost would have to meet the inevitable early-spring invasion with what forces were on hand.

Hoping to force the Americans to divert troops away from Canada, the British government instructed Admiral Warren in January to launch a series of raids along America's coastline in addition to maintaining the blockades. Liverpool's cabinet realized that Warren would not be able to fully blockade such a long coast riddled with small bays, coves, and inlets. Instead key ports would be blockaded, while the raids would spread panic throughout the coastal communities and create demands for defensive troops. Warren was also to corral as many U.S. naval ships inside blockaded ports as possible to prevent their putting out to sea where they might threaten British shipping and trade lines.

By early spring Warren had blockaded Chesapeake and Delaware bays, New York City, Charleston, Port Royal, Savannah, and the mouth of the Mississippi. No American ships, naval or merchant, were allowed in or out and were seized if possible. Neutral ships approaching these ports were warned off, while those caught within were denied exit. Attempts to elude the blockade resulted in seizure.

Another stricture the Admiralty imposed on the Royal Navy was that ship captains were to refuse single-ship engagements that they might lose. To ensure that his blockading forces could defeat any challenge issued by the U.S. Navy, Warren always had a ship of the line supporting every squadron of frigates and smaller ships. This was particularly the case at Boston, a favourite port for American frigate captains.[5]

While Warren sought to bottle up the American fleet, Secretary of the Navy William Jones struggled to get all his ships out to sea. Knowing the U.S. Navy was too weak to directly challenge the blockades, Jones ordered his captains to slip out to sea one by one and then scatter. His idea was simple. Working singly, each U.S. frigate or schooner would carve out a section of ocean as its personal hunting ground and capture or destroy any British shipping that strayed across its sights. If enough havoc was wreaked, the British blockades would have to be lifted so these squadrons could pursue the American warships or shepherd maritime shipping by convoy through the troubled waters. In this way, Jones was confident America could challenge British domination of the seas "without hazarding the precious gems of our national glory." Given their scant numbers, Jones was anxious to preserve every ship he had.

Some ships escaped the blockades. Others had already been at sea before the blockades were erected. The 32-gun *Essex* was among the latter. Having put out from Delaware in late October, by spring 1813 it had rounded Cape Horn to spread terror throughout the British whaling fleet operating near the Galapagos Islands.

Loose in the South Atlantic was the 18-gun sloop *Hornet*, under Capt. James Lawrence, which tangled with Capt. William Peake's brig *Peacock* in February. In a thirty-minute action fought at a range of 50 yards, Lawrence managed to swing *Hornet* so as to fire on *Peacock*'s starboard quarter with full effect while Peake could only counter with two after-guns. The Americans mauled the British ship. Grapeshot and sniper fire from the sails aloft slaughtered the sailors manning the after-guns. A cannonball tore Peake asunder, while a falling spar swept the ensign overboard, prompting the senior lieutenant to surrender the ship. A prize-crew jumped aboard only to find the ship foundering. Three Americans and eight British drowned trying to abandon her. Lawrence had lost only 1 man killed and 2 wounded during the fight itself, while the British had suffered 9 dead and 28 wounded.[6]

That the blockades were far from impregnable was effectively demonstrated by Commodore John Rodgers when, taking advantage of late-season heavy seas and a blinding snowstorm that had driven the British ships out of position, he slipped *President* and *Congress* out of Boston on April 23. Once at sea the two ships scattered per Jones's instructions. *Congress* achieved little over its eight-month cruise. But Rodgers took *President* on a great circle of the Atlantic that passed the Azores, the Shetlands, and the Orkneys, looped around Ireland, and then scoured through the Grand Banks off Newfoundland before dodging back into the shelter of Newport, Rhode Island, in September. Rodgers had taken a dozen prizes during his voyage, and every British attempt to intercept him had gone for naught.

Two other ships, *United States* and *Macedonian,* also slipped their tethers, escaping from New York at the end of May. Although these ships had luckless cruises, their elusion of the blockade exposed Warren to much criticism and added to the growing British public opinion that the American naval captains could run circles at will around their Royal Navy counterparts.[7]

That illusion was somewhat laid to rest when Capt. Philip Broke of the 38-gun *Shannon* met the much-lauded Capt. James Lawrence, who had just taken command of the American frigate *Chesapeake*—star of the 1807 impressment crisis—in a head-to-head contest. Although the ships mounted an equal number of guns and *Chesapeake* had a larger crew, Broke decided to bring the ship to battle despite Admiralty injunctions against single-ship engagements. For weeks he had been relentlessly training his gun crews and felt them ready to match the best of the U.S. Navy. On June 1, standing off Boston harbour, he issued a formal challenge for Lawrence to meet "ship to ship to try the fortunes of our respective flags." The challenge was issued too late, however, as before it reached the harbour, *Chesapeake* sailed directly toward *Shannon*. Both men were spoiling for a fight, even though Lawrence thought his crew green as grass and *Chesapeake* jinxed. Before leaving his cabin for the bridge, the American captain scratched out a hurried letter to a friend. "Should I be so unfortunate as to be taken off," he wrote, "I leave my wife and children to your care."

The two ships passed several hours manoeuvring for position, but at about four in the afternoon opened on each other with a broadside at close range. Broke had his guns loaded with double shot that tore into the American vessel with catastrophic result. Great holes were rent in the bulwarks, the sailing master fell dead, the fourth lieutenant lay dying, Lawrence was struck in the leg by a sniper's musket ball. The two ships veered and then collided, Shannon's after-port being caught by Chesapeake's anchor. The resulting position left the American upper decks completely exposed to Shannon's forward guns, which raked them with grapeshot. A group of British sailors jumped aboard Chesapeake but were driven back in a vicious fight, and Lawrence was wounded a second time when a bullet pierced his abdomen.

Before the Americans could clear the British from the deck, Broke jumped over Chesapeake's railing with a larger boarding party close behind. Seeing the danger, Lawrence struggled to his feet and shouted: "Don't give up the ship! Don't give up the ship!" Carried below to his cabin, now serving as the surgeon's operating theatre, Lawrence demanded that the surgeon rush up to the deck and order that the crew fight to the last, refusing to strike the colours. "They shall wave while I live," he gasped.

It was too late. The hand-to-hand melee ended when the senior American officer ordered his men to lay down their arms. A battle that had lasted a mere fifteen minutes had transformed the two ships into slaughterhouses. Broke lay dying, the victim of a sabre wound. 23 other British sailors were dead and another 58 wounded. The Americans had lost 61 killed and 85 wounded. Lawrence lived for four more days, but refused to speak or acknowledge the surrender. When he died the British officer commanding the prize-crew ordered his body wrapped in the ship's colours. Chesapeake was taken to Halifax, where the American commander was buried with full honours.[8]

The capture of Chesapeake did much to quell criticism of the Royal Navy at home and marked the end of the U.S. Navy's dominance of the sea that had marked the previous year, while the blockades and raids of its coasts demonstrated that America could do little to safeguard itself from direct naval attack. Repeated amphibious raids sent the clear message that the British could strike where and when they wanted with near impunity.

The first British raid was conducted in Chesapeake Bay by Admiral Sir George Cockburn in April. Intelligence reports showed that the Americans had such weak defences in place that Warren provided only a single frigate to support the landing of about 180 seamen, 200 marines, and a small artillery detachment. On April 28 the raiders struck Frenchtown on the Elk River and burned a large quantity of military stores and several small vessels. They escaped with only one man wounded.

Five days later Cockburn struck again, attacking and destroying an artillery battery at Havre de Grace along with several nearby homes. The raiders then pushed several more miles up the Susquehanna River and spent the ensuing day wrecking a cannon foundry. Again only one man was wounded during this escapade. On May 5, Cockburn went up the Sassafras River to Georgetown and Fredericktown, scattered some local militia and burned any houses from which their owners had fled. Cockburn established a pattern here that subsequent British raiders adopted. Those inhabitants who stayed and cooperated by accepting forced sale of goods the British wanted had their houses spared. Those who either resisted or took flight saw their homes looted and burned.

This early success, against what Warren described as the most vulnerable country to raiding he had ever seen, prompted the Admiralty to commit more resources to amphibious operations against the American coastline. Warren was allocated 2,400 men, consisting mostly of two Royal Marine battalions numbering 1,684. While Lord Bathurst saw these operations as a means to take pressure off Canada, the Admiralty instructed Warren to focus on objectives that would cripple the U.S. Navy.

The larger force's first attempt came on June 22, with an attack against a fort manned by about 700 Americans on Craney Island in Chesapeake Bay. Poor intelligence resulted in the landing boats running aground well offshore, and the attack crumbled. Forty men were dead, wounded, or missing when the attackers withdrew with nothing to show for the attempt. Warren ordered a less ambitious operation three days later against Hampton, where a small artillery battery and a couple of hundred militia were dug in facing the James River. The militia were quickly driven off, the guns captured, and the village pillaged. A company of

French prisoners of war recruited into the army ran amok. Wrote Lt. Col. Charles Napier, who had commanded one element of the raid, "every horror was committed with impunity, rape, murder, pillage: and not a man was punished." Col. Sir Thomas Beckwith reported to Warren that controlling the Frenchmen had proved impossible and that many were liable to desert at the first opportunity. In early July, Warren had them packed off to Halifax and shipped back to Britain.

More raids followed in July, with Cockburn leading a detached force south to attack Ocracoke Island and Portsmouth, North Carolina. Two American vessels were captured and the inhabitants forced to sell cattle and stores. Warren, meanwhile, continued running raids in Chesapeake Bay when and where he liked. In August, with malaria and other fevers running wild through the ranks of his soldiers and sailors, Warren abandoned the bay, sailing north to recoup his strength in Halifax. The success of the British blockades and raids had left no doubt in the minds of either the British or the Americans that the United States could prevail only by succeeding in its campaigns against Canada.[9]

Unlike his predecessor Paul Hamilton, who had concerned himself exclusively with seagoing matters, American Secretary of the Navy William Jones remained distinctly aware of the need to gain mastery of the Great Lakes. Operations against Canada, he wrote Commodore Isaac Chauncey at Sackets Harbor on Lake Ontario, "will depend absolutely on our superiority on all the lakes."[10] The two lakes that really mattered were Erie and Ontario, for it was around their shores that much of the 1813 land war would be fought. Chauncey realized the strategic importance of Lake Ontario. He also knew that the naval battle for control of the lake depended less on tactics one or the other side might develop than on sheer weight of numbers. Given that neither the Americans nor the British had a significant naval presence on the lakes, the side most likely to prevail would be the one that managed to float the most vessels after the spring thaw.

All through the winter shipwrights had been hammering together ships. On Lake Ontario the British laboured on two frigates, one at Kingston, the other at York. The Americans at Sackets Harbor had launched the 24-gun corvette *Madison* in November, purchased a number of schooners for refitting into warships, and laid the keel of another corvette, the 26-gun *General Pike*, which Chauncey hoped to launch in June. At Presque Isle on Lake Erie the Americans had established a small naval yard, and in March young Capt. Oliver Hazard Perry assumed command of that lake's fleet. Much to his chagrin, Perry discovered the work here was only in its infancy and he was unlikely to contest British control of the waters until mid- to late summer. Perry could not compensate in just a few months for the American failure to establish any pre-war naval presence on the lakes. So Jones's prescription that the United States must gain superiority over the lakes to ensure successful land operations was clearly beyond attainment.

The British, meanwhile, were hampered by a badly organized chain of command in their naval program for the Great Lakes. Initially Sir George Prevost, in his capacity of governor, controlled it through the offices of the army Quartermaster General's Department. With no shipbuilding experience, the army turned to local Canadians to both construct and man the fleet. Precious few of these men had any more experience with warships than the soldiers. In March 1813, a British officer reviewing the capabilities of the ships on the lakes lamented to Prevost: "I do not conceive there is one Man of this Division *fit* to Command a Ship of War."[11]

Prevost quietly agreed. The previous fall he had begged Lord Bathurst for naval supplies and, more importantly, qualified seamen. He also wanted the lake navy placed under Admiralty command. Bathurst agreed, but it took time for orders to this effect to reach Admiral Warren in Halifax. Consequently, it was not until March that Warren freed a small number of officers from sea duty and sent them to the lakes. Meanwhile the Admiralty dispatched 400 officers and men under command of Commodore Sir James Lucas Yeo, who was to command the lake navy. Only thirty, Yeo had gone to sea as a ten-year-old ensign, rising to the rank of post captain by his twenty-fifth birthday. He and his contingent of officers and men sailed from Britain in late March, but would not reach Quebec until May. The Admiralty had assumed responsibility of the lake fleets with little enthusiasm, arguing that defending the vast sea lanes of the empire was already barely within its capability given the resources at hand. What ordnance could be supplied would be, as well as a core of manpower, but the basic supply for the lake navy would remain an army responsibility. So Britain's lake navy became somewhat of an outcast over which neither Admiralty nor army cared to admit ownership. The result was that by early spring it posed no serious threat to Chauncey's claim to control Lake Ontario, and its superiority on Lake Erie was in doubt.

With superiority of the lakes, the Americans determined to again invade Canada. Secretary of War John Armstrong recognized Montreal as the objective of paramount importance—its capture would cut Upper Canada off from Lower Canada and reinforcement by British forces coming up the St. Lawrence River. But intelligence reports claimed that between 8,000 and 10,000 regulars were deployed at this bustling fur-trading centre. The Americans could never hope to defeat such numbers. So Armstrong turned his sights on gaining control of Lake Ontario's shoreline in Upper Canada and the Niagara Peninsula. He ordered Maj. Gen. Henry Dearborn to assemble a corps of 4,000 men at Sackets Harbor to join Chauncey's fleet for an amphibious assault on Kingston and thereafter the provincial capital of York. Rather than holding these communities, the intent was to destroy the shipping, shipbuilding facilities, and forts present at each, thus solving "by a single stroke every difficulty" the Americans faced in gaining control of Upper Canada. With Kingston and York in ruins, the British would be unable to supply or reinforce their troops west of Lake Ontario. Kingston was the real key, for it held the only harbour on the lake's northern shore that could provide a viable naval station. Armstrong made clear that Kingston was the prime objective around which the rest of the campaign turned.

Once Kingston and York were ransacked, Armstrong wanted the Sackets Harbor corps to swing westward to participate in an operation against the Niagara Peninsula. A second corps of 3,000 men would be waiting in Buffalo. In concert these two formations would overrun Fort George on Lake Ontario's shore and Fort Erie next to the lake for which it was named. Armstrong understood that there were no more than 2,100 regular troops concentrated around Lake Ontario, of which 600 were in Kingston and 1,200 garrisoned on the Niagara Peninsula. So the Americans should enjoy overwhelming numerical superiority.

Armstrong's plan was bold, but not as bold as it might have been. American estimates of British strength at Montreal were absurdly inflated. In fact, excluding militia, there were only a little more than 9,000 troops in all the Canadas, and 2,000 of these were provincials considered of dubious quality.[12] Nor were the British able to depend on significant numbers of Upper Canadian militia responding to a call to arms. Prevost had admitted to Lord Bathurst in May that call-ups were causing "growing discontent [and] dissatisfaction of the Mass of the People of Upper Canada, in consequence of the Militia Laws upon a population thinly scattered over an extensive range of Country, whose zeal was exhausted & whose exertions had brought want and ruin to the doors of many." A good number of the American settlers were packing up and crossing the border to the south. His only recourse had been to move more regulars out of Lower Canada to create a thin screen that might withstand the expected American assault. The militia, Prevost lamented, had "been considerably weakened by the frequent desertion of even the well disposed part of them to their farms, for the purpose of getting seed into the ground before the short summer of this country had too far advanced."[13]

If Armstrong had seriously overestimated the numbers of British regulars in the Canadas, his calculations were conservative in the extreme compared to those added up by Dearborn. Claiming sources "entitled to full credit," Dearborn reported that Prevost had assembled 6,000 to 8,000 men in Kingston alone. He expected Prevost to concentrate there for operations against Sackets Harbor, a fear he had harboured throughout the winter and which had been reinforced in his mind by a British raid in February against the small fort garrison at Ogdensburg—the only real base the Americans had managed to establish on the St. Lawrence River. In a daring attack out of Prescott, the fort standing on the opposite shore, British troops had crossed the frozen mile-wide river on foot, driven off the small garrison, burned several ice-bound ships, and carried off the military stores on sleighs back to Canada.[14] Dearborn was so rattled he was quick to believe any reports that large British forces threatened Sackets Harbor.

Chauncey little credited Dearborn's fears. Rather, he believed the British were massing in order to march against Maj. Gen. William Henry Harrison's army out on the western frontier. But he agreed that there were at least sufficient men garrisoning Kingston to ensure that an attack against its forts would bog down in a drawn-out siege that would limit the American ability to conduct further operations in 1813. He proposed instead to abandon the attack on Kingston and destroy only the ships and shipbuilding facilities at York. Chauncey believed this would sufficiently weaken the British on Lake Ontario to ensure America retained supremacy. Once York was reduced, the two corps would carry out Armstrong's Niagara plan. British loss of Fort Erie would free several American ships currently confined in Black Rock by its overlooking guns. Once these vessels were free, the Americans would control Lake Erie and be able to assist Harrison in recovering Detroit and capturing Fort Malden. With the British presence in the west eliminated, it would be a simple matter to sail the length of Lake Huron and reoccupy Fort Michilimackinac, leaving the Americans in control of the frontier. Harrison could then either eliminate Tecumseh's Indian confederacy at leisure or impose a new treaty should they sensibly decide to sue for peace. The British would be left with Kingston and Montreal, but little else.

Chauncey's was a tidy plan that looked good when little wooden boats and soldiers were moved about on a map, but it failed to address the fact that even if it succeeded the Americans would not have conquered Canada. And they were too sparse on the ground to hope to hold whatever they captured against a major British offensive. Great Britain would still be free to pour in more soldiers and supplies via the St. Lawrence River and carry out a campaign the following year to wrest back everything the United States might win in 1813. Only by seizing Montreal to create a blocking position on the St. Lawrence could the Americans hope to choke off British reinforcement of Upper Canada.

Dearborn embraced Chauncey's strategy and proceeded to listlessly gather troops for the planned operations despite Armstrong's urgings to make haste. The strategy the general determined to follow was, in the words of one analyst, akin to someone who, "desiring to fell a tree, should procure a ladder and begin cutting the outermost branches, instead of striking at the trunk by the ground."[15] Presented with the details of the revised plan, Armstrong reluctantly approved it on March 29.[16]

Not until April 24 did Dearborn rouse to action and lead 1,700 soldiers onto fourteen of Chauncey's vessels. Aboard the corvette *Madison*, the commodore then led the expedition out onto the lake. It was a foul day. The ships pitched and yawed wildly in heavy weather. Realizing some of the small, heavily laden vessels might founder, Chauncey soon ordered the fleet to come about and return to harbour. The next day the weather was better and the fleet sailed toward York. Below decks, hundreds of the soldiers became violently ill anyway because of the close confines they had to endure. There was a general sense of relief when York was spotted in the distance on the afternoon of the next day.

P. Finan, a soldier of the Royal Newfoundland Regiment stationed there, described York—which had a population of less than a thousand— as a "pleasant little town, the houses generally of wood, and containing some good shops. Being the seat of government of the upper province, it has a house of assembly, court house, etc. It is situated at the lower end of a long bay formed by a narrow peninsula stretching up the lake, parallel with the shore, about two miles. On the extremity of this, called Gibraltar Point, stands a light-house, and exactly opposite to it, on the mainland, the garrison is situated."[17]

That garrison was pathetically small: 700 militia, dockworkers, and a few Indians along with five under-strength companies of regulars. There was no fort, just a temporary munitions magazine, a two-storey wooden blockhouse, and a defensive ditch surrounding Government House. Several lightly entrenched batteries stood along the shore to the west of the town and another battery stood next to the blockhouse. In the Front Street shipyard a large frigate named *Sir Isaac Brock* was nearing completion and nearby the old schooner *Duke of Gloucester* was under repair. Although not in command of the garrison, Sir Roger Sheaffe took immediate charge of the town's defence.

Aboard *Madison*, Dearborn was seasick and disinclined to lead the amphibious assault. The old general's fighting days were well past. At 250 pounds, he could barely walk. When horse and carriage were unavailable, a couple of soldiers pulled him about in a two-wheeled cart. Dearborn passed command to thirty-four-year-old Brig. Gen. Zebulon Montgomery Pike, a professional soldier with nineteen years' service behind him. Ambitious and impulsive, Pike determined to attain glory taking York or die trying.[18]

As Chauncey's ships had clearly been sighted by the British, the landing was put off to the following morning. April 27 was a lovely spring day, and the sailing vessels glided across the calm waters of the lake with several boats full of troops preparing for the landing in tow. It was, P. Finan noted, "an elegant and imposing appearance."[19]

The first wave of Americans went ashore in flat-bottomed boats under covering fire from Chauncey's dozen warships, landing about two miles west of Government House and the blockhouse. Three companies hit the beach and quickly forced the single company of regulars to withdraw, but not before about half of its strength was eliminated in a fierce clash. The Royal Newfoundland Regiment was caught trying to reach the beach and thrown back with a loss of thirty-six men.

Disaster befell the British when they attempted to rally around the westernmost artillery battery only to have it accidentally blown apart when a gunner dropped his match into a wooden chest containing one of the gun's magazines. Confused and demoralized, the British retreated in disarray toward Government House. Pike drew his men up before the blockhouse shortly after noon, quickly knocked out the single artillery battery, and prepared to storm the remaining strongpoint. Realizing further resistance was futile, Sheaffe decided to run for it with his regulars to the protection of Kingston. He ordered that the British flag remain flying over the blockhouse to give his men time to get away and left a party to blow up the magazine. York would be sacrificed to save his precious regulars.

Pike was interrogating a British prisoner about a hundred yards from the magazine when there was a terrific detonation. Finan of the Newfoundland Regiment, near the rear of the British line, turned to see "an immense cloud" rising from where the magazine stood. "A great confused mass of smoke, timber, earth . . . assumed the shape of a vast balloon." A giant chunk of stone smashed Pike down and literally crushed the life out of him. British and Americans alike were killed and wounded by a deadly hail of debris.[20] The Americans estimated 40 of their own were killed and more than 200 wounded by the explosion. What few medical men were ashore "waded in blood, cutting off arms, legs, and trepanning heads," one surgeon wrote, who himself "cut and slashed for 48 hours without food or sleep" before all the injured were treated.[21]

Had Sheaffe not been in the midst of flight, he might have wheeled about and put in an attack after the explosion that could have carried the day. But he was already on the outskirts of York, pausing only so long as it took to tell the senior militia commanders present that it was their responsibility to contact the Americans and arrange terms for surrendering the town. This they did, but first they obeyed Sheaffe's additional order to burn *Sir Isaac Brock*.

The Americans were in a foul mood because of the casualties suffered when the magazine exploded and the fact that the ship they had hoped to capture was burned, but their commanders held them back from occupying York until terms of the capitulation were signed the next day. Under the agreement, private property was to be protected while all public property was subject to forfeiture. But the occupation soon turned sour as troops ran rampant looting empty houses, vandalizing property, and bullying unarmed citizens. The legislative building, Government House, and most of the military barracks were burned, the government printing press smashed, and the £2,000 in the public treasury commandeered. They floated *Duke of Gloucester* off as a prize. A large amount of military stores—much intended to resupply the British forces on Lake Erie—was loaded aboard Chauncey's boats.[22] On May 2, the Americans embarked their ships but were then trapped in the harbour until May 8 by a heavy gale.

Although Chauncey's fleet sailed that day to Fort Niagara and put soldiers ashore to carry out the planned attack on Fort George, they were too "sickly and depressed" to immediately carry out the operation. Dearborn sent Chauncey back to Sackets Harbor to gather reinforcements, for he had lost 320 killed and wounded at York. Meanwhile, he and his men would "recruit their health and their spirits." In a letter to

Armstrong, the general said his intention was "to collect the main body of troops at this place and, as soon as Commodore Chauncey returns and the forces from Oswego arrive, to commence operations in a spirited and effectual a manner as practicable."[23]

This effort was launched when Chauncey's fleet returned on May 25 and subjected the fort to a heavy bombardment. Before the American attackers could overwhelm the defences, Brig. Gen. John Vincent ordered the fort abandoned. After spiking the cannon and destroying the ammunition, the British and Canadian militia withdrew to the safety of a new position near Beaver Dams.

FIFTEEN

A Succession of Defeats

*T*he burning of York and the fact that Commodore Isaac Chauncey's fleet was "capable of commanding every port on the lakes and in actual possession of the Niagara frontier shores" cast a pall of gloom over Upper Canada. Settlers and British soldiers alike reflected on the loss of Fort George and the defeat at York and could hardly consider that anything "but the entire evacuation of the western peninsula seemed possible." Morale in the British ranks was low. Most of the militiamen were frantically sowing their fields and worried that the inevitable call-out would result in yet another crop going unharvested. If they did not die on a blood-soaked battlefield, they and their families were likely to starve in the coming winter.¹ There was little cause to think that the American tide could be turned back. Everywhere large American forces gathered, poised to cut through the thin red lines that could hardly be expected to hold back their onslaught.

On the western frontier, newly promoted Maj. Gen. William Henry Harrison had constructed a major fort just below the Maumee Rapids to serve as a strong base for his spring operations. At Presque Isle, Oliver Hazard Perry and a handful of men were hammering together several ships that would enable the Americans to challenge British domination of Lake Erie. From Amherstburg on the lake's northwestern shore Henry Procter, whose victory over James Winchester had brought promotion to brigadier general at the young age of twenty-six, watched this American industriousness with growing concern.

The British situation on Lake Erie was precarious. While Harrison had relatively secure supply lines stretching back to Ohio, and Perry could draw on the American West's main industrial centre of Pittsburgh only about 150 miles to the south, Procter depended on a supply route that passed through the threatened Niagara Peninsula. Normally he would feed his troops by local purchase, but the militia call-out the previous fall had resulted in serious losses to the autumn harvest. The forthcoming American attack could only worsen this critical food shortage.

Procter was short of men and supplies of every sort, but his appeals to Governor Sir George Prevost went largely unanswered. Not only did he lack supplies for his men, as the region's civil administrator he could not provide for the needs of either the settlers or the Indians. The latter had begun gathering at Amherstburg with the melting of the snows, responding to a call sent throughout the confederacy by Tecumseh. On April 17, the warrior chief had walked into Procter's headquarters. It had been seven months since the two men had last met. Always ambivalent about the Indians, Procter both respected and feared Tecumseh. Though he distrusted their loyalty, failing to recognize that the confederacy did not share British war aims, his lack of troops required him to rely on them as allies.[2] The British could never prevail on the frontier without Indian support, but their support came at a price. Procter must be seen to be carrying the fight to the Americans. Tecumseh and his chiefs saw no value in a defensive war. Only through offensive action could they regain the lands stolen by the Americans through war and deceit. Tecumseh came seeking word of where the next attack would fall, not to hear that Procter preferred to sit in Amherstburg and Fort Malden and wait for Harrison to strike.

Despite Prevost's instruction to Procter that a defensive strategy was preferred, the newly appointed brigadier had no intention of complying unless directly ordered. Nothing in his instructions restricted spoiling raids like those he had led against Winchester. An attack on Fort Meigs could nip Harrison in the bud, gaining Procter most of the summer to beg more supplies and men and also to give the militiamen opportunity to sow their seed for the autumn harvest.

Consequently, on April 28, Procter loaded 550 regulars, 464 militia, and 63 fencibles aboard two gunboats, six other vessels, and a flotilla of bateaux and crossed the lake to the mouth of the Maumee River. There, they joined 1,500 confederacy warriors under Tecumseh's command. While the troops and warriors moved toward the fort on a mud-drenched track with oxen dragging a small number of cannon, the two gunboats laboriously worked their way into the river to bring the fort into range of the nine-pounder gun each mounted.[3]

The British erected gun batteries on each side of the river and along with the gunboats pounded away at the fort while Tecumseh's warriors took up positions to the south of its walls and fired on the parapets with muskets. Investing the fort by direct assault would be suicidal, for it was stoutly constructed and Harrison's garrison appeared determined to fight. Procter hoped instead to subdue it through bombardment. Between May 1 and May 5, 1,600 shots hit the fort with little effect.

Harrison knew that help would soon arrive, if he could hold out. In the early morning hours, Brig. Gen. Green Clay and 1,200 Kentucky troops aboard eighteen flat-bottomed boats shot the rapids above the fort. Most landed on the north bank and overran the British batteries. Prevost counterattacked with the 41st Regiment supported by Tecumseh's warriors. A bloody melee ensued as the redcoats and Indians broke the Kentucky line and routed them into the forest. About 450 surrendered while only 150 of the 800 who had landed on that side of the river regained their boats and escaped. The surviving Kentucky troops soon withdrew into the safety of the fort, managing to carry in only a small amount of supplies. The rest were quickly plundered by the Indians.[4]

As had proved true after the Raisin River battle, Procter made poor allowances for protection of his captives, merely removing them to the ruins of Fort Miami on the river's mouth and placing them under the guard of a handful of men. Soon a party of Indians, who mostly had played no part in the battle, burst in and began tomahawking the helpless men. Hearing their screams, Tecumseh ran to the building and threatened to kill any warrior who continued murdering prisoners. About a dozen Americans were killed before Tecumseh's intervention. The warrior chief also had to prevent a party of Wyandot warriors from torturing and executing four Shawnee who had fought alongside the Kentucky troops. He shook each man's hand, promised them safe passage home, and provided them with protection.[5]

Procter won a tactical victory on May 5, but this success did little to alter the situation. Harrison was still unassailable inside his fort and had been modestly reinforced. Meanwhile, the Canadian militia, who made up almost half Procter's force, announced that they had to return home to start sowing crops—something the brigadier badly wanted, too. Great numbers of the Indian warriors were already departing, heading home to deliver the captured goods. Reluctantly, Procter lifted the siege on May 9 and returned to Amherstburg. Between those lost as prisoners and those killed or wounded, the Americans suffered 1,000 casualties, while the British counted only 15 killed, 46 wounded, and 41 taken prisoner.[6] But the inequity of the butcher's bill failed to mitigate the fact that Procter had failed in his purpose. Harrison still threatened the Erie frontier.

On the vital front of the Niagara Peninsula, critical to the continuance of British support for Procter, Brig. Gen. John Vincent—who now commanded the region—watched the American buildup at Fort Niagara with trepidation. Barely 1,000 yards of Niagara River separated the two forts, and ranks of cannon bristled on the opposing shores and along the fortress walls. The little village of Niagara, standing alongside the mouth of the Niagara, lay between Fort George and Lake Ontario. Directly opposite, the American bastion hulked. Seldom did either side bother firing shot across the water. Both husbanded their limited supply. Vincent was badly outnumbered, the Fort George garrison numbering only about 1,000 regulars and 300 militiamen. The fort itself was run-down. If Chauncey brought the American lake fleet into play its naval guns would easily demolish the walls. His only option was to anticipate where the Americans would land and to meet them on the beaches. That was where the battle would be decided.

The dawn of May 25 was signalled by the harsh thundering roll of cannon firing from the batteries directly facing Fort George—hot shot, designed to set anything wooden alight. Within minutes fires raged within every single barrack. The American guns fired for the next two days, sometimes continuously, more often by fits and starts.

Vincent anxiously watched the river for signs that the Americans might force a crossing under protection of the fortress guns. At the same time he nervously looked to his left, knowing that they more likely would come at him from there aboard Chauncey's damnable fleet that sailed Lake Ontario with smug impunity. He had to keep pickets out along both shores and man the gun batteries covering each line of approach. The British were stretched desperately thin. Fort Niagara's guns banged continuously, fraying nerves and setting more fires. On the second day of the bombardment thick fog cloaked the lake and river. Vincent could see nothing beyond the hazy shoreline. Then, shortly after dawn on May 27, the fog lifted and there stood Chauncey's fleet in a great arc.

The American soldiers had boarded the ships the previous day, using the covering fog to close on Fort George. Lacking breeze, the sailors had rowed the vessels toward the British shore. It had taken longer than hoped, the dawn had beaten them and the fog had lifted. No surprise was achieved. But Vincent's screen of troops was terribly thin, most held at the fort to meet an attack from either direction. Hundreds of Americans poured off the ships into landing boats and paddled hard for shore. Vincent sent 170 Glengarrians, light troops trained to move fast, to intercept them.

Typically, Maj. Gen. Henry Dearborn had claimed illness and turned command over to his brigadiers John Boyd, William Winder, and John Chandler. That was the order by which they were to take their respective brigades ashore in lifts—more than 4,000 troops. But the initial landing was led by Dearborn's adjutant general, the recently exchanged Col. Winfield Scott, who had been taken prisoner at Queenston Heights. Scott was at the head of a detachment of New York riflemen commanded by Capt. Benjamin Forsyth, sharpshooters clad in green uniforms.

The Americans landed east of the mouth of Two Mile Creek, about 1,000 yards west of Niagara. As they spilled from the boats and clambered up a steep bank, the Glengarrians met them with bayonets and musket shot. Narrowly dodging a bayonet thrust, Scott tumbled into the water. But others gained the high ground and pushed the light troops back, forcing them in on the lines of the reinforcing King's Regiment of Foot commanded by Maj. James Ogilvie.

Behind Scott's riflemen Boyd's brigade landed and spread out into fighting formation—too many for the British to repel. Vincent ordered a fighting withdrawal to delay the American advance long enough to spike the guns and destroy the ammunition stores. After three hours of intense fighting, Vincent's men retreated toward Queenston. They left behind 52 dead and another 300 wounded or missing. The Americans had taken Fort George at a cost of just 150 casualties. Vincent gave up the Niagara Peninsula, withdrawing to Burlington Heights at the head of Lake Ontario from where he could threaten their control of the region.

The Americans had achieved a major victory, but Dearborn failed to exploit it by reboarding Chauncey's ships and getting behind Vincent to force a battle that would eliminate the British army. Instead he allowed it to escape and remain a threat.[7]

Poor weather contributed to Dearborn's lack of initiative. Heavy rain and weak winds left Chauncey's sailors bedraggled and becalmed. Then, two days after the capture of Fort George, Chauncey received the news that Sackets Harbor was under attack, his precious base in jeopardy and even more the still-under-construction *General Pike*. Chauncey raised sails, deployed the sweeps and made best speed toward home, abandoning Dearborn's army.

Surprisingly, the attack on Sackets Harbor was Sir George Prevost's work. On May 25, hearing of the cannonade fired against Fort George, he decided on a diversionary attack of his own. With 800 men, he and Commodore Sir James Yeo sailed from Kingston. Prevost hoped to destroy the dockyard and the corvette under construction. Bedevilled by light winds, Yeo's ships did not near the fort until just before nightfall, so Prevost decided to delay landing until morning. Yeo, who had combined operations experience, argued that keeping soldiers in the holds through the night would wear them out more than landing them immediately. The element of surprise the British now enjoyed would also be lost, giving the Americans time to call up their militia. Blithely dismissing Yeo's concerns, the governor took to his bed.

Come morning, Yeo's prediction proved out as tired, dispirited British troops were met by a force of about 500 militiamen. Although the Americans were easily pushed back, every inch of ground was still contested, slowing the advance. Yeo, meanwhile, was prevented by an offshore breeze from bringing his ships into position to shell the dockyard. After three hours of hot fighting, Prevost ordered a retreat while declaring the enemy beaten. He seized three captured six-pound guns and 154 prisoners. The redcoats fell back unwillingly, bearing off 154 wounded and leaving 47 dead and 16 men missing. "Tired, hungry, wet and thirsty, highly mystified and looking very sheepish at one another," the veteran troops believed they could have won the day under a bolder commander.[8]

The attack on Sackets Harbor achieved nothing in real currency, but it succeeded in one sense by the panic it instilled in Chauncey's mind. On June 11, he wrote to Secretary of the Navy William Jones that he had been "prepared to proceed in quest of the enemy, but upon mature reflection, I determined to remain in this place and preserve the new ship at all hazards." Suddenly Yeo was master of Lake Ontario. At least until Chauncey mustered his resolve and ventured forth.[9]

Unable to move men by ship, Dearborn ordered his army to pursue Vincent marching along the shore of Lake Ontario while he remained in Fort George. Refusing to relinquish command despite increasingly failing health, he sent Chandler and Winder forward with about 3,500 men and no clear instructions as to which man was in charge. Both were political appointees—Chandler a congressman who had been a blacksmith and then a tavernkeeper, Winder a Baltimore lawyer.[10] Despite inarguable superiority of force, the two officers advanced gingerly, with cavalry well ahead, stopping at the slightest threat to conduct lengthy reconnaissance. Pausing at Forty Mile Creek, about two-thirds of the way between Fort George and Burlington Heights, they dallied to establish a supply depot to support the next stage of the advance. Then the Americans advanced another fifteen miles to Stoney Creek, encamping there on June 5.

Vincent's scouts kept him well informed of the American progress. When nineteen-year-old militia scout Billy Green found his brother-in-law hiding from the Americans who had tried to take him prisoner, the fugitive revealed the enemy's password. Green rushed this information to Vincent. Meanwhile, Lt. Col. John Harvey had been creeping about the edges of the American camp, finding it haphazardly placed and poorly guarded. Not cooperating with each other, Winder and Chandler had failed to tie their lines together. Men were strewn everywhere, companies setting up and lighting cooking fires wherever they liked. Harvey urged Vincent to attack at once.

At about 11:30 that night, Harvey returned with 700 men. Armed with the password, they closed on and bayoneted the first sentries. Then they formed a line and charged. The Americans sitting around fires recovered quickly, snatching up guns to meet the attack. Charge thrown into chaos, the British troops broke formation and became entangled with the Americans.

Chandler and Winder lost control over their men, as did Harvey. Vincent, who had accompanied the attack, got turned around in the dense woods and only reappeared at his headquarters the next morning, having lost horse and hat. Chandler kept yelling, "Where is the Line? Where is the Line?" until he was silenced by a British soldier from a twenty-man unit commanded by Maj. Charles Plenderleath of the 49th Regiment. The general was taken prisoner. Sgt. Alexander Fraser of the same unit came face to face with Winder, and when the general raised his pistol, calmly advised: "If you stir, Sir, you die." Winder lowered his gun. Plenderleath and his intrepid band bagged not only two generals but also five field officers and captains and more than 100 troops. Although the British suffered more casualties than the Americans—214 to 168, including the prisoners—by morning they held the field.[11]

Command of the Americans devolved to cavalry officer Col. James Burn, who later informed Dearborn that he had been "at a loss what steps to pursue in the unpleasant dilemma, occasioned by the capture of our Generals, finding the ammunition of the troops nearly expended." A hasty council of war produced the inevitable result. The American officers agreed to retire briskly to Forty Mile Creek. There they remained until the afternoon of June 7, when Yeo showed up and subjected them to a heavy naval bombardment that sent the column scuttling back to Fort George. Dearborn, thoroughly alarmed, ordered Fort Erie—which had been taken without a shot fired—burned and abandoned. He then drew his entire army in behind the dubious walls of Fort George and prepared to meet a siege.[12]

Believing he faced at least 6,000 Americans at Fort George, Vincent could do little to exploit this unexpected failure of will. A consequent lull ensued that Prevost put to good use by reorganizing his command. Maj. Gen. Roger Sheaffe's ignominious abandonment of York garnered no thanks from the inhabitants of Upper Canada, so the governor sent him packing to Montreal and brought in Maj. Gen. Francis de Rottenburg. The fifty-six-year-old baron had been born in Danzig and seen service in both the French and Polish armies before joining the British army in 1794. After several postings in various corners of the empire, he was promoted major general in 1810, sent to Canada, and had since held various commands in Lower Canada.[13] Cautious but competent, de Rottenburg kept his emotions and temper on such a short rein that he seemed unshakably calm no matter the crisis. No Brock, he was a commander who would husband his resources but not shy from giving battle.

Dearborn, meanwhile, finally admitted to ill health and handed off to his surviving senior officer, Brig. Gen. John Boyd. With Canadian irregulars and Indians roaming at will throughout the peninsula and routinely sniping at American foraging parties, Boyd decided some offensive action was needed. He also wanted to prove his worth as an officer and assuage American pride after the humiliation of Stoney Creek. On the road leading from Queenston to St. Davids, near a place known as Beaver Dams, the British had established a small outpost. Its commander, Lt. James FitzGibbon, was headquartered in a stone house. To the northeast, a gathering of Mohawk and Caughnawaga Indians was camped, and it was from here that the raiding warriors operated. Sending the redcoats off and then sorting out the Indians seemed easy enough to Boyd, a former soldier of fortune who had served in India and pretended to have great experience in handling troops. Winfield Scott distrusted the man's competency, thinking him more bully than soldier, but being subordinate held his peace.[14] The operation seemed straightforward, the kind of punitive strike frontier American soldiers had conducted for decades. Boyd assigned the job to Lt. Col. Charles Boerstler of the 14th United States Infantry, who sallied forth with a mixed cavalry and infantry force of 700 men and two field guns.

What followed was the kind of comic farce that had signified American performances during 1812. It also gave birth to a Canadian legend forever wrapped in mystery and the subject of countless debates regarding its credence.

On June 23, Boerstler set out, guided by a freebooter partisan from Buffalo named Cyrenius Chapin—who claimed to be a doctor—and his irregulars whom the regular soldiers disparaged as the "Forty Thieves." The American column slogged through the heaviest summer rains in twenty-five years, Boerstler increasingly disenchanted by his guide's blundering about in such a manner that it was evident he little recognized any of the country through which they passed. In addition to the unwieldy cannon trains, the soldiers dragged along wagons brimming with supplies as if on a protracted campaign rather than a hit-and-run mission. Wading through a miasma of mud, the column managed only eight miles the first day before stopping about midnight at Queenston. Boerstler commandeered a house and ordered its residents to serve dinner. The Americans were still about the same distance again from their objective and Boerstler issued instructions that come morning the force would bring the enemy to battle.

How then to explain, just before dawn on June 22, a day before Boerstler's arrival, the departure by a Queenston housewife and mother of five on a mission to warn FitzGibbon that the Americans were marching on his position? Thirty-five years old, Laura Secord could give FitzGibbon no other details. Despite this paucity of information, the lieutenant credited it sufficiently to warn the Indians and put his small garrison on alert.

Consequently, when the Americans started up the road to the Niagara Escarpment, the British, Indians, and Canadian militia lay in ambush at Beaver Dams. Boerstler and his men faced tough going, worse than the previous day's advance. Men slipped and slid in the mud that greased the road.

At nine o'clock that morning 300 Caughnawaga struck the rear of the column and were soon joined by 100 Mohawks. Disoriented by the dense woods lining the road, the Americans fired at shadows more than the fleeting Indians. After three hours of this harassment they were totally demoralized and would surrender but for fear of being massacred. That was when FitzGibbon and fifty redcoats materialized out of the woods. By his own account the British had not yet fired a single shot. But the Caughnawaga and Mohawk had "beat the American detachment into a state of terror, and the only share I claim is taking advantage of a favourable moment to offer them protection from the tomahawk and the scalping knife."[15]

FitzGibbon engaged Boerstler long enough in negotiations through various blustering proclamations to enable Maj. Peter DeHaren to hasten in from Twelve Mile Creek with three companies of regulars to enforce the lieutenant's claims that between the Indians and redcoats they could easily butcher the Americans. Sufficiently cowed, Boerstler surrendered. The American militiamen with the column were paroled, but 462 officers and men of the regular army were made prisoners and all the supplies and the cannon they had lugged with them were captured. Although in the confusion Boerstler managed to slip away, he was damned as a coward by the Americans despite his claims that the men were so exhausted that further fighting would have been futile.

Beaver Dams was truly an Indian victory for which they were barely thanked by the British despite suffering about 15 killed and 25 wounded. It was also the final straw for the Americans on the Niagara Peninsula. After this debacle Dearborn simply hunkered down in Fort George, waiting for inevitable attack. But, rather than the British coming for the old general that everyone now disdained with the nickname Granny, there came instead a short note from Secretary of War John Armstrong. "I have the President's orders to express to you his decision that you retire from . . . command . . . until your health be re-established, and until further orders."[16]

Despite her making little of it herself, Laura Secord's trek was soon enlarged into myth, and she became a Canadian hero of the war even as it remained unclear how she came about her knowledge. Over the years Secord provided contradictory and vague details. By one account her husband had overheard an American officer discussing the planned operation. But where he was at the time was never clarified. At other times the story was that she heard it personally from enemy soldiers while forced to serve them dinner. Who were these men? Certainly not Boerstler, as some accounts would claim, for he had not yet led the column out of Fort George. Perhaps, however, they were some of Chapin's scurrilous characters. Just as probable, Secord picked up nothing more than a rumour—for rumours flowed like water over Niagara Falls in this region because almost everyone knew someone or was related to someone on the other side of the border— and decided it warranted bearing to the nearest British officer.[17]

FitzGibbon little helped to clarify matters. His reports on Beaver Dams filed shortly after the action failed to mention her at all. Sometime after the war, when a debate as to the credence of her story was raised, FitzGibbon issued a signed certificate that a woman named Laura Secord, "a person of slight and delicate frame," did make the journey.[18] She would be the only hero to emerge on either side out of the seesaw of events that played out on the Niagara Peninsula in 1813.

In Washington, President James Madison had convened a special session of the Thirteenth Congress on May 24 primarily to enact legislation needed to keep the federal treasury afloat by introducing internal taxation and to have his appointed envoys to the Russian mediation offer endorsed. Typically, Henry Clay was elected Speaker by a hefty majority vote of eighty-nine to fifty-three. When news of the defeat at Beaver Dams and other failures on the Niagara Peninsula reached the city, Clay was so incensed that he sent Representative Charles J. Ingersoll to Madison with a formal demand that Dearborn be replaced. The president, who had fallen ill with a severe fever on June 11 that seemed at times life-threatening, was barely able to receive Ingersoll. Rising from his sickbed but briefly, Madison agreed that Dearborn must be replaced, and the bitter note had been duly issued under Armstrong's hand on July 6.

Armstrong's first instinct was to personally take command in the north, but there was little support among the rest of the administration for this notion. James Monroe and Armstrong were engaged in ever more public scraps over war policy. William Jones, the navy secretary, was disenchanted with them both but more so with Armstrong. Many, Jones wrote, "believe that the 'Old Soldier' is not a legitimate son of Mars.

He is descending very fast—and so are we all."[19] In Albert Gallatin's absence, Jones had assumed responsibility for the treasury and found the double duties extremely onerous. He begged Madison to appoint a new treasury secretary, but the president ignored him.[20] Madison was barely functional, laid out on what was alternately described, depending on the source of information, as his White House sickbed or deathbed. The latter prospect gave many a Federalist heart while adding to a general sense of demoralization in Republican ranks. A wet, searing summer gripped Washington in its maw. The House and the Senate sweltered. Their members bickered incessantly.

Madison had sought ratification of his appointments of Albert Gallatin, John Quincy Adams, and James Bayard for the Russian peace delegation. He also advanced the name of Jonathan Russell, whom he wanted endorsed at the same time as minister to Sweden.

The president had expected a rough reception to the taxation proposal, and that was exactly what he got. "Is this a dagger that I see before me?" demanded an editorial in the New York *Evening Post*. Macbeth, the editor wrote, "hardly felt less horror at the appearance of the bloody dagger staring him in the face, than must the good people of these United States at beholding a democratic President recommending internal taxes."[21] The taxes had been proposed by Gallatin, and when Jones presented the plan in the House he made this clear. One Federalist after another and many a Republican accused Gallatin of having fled his post by joining the Russian mediation delegation "to avoid the odium of the system of taxation." When the proposals were forwarded to the Ways and Means Committee for consideration and discussion, the Federalists launched an all-out attack on the administration by challenging the appointments of Gallatin and Russell.[22]

Gallatin, they argued, could not simultaneously serve as a peace mediator while retaining helm of the treasury. Without addressing the proposal that he serve on the Russian mission, the Federalist senators objected to Russell's appointment as minister to Sweden. The character and record of both men were impugned during the hearings that followed. Finally the Senate ended the matter of Russell by deciding there was no need to appoint any minister to Sweden at all. A covey of senators tried to mollify Russell by suggesting they would reverse their votes if he agreed to go to Sweden as something less than a minister. This proposal was "so pitiful in the parsimony . . . so incompatible with the national interests and dignity . . . that I did not hesitate for a moment in my refusal," Russell wrote.[23] Meanwhile, Gallatin's appointment was rejected by an eighteen-to-seventeen vote. Only Adams and Bayard were approved.

On August 2 Madison advised Gallatin of "the painful manner in which the Senate have mutilated the mission to St. Petersburg."[24] By this time, it was equally clear that the Ways and Means Committee would not recommend Gallatin's tax plan in full. Instead, a series of stopgap measures were accepted that would do little to raise significant amounts of money. The war would continue to be financed on the cheap.

While these debates had been under way, Armstrong confirmed Dearborn's replacement, a matter that received little attention in the House or Senate. Maj. Gen. James Wilkinson, another Revolutionary War veteran currently posted to New Orleans, would assume command in the north. Gearing up for this change for some time, Armstrong had sent word four months earlier for Wilkinson to report to Washington. Fifty-six, Wilkinson was not one of the Revolution's favoured sons. His was the reputation of a professional schemer and incompetent most notorious for participating in a cabal that had attempted to bring about the sacking of George Washington. Most U.S. senior officers despised him. His health in recent months had been poor.[25] Sensing no urgency in Armstrong's summons, Wilkinson turtled northward and had yet to pass all the way through Georgia, stopping here and there to visit acquaintances and take long rests, when he learned that Armstrong had fired Dearborn and he was to make haste to Washington. Picking up the pace to a shuffle, Wilkinson passed another four weeks moving along the banquet circuit, making speeches and currying favour as he went, before reporting to Armstrong in early August.

Meanwhile, the hot, dry summer of 1813 on the Canadian border had passed with the Americans doing little of anything. At best a stalemate had been allowed to develop. While this might suit the British, allowing them to continue building defences and assembling reinforcements, it did nothing to advance the American cause.

Hull, depicted much younger-looking than he actually was, surrenders his sword and Detroit to Brock. (Library and Archives Canada C-16404)

Brock is pictured here urging on the main counterattack that turned the flank and gave the British a victory at Queenston Heights but he actually died much earlier during an ill-fated charge against the American line. (Library and Archives Canada C-00273)

British boarders from *Shannon* fight hand-to-hand with the American crew
of *Chesapeake* on June 1, 1813. (Library and Archives Canada C-974)

Laura Secord delivers her warning that the Americans are advancing on Beaver Dams to
Lieutenant James FitzGibbon. (Library and Archives Canada C-11053)

The American and British fleets collide on Lake Erie in a decisive battle for control of the western frontier on September 9, 1813. (Library and Archives Canada C-7762)

Tecumseh is shot down by a Kentucky horseman during the final stage of the Battle of Moravian Town on October 5, 1813. With him dies the dream of a self-governing Indian confederacy. (Library and Archives Canada PA-21304)

Lt. Col. de Salaberry leads French-Canadian voltigeurs and militia to victory at Châteauguay on October 25, 1813. (Library and Archives Canada C-3297)

Although the British carries Fort Oswego on May 6, 1814, the raid fails
in its purpose to capture the guns bound for arming the 62-gun frigate *Superior*.
(from *The Pictorial Field Book of the War of 1812* by Benson Lossing
[New York: Harper & Brothers Publishers], 1868)

The American failure at Lundy's Lane on July 24, 1814, spells the end of attacks on Canada.
(Library and Archives Canada C-12094)

This American cartoon accuses the British of waging uncivilized warfare by
inciting Indians to massacre and slaves to revolt, and setting Washington to the torch.
(Library and Archives Canada C-40831)

The Peace of Ghent comes too late to avert the Battle of New Orleans. (from *The Pictorial Field Book of the War of 1812*)

The picturesque and ancient city of Ghent offers an amenable setting for the negotiations to end the war. (from *The Pictorial Field Book of the War of 1812*)

Admiral Sir James Gambier and John Quincy Adams shake hands after the signing of the treaty on December 24, 1814, while the other negotiators and commission secretaries look on. Henry Goulburn is in the foreground with back mostly turned so that his features and expression are hidden. (Library and Archives Canada C-5996)

This allegorical American treaty montage represents the negotiated end of the war as a triumph for America. (from *The Pictorial Field Book of the War of 1812*)

SIXTEEN

Have Met the Enemy

The failed British attack on Fort Meigs in early May rendered both commanders on the Lake Erie frontier unduly cautious. Maj. Gen. William Henry Harrison cancelled an attack on Fort Malden and instead passed the spring recruiting and training new regiments. Harrison waited for Oliver Hazard Perry. The young master commander at Presque Isle was busily constructing a small fleet to contest control of the lake. Once there were ships, an amphibious operation could be mounted.

Elsewhere on the western frontier developments indirectly strengthened his position at Lake Erie. Illinois governor Ninian Edwards spent a busy spring building forts at Peoria, Fort Madison, and Prairie du Chien and at Rock Island Rapids. The last three, on the Mississippi River, marked the outer limits of American influence in Indian territory. On the negative side of the ledger came word that the tenuous claim America had made to any presence on the Pacific coast had been erased by the surrender that April of Fort Astoria on the Columbia River mouth. North West Company traders had appeared at the fort to inform the American fur traders there of the war and the inevitability of an imminent attack by the Royal Navy. To avoid bloodshed, the Canadian traders offered to buy the fort, and the American Pacific Fur Company manager astutely accepted. American colours were exchanged for the Union Jack.[1]

Back on Lake Erie, Perry was well aware that the fate of American operations rested on his ability to float a fleet and destroy the British

ships. Under construction were two brigs to be called *Lawrence* and
Niagara. Weighing 500 tons and brig-rigged with two masts that mounted
square sails, the two ships were to be fitted with eighteen 32-pounder
carronades and two long 12-pounder guns. Perry also had eight smaller
schooners, some built from scratch and others, like *Caledonia*, that had
been captured earlier. Most of these vessels had been trapped at Black
Rock until Fort Niagara's fall. But he lacked sufficient sailors to crew
them all. Naval reinforcement flowed through Commodore Isaac
Chauncey at Sackets Harbor and most were kept there.[2]

More immediate was the problem that the British had Presque Isle
blockaded. Because Lake Erie's southern shore lacked an ideal harbour,
Presque Isle had been selected only out of necessity. A long sandbar that
choked the mouth of the bay to a width of only eight-tenths of a mile
and a depth of only five to seven feet made it too shallow for the British
warships to enter. But this protection came at a distinct disadvantage.
When fully loaded with armaments, Perry's new brigs had insufficient
draft to cross over the sandbar. So long as the British maintained the
blockade, any attempt to float the vessels over the bar and then mount
the guns could be easily thwarted.[3]

Knowing this, the British naval commander, Capt. Robert Heriot
Barclay, kept vessels standing off the bay at all times. An experienced
officer, Barclay had lost an arm at Trafalgar and his career had since
suffered. Middle-aged, he was still only a commander, his captaincy temporary and contingent on continued command of the Lake Erie fleet—
a fleet that was poor at best. Barclay had two main fighting ships afloat,
the 12-gun *Lady Prevost* and the 18-gun *Queen Charlotte*. At Amherstburg
he was building the larger *Detroit*. But Barclay was hampered by the
same personnel shortages that dogged Perry. Worse, the ship's guns had
been lost during the American raid on York, along with many stores
Barclay's little fleet sorely needed.[4] If Perry got loose from Presque Isle,
Barclay would be hard pressed to retain control of the lake. So he had to
keep the blockade cork firmly in place.

While the two naval commanders glared at each other across the
sandbar, Maj. Gen. Henry Procter had come to the demoralizing conclusion that his superiors were ready to cede the Lake Erie frontier, at least

temporarily, to the Americans. When Maj. Gen. Francis de Rottenburg assumed command in Upper Canada, he advised Procter that should the Americans gain control of Lake Ontario he intended to withdraw east of Kingston. Procter and his men, de Rottenburg said, would escape via Lake Huron to Lake Superior. There they could commandeer North West Company canoes and follow a tortuous old river route that would eventually bring them safely to Montreal.

Stunned by these defeatist instructions, Procter had immediately gone over de Rottenburg's head to Governor Sir George Prevost. If the British abandoned Lake Erie, he argued in a July 11 letter, they would lose the support of Tecumseh's confederacy. Procter wanted to seize the initiative on Lake Erie by capturing Perry's fleet at Presque Isle. But that demanded reinforcement from the east.[5]

Over the next two days, Procter discussed matters with Tecumseh. As the warrior chief preferred, they met in the open. Tecumseh sat comfortably on the ground, legs crossed, smoking his tomahawk-pipe. Both men treated the other coolly. The failure at Fort Meigs had distanced them more than ever. Never sure what to think of his ally and always a poor communicator, Procter found explaining his strategy difficult. Tecumseh little trusted the British general and doubted his competency. The Fort Meigs failure, he believed, had resulted from a lack of both skill and will on the part of the British. Tecumseh wanted to try again and was uninterested in Procter's notion that attacking the smaller Fort Stephenson on the Sandusky River would be easier. What would success there accomplish? Presque Isle and Fort Meigs were where the Americans were concentrated. Even most of Procter's officers saw no utility in an operation on the Sandusky.

Procter argued that it was impossible to transport heavy siege guns to breach the walls at Fort Meigs, but Fort Stephenson was poorly constructed and its garrison small. A victory there would keep Harrison on the defensive.

Tecumseh wanted to destroy Harrison and his army. Scouts kept him informed of the American dispositions. At Fort Meigs there were about 2,000 troops under command of Brig. Gen. Green Clay. Harrison was nine miles up the Sandusky River at Seneca Town with about the same number. From here the American commander could reinforce either Fort Meigs or Fort Stephenson. Although Harrison had overall numerical superiority, Tecumseh had more warriors than Clay had soldiers.

For the past two months the confederacy had been gathering at Amherstburg and Fort Malden, and now 3,000 warriors waited impatiently for action. The warriors would not stay put for long unless given a chance to fight. Looking at Procter, Tecumseh lowered his pipe and sardonically suggested that if the British could not breach the walls at Fort Meigs they should supply his warriors with shovels to dig a trench into the fort.

Procter started hectoring the chief. Suddenly Tecumseh angrily shook the tobacco from his pipe and jumped to his feet. "What does he say?" the warrior harshly demanded of the Indian agent who was translating. The agent put a restraining hand on Tecumseh's arm. "Never mind what he says," the man said gently.

Finally Tecumseh, who had proposed the trench merely to embarrass Procter and truly doubted a siege could succeed, proposed a deception plan. The appearance of a large force before the fort must prompt Clay to ask Harrison for reinforcement. So the aim would be to ambush the relief column. If, however, Harrison did not immediately send troops, the Indians and British would conduct a mock battle along the reinforcement route. Clay, believing the relief force under attack, would undoubtedly come to its rescue. Outside the safety of their walls, the Americans could be destroyed.

Procter reluctantly agreed to the plan.[6] But his lack of enthusiasm was expressed by the token numbers he committed. On July 20, Procter set out with just 300 men and a few small guns. Moving alongside the boats carrying the British were 3,000 warriors in canoes, a vast flotilla that darkened the water and warned Clay that Fort Meigs was in jeopardy.[7] The general sent a courier to inform Harrison that he was about to face a siege. Shortly before the British and Indians appeared in the woods around the fort on July 25, Harrison's reply arrived. Help would soon be on its way.

The next day, Tecumseh's warriors divided into two groups on each side of the track that a relief column would travel and embarked on a good imitation of a battle. Muskets fired, warriors whooped and cried. Inside the fort the troops could well imagine their comrades being massacred. Guns were shouldered, the men anxious to run to their rescue. But Clay ordered them to stand down. He smelled a rat. How could Harrison have responded so quickly? Hours passed, the gunfire and shouts became more ragged, and then stilled entirely. The deception had failed.[8]

Procter and Tecumseh kept the fort surrounded for two days, but clearly the Americans intended to stay put. Nor did a relief column present itself for ambush. Harrison would not move unless forced to do so. Too many Americans had been slaughtered in the past trying to march in column through this country's dense woods. Soon his scouts reported that the British and Indians had moved instead, heading toward Fort Stephenson.

The fort was a cluster of little wooden buildings linked by a weak palisade around which a ditch had been dug. Inside were just 160 United States regulars commanded by twenty-one-year-old Maj. George Croghan, who had fought with Harrison at Tippecanoe. His artillery consisted of a single six-pound gun. Against the thousands of Indians headed his way Croghan stood little chance. Harrison ordered the major to set the fort alight and fall back on Seneca Town, seven miles upriver. The courier carrying the order, however, lost his way and the message did not reach Croghan until after nightfall. Nearby the British gathered, and Indians were detected in the woods. Croghan read the note in a fury. He sought glory, had sworn to "defend this post to the last extremity." His reply to Harrison was terse. The orders were too late, there was no time to retreat. "We have determined to maintain this place and by heavens we can."[9]

Upon receiving the message, Harrison ordered Croghan relieved of command for disobedience, but it was too late to withdraw the garrison. Battle was joined on August 1 when Procter opened with a barrage by three six-pounders and two five-and-a-half-inch mortars. The shot bounced ineffectually off the palisade. Procter by now had little faith in success. Once he left Fort Meigs the majority of the Indians, including Tecumseh, had drifted off into the woods. Tecumseh still thought an attack on Fort Stephenson pointless and would play no part in it. Only about 300 warriors remained.

In the mid-afternoon the British general decided that the guns had achieved all they could and formed his infantry and the Indians into three columns that moved toward the fort at "double-quick time" under the lingering cover of cannon smoke. Croghan ordered the defenders to hold fire until the British were within 150 feet. As the redcoats and warriors reached the defensive ditch Croghan unleashed the first volley. Muskets flared along the length of the palisade's top and out of loopholes lower down, and the single cannon loosed a devastating cluster of grapeshot. Immediately the Indians realized the hopelessness of the situation and withdrew. But the redcoats kept coming on. They were of the 41st Regiment of Foot, tough troops with long service in Canada and great discipline. Into the smoke and rain of steel they pressed, some even reaching the fort wall. But there were no fascines or ladders to climb it, the axes too dull to hack through it. Many suffered multiple wounds before finally falling. With darkness the attack collapsed.[10] Procter retreated to Amherstburg. The losses were horrific. Of approximately 250 British that went into the attack, 96 were killed or wounded.[11] The Americans claimed to have found 50 corpses in the ditch. Croghan went from facing summary court martial for disobeying a direct order to being a national hero and celebrity.[12]

Procter left the battlefield with tears running down his cheeks at the sight of so many of his men dead on the ground. But his subsequent reports on the action expressed little remorse for launching an obviously doomed attack that had sent his men into "the severest fire I ever saw." Instead he claimed that the Indians had deserted the British, in fact "scarcely came into Fire, before they ran off out of its Reach." Yet the attack had been made at their insistence and to not have done so "would have ever stigmatized the British Character." Finally the losses suffered, he argued, represented "a more than adequate sacrifice . . . made to Indian opinion." He closed by appealing for more men.[13]

Prevost's response was scathing. "I cannot refrain from expressing my regret at your having allowed the clamour of the Indian Warriors to induce you to commit a part of your valuable force in an unequal & hopeless combat.

"You cannot be ignorant of the limited nature of the force at my disposal, for the defence of an extensive frontier & *ought therefore* not to count too largely upon my disposition to strengthen the right division [Procter's command]." He urged Procter and Captain Barclay to work together "in honourably surmounting . . . the numerical superiority of the enemy's force." In closing he pointed out that Commodore James Yeo's conduct on Lake Ontario should inspire Barclay "only to dare & the Enemy is discomfited."[14]

Prevost's claim that Yeo had engaged in an act of daring greatly stretched the truth. Throughout July the British commodore had trolled Lake Ontario in a vain attempt to embarrass Commodore Isaac Chauncey into coming out of the shelter of Sackets Harbor to give battle. But the American refused the challenge, content to wait until his flagship *General Pike* was ready. While Yeo could claim mastery of the lake during the early summer, there was scant value in it as the army was in no position to carry out offensive operations. And inevitably Chauncey would venture forth. When he did, control of the lake would shift to the Americans.

There was nothing Yeo could do to prevent this unless he was blessed with inordinate good fortune. It was simply a straightforward outcome of the strength of the American squadron on the lake compared to that of the British. Yeo had six vessels that varied in size and sailing rig but were all able enough warships and capable of working well together in formation. Chauncey had more vessels, but they were a hodgepodge of types. Ten were civilian schooners of various sizes that had been converted into fighting ships simply by loading them up with cannon. There were also three corvettes, including *General Pike*, which were fighting ships. The great weight of the guns rendered the schooners sluggish in response to their sails, and all the crews were poorly trained, so the ability of the ships to manoeuvre as a squadron was poor. This reduced the value of Chauncey's superior numbers. The American's trump card lay in the type of guns his ships carried, for of the two principal classes of naval cannon available in 1813, Chauncey had the type best suited for lake warfare. His ships mounted long guns, which in accordance to their designation had long range but fired a fairly light shot. Yeo's ships were fitted out with carronades, short-ranged cannon that fired heavy shot.

So long as Chauncey stayed beyond range of Yeo's ships, he could batter the British at will. Yeo's only chance was to get right in among the American vessels, and to achieve that he would require a strong breeze combined with an advantageous position to enable his ships to close before Chauncey could escape. Another advantage would come Yeo's way if he could force a fight at extremely close range. The cannon on the American schooners were mounted on the decks, and these ships, having not been intended for combat, lacked the bulwarks common to warships that protected crews from enemy fire. Sailors on the schooner decks were exposed from the feet up, and carronades fired a type of shot perfect for butchering ships' crews—canister. A case usually packed with small iron balls—when these were unavailable, nails, spikes, or any scraps of iron sufficed—canister separated upon being discharged to spray a wide area in the same manner as buckshot. Its ability to maim or kill men caught in the open was terrific. But its range was extremely short and it was easily blunted. A six-inch-thick bulwark was sufficient armour.

The long gun was not as good a killing weapon. It generally fired solid shot intended to smash holes in hulls, split masts, and tear down rigging. Cumulative damage, literally bashing the opposing ship into bits and pieces, was the key to success. Each American schooner carried only a small number of guns, so had only limited hitting power. *General Pike* was entirely different. She was big: displacement 875 tons, length 146 feet, beam 37 feet, crew 300. Twenty-six guns that fired shot weighing 24 pounds. A single broadside striking any of the British ships would wreak havoc.[15] In the right circumstance, this colossus could single-handedly sink Yeo's entire squadron. Yeo determined to avoid a direct contest.

On July 20, Chauncey boarded *General Pike* and led the American squadron out onto Lake Ontario. About 2,000 sailors manned the ships. Chauncey sailed with a purpose. Stopping at Fort Niagara, he took on board almost 2,000 soldiers, intending to carry out an amphibious assault on Brig. Gen. John Vincent's supply depot at Burlington. When the depot appeared too strongly defended,

Chauncey cancelled the attack, sailing instead to York. Left defenceless after the last raid, the town was easily occupied on July 31. A few storehouses were burned and some property seized, but there was little profit in the action. Chauncey attacked York not for its worth but to throw a gauntlet in Yeo's direction.

Chauncey returned to Fort Niagara and unburdened his vessels of the soldiers and plunder. When he turned about on August 7, Yeo was there with his two corvettes, two brigs, and two large schooners. Chauncey had the corvettes *Madison* and *General Pike*, the brig *Oneida*, and ten schooners. As night fell the two commanders manoeuvred for advantage, Yeo trying to close and Chauncey seeking to bring the British into range of the long guns but avoid getting tangled in a dogfight. At two in the morning a heavy squall started battering both squadrons. Suddenly the two schooners *Hamilton* and *Scourge*, which collectively mounted nineteen guns and were Chauncey's best vessels of this class, capsized. This calamity resulted in part because the weight of the guns rendered the vessels top-heavy. All but sixteen men aboard drowned. After this accident Chauncey decided that Yeo enjoyed superiority, but breaking would look like running. In his calculations, Chauncey neglected to factor in the vast firepower of *General Pike* or even that of *Madison*, with its fourteen 18-pounders.

Seeing matters more clearly, Yeo carefully kept the wind to his advantage and avoided closing on the big ships. Instead he prowled out of range, seeking an opportunity to cut a couple of the schooners out of the pack. His opportunity came late the night of August 10, when *Growler* and *Julia*, appearing to bore of the long and tedious exercise in manoeuvre, broke out of Chauncey's formation and cut across the British line. Yeo immediately came about and all six British ships bore down on the schooners, which were now hopelessly separated from the American squadron. Their commanders ordered the colours struck, and Yeo had a couple of prizes.[16]

He failed, however, to bring Chauncey to battle. Nor could the American force a contest that ensured the advantage he sought. All the rest of August and then most of September the two squadrons warily circled each other to no effect. Chauncey reported that it seemed Yeo was intent on picking off the schooners one by one, "and as his vessels in squadron sail better than our squadron, he can always avoid an action."[17]

On Lake Erie, Capt. Robert Barclay could not avoid battle. Critically short of seamen to crew his ships and needing provisions, Barclay had rolled the dice in a calculated gamble and lost. For three days, from August 2 to 4, he lifted the blockade at Presque Isle, thinking that Perry was not yet finished constructing *Lawrence* and *Niagara*.

Realizing the opportunity presented, the young American officer ordered the guns stripped from the two big ships to reduce their draft and wrapped anything he could find that might serve as a float around the hulls. On August 5, before Barclay's return, Perry floated the ships over the sandbar. The American squadron was loose.

Too weak in ships and sailors to immediately challenge Perry, Barclay concentrated on finishing the brig *Detroit*. He also wanted to avoid a fight until the arrival of a party of one naval officer and about fifty British seamen reported to be en route from Kingston. This would much bolster his ranks, which numbered just seven British sailors and 108 Canadians of the Provincial Marine. Added to these men who knew boats were 160 British regulars provided by Procter to fill out the crews. But they were all infantrymen with no experience handling cannon, rigging sails, or much else in the way of useful skills.

Perry was not much better off. Chauncey had agreed that a complement of 740 seamen was needed to man the new brigs and eight schooners that formed the Lake Erie squadron. Yet he detailed only 490 men, 140 of whom were soldiers. Still, game to draw Barclay out to fight, Perry established a makeshift base at Put-in-Bay, about 30 miles southeast of Amherstburg, and spent the end of August parading past the village and Fort Malden in a clear demonstration of his mastery of the lake. Barclay refused to be drawn.

But the British could not entirely avoid the contest. Supplies were desperately short, a point Procter impressed upon Barclay with monotonous regularity. The only way supplies and reinforcement troops reached them was by the lake. On September 6, Barclay gloomily spelled out his dilemma in a letter to Yeo. Something "must be attempted by me to enable us to get Supplies. . . . I shall sail and risk every thing."[18] Three days later, Barclay sailed forth aboard *Detroit*. *Queen Charlotte*, *Lady Prevost*, and three schooners, *Chippawa*, *Hunter*, and *Little Belt*, followed. *Detroit* was fit for sea, but barely for combat. Lacking naval guns, Barclay had man-handled a mixed array of cannon from the ramparts of Fort Malden and lashed them to her deck. Seventeen of her nineteen cannon were long guns, ranging from two 24-pounders to eight 9-pounders, the remaining two medium-weight carronades.

The next day, a Thursday, the British squadron sighted Perry's ships off Put-in-Bay. Knowing he was outnumbered, Barclay formed his squadron so *Chippawa* with her single 9-pounder long gun led, followed by *Detroit*, *General Hunter*, *Queen Charlotte*, *Little Belt*, and *Lady Prevost*. *General Hunter* mounted six lightweight long guns and two carronades, *Queen Charlotte* three 12-pounder longs and, making her formidable in a close fight, fourteen 24-pounder carronades. *Lady Prevost* had three 9-pounders and ten 12-pounder carronades, while *Little Belt* had one 9-pounder and two 6-pounder longs. By interspersing schooners between his brigs, Barclay hoped to increase the squadron's overall firepower directly against the two ships in the American squadron that were of concern—*Lawrence* and *Niagara*. His approach was from leeward of the Americans, riding slowly on an advantageous wind. It was 11:45 a.m.

Aboard *Lawrence*, Perry hoisted a fighting flag bearing its namesake's dying entreaty, "Don't give up the ship." His squadron was strung out in a long column with two schooners, *Scorpion* and *Ariel*, in the van, then his flagship followed by *Caledonia*, *Niagara*, and the remaining four schooners in trail. *Scorpion*, *Ariel*, and *Caledonia* all mounted long guns, which Perry hoped would make up for the deficiency of guns aboard his bigger ships.

The wind was light, but fickle. At the pivotal moment the breeze turned, giving the Americans the weather gauge. Perry ordered his ships to close on the British. Barclay opened with the long guns, firing at *Lawrence*. Ten minutes passed before Perry was able to reply with his two 12-pounder long guns. This interlude dragged fearfully for the American crew as British shot from *Detroit*'s three longer-ranged guns tore into their ship with surprising accuracy. Finally the two ships stood just 250 feet apart. Canister range, but just. Perry could get no closer, his rigging almost entirely shot away. Behind, *Niagara* and *Queen Charlotte* ineffectually banged away at each other with carronades, the shot falling harmlessly into the water. Then Commander Robert Finnis, aboard *Queen Charlotte*, gave the order to make sail and a few minutes later joined *Detroit*'s attack on *Lawrence*.

By 2:30 both flagships were in a bad way. Only one of the ten guns mounted on the broadside of *Lawrence* facing *Detroit* still fired. Eighty-three of her 142 men were dead or wounded. Blood ran like water across her deck, staining the canvas of the fallen sails. Men lay crushed under tangles of rigging, others had been torn asunder by canister. Yet Perry, remarkably untouched, refused to strike the colours.[19]

Detroit was little better off, Barclay later describing her as "a perfect wreck." The squadron commander was weak from loss of blood, one thigh ripped open. On *Queen Charlotte*, Finnis lay dead. Lt. Robert Irvine of the Provincial Marine, too inexperienced to competently manoeuvre such a large ship, was in command. The wind was so weak that barely any of the vessels could make way. The three larger vessels locked in their deadly firefight had sails so badly rent that what breeze there was passed uselessly through the many holes.[20] Farther back in the line, *Lady Prevost* drifted helplessly leeward with a damaged rudder, her captain rendered senseless and near insane by a splinter that had pierced his skull.[21]

Throughout the fight Lt. Jesse Elliott, commander of *Niagara*, kept his ship alternately out of line or range of any serious fire from the British. Bad blood existed between Perry and Elliott, who believed command of the Lake Erie squadron had been unfairly passed to the other man despite the lieutenant's having captured *Caledonia* and burned the first *Detroit* the year before.

Finally, recognizing that *Lawrence* was finished, Perry took to a boat with four sailors after ordering the colours struck and the ship surrendered. Covered by the thick blankets of gunsmoke drifting on the lake surface, Perry was rowed to *Niagara*. Soon his personal flag was hoisted and he ordered *Niagara* to bear directly on a suddenly rising fresh breeze toward the British line so as to cut across *Detroit*'s bow.

Barclay, his leg wound wrapped in a thick bandage, stood on his bridge watching the approaching American ship with angry frustration. If *Niagara* crossed in front of *Detroit* he faced a raking broadside. Desperately, he ordered *Detroit* brought around, trying to bring the guns on his undamaged side into broadside position. But suddenly a volley of loosed canister shrieked across the deck. An iron ball ripped the shoulder blade of Barclay's surviving arm open, blood gushed from a large open wound, and the captain collapsed. Nearby, his second-in-command, Lt. John Garland, lay dying. Lt. George Inglis tried to carry out the captain's order, but just as the ship began to come about disaster struck. *Queen Charlotte*, blundering about under the uncertain hand of Lieutenant Irvine, strayed too close to the flagship, and the masts and bowsprits of both ships became entangled.

At this moment Perry achieved his purpose, crossing in front of the bows of the two ships. All the facing cannon aboard *Niagara* were double-shotted. The guns belched flame and smoke, causing carnage aboard the two ships. Some of the broadside struck *General Hunter* as well. On *Niagara*'s port side the guns also spoke, tearing into the tiny *Chippawa* and disabled *Lady Prevost*.

Detroit's masts were gone, *Queen Charlotte*'s mizzen down. An officer aboard *Detroit* hoisted a white handkerchief on a pike to signal the ship's surrender. *Queen Charlotte*, *General Hunter*, and *Lady Prevost* all struck their colours. *Chippawa* and *Little Belt* attempted to flee but were soon overtaken and rounded up. Perry, exultant, scribbled a signal to Harrison. "We have met the enemy and they are ours."[22]

American losses were almost entirely confined to the *Lawrence*. Twenty-two of the 27 killed in the engagement fell aboard the flagship, as did 61 of the 96 wounded. British casualties were fewer, 41 dead and 94 wounded, but this was almost half the squadron's entire strength.

A year after the battle, Barclay appeared before a court martial required whenever a naval officer lost an entire squadron. His ruined shoulder was still wrapped in bandage. He was absolved.

When rumours persisted that Elliott had shown cowardice and failed to come to Perry's support, he demanded a court of inquiry be held in 1815. The court found no basis for the claims. Then in 1818 Perry rekindled the controversy by bringing formal charges against the officer.

Perry's death within a year of the charges being laid resulted in the matter not being pursued, but the question lingered on long after both officers had been laid in their graves.

The effect of what would be known as either the Battle of Lake Erie or the Battle of Put-in-Bay was immediate. Two days after the fateful engagement, Major General Procter wrote his superior, Major General de Rottenburg, proposing an immediate retreat east to the Thames River, which flowed into Lake St. Clair north of Amherstburg. About seventy miles up the river was Moravian Town, a small village where a stand against the Americans might be possible. But his heart was more into a further retreat that would take him overland to the British lines established by recently promoted Maj. Gen. John Vincent on the Niagara Peninsula. While awaiting an answer, Procter declared martial law to enable his commissary officers to confiscate cattle and other supplies sufficient to supply his garrison of about 900 men on an almost 200-mile-long trek through dense wilderness. Procter's letter reached de Rottenburg the evening of September 16 and caused great consternation. First there was the disastrous loss of the Lake Erie squadron, but the general could not believe that cause for "precipitate retrograde movement," as he called it in a hurried reply the next morning. Procter was ordered to consult with Tecumseh to gauge the effect of the naval defeat on the confederacy and meanwhile concentrate his remaining force in such a way as to "prove to them the sincerity of the British Government, in its intention not to abandon them."[23]

But Procter was panicked. He feared the Americans would soon be nipping at his heels. There was no time to await further instruction from de Rottenburg. The only course was obvious. On September 18, Procter called a meeting at the council house in Fort Malden and explained to Tecumseh and his chiefs the need to retreat.

When the British officer finished, all eyes turned to Tecumseh, who stood holding a wampum belt in his hands marked with symbols to remind him of the points he wished to make. Sixteen-year-old John Richardson, the volunteer with the 41st Regiment of Foot, described him as wearing leather jerkin and pants, "while a large plume of white ostrich feathers, by which he was generally distinguished, overshadowing his brown, and contrasting with the darkness of his complexion and the brilliancy of his black and piercing eye, gave a singularly wild and terrific expression to his features."

Through an interpreter Tecumseh spoke. After recapping the events of battles fought since the war's outbreak, he turned to the British promises. "Listen! When war was declared, our father stood up and gave us the tomahawk, and told us that he was now ready to strike the Americans—that he wanted our assistance; and that he would certainly get us our lands back, which the Americans had taken from us." The entire history of British guarantees was trotted before an embarrassed Procter. "You always told us to remain here and take care of our lands; it made our hearts glad to hear that was your wish. Our great father, the king, is the head, and you represent him. You always told us you would never draw your foot off British ground; but now, father, we see you are drawing back, and we are sorry to see our father doing so without seeing the enemy. We must compare our father's conduct to a fat animal, that carries its tail upon its back, but when affrighted, it drops it between its legs and runs off.

"Listen, father! The Americans have not yet defeated us by land . . . we therefore wish to remain here, and fight our enemy, should they make their appearance. If they defeat us, we will then retreat with our father."[24]

But Procter was in no mood to be bullied by Tecumseh into standing and fighting. Even though he still had 900 men and a formidable defensive bastion in Fort Malden, as well as about 1,500 confederacy warriors, Procter viewed the situation as already lost. He soon realized, however, that the support of Tecumseh's Indians upon which the British government staked such importance would be lost if he fled to Vincent's lines. So he proposed a compromise. The withdrawal would be only to the lower Thames. There they would turn and fight. Would Tecumseh come with him?

After some discussion with his chiefs Tecumseh assented to the plan. Supplies for the Indians and soldiers were extremely short. Together they consumed fourteen head of cattle and 7,000 pounds of flour daily, which was more than could be collected locally.[25] There was the real possibility that the retreating force would starve, but Procter thought that prospect even more likely if they stayed. And he could easily imagine being surrounded in Fort Malden. All the Americans had to do was wait them out. Eventually there would be no food and surrender inevitable. Better to retreat and save his army.

Once the decision was made, an exodus slowly began taking place. Over the next few days, as the British destroyed the Lake Erie fortifications, hundreds of Indians moved into the forests. Most headed for the Thames, others simply went their own way. About 1,200 warriors and their families announced their intention to go with the British. They represented the diversity of Tecumseh's great confederacy of tribes—Shawnee, Winnebago, Kickapoo, Wyandot, Sac, Miami, Munsee Delaware, Potawatomi, Ojibwa, Ottawa, Seneca, and Creek.[26] Also accompanying the British were many of the Canadian settlers, fearful of being left to the questionable mercy of the Americans. A great line of carts, wagons, cattle, and horses was gathered together by all these people.

On September 24, Detroit was torched, and two days later Fort Malden was set alight. That same day Perry's squadron was sighted probing carefully up the Detroit River. The morning of September 27 the retreat began in earnest. It was a miserable day. A continual, heavy rain soaked everyone. The downpour combined with the advance of wagons, people, and animals churned up the narrow track, so that the farther back in the line one was, the harder the going. Wagon and cart wheels sunk to the axles and had to be wrestled free. The dresses of the women were sopping with mud as they struggled through knee-deep bogs. Men cursed and swore and pulled and shoved, sweating and shivering at the same time.

Each day that followed only increased the misery of the straggling column. Many civilians had insisted on bringing with them vast amounts of personal belongings. One family alone had thirty horses straining to pull nine heavily laden wagons that carried among other things 1,500 pounds of silver plate. For ten days the retreat went on until the vanguard reached Moravian Town, about seventy miles from Detroit, and Procter decided to make his stand against the Americans. At the opposite end of the long column, a rearguard of soldiers had become so disorganized and demoralized that it failed to carry out the primary assignment of destroying the bridges to slow the American pursuit.

That the Americans would pursue was never in doubt, and Procter was amazed not to be overrun while on the march. The last pickets to abandon Fort Malden had reported troops coming ashore just as dusk fell. Expecting a fight, Harrison had landed 3,000 regulars and Kentucky Volunteers, and been surprised to find the fort a smouldering ruin. Although Procter had no more than a few hours' head start, the American general did not immediately pursue him despite his estimation that no more than 580 redcoats remained and that Tecumseh's warriors could be easily scattered. Instead, that night he wrote to Secretary of War John Armstrong: "I will pursue the enemy to-morrow, although there is no probability of my overtaking him, as he has upwards of 1,000 horses, and we have not one in the army."[27]

This was gross exaggeration, of course. Harrison faced mostly infantry, who had neither the ability to master horsemanship on short notice nor the inclination. Most would rather walk than try saddling a horse. There were also far fewer horses than oxen and cattle, and the number of heavily burdened carts moved slower than a man taking a leisurely stroll. This was a gruelling retreat that mimicked the flight of Napoleon from Moscow. And Procter led his people toward a semblance of the same tragedy that had befallen the Grande Armée.

SEVENTEEN

———

Fields of Victory, Fields of Shame

OCTOBER 1813

M aj. Gen. William Henry Harrison's lack of enthusiasm for a quick pursuit of Maj. Gen. Henry Procter's retreating army was as nothing compared to the state of torpor that had settled over the rest of the American northern command as the campaign season of 1813 entered its final months. In early August, Secretary of War John Armstrong had derided operations so far conducted west of Kingston as having left "the strength of the enemy unbroken." Kingston was "the great depot of his resources," he advised the new commander of the north, Maj. Gen. James Wilkinson, on August 8. "So long as he retains this, and keeps open his communications with the sea, he will not want the means of multiplying his naval and other defences, and of reinforcing or renewing the war in the West." Kingston should be either captured directly or cut off from Montreal by an army driving up each side of the wide St. Lawrence River to blockade this vital link in the British communication lines. Once the blocking position was secure, the army could march east to join a second army coming toward Montreal from the south via Lake Champlain and seize the important trading centre. Success in this venture would well position the Americans to drive the British out of Upper Canada and all of Lower Canada west of Quebec in the spring of 1814. With luck even the fortress city itself might be taken and the conquest of Canada completed. "In conducting the present campaign," Armstrong ordered, "you will make Kingston your primary *object*, and that you will *choose* (as circumstances may warrant), between a *direct* and *indirect* attack upon that post."[1]

Wilkinson, who had only recently concluded his Odyssean banquet-hall journey from New Orleans to Washington, virtually scurried toward his new command after this meeting—arriving at Sackets Harbor on August 25. On paper his was a formidable army consisting of 14,357 regulars. But that included 2,528 unfit for duty. And the rest were spread out into three separate forces. On Lake Champlain there were 4,053 men, on the Niagara Peninsula at Fort George he had 3,668, and on the Erie frontier another 6,636.[2] The latter were with Harrison at Lake Erie and so of no use in the coming campaign.

More problematic was the fact that almost every officer under his command either hated Wilkinson or held him in contempt. In addition to his role in the conspiracy against George Washington, there was an open and bitter quarrel with the popular "Mad Anthony" Wayne, his former collusion in the Aaron Burr scheme that had sought to carve Louisiana away from the United States to create an independent nation, and various lesser intrigues for which he had faced courts martial only to be exonerated for lack of evidence. As well, Wilkinson's health was poor; he was plagued by fevers that he remedied with a regularly consumed self-prescribed mixture of laudanum and whisky.[3]

The commanding general with whom Wilkinson must cooperate to realize Armstrong's objective was also his archrival. Maj. Gen. Wade Hampton, commander of the army at Lake Champlain, was a big, stiff-necked Virginian of sixty years. Hampton's temper was as legendary as his impatience with those who got in his way. Orphaned by a Cherokee raid, Hampton scrabbled his way through a mixture of cunning, good fortune, and bloody-minded determination up from poverty to become one of America's wealthiest plantation owners. His holdings encompassed thousands of acres and were worked by even more slaves.[4] A tough disciplinarian, Hampton imposed a strict training regimen on the Champlain command. *Niles' Weekly Register* reported that even officers were "given to understand that they must and shall ascertain and perform their several duties."[5]

But his army was still painfully raw. Col. Robert Purdy, commanding the 4th U.S. Infantry Regiment, described it as "composed principally of recruits who had been but a short time in the service, and had not been exercised with that rigid discipline so essentially necessary to constitute the soldier. They had indeed been taught various evolutions, but a spirit of subordination was foreign to their views."[6]

Hampton had accepted this command reluctantly, consenting only when promised that he would be independent and report directly to Washington. But when President James Madison approved Armstrong's new operational plan, he did so with the proviso that Wilkinson would be in overall command of the newly designated Military District No. 9, which included the commands of Harrison and Hampton. "I ask from the President . . . my immediate discharge," an infuriated Hampton demanded.

Armstrong responded with mollification. His command would be separate and distinct, just not independent. Surely he must understand that Wilkinson, as the United States Army's most senior officer, could not be embarrassed by having the more junior Hampton commanding on an equal footing. That would run against convention. What Armstrong could do, however, was directly oversee the entire operation—something he had sought since taking over the War Department. "I shall be with you throughout the campaign and I pledge to you my honor as a soldier that your rights shall not be invaded. I forbear to transmit your letter to the President until I receive your reply."

"He has locked the door on me," Hampton growled. The general would serve, but only until the campaign's end. Then he would resign. Meanwhile he promised to be ready to march on September 20 with 4,500 regulars and 1,500 militiamen.[7] The objective would be Montreal.

The most obvious route was a direct one from Champlain northwest of the lake bearing its name across the Canadian border at Odelltown and from there almost due north to L'Acadie and then through country that was primarily a scruffy mix of swamps and woods to gain the St. Lawrence across from Montreal. On reaching Odelltown, however, his scouts brushed up against a mixed force of French-Canadian militia supported by a small band of Iroquois, and Hampton abruptly called a halt. His soldiers groused anxiously about the dangers inherent in fighting a large force of Indians. After a personal reconnaissance, Hampton reversed course back to New York. He wrote Armstrong to say that the unusually dry summer had dried up most of the wells and streams, so persisting would have exposed his army to death by thirst.[8]

But Hampton was not going to give up. Instead, he advanced west along the Chazy River to Four Corners. From here he would pick up the easterly coursing arc of the Châteauguay River to where it joined the English River and then follow this stream's descent to the St. Lawrence. This would place his army opposite Lachine, within a day's march of Montreal, while always having water close at hand. Hampton set off at a leisurely pace, reaching Four Corners on September 25. Here, he received orders from Armstrong to hold, as Wilkinson would not be able to move for several weeks.[9]

Wilkinson, meanwhile, was still puzzling over whether to attack Kingston or advance up the St. Lawrence. The day after his arrival at Sackets Harbor he convened a council of war where his intentions, he later wrote, met unanimous endorsement from the officers present. The troops stationed on Lake Ontario would concentrate at Sackets, most having to be moved from Fort George. In cooperation with Commodore Isaac Chauncey's squadron, "a bold feint" would be made on Kingston while the main army would "slip down the St. Lawrence, lock up the enemy in our rear to starve or surrender, or oblige him to follow us without artillery, baggage, or provisions, or eventually to lay down arms; to sweep the St. Lawrence of armed craft, and in concert with the division under Major-General Hampton to take Montreal."[10]

Having clearly stated his plan, Wilkinson made no haste to implement it. Only on August 30 did he move to Fort Niagara to assemble the soldiers on the Niagara Peninsula for the move to Sackets Harbor. Immediately upon arrival there a fever rendered him bedridden. Although he could have put peninsular commander Brig. Gen. John Boyd in charge, Wilkinson refused. Instead, nothing further was done until October 1, when Chauncey began ferrying troops from Fort George to Sackets Harbor. Over the next two days 3,500 men were shifted, as Wilkinson effectively stripped the peninsula of its occupation force except for an unruly garrison of New York militia commanded by Brig. Gen. George McClure and some Canadian irregulars led by Joseph Willcocks who had cast their lot in with the Americans. On October 2, the commander returned to Sackets Harbor with the final lift of soldiers. He now had about 8,000 men.

Back on the Niagara Peninsula, McClure and Willcocks either exerted little control over the actions of their men or actively encouraged them to pillage farms and burn the barns in areas they controlled. Finally, in November, as the depredations increased and came to the attention of Maj. Gen. John Vincent at Burlington Heights, he detached a force of 378 regulars of the 8th Regiment of Foot along with some volunteers and Indian warriors under Col. John Murray. Establishing an outpost at Forty Mile Creek, they harried McClure's men, slowly regaining control of more of the peninsula. At the same time, the New York militia were taking their leave the moment their short-term enlistments expired. McClure could soon barely maintain any form of occupation. He began to consider a withdrawal across the Niagara River to Fort Niagara.[11]

Wilkinson, meanwhile, no sooner re-established himself in Sackets Harbor than a rather unwelcome visitor arrived in the form of Secretary Armstrong, who announced his plan to run the War Department from there in order to better oversee the forthcoming operation. Armstrong was fed up with delays. Wilkinson seemed no more inclined to engage the British than Dearborn. Hearing that Kingston had been reinforced, he fumed. "With nine days' start of the enemy what might not have been done? At Kingston we shall no longer find him naked and napping."[12] Wilkinson was dismayed to realize that Armstrong was effectively usurping his command, and the two men began to bicker over details of the operation and its whole purpose. Always obsessively secretive, Armstrong began issuing directives and orders that affected the commands of his generals without informing them of what he was about. Chief among these was an instruction to the quartermaster general to construct winter quarters for Hampton's army on the Châteauguay River just inside Canada. If Armstrong expected to carry Montreal, what purpose did such quarters serve? Hampton would winter in the town. Only if the offensive failed should this preparation "against contingencies," as Armstrong described it, be necessary.

The war secretary, who had repeatedly prodded Wilkinson to attack Kingston rather than move on Montreal, abruptly reversed course.

Perversely, Wilkinson, too, switched about. Bring Hampton's army here, he argued, and with 12,000 men he would overwhelm the 4,000 troops he believed garrisoned at Kingston. Lake Ontario would be theirs, Upper Canada finished. Armstrong icily replied that at least 300 scows and other small boats would be required to carry such an army to the Canadian shore and the landing easily repulsed. Montreal was more weakly defended than Kingston, so the trading centre it would be.[13] But Wilkinson would not march immediately. Not before early November, he decided, could the army be ready.

While Armstrong, Hampton, and Wilkinson nudged slowly toward Montreal, Maj. Gen. Wiliam Henry Harrison had spent the last days of September consolidating his hold on the Detroit River. He found Amherstburg empty and raised the American flag once more over Detroit. Only on October 2 did he begin pursuit of Maj. Gen. Henry Procter. With him marched 3,500 men, including 1,500 mounted Kentuckians under Lt. Col. Richard M. Johnson. Another 1,500 troops were left behind to occupy Amherstburg and Detroit.

Harrison initially tried using boats, but soon realized that the twisting and turning course of the Thames slowed his troops down. The boats were abandoned, and with the aid of a Canadian militia deserter, Harrison followed tracks that cut directly through the woods. Each time they came back onto the main track, Harrison saw increasing amounts of discarded military equipment, burned boats, and dead animals. The British were obviously not far ahead. And their failure to destroy bridges allowed Harrison's men to move quickly. On October 5, the Americans overtook and captured two British gunboats loaded with ammunition. A captive confessed that the British column was only a short distance ahead. The Americans paused to work out a hasty plan of attack.

Procter was waiting with his men deployed across a 1,000-foot-wide gap of open ground, with the Thames to his left and a dense swamp choked with scrub to the right. He hoped the narrow frontage would prevent Harrison committing more troops than his 1,000 redcoats could handle. Not wanting Tecumseh's warriors disrupting his regimented thin red line, Procter sent them to the extreme right to form a blocking force in the swamp. His single six-pounder, loaded with grapeshot, was positioned square in the middle of the track. Procter formed his men in the open, but had to break them into two groups separated by a swamp that mired the centre ground. The woods to their front were dark and impenetrable. There would be little warning when the Americans struck. To their right, the swamp was "dark and dreary and littered with fallen and rotting trees." In their glaring red uniforms, the soldiers felt terribly exposed. Somewhere Indians and Americans lurked, each equally invisible. Behind their lines the woods and swamp intermingled into a confused jungle. There was nowhere to retreat if the line needed to move back to regain cohesion.

The British were demoralized. The 41st Regiment of Foot had lost confidence in Procter, been dispirited by the retreat, and were short ammunition. All they had was in their pouches.[14]

Procter prepared to meet a European-style attack where infantry marched toward infantry. The American cavalry, he expected, would attempt to move around the flank, where Tecumseh's warriors should repel them. Harrison, however, decided to fight like a frontiersman. The Kentucky troops were unsuited to conventional tactics. They liked a fight that was hard and plain, with no fancy manoeuvring.

Looking from the woods at the thin line of redcoats, Lieutenant Colonel Johnson suggested that Harrison bring his infantry out in line toward the British while at the last moment he and the mounted Kentucky riflemen would charge from the flank. Nothing stood between his horsemen and the British infantry. Procter had lacked time to construct any abatis or other works. The British, Johnson said, might get off one volley. But that would be all. Harrison thought on it and then agreed.

As the first American skirmishers began to snipe at the British, Procter swung up onto his magnificent charger with his personal staff mounting behind him. Coming on hard were the Kentucky horsemen screaming at the top of their lungs, "Remember the River Raisin!" Thick gunsmoke erupted from the British line, but the horsemen never faltered. A second volley was loosed. Then the Kentuckians were among the British, muskets cracking and swords slashing. Procter and his staff galloped from the field. British soldiers everywhere threw down their guns; the cannon had not been fired.

British finished, Johnson wheeled his horsemen about. Leaving Harrison's infantry to sort out the prisoners and kill any redcoats that offered further resistance, the Kentuckians pushed into the swamp to wipe out Tecumseh's warriors. The heavy musket fire they met soon forced most of them to dismount and take cover. Both sides fought with fierce determination. Whenever the thunder of gunfire abated for a few seconds Tecumseh's voice was heard, rallying his men and urging them to stand firm.

Johnson was equally ferocious, galloping from one hot spot to another, refusing to get off his horse. Four times he was struck by a musket ball but carried on. Then a bullet shattered his left hand, but he killed his assailant with a pistol shot. In the confusion of the battle many thought that the warrior shot was Tecumseh, but no one could prove this afterward. But Tecumseh was dead, and as the life left his body the dreams of the great tribal confederacy he had laboured so long to build died with him. The surviving warriors were in flight, escaping the vengeance of the Kentuckians.[15]

When Tecumseh's body was identified by an American who knew him and by some of the captured British officers, they found he had been wounded repeatedly. Near the heart was a bullet hole probably made by a pistol. Buckshot had struck him in several places. There was a deep cut on his head.

The body was scalped and stripped of clothing by some Kentuckians. Others later slashed pieces of skin from his back and thighs to make razor strops. A rumour was soon born that Henry Clay had proudly displayed one of these souvenirs to some fellow congressmen in Washington.[16]

After darkness a warrior named Black Hawk and several others crept back to recover their leader's body. Having seen Tecumseh die, Black Hawk knew where to look and quickly located the chief "lying where he had first fallen; a bullet had struck above the hip, and his skull had been broken by the butt end of the gun of some soldier, who had found him, perhaps, when his life was not yet quite gone. With exception of these wounds, his body was untouched: lying near him was a large fine looking Potawatomi, who had been killed, decked off in his plumes and war-paint, whom the Americans no doubt had taken for Tecumseh, for he was scalped and every particle of skin flayed from his body. Tecumseh himself had no ornaments about his body, save a British medal. During the night, we buried our dead, and brought off the body of Tecumseh, although we were in sight of the fires of the American camp."[17]

Whether Black Hawk correctly identified Tecumseh's body was uncertain. Over the years there would be many accounts that reputed to accurately describe Tecumseh's death. Of eight accounts given by Indians, four (including Black Hawk's) attested that Tecumseh was killed in the opening volley of the battle. An equal number supported the claim commonly agreed on by the Kentuckians present that Johnson shot him after being wounded by Tecumseh. Complicating matters further, the only American officer who had ever met Tecumseh was Harrison, and he did not visit that part of the battlefield until the following day. Shown the body that had been scalped and flayed, he was unable to confirm its identity. But his observation that it was either Tecumseh or a Potawatomi chief who had always accompanied the confederacy leader during visits to Harrison at Vincennes, lent credence to Black Hawk's account.[18]

Moravian Town had been as disastrous a defeat for the British as it was for the Indian confederacy, but not because of the death of their leader. Twenty-eight officers and 606 men were killed or captured. Harrison counted only 7 men dead and 22 wounded. Nobody knew how many Indians fell, for they carried away all but 33 of their dead and later recovered most of these. Procter gathered his surviving 246 officers and men. Accompanied still by many civilians and about 400 warriors, he led an orderly retreat to the head of Lake Ontario.

Harrison did not pursue. He returned to Detroit, where he discharged the Kentucky Volunteers on October 13. The following day he signed an armistice with some tribal chiefs, taking a number of their women and children hostage to ensure they honoured it. On October 17, the major general issued a proclamation pledging that private property and the security of the settlers would be guaranteed.[19] The same day, he turned command over to Brig. Gen. Lewis Cass and set off to receive due accolades during a triumphal progress via Buffalo, Sackets Harbor, New York City, and Philadelphia to Washington. Crowds turned out by the hundreds to cheer this hero who had given America its first major victory. Armstrong, resenting being upstaged by a subordinate, snubbed the hero by assigning him a modest command at Cincinnati. In a fit of pique, Harrison tendered his resignation in the new year. Armstrong accepted with satisfaction and President James Madison, hesitant to confront his secretary of war, confirmed it.[20]

Procter's career was also destroyed by the Battle of Moravian Town, but for more obvious reasons. For a while he retained command of his troops after reaching Maj. Gen. John Vincent's lines at Burlington Heights. But he was soon ordered back to England to face court martial for his conduct. Reduced in rank, docked six months' pay, and put on the army's unattached list until his retirement, he died nine years after the battle, at Bath, England.[21]

In Kingston, Major General de Rottenburg was initially so alarmed by the defeat that he ordered Vincent to fall back on his position. But learning that Harrison had failed to march on the Niagara Peninsula and Lake Ontario, he ordered Vincent to stay put for the time being. On November 1, he advised Vincent that whether the British continued to defend what remained to them of Upper Canada would depend on the outcome of the American campaign beginning to unfold in the St. Lawrence River region.[22] Vincent acknowledged this instruction but did not go out of his way to report that Colonel Murray was already loose on the peninsula and slowly pushing the Americans out.

When it had become obvious that the Americans planned an offensive against Montreal, Prevost moved his headquarters there and divided his command so that de Rottenburg had authority for Upper Canada while he would concentrate on defending Lower Canada. Given the paucity of regulars, saving Montreal would largely depend on the province's militia, mostly French Canadians. The militia in Lower Canada were quite strong and well organized. Maj. Gen. Roger Sheaffe had earlier called out 3,000 men south of the St. Lawrence and established a main line of resistance along the Châteauguay River. Prevost quickly summoned another 5,000. With him from Kingston was the 1st Light Infantry Battalion, commanded by Lt. Col. "Red" George Macdonell—so named to distinguish him from the scores of other George Macdonells, serving officers or otherwise, to be found in the Canadas.

British army surgeon Dr. William "Tiger" Dunlop, on seeing his first French-Canadian militia, was openly impressed. "They . . . had been pretty well drilled and their arms . . . were in perfectly good order, nor had they the mobbish appearance that such a levy in any other country would have had. Their capots and trowsers of home-spun stuff, and their blue *toques* (night caps) were all of the same cut and color, which gave them an air of uniformity that added much to their military look, for I have always remarked that a body of men's appearance in battalion, depends much less on the fashion of their individual dress and appointments, than on the whole being in strict uniformity.

"They marched merrily to the music of their voyageur songs, and as they perceived our uniform as we came up, they set up the Indian War-whoop, followed by a shout of *Vive le Roi* along the whole line. Such a body of men in such a temper, and with so perfect a use of their arms as all of them possessed, if posted on such ground as would preclude the possibility of regular troops out-manoeuvering them, and such positions are not hard to find in Canada, must have been rather a formidable body to have attacked."[23]

The willingness of Lower Canada's French-Canadian majority to fight for Britain had baffled Americans since the Revolutionary War, when it was expected they would welcome the 1775 invasion of Quebec. After all, were these not the sons and daughters of New France conquered by the British in 1760 and since reduced to a subjugated people? But they failed to grasp that the victorious British had been careful to foster loyalty by allowing the French Canadians to retain their land-ownership system and their Roman Catholic religion, including continuance of the secular role the church played in society. While resentment toward the British for having conquered them might linger, few saw anything in the way the United States had shaped its government and society that made them feel they would be better off under the American flag.

The formidable ability of the French Canadians was quickly made evident on October 25, when Hampton came up against a thin line of about 300 Provincial regulars and militia alongside the Châteauguay. Hampton had finally pushed off from Four Corners on October 21 and crossed the Canadian border. For the past four days he had advanced cautiously and made little more than 40 miles before scouts discovered a defensive line barred the way.

Hampton had 4,000 regulars, 200 dragoons, and ten field guns, so was little concerned. Further reconnaissance confirmed that the defences were held by only 350 men, who appeared to be mostly militia commanded by a militia officer. If a flanking force skirted the right bank of the river and passed the defenders on the opposite shore, they would find a ford that could be waded, effectively turning the militia position. Hampton ordered Col. Robert Purdy to take 1,500 men through the woods under cover of darkness to gain the ford and attack in the morning while Hampton would hit the position head-on with the remainder of his force. It should be easily rolled up.

The Americans had correctly estimated the number of men holding the line, but they were wrong about the identity of its commander and unaware of the presence of reserve forces totalling 980 men and 150 Kahnawake Iroquois warriors. Lt. Col. Charles-Michel d'Irumberry de Salaberry was no militia officer. Just shy of his thirty-fifth birthday, de Salaberry had been born in Lower Canada's Beauport and was commissioned into the British army at the age of sixteen. He served in Ireland and the West Indies and fought Napoleon's armies in the Low Countries before returning to his birth colony in 1810 to become de Rottenburg's aide-de-camp. Short, barrel-chested, powerfully muscled, he was as strict a disciplinarian as Hampton and far more impetuous. "My dear Marquis of cannon powder," de Rottenburg fondly described him. Technically de Salaberry commanded the Canadian Voltigeurs, of which there were 150 in the front line and another 300 back in reserve, but as senior officer the defence was in his hands.[24]

There was nothing about Hampton's force de Salaberry did not know. Scouts had carefully gathered intelligence on them for weeks, slipping across the American border to spy on the Four Corners camp at will. The position chosen for the fight was selected with this intelligence in mind. Reserve positions were established in a series of ravines cut through the sandy soil by creeks flowing into the Châteauguay from the northwest. A mile ahead of the first of these ravines was a 40-foot-deep coulee that extended about 1,000 yards from the river to swampy woods. Here de Salaberry had erected a massive abatis behind which the 350 front-line troops were positioned. The reserve units were divided among four of the ravines at his back, erecting formidable abatis along the edges facing the American line of advance.

Hampton was still preparing his attack on October 25 when a courier arrived with puzzling orders from Armstrong directing him to take his men into winter quarters. What did this mean? Was the invasion called off? Was Wilkinson on the march up the St. Lawrence or not? If he carried on against Montreal would his army be sacrificed? These troubling questions swirled through his mind and there was no immediate answer for them. Hampton would fight on the morrow without knowing whether there was any point to giving battle.[25]

Meanwhile in the inky darkness Colonel Purdy and 1,500 men struggled to pass the Canadian front line by flanking it on the southern bank. They blundered through a dense hemlock swamp, unable either to find a trail to advance by or to locate the ford. Purdy had expected to go nine miles past the defensive work and find the ford there—a total marching distance of about 15 miles. By daylight he was barely abreast of de Salaberry, well away from the riverbank, and completely lost. To this point he had relied on a couple of Canadian scouts who claimed to be deserters but could as well be spies. Purdy had to trust them, for he would never be able to lead his men out of the confused quagmire into which they stumbled. It was impossible to tell north from south, east from west. Trailing the scouts, he struggled onward.

By now it was 2:00 in the afternoon and Hampton's main body, commanded not by the major general but by his second-in-command, Brig. Gen. George Izard, had advanced to face de Salaberry and been waiting impatiently for several hours for Purdy's signal that he had gained the ford. Deciding he could wait no longer, Izard ordered the attack. Seconds later, de Salaberry started the fight by coolly raising a musket to his shoulder and shooting down a mounted American officer. At about the same moment

Purdy suddenly emerged out of the woods directly across from the Canadian position. Jumping onto a stump, which exposed him dangerously to the American fire, de Salaberry shouted encouragement to his men and directed their fire so that they hit the soldiers advancing against their front and also Purdy's men on the opposite shore.

For two hours the gunfire crackled. It took this long for two companies of militia and some light cavalry that de Salaberry had positioned on the opposite bank of the river to guard the very ford that Purdy sought to come forward and attack the American colonel's force. Purdy and his men retreated briskly, abandoning the field. Izard had not been pressing his men forward with any determination, so they were mostly hunkered behind trees and logs sniping at the Canadians without intention to carry the defensive works with a frontal charge. Seeing Purdy's hasty withdrawal and Izard's lackadaisical approach, Hampton lost his resolve and ordered a withdrawal all the way to Four Corners. Purdy, still stuck in swamps and being sniped at the entire way by Indians and militiamen, followed. Hampton's part in the invasion of Canada was over. His army had suffered only 50 casualties in the action. After settling his men into their winter quarters, Hampton tendered his resignation as promised.

The Canadians lost only 5 men killed, 16 wounded, and reported 4 missing in an action that turned back an entire American army. Almost to a man his troops had been Lower Canadians, most of whom were French-speaking. Their colonel knew this was a battle that should not have been so easily won. That evening in a letter written to his father, de Salaberry reported in near wonder, "I have won a victory mounted on a wooden horse."[26]

EIGHTEEN

Under Great Danger

FALL 1813

October 26 found Maj. Gen. James Wilkinson and his 300 supply-laden boats protected by a dozen gunboats trapped on Grenadier Island at the head of the St. Lawrence River by a ferocious storm. Icy rain and screaming winds foretold an early onset of winter. Many of the boats were reduced to so much worthless kindling by pounding waves. Marching along the river's south bank, the thousands of troops, chilled and soaked to the bone, became increasingly despondent. At Ogdensburg they halted to await the boats. Not until November 6 did the weather lift and, under cover of darkness, Wilkinson and the remains of his flotilla quietly drifted past British sentries standing on the ramparts of Fort Wellington.

The only positive development Wilkinson could detect so far was that Armstrong no longer looked directly over his shoulder to counter his every plan with one of his own. Just before Wilkinson boarded one of the scows, the war secretary had announced his intention to return to Albany, where he would await word from both generals as to their progress toward Montreal. "I shall forbear my visit to Canada until a future day," he wrote airily to President Madison.[1]

Having arrived in Albany on November 8 and being entirely out of contact with Wilkinson, he wrote Madison again to say that the general and his 8,000 troops should be well along down the St. Lawrence "and I have no doubt but that by today the army will be near Montreal." As for Hampton's defeat, of which he had just been informed, Armstrong declared that the general had "wisely declined the invitation" to battle.

The following day Armstrong read in a Canadian newspaper that Hampton's 4,000 had been routed by only 460 French Canadians. He dashed off a pre-emptory note to the president explaining Hampton's action as necessitated by his facing a heavily fortified fortress that forced his withdrawal to seek a better route to Montreal. He also thought that Prevost's regulars had bested Hampton at Châteauguay rather than French-Canadian militia—this claim being merely propaganda—and consequently the British commander stood between Hampton and Wilkinson. So positioned, Prevost could be easily dealt with by either army or by both coming together like a hammer striking an anvil with the British smote in the middle.² This was, of course, all prattle. Prevost was in Montreal. Brilliant general he might not be, but neither was Prevost fool enough to allow his forces to be so trapped.

At Ogdensburg, Wilkinson dithered and vacillated. He was sick again, racked by dysentery and quaffing hefty doses of laudanum and whisky. Illness, alcohol, and drugs rendered the general at times incoherent; next moment he became "very merry, and sung, and repeated stories."³ Often he issued orders contradicting those he'd given shortly before.

Before him lay the 8-mile Long Sault rapids, behind a little pack of about 600 British regulars from Kingston commanded by Lt. Col. Joseph W. Morrison of the 89th Regiment of Foot. These soon picked up about 200 or more Canadian Fencibles, Voltigeurs, Indians, and even some gunners from a militia artillery unit who dragged with them a six-pounder field gun. This force nipped at Wilkinson's heels, like some nasty terrier that no amount of rearguard forces could shake off. Should he turn and fight them? Or were they best ignored? A nuisance certainly, but surely not a deadly threat. The rapids were another matter. It would be a trick getting all the boats down safely, impossible if the British manned their side of the river. To guard against that he had to put soldiers over there.

As reported by scouts who had interrogated local farmers, what lay ahead was fearful. Endless savage rapids went all the way to Montreal, batteries of cannon covered every narrows, packs of bloodthirsty Indians lurked in the woods, 5,000 redcoats and 20,000 militia blocked the way. There were also troubling reports that Morrison's small force would soon be reinforced by gunboats commanded by Capt. William Howe Mulcaster, the British second-in-command of the Lake Ontario fleet. On board the vessels were 1,500 regulars from Kingston. If that proved true, where would Wilkinson be?

Wilkinson wanted most to turn around and retreat to Sackets Harbor, return to a warm bed and a toasty fire, settle in for the winter. He had no faith in this venture, could not possibly see how they were to get to Montréal. Having received orders about setting up winter quarters, Wilkinson doubted Armstrong seriously thought the operation would succeed. Of Hampton there was no word. Had he crossed the border? Was he even now closing on Montreal?

Unable to come to any decision, wishing to pass responsibility to others, Wilkinson convened a council of war on the night of November 7. Propped up in his bed, he outlined his many concerns. Wilkinson asked his six most senior officers to vote on whether to proceed or turn back. To his dismay, four voted to continue, more to preserve honour than from expectation of success. Gloomily, Wilkinson commented, "we proceed from this place under great danger . . . we know of no other alternative."[4]

To cover the movement down the rapids, Wilkinson deployed Brig. Gen. Jacob Brown's brigade of 2,500 along with some artillery and dragoons to join a detachment of 1,200 sent earlier to the Canadian shore. Rain and sleet fell in unrelenting sheets. Canadian militia sniped at the columns from woods and melted away before American skirmishers could respond. To Wilkinson's horror, a couple of gunboats closed on the rear of his flotilla and brought it under fire. Although they caused no damage, the general realized that Mulcaster had caught up. Had he landed more troops? The threat to his rear was too serious to ignore. Late on the evening of November 10, Wilkinson sighted the head of the rapids. On the Canadian shore, Brown worried over the slow pace, 80 miles in eight days. His men were drenched, freezing, and already exhausted. He boarded Wilkinson's cramped passage boat to hurry things along. The general was too ill to see him, issuing written instruction "from my bed." The flotilla would enter the dangerous rapids in the morning. Brown was to cover the move. But Brig. Gen. John Parker Boyd would put 2,000 regulars across the river and clear the British from off his tail.

Morrison, meanwhile, passed the night in the spacious comfort of John Crysler's farmhouse hard by the river and King's Highway that ran from Kingston to Montreal while his men huddled under whatever shelter they could find. A good night's rest gave the fifty-year-old officer heart. Half his life had been spent as a soldier. Morrison had marched to battle in Holland, the Caribbean, and now Canada. This was his first time at the head of a battalion-sized unit, though, and every moment passed added confidence. Just after dawn, Morrison was considering whether it was likely they would fight today or continue the wearying pursuit when his scouts reported the Americans approaching.

Although they were soon revealed as only a small reconnaissance party, Morrison decided to deploy for battle. If the Americans came in force he would be outnumbered, so best use the ground to advantage. On his right lay the river with Mulcaster's gunboats just behind the front line, to his left a dense wood of black ash grew out of swampy ground. A rutted track from the farmhouses to the forest was at his back. A stout fence built of cedar logs paralleled the track and presented a formidable wall behind which his men faced east toward the Americans. In that direction a half-mile of open field extended to a ravine cut by a small stream that stretched from the woods to the river. Half of the muddy field closest to the British sprouted winter wheat while the rest was ploughed. Two small gullies thrust westward like crooking fingers into the field from the river's edge but petered out a third of the way to the woods.

Morrison had 600 regulars of the 49th and 89th regiments behind the fenceline, with the 89th standing closest to the woods. Between the two gullies, by the King's Highway, 240 men commanded by Lt. Col. Thomas Pearson were positioned. This was a mixed force of two companies of the 49th, three companies of Canadian Voltigeurs, a detachment of Canadian Fencibles, and the score of militia gunners who served the six-pounder gun. Out as far as the ravine more Voltigeurs and some Indian warriors formed a thin skirmish line. They were not to stand and fight. Rather, Morrison's instruction to the skirmishers was that they draw the Americans toward his centre by luring them into a running fight.[5]

It was not until two that wet, dreary Thursday afternoon that the Voltigeurs—almost invisible in a grey light coloured much like their uniforms—spotted advancing infantry. When the Americans were in range the Voltigeurs popped up from behind shrubs and out of folds in the ground to loose a light volley of balls. Quickly another volley followed and then the men fired at will. The Americans hesitated, those in the lead turning to withdraw, those behind pressing forward. Officers shouted, the line stiffened, came on. The Canadian skirmishers gave ground quickly, pausing to fire, reloading on the run at times, turning again to fire, until they were back inside the British lines.

The Americans put a brace of cannon close by the river so that they could pound Pearson's men, knock out the little six-pounder, and force this forward group back. Boyd then massed his infantry by brigades into three columns about 250 feet apart with the leftward column following a line that would turn Pearson's flank. Each column moved toward Morrison's regulars at the fence, coming on in a deep, closely grouped formation with one line of men treading closely behind the next. This was a formation favoured by Napoleon's Grande Armée, one that required great discipline and fearlessness under fire. Stumbling through the mud, it was also hard for each man to maintain his interval.

And then Morrison's regulars opened fire with a continuous rain of volleys, while Pearson's men opened from closer range. The Americans pushed into the hail of balls until they were almost parallel with the first gully, close to Pearson's flank, but then halted and each column widened out. Standing in the field, the Americans returned the British volleys with their own. The cannon were dragged up alongside the column closest to the river and the Americans engaged the six-pounder at a range of less than 1,000 feet.

Boyd, realizing his infantry could not gain the British main line unaided, ordered Brig. Gen. Robert Swartwout's brigade to cut alongside the edge of the woods and turn the flank of the regulars holding the fenceline. Once in the British rear the column would roll the redcoats up by driving them toward the river.

Morrison realized the threat Swartwout posed the moment he appeared. Remain as he was and the battle would be lost. But the regulars were well trained and the battle being fought was one that allowed for parade-ground manoeuvres. He ordered the 89th to wheel a full 90 degrees to meet the threat. Officers and sergeants barked commands and each company in unison stepped crisply back from the fence, the man closest to the wood becoming a virtual pivot point, the rest moving like an opening door until they faced north rather than east. It all happened quickly. Suddenly a line of men in long scarlet coats massed before the advancing Americans where none had previously been. Then the British muskets fired and Swartwout's advance collapsed, the soldiers reeling back across the field.

Meanwhile, two companies of the 49th charged from Pearson's position toward the closest cannon. Momentarily checked by a cavalry counter-charge, they soon drove the horsemen off and seized the gun. It was a few minutes past four, the battle two hours old. And the Americans abandoned the field. The Battle of Crysler's Farm cost Morrison dearly: 22 dead, 148 wounded, 9 missing. But he had held the field, and strewn in the mud were the bodies of 102 Americans. Another 237 had been wounded. The British rounded up more than 100 prisoners.[6]

Downriver from Crysler's farm Major General Wilkinson received Boyd's report grimly. How could he continue toward Montreal after this? How could he not? The advance had gone well enough this day. They were positioned to shoot the Long Sault Rapids in the morning. But there was this defeat, and the sure knowledge that Morrison's pursuit would continue. Through the night he brooded.

At dawn, the American boats easily shot the rapids. On the other side, Wilkinson learned of Hampton's whereabouts. Earlier, Wilkinson, asserting his position as commander of the whole northern army, had imperiously ordered Hampton and his army to rendezvous with him at St. Regis, on the south bank of the St. Lawrence across from Cornwall. Having passed through the rapids, Wilkinson could easily reach St. Regis the following day. Hampton's message was brief. Hampton would not come; his army was taking its winter quarters. Relief mixed with indignation at this blatant disobedience. Wilkinson's breathless response, copied to Armstrong, sought to shift to Hampton blame for abandoning the Montreal offensive. Such lack of "resolution defeats the grand objects of the campaign in this quarter, which, before the receipt of your letter, were thought to be completely within our power, no suspicion being entertained that you would decline the junction directed."[7] Abandoning most of his boats, Wilkinson crossed the American border and established winter quarters at French Mills on the Salmon River. There would be no further American offensive action in 1813.

But there would be another defeat. On the Niagara Peninsula, Brig. Gen. George McClure's New York militia were increasingly hard pressed by the little 8th Regiment detachment led by Col. John Murray. Less interested in fighting than looting, the militiamen who had not yet marched homeward were increasingly on edge. Murray's men seemed to crop up anywhere at any time. McClure decided he had too few men to hold the Canadian side of the river, but he was loath to just hand everything back to the British. So on his own initiative—but claiming a letter from Armstrong had authorized him to destroy Niagara, if necessary— he decided to burn the peninsula's main community. On December 10, he informed its inhabitants that their town was to be torched. Everyone was stunned. For the most part the townspeople, with a fort on either side of them, had meticulously striven to offend neither the British nor the Americans. It was obvious that they could easily be on one side of the front lines or another at almost any moment.

Niagara was a pleasant, prosperous town of more than 300 buildings. It was the peninsula's commercial and government centre, with a public library and two churches. No appeal to reason could sway McClure's resolve, but he also left the dirty work to Joseph Willcocks and his Canadian irregulars. While McClure abandoned Fort George in favour of Fort Niagara across the river, Willcocks's men kindled fires among the houses. At least 130 buildings were destroyed and almost 400 hundred residents, mostly women and children, were "exposed to all the severities of deep snow and a frosty sky, almost in a state of nakedness," as one shocked New York newspaper editor put it. "How many perished by the inclemency of the weather, it is, at present, impossible to ascertain."

In Upper Canada news of Niagara's burning caused immediate demands for reprisal. Colonel Murray was instructed to take Fort Niagara and exact revenge on the Americans. On the night of December 18, Murray led 500 men in a swift attack. With scaling ladders and axes the men climbed or hacked their way through the walls. Completely surprised, the Americans were quickly overwhelmed. At a cost of 6 killed and 5 wounded, Fort Niagara was taken. Only 20 Americans escaped. The remaining 422 officers and men were either killed or captured, but McClure escaped.

The capture of Fort Niagara failed to quell the Upper Canadian desire for vengeance. Buffalo, Black Rock, and Lewiston were all carried by British raiders and torched. In every case most of the inhabitants of these communities had fled before the soldiers arrived, and McClure's militia made only a token attempt at defence. By year's end the entire Niagara frontier on the American side was a scene of desolation. Everyone involved in the December fighting there noted that the war had taken on a new shape. Scalping was common, private property looted without regard to the hardship its loss might cause civilians, buildings similarly burned. There were fewer prisoners. Soldiers, militiamen, and Indians fought to the death. The manner in which the fighting of 1813 closed portended the way of the war in the year to follow.[8]

In Washington consternation greeted the failure of the campaign against Montreal. Presiding over the second session of the Thirteenth Congress, Henry Clay bemoaned that he had been "waiting to bear . . . the tidings of the reduction of Montreal. That event was wanted to enable the President to give to his message a finishing stroke, & why it was not permitted to him to announce it I confess has not been satisfactorily explained."[9] There was no end of unconvincing excuses offered by the principals involved. Secretary of War Armstrong and Generals Wilkinson and Hampton blamed each other, with Hampton hung out to dry by the others. His earlier resignation rendered Hampton almost powerless to fight back. Although Wilkinson's competency was publicly questioned, he retained command. Both he and Armstrong guaranteed the next campaign would prove more successful.[10]

Lack of military success made an unpopular war more so, a fact reflected by the fall elections. While the Republicans won the lower houses in the state legislatures of Maryland and Vermont, the Federalists gained control of both senates. Vermont's new governor,

Martin Chittenden, recalled the state militia from Canadian frontier service, effectively removing it from the war.[11]

On the international front there was nothing to suggest that the British were inclined by events to seek negotiation. Over three days in October an allied Austrian, Russian, Prussian, and Swedish army of 320,000 had mauled Napoleon's 185,000 troops near Leipzig in Saxony. The French lost 68,000 men and with them control of any lands east of the Rhine. Napoleon's continental empire was torn asunder.

Tsar Alexander I had been in the field with his army during those fateful days, bent on bringing Napoleon down. So preoccupied, he gradually became less concerned with playing mediator. Inside his court, the influence of the mediation proposal's architect, Count Rumyantsev, waned while that of competitor Count Vasilievich Nesselrode rose. The latter sought good relations with Britain and saw no coin to be gained from facilitating negotiations.

When Albert Gallatin and James Bayard concluded their long voyage by arriving at St. Petersburg on July 21, they had learned that the British government was "discouraging arbitration altogether." Gallatin confided to his son James, the "English Government resent the offer of mediation." He feared "the President was a little hasty in sending the mission." On July 29, young Gallatin lamented: "Our position is a very embarrassing one. We plainly see we are not wanted."[12]

Hoping to revive the mediation offer and regain his status at court by doing so, Rumyantsev was at pains to make the newcomers feel welcome. At endless banquets they were fêted by high society and spent long days touring the city's grand sights. Rendered ill by the local water, Bayard alternately gushed about all he saw and experienced or longed for home—mood dependent on the ebb and flow of bowels.

On August 1, Gallatin and Bayard met with Rumyantsev. Adams was not invited, an oversight that irritated him. He did not feel treated as a colleague in the negotiations. The British, the count told them, considered "the pretensions of the U[nited] States were of such a nature that the intervention of a third Power however friendly to both Parties must necessarily fail of a successful issue." Impressment remained the irresolvable issue, but Rumyantsev still believed that mediation could bear fruit. After all, the Americans were here, empowered to negotiate, and there was nothing unequivocal about the British position. It was worth renewing the offer.[13] Not knowing what other course to take, the Americans agreed.

Rumyantsev had not been honest. Lord Cathcart, Britain's Russian minister, had emphatically rejected the proposal in a July 6 letter to Alexander.[14] In conversation with the tsar, Cathcart added that cabinet had twice considered Russia's mediation offer, unanimously rejecting it each time. There was no future in the proposal. But the count refused to give up, and to keep the Americans in the game he held back the fact that Cathcart had indicated that if they were willing to negotiate directly with a British peace commission then Viscount Castlereagh would approve this course.

Independently Gallatin had concluded that direct negotiation was the only path to peace. He wanted to go directly to London and ask Castlereagh to negotiate. Privately he opened a line of communication through Alexander Baring, the London banker who handled the U.S. government's accounts in Europe (and viewed the fact that his nation was at war with a favoured client with dismay), to test the waters. Baring had tried earlier to get Castlereagh to accept Russia's mediation offer, without success. Such a process, the foreign secretary declared, would enable America "to mix directly or indirectly her maritime interests with those of another state."[15]

Knowing that Gallatin was considering either coming to England or returning to the United States, Baring argued that if America's negotiators were "desirous of endeavouring, by mutual explanation and concession, to consult the security and apprehension of both countries," such an approach would "find a corresponding disposition here" that led him to "anticipate every reasonable degree of success from the joint efforts of yourselves and those persons whom our government will be prepared to appoint to meet you." Baring urged Gallatin "not to return to America without at least making an experiment in the manner most likely to lead to success."[16]

Not dissuading Rumyantsev from further Russian overtures, Gallatin advanced the discussion with Castlereagh through Baring.

While ostensibly the letters exchanged were purely private correspondence, the British banker's thoughts seemed at times to come almost directly from Castlereagh's hand. Gallatin's were more formal, a result of being drafted in committee by the three Americans. The first hurdle Gallatin raised was that the three Americans were empowered by their government only to participate in mediation. Direct negotiation had not been authorized. For this reason alone mediation might be the best course.

While raising this problem with Baring, Gallatin began the laborious process of trying to get the commission's powers expanded to include direct negotiation. Though it would be months before a response arrived from Washington, he set the wheels in motion for the president to expand their role by reporting Baring's approach to Secretary of State James Monroe. If mediation was bluntly refused or accepted, he said, the envoys would either return home or enter into mediation. But what if the British response was ambiguous? "It is for the President to decide what should be done in that case," Gallatin decided.[17]

Summer drained away into autumn and the fitful correspondence between Baring and Gallatin continued while no decision was forthcoming from London on the mediation proposal. In fact, Prime Minister Liverpool's cabinet considered the renewed offer in mid-October and again rejected it. Baring hinted at the finality of this decision in an October 12 letter. This time the language of the letter sounded even more like Castlereagh. "We wish for peace. The pressure of the war upon our commerce and manufactures is over; they have ample relief in other quarters; and, indeed the dependence of the two countries on each other was, as it usually is, overrated. But the war has no object; it is expensive, and we want to carry our efforts elsewhere. Our desire of peace, therefore, cannot be doubted and you can rely on it." A possible resolution to the maritime issue was proposed without setting out specifics, but if Gallatin considered the commissioners empowered to negotiate directly, Baring wrote, "I think you would soon complete the work of peace without the help or hindrance of any mediator."[18]

That decided Gallatin. Summoning private secretary George Dallas on October 18, Gallatin told him to pack his bags and leave that very day for London. Once there he was to discreetly, through Baring and the Russian ambassador Count Lieven, determine whether either direct negotiation or mediation was remotely possible.

Gallatin wanted to go himself, but could not without the president's blessing—something he hoped to attain once his letter to Monroe reached Washington. But the day after Dallas left St. Petersburg came news from Monroe that struck Gallatin like "a thunderclap. Letters from Washington; one announcing officially that the Senate had rejected father's nomination as head of the Commission by one vote," young James Gallatin scribbled in his diary.[19] A distraught Rumyantsev begged Gallatin to remain in St. Petersburg. Surely the American Senate would reverse this inane decision. Gallatin considered rushing home to confront his political enemies, but confessed more to being "strongly impressed with the idea that he ought to resume the negotiations."[20] Peace was what America needed most; was it not his duty to try to achieve that?

On the last day of October further bad news arrived in the form of Lord Walpole, the new British ambassador to Russia. Ignorant and coarse, Walpole told the Americans "he never heard from his government, he never wrote to them, he never read newspapers excepting articles about murders, could not bear to look at births or marriages, he never wore boots, never walked, hated music and dancing."[21] And, by the by, the cabinet had scotched any idea of mediation. They should not be further misled by Rumyantsev's "intrigues."

The count must have already known the news, for only the day before he had told Gallatin that once the American mission to St. Petersburg was closed it was his intention to retire from office. November 1 brought ice to the Neva River, precluding any chance of leaving Russia by sea. The weeks dragged by, snow lay thick upon the land, and no further news reached the Americans in St. Petersburg. Tsar Alexander seemed to have forgotten them, not notifying them whether the mediation offer was withdrawn or to be renewed. Gallatin finally decided there was no further point in waiting. On January 12, he informed Rumyantsev that he and Bayard were leaving St. Petersburg. Adams would remain, continuing to represent America in the Russian court.

Two weeks later the two envoys and their secretaries climbed into horse-drawn sledges and set out on a long journey to Amsterdam. There they would await word from Washington on whether to try negotiating directly with the British. The journey took two months. March 5 brought them to Amsterdam, where James Gallatin—having abandoned his diary entirely during the long trip—entered a single sentence. "After a terrible, cold, and weary journey we arrived here last night."[22]

Part Four

—

QUEST FOR A JUST PEACE

NINETEEN

Destitute of Military Fire

The correspondence between Albert Gallatin and Alexander Baring encouraged Castlereagh to approach James Monroe with an offer of direct negotiations. His letter, written on November 4, 1813, was carried to America by the British schooner *Bramble*. After its arrival under flag of truce at Annapolis on December 30, a courier galloped through the dark night and placed the message in Monroe's hands just as the clock struck midnight.

"To avoid an unnecessary continuance of the calamities of war ... I can assure you that the British government is willing to enter into discussion with the Government of America for the conciliatory adjustment of the differences subsisting between the two States, with an earnest desire on their part to bring them to a favourable issue, upon principles of perfect reciprocity, not inconsistent with the established maxims of public law, and with the maritime rights of the British empire," Castlereagh wrote. He guaranteed for the American commissioners safe passage to wherever in Europe was agreed for the talks.[1]

While maintaining the impression that the United States remained determined to continue the war, Monroe and President James Madison leapt at the offer. On January 5, the secretary of state sent a reply back to London on *Bramble*. Although he regretted Britain's refusal of mediation through Tsar Alexander, Monroe imagined that the Russian emperor would recognize that direct negotiation "affords the best prospect of attaining speedily what was the object of his interposition. I am accordingly instructed to make known to your lordship . . . that the President accedes to his proposition." Madison suggested Gothenburg, Sweden, thinking the Swedish king would "readily acquiesce in the choice of a place for their pacific negotiations within his dominions."[2]

Madison reported the news to Congress on January 7, 1814, and forwarded for Senate approval John Quincy Adams, James Bayard, Henry Clay, and Jonathan Russell as envoys. Under the mistaken impression that Albert Gallatin was somewhere on the high seas bound for home, Madison did not advance his name. Instead, Adams was proposed as the commission's chairman. Gallatin was added to the list on February 8, but Adams retained the chair. Madison emphasized that Gallatin would not continue as secretary of the treasury. Mollified, the Senate endorsed his appointment the next day. The appointment of Adams and Bayard passed unopposed. Clay's nomination alarmed Federalists, who thought the congressional Speaker too fervent in his desire to annex Canada, and that insistence on this point would defeat the negotiations. Bayard, however, was presented as sufficient counterweight to keep the commission balanced toward a spirit of compromise. Because Russell's appointment was once again tied to his also being America's minister to Sweden, it initially met Senate resistance. In the end, the Senate capitulated because the discussions were likely to occur in that country, making a diplomatic presence there necessary. Russell's approval squeaked through.[3]

Federalist concerns over Clay were valid. Support for the Kentuckian in Republican and western circles was anchored on the certainty that he would never sign any treaty that failed to uphold American honour or prohibited Canada's annexation. Although there remained almost no support for the war in New England, in the west the war's purpose was perceived as necessary to end British influence over the Indians—considered the only cause of their uprisings against American settlers. This meant that Canada must be taken.

While the Federalists correctly divined the mood of the western frontier, they misjudged Clay's commitment to peace. Having brought about the war, he now equally and without apology was determined to hold centre stage in negotiating an armistice that achieved the goals for which so much blood had been spilled. The ink was barely dry on the papers confirming the appointments than Clay departed for New York City to hasten across the sea to begin proceedings.

Clay wrote Monroe from a New York hotel on February 13 to express his "satisfaction that . . . our mission has acquired the benefit of Mr. Gallatin's services, tho' I confess I am sometimes afraid that we shall find neither him nor Bayard at Gothenburg."[4] The possibility that Gallatin and Bayard might pass the ship bearing Clay and Russell to Europe was an anxiety for Clay and Madison's executive. It was imperative that the Europe-bound Americans reach their destination with news of the reconstituted commission before the other two abandoned hope and caught a ship homeward.

The corvette *John Adams* stood in harbour, its captain had in hand a safe-passage passport from Vice-Admiral Sir Alexander Cochrane, Clay was present with bags packed. But there was no word of Russell. By the 18th, Monroe instructed Clay to sail alone if Russell had not appeared by the time his letter was received. Clay stalled, and finally reported on February 23 that Russell had arrived. The ship would sail later that day.[5] It would, however, take until April 13 for *John Adams* to reach Gothenburg.

While hoping that negotiations would bear fruit, Madison positioned the government in an awkward middle ground aimed at preventing the deep schisms that existed over the war from crippling the nation. The war would continue, he assured the House and the Senate, while at the same time the effort to negotiate a peace treaty would receive equal attention. He therefore rejected calls from the seaboard states to suspend further military action pending outcome of the talks. Yet his vision of waging the war was judged insufficiently fervent by John Armstrong. Under increasing criticism for the failures of 1813, Armstrong demanded a vast increase in forces dedicated to conquering Canada: expanded fleets on Lake Ontario and Lake Champlain, the launching of vessels on the St. Lawrence River to gain control of Lake St. Francis, 55,000 men added to the army through classification whereby the nation was divided into sections with each required to provide a specific number for military service.

The army faced a manpower crisis. Most five-year enlistments would expire in a few months, as would the twelve- and eighteen-month enlistments of men who had joined in 1812 or 1813. This convinced Armstrong of the necessity for classification, but the plan was little more than thinly veiled conscription—something akin to slavery to average Americans. Faced with congressional opposition, Armstrong compromised: introduce classification or offer increased premium payments to those who enlisted. One way or the other, the army must be stronger to conquer Canada in 1814.

The fact the British had laid waste to the Niagara River country in December added urgency to Armstrong's calls for an all-out campaign against Canada. But the devastation in this area also hobbled his efforts, for the Republican majority insisted that regaining control of the Niagara Peninsula must be the priority. This left Armstrong precisely where he had been in 1812 and 1813, waging a war of limited strategic value in western Upper Canada. Kingston, Montreal, and Quebec City were where British power was concentrated, yet there was little support for concerted efforts against these objectives.

Wherever the army marched it would not do so under Maj. Gen. James Wilkinson. Early in the new year, the old general had requested a court of inquiry into his conduct of the 1813 campaign—a request granted by Armstrong on March 24. By then, however, he had presided over another defeat. In mid-March, Wilkinson had led 4,000 men north from Champlain into Lower Canada. Within a week, the Americans met 180 Canadian militia, redcoats, and Royal Marines barricaded inside a stone mill on the Lacolle River. A fitful siege brought the defenders perilously close to exhausting their ammunition, but Wilkinson's nerve again deserted him. Retreating across the border, Wilkinson left for Washington to face his critics.[6] Declaring that he would submit only to the judgment of a court of senior generals—none of whom could be spared from active duty—Wilkinson was placed on the unassigned list, never again to hold command.[7]

That suited Armstrong, left free to promote younger officers and to pursue his personal ambition to be appointed lieutenant general and the nation's highest-ranking officer. Standing in the way of the latter ambition because of seniority issues were just two officers—Maj. Gen. Andrew Jackson and Brig. Gen. Jacob Brown. The former was engaged in a brutal Indian war on the Tennessee frontier, while the latter had arrived at Sackets Harbor on February 24 with 2,000 men and authority to lead the forthcoming spring campaign against Upper Canada. A regular army officer, Brown was a logical choice for promotion to major general. Despite an erratic and cruel disposition when it came to Indians, Jackson had personally led Tennessee militia and volunteers to quell the 1813 Tecumseh-inspired Creek uprising in Alabama and Florida. On March 27, the final stage of this brutal war, in which neither side showed the other mercy, concluded when Jackson led about 2,000 men against some 900 Creek warriors and 300 women and children sheltered in a fortified position on the Tallapoosa River. By sunset, 700 of the warriors and many of the women and children were dead.[8] The victory freed Jackson for service in the north, and Armstrong could easily have converted his militia rank into a regular army commission.

Jackson's immense popularity in Tennessee held no coin in Washington. Although Republican to the core, Jackson had ensured his unpopularity by denouncing President Jefferson's administration and backing Monroe over Madison for the presidency. Armstrong was determined to prevent the man's rise. But Madison was equally intent on thwarting Armstrong's ambition to gain overall command of the army. So he nominated Brown for promotion to major general, and Congress readily agreed.

Armstrong did breathe new life into the flagging army by promoting six young colonels—among them Winfield Scott—assuring the troops marched to battle behind more competent officers than before. But better officers could little offset the fact that Madison's executive lacked a viable strategic plan for the 1814 campaign.

Madison was lukewarm to major offensive operations. With negotiations about to begin, he preferred a defensive war over one of conquest. This put him at odds with Armstrong, also engaged in a bitter dogfight with Monroe for executive dominance. Yet Madison refused to fire Armstrong, as advocated by his secretary of state.

In the end, Congress scuttled Armstrong's grand campaign by rejecting the classification scheme and merely increasing the bounty paid for men willing to enlist for five years or the war's duration. Existing regular army troops were automatically re-enlisted until the war ended.

Congress also failed to finance the war, projected at $45.3 million in 1814. William Jones, serving as secretary of both the navy and treasury, estimated a $29.3-million shortfall. Yet, after three weeks' debate, Congress authorized borrowing only $25 million, the consensus being that raising such a sum clearly exceeded the government's credit. Despondent, Jones asked to resign the treasury. Madison soon consented, appointing Tennessee senator George Washington Campbell— providing Federalists opportunity to coin a new jeer hinged on his initials, GWC. "Government Wants Cash!" cried Massachusetts congressman Samuel Taggart. Campbell brought no real qualifications to the job and lacked any clout with the New England bankers who were the essential lenders upon whom the government depended. In the absence of any fiscal policy, the treasury limped from one short-term loan to another, never assured that the next infusion of cash would be forthcoming.[9]

On the military front, gaining any ground in Canada seemed doubtful. The better hope was that the navy might achieve some victories at sea, but even there prospects looked bleak. Only a successful negotiation could retrieve the nation's fortunes, so the peace talks were the most critical component of the government's 1814 strategy. Madison's commissioners must secure for America what her army and navy could not win by battle.[10]

At no point had the prospect for defending Canada looked brighter, yet neither the victories won the previous fall nor reinforcements received from Britain, nor assurances from Lord Bathurst and Henry Goulburn at the War and Colonial Office in London that more men and supplies were to be provided, brightened Sir George Prevost's gloomy countenance. On January 14, he had written Bathurst that experience "has taught me that reinforcement even by the most direct route to this Country cannot arrive in time to give a decided Character to the Campaign, as inevitably the principal events must have occurred before they can ascend the St. Lawrence to their destination." While the number of British regulars and Canadian Voltigeurs available were reported at 900 officers and about 15,000 other ranks, many were sick or recovering from wounds.[11] All had been exhausted by the 1813 campaign. Not even the rapid development of events in Europe could boost his spirits.

Following Napoleon's defeat at Leipzig in October, the French Empire had simply collapsed. Napoleon had fled into France with an army led by Tsar Alexander I hot in pursuit while the Duke of Wellington broke the French in Spain and chased them across the Pyrenees to occupy Toulouse. On March 31, Russian, Prussian, and Swedish troops marched triumphant into Paris. Six days later, Napoleon abdicated and accepted exile to Elba, an island off the western coast of Tuscany. After more than ten years of war, Europe was at peace. And Britain was free to unleash its military juggernaut against the United States.

That might was formidable. The army and Royal Navy had more than a million men in service. While anxious to stem the drain war had imposed on the treasury by discharging most of this strength, Lord Liverpool's cabinet was determined to give Prevost sufficient means to not only defend Canada but assume the offensive. "It is the wish of His Majesty's Government to press the war with all possible vigour up to the moment when Peace shall be finally concluded," Bathurst informed Prevost.[12] Within a week of Napoleon's abdication, Wellington received instructions to ready 13,000 Peninsular Army troops for redeployment to Canada. By early May, London's *Morning Chronicle* crowed, the Americans must soon face the *"elite of the army."*[13]

The British government intended to settle the matter of mastery of the Great Lakes, control of which Bathurst and Goulburn considered essential to securing Canada from further invasion. Ill-pleased with Admiral John Warren's performance, the Admiralty had eased him out of command early in the year. His replacement, fifty-five-year-old Vice-Admiral Sir Alexander Cochrane, had taken up his duties at Halifax Station on April 1. Whereas Warren, like Prevost, had favoured defensive strategies that verged on inaction, Cochrane promised to take the war to the enemy. "I have it much at heart," he informed Bathurst, "to give them a complete drubbing before peace is made, when I trust their northern limits will be circumscribed and the command of the Mississippi wrested from them."[14]

Cochrane had fought America during the Revolution, and little regarded its citizens or its institutions. He particularly disliked slavery and believed that many of the teeming thousands toiling on southern plantations would welcome an opportunity to escape aboard British ships and to fight their former masters. Certain that by genetic disposition all slaves were natural horsemen, Cochrane envisioned a large force of cavalry that would "be as good Cossacks as any in the Russian army, and more terrific to the Americans than any troops that can be brought forward."[15] Accordingly, he spent his second day on the job writing a proclamation that slaves would be welcomed aboard Royal Navy ships and could choose between "entering into His Majesty's sea or land forces, or of being sent as FREE settlers, to the British possessions in North America or the West Indies."[16] Throughout 1814 many slaves did manage to reach the safety of British ships and most were transferred to Nova Scotia, much to the alarm of southern plantation owners.

Cochrane knew, however, that while encouraging the flight of slaves might alarm plantation owners, it would discomfit few other Americans. Some, mostly northerners, would even welcome this potential weakening of the "peculiar institution." Cochrane wanted to cripple America so badly that its citizens would demand peace on whatever terms Britain cared to insist. To that end, on April 25, he ordered the entire U.S. coastline blockaded. This brought to an abrupt end the cozy arrangement that spared northern ports from the blockade imposed on ports to the south in order to allow export from New England of trade goods needed by the British. "I have stationed off the said Ports and Places," Cochrane declared, "a Naval Force adequate to maintain the said Blockade in the most rigorous and effective manner."[17]

British ships seemed to be everywhere along the American coast. "With ceaseless vigilance they traversed continually the allotted cruising grounds, capturing the privateers, harrying the coasters, and keeping the more powerful ships confined to port; no American frigate could proceed singly to sea without imminent risk of being crushed by the superior force of the numerous British squadrons," observed one commentator.[18]

Niles' Weekly Register complained: "The eastern coast is much vexed by the enemy. Having destroyed a great portion of the coasting craft, they seem determined to enter the little outports and villages, and burn everything that floats."[19] While coastal commerce was seriously disrupted, the blockade was less effective in bottling up the small sloops-of-war. Many managed to escape, usually under cover of night during heavy storms, to stalk British merchantmen on the high seas. Knowing it would be futile to try sailing prize-ships past the blockades into American ports, the U.S. naval commanders and privateers looted what they could from the cargoes and burned the ships. In the words of one naval expert: "Damage done and consternation caused were very great."[20] Despite these successes, the fact remained that the U.S. Navy was too small and too outgunned on the American coast to tip the scales in its favour. In 1814 the British had undisputed naval supremacy at sea.

Cochrane also tried to ensure supremacy on the Great Lakes, capitalizing on steps taken by Warren and Bathurst during the winter. In January, the Admiralty had agreed to assume complete responsibility for naval operations on the lakes. Earlier, Bathurst had sent 300 sailors from England and ordered Warren to match this force with seamen from Halifax. Those from Britain reached Quebec in November while the Halifax detachment, consisting of two battalions of marines, two companies of marine artillery, and a company of rocketeers, had arrived a few weeks earlier. In December, 250 seamen were sent overland from Halifax to help crew two new frigates being built at Kingston, the 58-gun *Prince Regent* and the 43-gun *Princess Charlotte*. Combined with the six vessels already afloat, of which the largest was the 23-gun *Wolfe*, Yeo believed he could gain mastery of Lake Ontario.

The Admiralty provided Yeo with even more resources in March, sending a convoy of 600 sailors and dockyard workers. In the holds were four prefabricated warships, complete with all fittings and armaments, to be assembled at Kingston. Although these ships-in-frame reached Quebec in April, they were delayed there by Prevost's inability to spare the men and resources to move them farther west. While the men went on to Kingston, the ships languished in their crates until July, when he was finally able to persuade a private contractor to deliver one of them. The delay meant the boat would not be ready for action until December 1814.[21]

But the increased manpower enabled Yeo's completion of the two frigates. And, as soon as they cleared the dockyard in mid-April, work began on a larger ship of the line that would mount 102 guns.[22]

Although aware of the great activity under way at Kingston, Yeo's nemesis, Commodore Isaac Chauncey at Sackets Harbor, had been slow to start new construction during the winter and had only two 22-gun brigs, *Jefferson* and *Jones*, laid down by February. Construction then began on the frigate *Superior*, initially fitted with 62 guns until Chauncey ordered four removed in August in a curious challenge to Yeo to give battle on the grounds that the ship no longer was superior in firepower to anything the British had on the lake.

Despite the British shipbuilding efforts, by May they still remained at a slight disadvantage in overall strength on Lake Ontario. Yeo had 1,517 men and eight warships with guns capable of combined weight of broadside firepower of 2,752 pounds of metal. Chauncey mustered eight ships capable of delivering broadsides weighing 4,188 pounds, and 2,321 men.[23]

But Yeo's ships were ready sooner and he decided to commit them to action in a joint operation with the new army commander and administrator of Upper Canada, Lt. Gen. Sir Gordon Drummond, before the Americans could venture out. Having come from Britain to relieve Maj. Gen. Francis de Rottenburg, Drummond was no stranger to Canada. Born and raised in New Brunswick, he had been posted to Canada from 1808 to 1811 while a major general. A soldier since age seventeen, Drummond had rocketed up through the ranks from lieutenant to colonel in his first three years of service. The forty-one-year-old officer was a stern, handsome man who had fought battles in the Netherlands, West Indies, and Egypt and since 1811 had commanded the troops garrisoning southern Ireland. But he was no firebrand, and one leading Upper Canadian suspected that he was "destitute of that military fire and vigour of decision which the principal commander of this country must possess in order to preserve it."[24] Accompanying Drummond to Canada had been thirty-eight-year-old Maj. Gen. Phineas Riall, who assumed the ailing Maj. Gen. John Vincent's command of British forces west of Kingston. Riall's only battle experience had been in the West Indies. Not that this short, stout Tipperary Irishman considered himself inexperienced. Brave to the point of impetuosity, Riall never shied from a fight.[25]

Although Drummond worried that he had insufficient men to defend Upper Canada, he was confident that the Fort Oswego raid would succeed. Spies reported the small fort only recently occupied by 290 regulars, and that it was here most of the guns intended for *Superior* had been delivered by river for transport to Sackets Harbor. Capturing the guns would render the large ship toothless.

On May 5, Yeo's fleet hove to off Fort Oswego in the middle of a heavy gale that prohibited landing until the following morning. With the ship's guns pounding the fortress, about 750 redcoats, marines, and sailors—armed with nothing but pikes—stormed ashore. They advanced up a long, steep hill swept by cannon fire without pause, but losing 18 killed and 73 wounded before the crest was gained and the American commander withdrew into the countryside. He reported 6 dead, 38 wounded, and 28 missing. To Yeo's frustration only seven long guns were found, the majority of *Superior*'s cannon having not arrived. But he was able to carry these guns off along with 2,400 barrels of welcome provisions.

Soon receiving word that *Superior*'s guns had arrived at Oswego Falls and the Americans were planning to move them by boat to Sackets Harbor, Yeo set up a close blockade of the American base. On May 20, Chauncey lamented to Washington that five British ships stood offshore "completely blocking both passes. . . . This is the first time that I have experienced the mortification of being blockaded on the lakes."[26]

At Oswego, Master Commandant Melancthon Woolsey fretfully bided his time, seeking opportunity to slip past the blockade with gun-laden bateaux. He had twenty-one long 32-pounder guns, thirteen smaller cannon, and ten heavy cables for *Superior* aboard nineteen boats. On the night of May 28–29, Woolsey set out and by daybreak was 20 miles from Oswego with eighteen boats. Of the other boat there was no sign. Gingerly the party moved slowly along the lakeshore, putting another 10 miles behind them during the morning. Just 8 miles from Sackets Harbor they took shelter in the mouth of Sandy Creek, and Woolsey sent for marines to escort them in.

The missing boat had been captured by the British during the night, and under questioning the crew betrayed the operation. Consequently Commander Stephen Popham was prowling the shoreline with three gunboats and several smaller craft. Aboard were 200 Royal Navy personnel. Spotting the masts of the American boats well up Sandy Creek on the morning of May 30, Popham decided to capture them by advancing up the creek by land—despite Yeo's long-standing directive prohibiting entering creeks to capture suspected stores for fear of ambush. Popham was confident that he enjoyed numerical superiority. But Woolsey had not sailed with just the men crewing the boats. He also had 130 regulars and 120 Oneida Indians, who had advanced alongside the boats on foot. Also that morning a force of marines and dragoons from Sackets Harbor arrived and established a defensive position between the creek mouth and the boats. Popham led his men right into the kind of ambush Yeo feared. Fourteen men were killed, 28 wounded in short order. Popham surrendered the rest.

The American boats slipped into harbour and the guns were hoisted aboard *Superior*. Maintaining the blockade would only expose the British ships to possible attack, so Drummond and Yeo abandoned it. Yeo was in low spirits. The capture of Popham's gunboats was a setback, but not as serious as the loss of men. These could not be replaced. Another misstep, Yeo feared, would give the Americans supremacy. Better, he decided with Drummond's concurrence, to husband his fleet so that it remained capable of carrying out whatever campaign orders Prevost might direct. Drummond cautioned Yeo to do nothing to jeopardize his fleet. Eventually the ship of the line would be completed and then "you may bring the naval contest on this Lake fairly to issue, or by a powerful combined Expedition (if the Enemy, as is probable, should decline meeting you on the lake) we may attack and destroy him in his stronghold."[27]

While the British went back on the defensive, the Americans frittered away the spring deciding what part of Canada to attack. Armstrong realized any advantage the United States enjoyed was likely to disappear sometime in the summer. On April 30, he proposed that Maj. Gen. Jacob Brown assemble 5,000 regulars and 3,000 militia and volunteers on

Lake Erie, to be ferried to the Canadian shore and then marched on Burlington Heights and York. Once these two objectives were captured, the British would be cut off from their Indian allies and forced to evacuate the Niagara Peninsula.

Madison was reluctant to endorse the operation. Reports from Lake Ontario showed that the British fleet was at least for now supreme. How could Brown concentrate troops anywhere along its shores without exposing them to combined attack by British troops and ships? Especially as American intelligence indicated that Drummond had 5,000 redcoats on the lake that could "be moved at pleasure by their fleet."

Ignoring the president's concerns, Armstrong fired off instructions to Brig. Gen. Winfield Scott, who commanded the Lake Erie front, outlining the campaign rather than sending it through channels first to Brown in Sackets Harbor. At the same time as he authorized Scott to "go to Burlington and destroy the land communication" with York, Armstrong asked Brown what forces he could move to support Scott's operation. Brown was incensed and Scott embarrassed by this breach of protocol.[28]

The secretary of war quickly confessed his impetuosity, but he never told Brown that his orders had been issued without presidential approval. After some minor fussing over details, however, Madison could do little but approve Armstrong's scheme and hope that Chauncey would prove able to support the operation with his fleet. The only serious change made to the plan was that Maj. Gen. George Izard's army at Plattsburgh would march toward Montreal in a feint to pin Prevost's forces there while Brown carried off the Upper Canada attack. Armstrong, however, either forgot or omitted to issue any instructions to Izard, so the feint never transpired—an oversight that Yeo later declared an act of such "extreme stupidity" that it cost the Americans the war.[29]

The always strained relationship between Madison and Armstrong was breaking into open animosity. In a directive to all executive "heads of departments," Madison issued the clear reminder that in the United States there was no such thing as government by cabinet. He was commander in chief, the others merely advisers and functionaries. On June 7, Madison demanded an accounting from Armstrong and Jones on the precise numbers of American land and naval forces and their distribution, with comparative estimates of British forces.

Armstrong, who had been tossing about figures in the many thousands, dourly confessed that he had 20,000 effectives and about 7,000 recruits expected to report any day. But the effectives were draining away as thousands of one-year men headed home. Half of the effectives were required for coastal defence. On the Niagara frontier were 2,121 men, about 5,000 were with Izard at Lake Champlain, and Brown had 3,000 concentrated at Sackets Harbor. The recruits were to be divided so that 4,000 went to Izard, 3,000 to Brown.

Looking at these grim numbers, Madison said Brown's attempt to capture Burlington Heights would have to "depend on Commodore Chauncey's gaining the command of the lake." In the meantime, while the army waited for Chauncey to finish constructing *Superior*, Armstrong was to instruct Brown to establish a toehold on the Niagara Peninsula by capturing Fort Erie and the bridge over Chippawa Creek, near Niagara Falls. Success in these two ventures would enable him to seize Fort George and gain access to Lake Ontario for further operations in concert with Chauncey's fleet. Capture of Burlington Heights and York should then follow. And that was the sum of the proposed campaign in Canada for 1814. If successful, Madison admitted, it was hardly going to pressure the British to negotiate on American terms.

Not that Madison had any idea what was transpiring across the Atlantic, for there had been little but silence from the commissioners there since Clay and Russell sailed from New York City. A few letters from individual members had trickled in aboard this or that ship, giving the impression that they were to have assembled in Gothenburg sometime in May. When negotiations would finally begin was anybody's guess. For all the president knew, the negotiations might have already failed. Had the instructions Madison and Monroe given to Clay and Russell been too confident and demanding? Over two days in June—the 23rd and 24th—Madison and his five-man executive discussed what they should seek in a treaty.

Britain's ending impressment would no longer be an ultimatum, they agreed, but the subject must somehow be addressed in the treaty even if only to refer the issue and that of commerce to a separate negotiation. Deferment of major grievances and issues such as those regarding fisheries and Louisiana's boundaries could be deferred if an article stating that "the essential causes of the war between the United States and Great Britain, and particularly the practice of impressment, have ceased" were inserted to explain the deferment.[30] Begging to be asked was how such a treaty could justify having gone to war at all. And there was the worrisome point that the British commissioners might logically wonder why, if the causes of the war no longer existed, they should be mentioned in a treaty. But without such a clause America would have to admit that the war had failed in its purpose.

These new instructions were incorporated into a dispatch on June 25 that was to be carried to Europe aboard France's *Olivier*, whose sailing the French minister Louis Sérurier had delayed for this purpose. The next day, however, Monroe requested that its sailing be again delayed as a communiqué written by Albert Gallatin and James Bayard, who reported they were in London and soon on their way via Amsterdam to Gothenburg, had arrived. Its news disturbed Madison and his executive, for it seemed peace on anything resembling American terms might be impossible. In fact, the British might not wish to negotiate at all.

TWENTY

Great Obstacles to Accommodation

APRIL–JULY 1814

*A*lbert Gallatin had gone to London on April 9 as a private citizen rather than a government representative soon after he and Bayard concluded their 1,500-mile trek from St. Petersburg. Lacking anything better to do, Bayard tagged along. London streets thronged with jubilant crowds. Just three days before, Napoleon had abdicated. Gallatin's son, James, thought the city dull after Paris and St. Petersburg. He also found their position "not a very pleasant one; we have many kind invitations, and I think all mean to be civil and kind, but there is always a feeling of constraint . . . . The only house where we seem to be really welcome is Mr. Baring's."

Despite the chilly treatment, Gallatin proposed shifting the negotiations from Gothenburg to London so that he could "be in direct touch with Lord Castlereagh."[1] Alexander Baring, still acting as an unofficial conduit, reported that British peace commissioners would be appointed only when the U.S. commissioners were officially announced and a location agreed. As the political landscape of Europe had undergone an abrupt change, Castlereagh no longer considered Gothenburg appropriate. Rather, London or someplace in the Netherlands would better suffice.[2] Unspoken was the fact that either location ensured the British cabinet, particularly Castlereagh and Lord Bathurst, could easily follow the course of negotiations.

Both Gallatin and Bayard were alarmed that rather than being weary of war, "the English people eagerly wish that their pride may be fully gratified by what they call the 'punishment of America,'" Gallatin noted in a letter to Washington. "They do not even suspect that we had any just cause of war, and ascribe it solely to a premeditated concert with Bonaparte at a time when we thought him triumphant and their cause desperate." He was little surprised, as various Federalist congressmen and senators had fed this view in speeches and editorials. While Gallatin was sure that Lord Liverpool's cabinet did not share this belief, "it will certainly require an effort on their part against popular feeling to make peace with America. It must be added that even there a belief is said to be entertained that a continuance of the war would produce a separation of the Union, and perhaps a return of the New England states to the mother-country." While the government would certainly move to reduce "the immense military and naval establishments" built up during the war with France so that war taxes could be cancelled, "a prosecution of the war against the United States would afford a convenient pretence for preserving a much more considerable standing force than is necessary and would otherwise be allowed by Parliament."[3]

In an April 20 letter, Bayard echoed Gallatin's concern. The "great augmentation of their disposable force presents an added temptation to prosecute the war. You must also know that the temper of the country is highly excited against us and decidedly expressed in favor of the continuance of hostilities."[4]

"The numerous English forces in France, Italy, Holland, and Portugal," warned Gallatin, "ready for immediate service, and for which there is no further employment in Europe, afford to this government the means of sending both to Canada and to the United States a very formidable army, which we are not prepared to meet with any regular, well-organized force; and they will also turn against us as much of their superabundant naval forces as they may think adequate to any object they have in view."[5]

Bayard and Gallatin expressed these anxieties in a joint letter to James Monroe on May 6. Requiring that the British agree to end impressment would assure failure, they insisted. "We think that . . . for our government the alternative only remains either to resolve on a vigorous prosecution of the war under an expectation of probable success or to forego for the present the assertion of our rights on what was the principal remaining object of the war." They urged Washington to agree to negotiate in England or, if that was unacceptable, somewhere in Holland.[6]

Gallatin was uneasy over the seeming lack of urgency that prevailed among Liverpool's cabinet members. Even when dining privately with Gallatin, Bathurst remained "stiff and formal." On April 30, a Saturday, he and James dined with Liverpool, but the prime minister never allowed the discussion to stray toward business.[7]

"Unfortunately, whilst the greater part of the civilized world rejoices at the restoration of a general peace, the United States alone remains at war, and are placed in a more critical situation than ever they were since the first years of their revolution. Pride, avarice, and ambition will throw here great obstacles to an accommodation for which there has ever been, on our part, the sincerest disposition," Gallatin wrote his friend the Marquis de Lafayette.[8] He could imagine that the British deliberately stalled in anticipation of military successes over the summer campaign. Each day passed could reduce the American commissioners' negotiating power.

Clay responded from Gothenburg. Russell was in Stockholm presenting credentials to the Swedish court. He had no news of John Quincy Adams's whereabouts save that he was en route from St. Petersburg to Stockholm and expected in early May. About the change of venue, Clay would agree to relocate to Holland only if the Swedish government were notified that this was "at the instance of Great Britain." As to negotiating in London, Clay refused "to submit to further condescension, especially when we have yet to see in British history the example of their haughty people having been conciliated by the condescension of their enemy . . . we shall best promote the objects of our mission and acquit ourselves of our duty by preserving a firm and undismayed countenance."[9]

Clay forwarded papers officially accrediting the five American commissioners, which Gallatin and Bayard presented to Bathurst on May 16 along with a proposal that the negotiations transpire either at Amsterdam or The Hague. Bathurst countered with the old Flemish capital of Ghent. Recently liberated from French rule, the Flemish provinces were about to unite with Holland. The two men replied that Ghent was acceptable to them as Gothenburg had been. They would advise the other commissioners "to repair immediately to Ghent." Bathurst assured them that the Prince Regent would promptly appoint his commissioners.[10]

When Adams, prevented from sailing from Reval, Estonia, to Stockholm for two weeks by unfavourable winds, arrived on May 25 and learned of this change, he was infuriated. He thought the journey to Sweden from Russia a wasted effort. On May 28, he wrote Monroe from Stockholm: "I cannot entertain a doubt that our conferences, wherever held, will be arrested at the threshold by an utter impossibility of agreement upon the basis of negotiation."[11]

Resigned to going through the motions, Adams hastened to Gothenburg, where on June 6 he found Clay had departed for Ghent five days earlier via coastal packet to Copenhagen and then overland coach. Clay had left John Adams to transport Adams and Russell, who reached the city four days later. In the early hours of June 12, the ship sailed on a fair breeze.[12]

From London, Gallatin reported to Monroe that Bayard had left London on May 23 with plans to visit Paris before proceeding to Ghent. Gallatin remained, fretfully waiting for word from Castlereagh as to when the British commissioners would travel to Ghent. Although the Prince Regent had confirmed three commissioners proposed by the foreign secretary, there was no sign they were going to depart any time soon. On June 9, Gallatin advised Castlereagh that Clay had departed Gothenburg, Adams and Russell would soon leave Sweden, Bayard was gone. All that held him in London was a desire to know when the British commissioners would repair to Ghent. The note languished at the Foreign Office for more than a week before one of Castlereagh's undersecretaries replied that he expected the British commissioners to depart London about the first of July. Satisfied that he had done all possible to hurry the British along, Gallatin and James left for Paris on June 21 with plans to remain there a week.

Gallatin reported to Monroe that the commissioners were finally gathering. "This does not bespeak any wish [by the British] to hasten the negotiations."[13] In past letters he had reported continuing naval and army reinforcements being sent to North America and predicted that between 15,000 and 20,000 troops could soon be landed on the nation's Atlantic coast. A confidant had informed Gallatin that Castlereagh and other ministers now agreed with the national sentiment that they should "inflict on America a chastisement that will teach her that war is not to be declared against Great Britain with impunity."[14]

Gallatin was not far off the mark. While Castlereagh truly desired an end to the war in North America and so hoped the negotiations bore fruit, he also believed the tide ran against the Americans. So while the British government inched through the early summer toward the talks, it simultaneously sped the flow of troops and ships across the Atlantic and urged its commanders there to carry the war to American soil.

In a secret dispatch sent on June 2 to Governor Prevost, Bathurst advised that before year-end more than 13,000 troops would arrive in Quebec. "His Majesty's Government conceive that the Canadas will not only be protected for the time against any attack which the enemy may have the means of making, but it will enable you to commence offensive operations on the Enemy's Frontier before the close of this Campaign. . . . The object of your operations will be; first, to give immediate protection: secondly, to obtain if possible ultimate security to His Majesty's Possessions in America."

To fulfill the first object, Bathurst ordered the "entire destruction of Sackets harbour and the Naval Establishments on Lake Erie and Lake Champlain." Fort Niagara was to be retained and Detroit and Michigan Territory occupied as part of the second object. Success on this front would restore "Detroit and the whole of the Michigan Country to the Indians," rendering "the British Frontier . . . materially improved." Prevost should also extend the British lines south to gain as much country around Lake Champlain as possible, but with the proviso that he not extend his line of advance so far that his troops were exposed to being cut off. To secure the St. Lawrence River from Halifax to Quebec, Bathurst ordered Lt. Gen. Sir John Sherbrooke, commanding the British army in Nova Scotia, to occupy a corridor of the District of Maine— part of Massachusetts State—paralleling the shoreline.

While these operations were conducted in the north, four regiments from Europe would assault America's coastline. The government also planned to collect "a considerable force . . . at Cork without delay" that would "make a more serious attack on some part of the Coasts of the United States."[15]

This rapid escalation of British strength in North America would not, of course, happen overnight. Ten thousand troops bound for Quebec would be moved in three convoys spaced several weeks apart because of difficulties assembling sufficient ships. But even to the defensively minded Prevost the intention was clear. He was to seize the initiative from the Americans and occupy territory that the British government would retain either for the Indians or as part of an expanded British North America. The adjustment of boundaries enabling this would be imposed on the Americans as a condition of peace.

Bathurst held no illusions that the negotiations would proceed smoothly, with the British commissioners simply submitting the government's settlement to the Americans and having it confirmed. There must be some give and take. Compromises were likely. Demands would necessarily require adjustment and clarification. He and Castlereagh concurred that they must approve any changes in the British position. The commissioners, therefore, were selected to ensure they would do nothing intemperate that might commit Britain to an unapproved course.

As the alleged causes of the war primarily regarded maritime issues, it was deemed that the commission's head should not only be a member of the House of Lords but also a senior ranking officer of the Royal Navy. Vice-Admiral James Gambier was appointed to this role. Also included was an expert in maritime and naval law, William Adams, who would be responsible for drafting the treaty's clauses. Gambier and Adams, however, were not expected to lead negotiations. That fell to the third member, War and Colonial Office Undersecretary Henry Goulburn. Trustworthy and loyal, he could be relied on to resolutely advance the British position with clarity and precision. He would also maintain strict lines of communication through Bathurst with Castlereagh and other senior cabinet members.

Despite Goulburn's being junior to Gambier and Adams in both age and social position, neither man was likely to protest his degree of influence over the proceedings. The forty-two-year-old Adams was noted for his mastery of legal details, but had no diplomatic experience. Like Goulburn, he was a graduate of Trinity College and had begun to practise law in 1800. His foray into naval law had come in 1811, when he was appointed by the Admiralty to a commission charged with regulating how vice-admiralty courts were conducted at stations abroad.[16]

Gambier's forty-seven-year career had concluded in 1811, when his term as commander of the Channel fleet expired and the Admiralty offered no other posting. Born on October 13, 1756, in Bermuda, where his father served as the colony's lieutenant governor, Gambier had been signed on as a midshipman aboard *Yarmouth* when he was eleven. Fifteen years later he gained command of the frigate *Raleigh* and fought several small engagements against French and American ships until 1781, when he asked to be relieved of command because of illness. By now Gambier had grown into a spare-framed man with a square face, his expression seemingly fixed in thought, his hairline receding. He was noted as a humourless soul who tended to tilt his head in a manner that some thought concealed a sinful measure of pride.

This observation would have horrified the devoutly religious Gambier. In the early 1800s he penned a tract defending the Church of England's right to impose tithes, and he insisted on the Sabbath services being properly conducted aboard ship at a time when such observances were normally perfunctory. In another departure from the norm, he denied women from coming aboard unless they could prove they were seamen's wives. Until a sailor was injured by the practice, anyone overheard swearing had to wear a wooden collar to which two 32-pound balls of round shot were attached by short lengths of chain. Such practices earned Gambier the nickname Dismal Jimmie.

On June 1, 1794, Gambier distinguished himself during a battle with the French near Ushant. At the helm of the 74-gun *Defence*, Gambier charged the French line with such dash that fleet commander Lord Howe cried, "Look at the *Defence*, see how nobly she goes into action!" Soon all *Defence*'s masts were shot away, her decks running with blood, but Gambier refused to strike the colours while the superior 110-gun *Républican* pummelled her. When the French ship turned to meet another threat, *Defence* was towed to safety. Gambier's casualties totalled 17 killed and 36 wounded, but his fellow officers lauded this resolute stand. A fellow captain remarked jokingly, "Jemmy, whom the Lord loveth He chasteneth!"

On the first anniversary of the battle Gambier was promoted to rear admiral and four years later to vice-admiral. In 1802, he undertook a two-year posting as governor of Newfoundland and then returned to serve as First Lord of the Admiralty. Three years later he assumed command of the 98-gun *Prince of Wales*.

When France entered into a secret treaty with Russia that would bar British ships from using the ports of Portugal, Denmark, and Sweden and hand the fleets of each nation to the French, the Admiralty was ordered to either capture or destroy the Danish fleet. Gambier sailed from Yarmouth on July 26, 1807, with seventeen ships of the line. Copenhagen was subjected to a long siege that included a three-day bombardment that resulted in the Danish surrender on September 7. Gambier's performance brought him a peerage. Given command of the Channel fleet in May 1808, he led it in one major battle off Isle d'Aix near Lorient. Aided by fireships under command of Lord Cochrane, the British ships of the line either destroyed the French ships or drove them aground. Gambier, however, was not accorded the glory that would normally be his for such an achievement because of accusations by Cochrane that the entire fleet could have been destroyed had the admiral shown more vigour. A court martial convened at Gambier's request exonerated him. Cochrane's career was ruined while Gambier returned to command the Channel fleet until his term expired. But his reputation remained sufficiently clouded to ensure that he would not again see active service.[17]

Retiring to his estate in Buckinghamshire, Gambier set to gardening with a passion. He avidly oversaw efforts by head gardener T. Tomson, who made botanical history in about 1811 by producing the first pansies by hybridizing varieties of *Viola tricolor* with the yellow *Viola altaica* common to Crimea. Gambier was deeply immersed in this project when called by Castlereagh to head the peace commission.

Gambier, Adams, and Goulburn had all accepted their commissions in mid-May, but, despite the assurances to Gallatin that they would move promptly to Ghent, they remained in England after the promised departure date of July 1 had passed. In part this was due to Castlereagh's being in Paris concluding the final peace treaty with France and his insistence on personally drafting their final instructions. As the House of Commons spokesman for the War and Colonial Office, Goulburn had to be present to answer the many questions regarding the war with America and other colonial matters.[18] The House would not rise until the end of the month, so it would be early August before Goulburn was free to depart for Ghent—a fact of which the American commissioners were not advised.

John Quincy Adams and Jonathan Russell had reached Ghent on June 24. Unwell, Russell immediately took to bed in the sumptuous Hôtel des Pays-Bas, while Adams dined alone in his room, strolled through the ancient city, and started a letter to his wife, Louisa, which he finished the next day.[19] Adams was in foul temper, bitterly resenting the move to Ghent. Had the winds not delayed his departure from Reval, he would have been at Clay's side when the letter from Bayard and Gallatin was delivered "and in that case none of us would ever have come to Ghent. . . . I never would have consented to come here. If a majority of my colleagues had concluded upon the measure, I would have returned immediately to St. Petersburg, and left them to conclude the peace as they saw fit." The negotiations, he believed, would either succeed or fail in three weeks, but the change of venue meant that discussions would not begin until mid-July. The move to Ghent had wasted two months, "to no useful purpose whatever."[20]

Adams also feared that the British had successfully played the Americans for fools. In a letter to Monroe, he charged that by effecting the move from Gothenburg to Ghent the British were able to "remove us from neutral territory to a place occupied by a British garrison." All the Allied powers coveted Belgium, Adams believed, but the presence of British troops on its soil and the influx of British gold into its economy made it inevitable that it would become a British province—a fate he considered to have already befallen Holland. Although as yet no redcoats paraded through the streets of Ghent, Adams reported that both Brussels and Antwerp were under their occupation and troops were expected to move into Ghent any day.[21]

While Adams groused to Monroe and Louisa, he knew that to move the talks yet again would only delay matters. Bayard had arrived on June 27, Clay the following day. Gallatin was expected shortly. On the 30th the four met in Adams's hotel room. "The conversation was desultory," Adams confided to his diary. They agreed only to soon send *John Adams* home and drafted a letter to acquire a British passport allowing her safe passage.

While they waited for Gallatin, the four did their best to treat each other cordially. They visited the city's mayor, walked its narrow cobble-stone streets or strolled along the canals either singly or as a group, and shared meals together until Adams suddenly chose to dine alone at the hotel's midday table d'hôte. "They sit after dinner and drink bad wine and smoke cigars, which neither suits my habits nor my health, and absorbs time which I cannot spare. I find it impossible, even with the most rigorous economy of time, to do half the writing that I ought," Adams grumbled. The next day, however, Clay took him aside and expressed regret that Adams had not joined them. He decided to hence-forth make a point of sharing meals with his colleagues, no matter how unpleasant he found their behaviour.[22]

In early July his prophecy that the city would be garrisoned by British troops came true. When Gallatin's entourage arrived on July 7, young James noted how the many men in scarlet uniforms made "the streets very bright."[23] Albert Gallatin met with the other commissioners on the 9th. A major topic of discussion during the four-hour session was whether they should continue lodging at the hotel or lease a house. Adams alone wished to remain at the hotel because he thought their time in Ghent would "be very short; but the other gentlemen are all of a different opin-ion. They calculate upon passing the winter here. It is impossible to form a decisive opinion upon the subject until the British commissioners arrive."[24] Adams announced that the commissioners would meet daily at noon, a decision with which the others reluctantly agreed.

On July 11, Adams turned forty-seven and lamented: "Two-thirds of the period allotted to the life of man are gone by for me. I have not improved them as I ought to have done." His personal disillusionment intruded on the day's meeting when he accused the others of having wasted government money sending special messengers about Europe on various unimportant diplomatic missions. Clay remarked that he had understood from Monroe that they should make use of special messengers as often as necessary rather than risk miscommunications. There the matter rested, but Adams was determined to raise it again at the first opportunity. "I should not have sent one of the messengers hitherto employed, neither were they . . . at all necessary."[25] That evening Adams was embarrassed when Bayard rose and offered a toast acknowledging his birthday. The Delaware Federalist, whom Adams had been predisposed to dislike because of his politics, was disarmingly polite and congenial.

The daily meetings quickly disenchanted everyone. Adams attempted to breathe vigour into the process by assigning each member to analyze how a particular part of their instructions might affect negotiations. It was a hopeless task, likely to be rendered irrelevant during the first meeting with the British.[26] On July 15, James Gallatin recorded that there was "nothing to do. Mr. Adams in a very bad temper. Mr. Clay annoys him. Father pours oil on the troubled waters."[27] Gallatin generally sided with Adams while Russell tended to back Clay in a manner that bespoke a growing sycophancy.[28]

While struggling for days over the wording of a joint communiqué to Monroe, each man wrote his own private letter to the secretary of state. They concluded a protracted and delicate negotiation among themselves on July 19 that resulted in agreement to rent a house on a monthly basis. "Although," Adams confided to Louisa, "we had all agreed . . . to live together, yet when it came to the arrangement of details, we soon found that one had one thing to which he attached a particular interest, and another another, and it was not so easy to find a contractor who would accommodate himself to five distinct and separate humors." They settled on the Hôtel d'Alacantara, which despite being called a hotel was a private residence because of a quirk in Flemish expression.[29] It was a large, three-storey house on the Rue des Champs that provided each commissioner with a private apartment. Their landlord had trained as a professional cook and promised satisfactory daily meals. He was also to provide the best liquors to be found in Ghent. "This was the article that stuck hardest in the passage, for [Adams] was afraid that he would pass off upon us bad wine, and make us pay for it as if it was the best." Finally the landlord agreed that if the wine provided was not acceptable "we shall look further, and draw the corks without paying him any tax or tribute for it at all."[30]

Having resolved their housing issues, the commissioners idled about awaiting the British. The Americans soon read in the British newspapers a report that during Commons debate on July 20 Castlereagh had been asked "whether the persons sent to Gothenburg from the American government were quite forgotten by his Majesty's Ministers, or whether any one had been appointed to treat with them?" Castlereagh replied that the British commissioners would travel to Ghent immediately upon being informed that all the Americans were in place and that it was known that Gallatin was lingering in Paris. This was crock, Adams told Louisa, for the British papers had announced Gallatin's departure from Paris on July 4 and "Lord Castlereagh had special and precise information that he had been here at Ghent, a full fortnight, on the day of the debate."

During the same Commons debate the chancellor of the exchequer, Nicholas Vansittart, argued that the delay was irrelevant as "the war with America was not likely to terminate speedily, and might lead to a considerable scale of expense." There was in the Commons, Adams noted, a disposition to continue the war "to accomplish the *deposition of Mr. Madison*." The Federalist Party was fuelling this notion, he believed, by claiming that Britain would not "treat with a person from who she has received such unprovoked insults, and such deliberate proofs of injustice." Impeachment was likely, according to the British newspapers, because Madison "had deceived and misled his countrymen by gross misrepresentations [and] abused their confidence by secret collusion with the late Tyrant of France."[31]

To a man the American commissioners worried that the British had no intention of coming to Ghent at all. Rather, they were stalling in the hopes that the United States would be so humbled by battle that the Federalists would succeed in ousting the president.

—

TWENTY-ONE

Summer of Stalemate

JULY–AUGUST 1814

*A*lthough many Federalists and New Englanders grumbled and postured, in fact no organized plan to impeach James Madison existed. While northerners remained ill disposed to support the war, there was little popular support for bringing Madison down.

There was also no forum for Federalists so inclined to argue their case. Congress was in recess until October. Despite the crisis posed by the British reinforcement, Madison had no intention of issuing an early recall. Doing so, he feared, would only "uselessly spread alarm."[1]

Yet Madison was personally alarmed. At a July 1 executive meeting, he warned that the "fierce aspect which British military power now had" made it almost a certainty that "the capital would be marked as the most inviting object of a speedy attack."[2] He wanted 10,000 men, including at least 1,000 regulars, raised to defend the District of Columbia. Madison created a special capital military district commanded by Brig. Gen. William H. Winder of Maryland. A peacetime Baltimore lawyer and nephew of the state's Federalist governor, Winder's appointment was intended to facilitate cooperation between state and federal officials in developing the district's defences.[3] Everyone except John Armstrong concurred. Armstrong countered that Baltimore more likely faced attack because of its strategic naval importance. Protect both cities, Madison replied. Clearly the British could strike anywhere along the eastern seaboard or even at New Orleans. Madison ordered the drafting of a defensive plan for all the ports from Boston to New Orleans and issued a call to "invite" the state governors to raise an army of 93,000 militiamen to provide coastal defence.[4]

Armstrong had no intention of complying. He merely issued a circular inviting the governors to call out thousands of militia, left Winder to prepare Washington's defences while providing no resources to do so, and turned his attention to the campaign against the Niagara Peninsula, over which he could exert no meaningful control. Maj. Gen. Jacob Brown's northern army was too distant from Washington for Armstrong's furtive directives to influence events. News from this front was scant and generally weeks out of date by the time it arrived. Armstrong downplayed the threat to coastal cities, declaring that excessive "bustle" would convince the British that the populace was afraid. Panic must be avoided. Pleas from coastal city councils for federal assistance building fortifications were ignored. Repeatedly, the Washington mayor sought Armstrong's commitment to mobilize the local militia only to have his concerns dismissed by assurances that the city was not at risk.[5] The secretary of war's attention remained firmly fixed to the northwest.

The campaign in Niagara had begun on July 3, when Brown bypassed Fort Niagara by crossing upriver of the falls, with Brig. Gen. Winfield Scott's brigade landing below Fort Erie and Brig. Gen. Eleazer Ripley just above. Brown's entire force consisted of only 3,400 men, of which about 2,400 were New England regulars divided evenly between the two brigadiers. The rest consisted of more than 300 artillerymen and some 600 Pennsylvania volunteers. There were also about 600 friendly Indians. Although small it outnumbered the fewer than 2,500 British troops divided into several garrisons. Most of the redcoats manned Fort George or Fort Niagara. Only 137 were posted to Fort Erie.[6]

Brown's troops were better trained than those of previous campaigns—credit for this going to Scott. Previously the troops had been barely trained in marching and battle-formation drill, the assumption being that accurate musketry was what mattered. Relying on a tattered copy of Napoleon Bonaparte's regulations for the French army, Scott relentlessly trained officers and men. Ten hours a day, virtually every day, drill was conducted until the men were not only thoroughly competent with musket and bayonet but could also efficiently perform in squad, company, and battalion formations. Strict discipline and maintenance of hygiene were emphasized so successfully that dysentery all but disappeared from the military camp and the men's morale increased greatly.[7] Despite a lack of blue cloth for standard army uniforms, the men marched to battle sharply turned out in grey jackets and white trousers—an outfit that would become known as Cadet's Grey after it was adopted as standard dress for West Point cadets.[8]

Fort Erie fell to Brown's Indians, who discovered that the rear of the fort facing away from the water was almost undefended and managed to fight their way inside. After firing several cannon rounds to maintain their honour, the British surrendered.

Learning of the American crossing at mid-morning, Maj. Gen. Phineas Riall sent five companies of the Royal Scots from Fort George to reinforce the now threatened garrison at Chippawa. Riall galloped ahead, gathering up troops scattered among various outposts. Long lines of redcoats soon double-timed along the river road.

At sunrise on July 4, the Americans marched from Fort Erie toward Chippawa. Clear skies promised a warm day. Before them British light troops under Chippawa's commander, Lt. Col. Thomas Pearson, exchanged musket fire with Scott's advance scouts and damaged bridges crossing the many creeks and ditches. Despite this harassment, Scott reached Chippawa by sunset. Realizing he had outdistanced Ripley's brigade and the combined Pennsylvania volunteers and Indians under Gen. Peter Buel Porter, he fell back a mile to put Street's Creek between himself and the British. The rest of the American force encamped close by.

Thinking the British would remain on the defensive, Scott decided to throw a belated July 4 dinner followed by a dress parade. For security, Porter's force was sent to drive away the British light troops who had been harassing the American lines. The festivities were just being readied when Scott learned the British had crossed the Chippawa and were headed his way.

Riall's attack represented a gamble, for he had only 1,500 regulars and about 300 militia and Indians. But he assumed the Americans would be as disorganized as always. Hit them hard and they should bolt.

Instead, Scott's brigade moved to meet him. The Americans stood with backs to the creek, formed into the long firing line that the redcoats favoured. Riall's men were on the road, packed in columns rather like the formation common to French assaults. Disconcerted by this reversal of form, Riall was heartened to see the Americans wore grey uniforms, assuming them to be militia. Just then the facing troops wheeled their line with uncanny precision as if conducting a parade-ground drill. "Those are regulars, by God!" he exclaimed.

Muskets fixed with bayonets were quickly raised as the Americans let loose a devastating volley. Holding back his centre, Scott threw both his flanks slightly outward so that the musketry slashed into the advancing columns from three sides. Riall galloped about trying to rally his troops, but soon gaps opened in the British lines. Unable to close with the Americans, they faltered and then broke. Riall was one of the last to leave the field.[9]

The British lost 148 killed, 22 wounded, and 46 taken prisoner. American casualties were overall higher at about 300, but only 60 were fatal. With only Scott's brigade involved, Riall's troops had enjoyed numerical superiority, but American steadiness won the day.[10]

Scott's victory at Chippawa forced a general withdrawal to Fort George. The Americans pursued as far as Queenston, where they paused on July 10 to fortify the heights. Brown ordered the army halted until Commodore Isaac Chauncey could bring up the naval squadron. He hoped Chauncey would supply some heavy guns for reducing Fort George and Fort Niagara.

Three days later not a single sail had yet appeared on Lake Ontario. Brown sent an urgent appeal. "Meet me on the lake shore north of Fort George with your fleet, and we will be able, I have no doubt, to . . . break the power of the enemy in Upper Canada. . . . At all events let me hear from you. . . . For God's sake let me see you."

Chauncey ignored him. Claiming to be laid low by fever, but more determined not to subordinate his fleet to the army or risk leaving Sackets Harbor undefended, the commodore allowed the American offensive to crumble. Knowing Riall was receiving more reinforcements in the form of local militia and redcoats marching from the east, Brown withdrew on July 24 to the south bank of the Chippawa. His army was in an ever-weakening state. Casualties and illness had reduced it to 2,644 effectives, and there was no prospect of reinforcement.[11]

Riall sent an advance guard of 1,000 men under Lieutenant Colonel Pearson after them. On Monday morning, July 25, Pearson established his troops atop a hill where Lundy's Lane intersected the road paralleling the Niagara River. At the same time, Lt. Gen. Gordon Drummond reached Fort George from York with about 500 reinforcements. Drummond moved this force to the American side of the river to threaten Brown's supply base at Fort Schlosser. No sooner did they cross over than Drummond changed his mind and recalled them. Instead, he ordered Riall to take everyone and join Pearson. By noon, the British had about 1,600 men at Lundy's Lane. Another 1,200 regulars and militia with two six-pound guns were on the way from Burlington.

Brown had, meanwhile, learned of the British move on Fort Schlosser. Knowing he was helpless to defend his supply base, Brown decided to advance on Fort George in the hope that the British would turn about to protect their own supply line. Accordingly, at about four in the afternoon, Scott wheeled his brigade about and made for the fort. Two hours later, he approached Lundy's Lane with 1,072 men. Across an open plain, a ribbon of scarlet lay unfurled across a low hill. Bayonets and the brass of several cannon close to the summit glistened in the sun.

No sooner had Drummond arrived on the scene than, as he laconically put it, "the whole front was warmly and closely engaged."[12] Throwing his men at the British with fierce determination, Scott achieved initial success on the left flank, where the line was driven back. Suffering from a bad wound (which eventually led to the amputation of an arm), Riall was captured. In the twilight's gathering gloom the Americans attacked repeatedly, trying to take the British guns. Hand-to-hand fights developed and gunners were bayoneted, but each time counterattacks drove Scott's men off.

By nine o'clock Scott had barely 600 men, but reinforced by Porter's and Ripley's brigades, the fight continued. Using the cover of shrubs, one of Ripley's regiments overcame the guns with a flank attack. Ripley's men slowly began to push the British line back. At this pivotal moment the 1,200 men from Burlington arrived and the line straightened.

The fighting raged on, confused by darkness. Cannon were exchanged repeatedly as attack met counterattack. Men fired muskets at point-blank range. Scott was bleeding heavily from a musket ball that shattered his left shoulder joint. Brown was shot in the right thigh and then stunned when a spent cannonball struck him.[13] Ripley had taken command, but the Americans were so cut up he ordered a withdrawal to the camp across the Chippawa. The dead-tired British and Canadians let them go; a pursuit in the darkness was likely to achieve nothing. From his stretcher, Brown claimed victory on the grounds that the British did not pursue. Yet the Americans had surrendered the field, giving Drummond a tactical victory. American casualties totalled 171 dead, 572 wounded, and 110 missing. Of these, 560 were from Scott's brigade. The British fared no better, with 84 killed, 559 wounded, 193 missing, and 42 taken prisoner. Lundy's Lane was the war's bloodiest battle.[14]

Ripley retreated to Fort Erie and strengthened its defences, expecting any moment to face a British attack. But Drummond decided to await reinforcements from Kingston, which had to come overland rather than aboard Commodore Sir James Yeo's fleet because Commodore Chauncey had finally sortied out of Sackets Harbor aboard *Superior* on August 1 to assert American dominance of Lake Ontario. Ironically, Chauncey now controlled the lake when it was too late to support the American offensive, while Yeo conceded the issue just as his ability to reinforce Drummond's advance on Fort Erie could have sped the pace of events to British benefit.

Chauncey's ships demonstrated off Fort George on August 5 and he haughtily dismissed all criticism for failing to sail earlier by pointing out that Brown's troops never got closer to the lakeshore than Queenston, so his presence one way or the other would have been immaterial. Leaving several small schooners to blockade the mouth of the Niagara, Chauncey sailed to the eastern end of the lake and blockaded Kingston.

Much vexed by this development, Governor Prevost wrote Lord Bathurst on August 14 to complain that whereas reinforcements could have reached Drummond in two days by water, the troops now had to march more than 250 miles overland through "a tract of Country impenetrable for the conveyance of Extensive supplies." After sixteen to twenty days' marching they arrived "fatigued, and with an exhausted equipment." By comparison, American reinforcements arrived fresh and ready for battle.[15]

This last observation evidenced Prevost's predilection to exaggerate American strength. Other than receiving a new commander, Brig. Gen. Edmund P. Gaines, who arrived at Fort Erie from Sackets Harbor, the Americans received few reinforcements and numbered just 2,200 men, who were poorly supplied.

Drummond first attempted a raid on Buffalo to destroy the enemy supply depot there, hoping to force the Americans to abandon the Canadian side of the Niagara in order to protect their vulnerable supply lines. Although his thinking was sound, the operation proved a fiasco. Six hundred redcoats gained the American shore uncontested, but soon encountered a lightly defended breastwork where a firefight broke out. Although half of the British troops were veterans, the orderly line crumbled. Men crouched, ducked, lay down, crawled behind fallen logs or into bushes, and altogether displayed, in the words of Lt. Col. J. Tucker, an "unpardonable degree of unsteadiness, without possessing one solitary excuse." Unable to control them, Tucker abandoned the attack and returned to the British camp two miles north of Fort Erie.[16]

Still, Drummond delayed laying siege to the fort, waiting instead for heavy guns to be dragged up from Fort George for use in breaching the walls. Finally, on August 13 the siege began in earnest. It was quickly realized that the guns were too far back to have much effect. Only one shot out of ten reached the ramparts, and these, observed Briton Dr. William Dunlop, harmlessly bounced off.[17]

After two days of this fitful bombardment, Drummond ordered a general assault on the night of August 14–15. The attack was to strike the defences simultaneously at three points under cover of darkness. Drummond divided his 2,200 men into three columns, of which one numbered 1,200, another 650, and the third 250.[18]

At 2:00 a.m., the main column stepped out toward Snake Hill, a sandy mound right of the fort dominated by an American battery. Ripley's brigade faced them and he expected the attack. The column marched into withering fire and then found its path blocked by an abatis the men were unable to breach. Although some got around this obstacle by wading along the Lake Erie shoreline, they were quickly cut off and captured. The column was forced to retire.

Meanwhile, the smallest column attacked Douglass Battery, but its commander was soon killed. Disorganized, the soldiers drifted toward the centre in the face of relentless fire and mixed in with the central column attacking the fort itself. Three times this combined force tried to breach the defences, only to be thrown back. A fourth effort gained the northeast bastion and overran the cannon, but, unable to advance farther, the redcoats could only try to hold the bastion until reinforced. The reserves never came, and shortly after daylight tragedy struck when an ammunition chest caught fire and "a most tremendous explosion followed by which almost all the troops which had entered the place were dreadfully mangled." Dr. Dunlop, caught inside the bastion, miraculously escaped unharmed. He was soon "scouring along the road at the top of my speed, with a running accompaniment of grape, canister and musketry whistling about my ears."[19] Those who survived retreated.

Drummond's assault was in ruins. Casualties totalled 905, of which 57 were killed, 309 wounded, and another 539 reported missing. In the aftermath, the Americans found 222 British dead on the field—most inside the destroyed bastion. How many others had been reduced to uncountable body parts or had taken the opportunity to desert was impossible to determine. Drummond suspected more deserted than were killed, for he had noted that the morale of the British regulars was falling dramatically. Many troops were undisciplined and openly rebellious. In a letter to Prevost, he assumed responsibility for the attack's failure. But he also attested that the "agony of mind I suffer, from the present disgraceful and unfortunate conduct of the troops committed to my superintendence, wounds me to the soul!"

American casualties were just 84 officers and men.[20]

The siege continued, with Drummond receiving another 1,200 reinforcements. Slowly the guns were pushed up to a battery closer to the American lines and inflicted real damage. Yet morale among the Americans remained high even after a shell wounded Brigadier General

Gaines on August 29. Recovered from his wounds, Major General Brown returned to the fort and resumed command.

Meanwhile, the British situation steadily worsened. September brought incessant rains that reduced the camp into "a lake in the midst of a thick wood." Chauncey's blockade reduced the flow of supplies that reached Drummond to a thin trickle. Ammunition was particularly short. Hundreds of men were sick and the rain depressed them all. Yet they laboured on and by mid-month had placed guns in a third battery only 500 yards from the fort, from which their fire could tear great holes in its breastworks.

Recognizing the threat on the afternoon of September 17, Brown ordered 1,600 troops to destroy the battery standing on the extreme British right flank facing Snake Hill. Another 400 ventured from the fort to eliminate the second, more distant battery. Under cover of a veritable deluge, Gen. Peter B. Porter led the 1,600 men from Snake Hill through woods toward the battery. With the guns of Fort Erie bombarding the battery with covering fire, Porter's men achieved complete surprise. The guns were quickly spiked and the magazine blown, and the large column swung to assist the smaller force assaulting the second battery. A fierce fight ensued and much damage was caused before the Americans withdrew to the protection of their fortifications.

Three of Drummond's six siege guns were disabled. He also lost 115 soldiers killed, 178 wounded, and 316 missing. The Americans counted 79 dead and 432 wounded or missing. But they had checked Drummond's efforts.[21] To Prevost on September 21, Drummond reported that because of sickness among the troops and "their situation . . . of such extreme wretchedness from the torrents of rain . . . I feel it to be my duty no longer to persevere in a vain attempt to maintain a blockade of so vastly a superior and increasing force of the enemy."[22] Drummond lifted the siege and retreated to the Chippawa that night.

The Americans, reinforced by 3,500 men under command of Maj. Gen. George Izard, who had marched overland for weeks from Lake Champlain to reach Brown, now numbered 6,300. This was the strongest and undoubtedly most efficient force the United States had yet managed to deploy inside Canada. With Izard in command, they set off on September 28 in pursuit of Drummond, who could do little but delay them by destroying bridges as he surrendered ground without offering a fight. Soon the Americans were again camped at Sandy Creek, intent on forcing the Chippawa the next morning. In a few days Izard expected to carry Fort George with supporting fire from Chauncey's fleet.

Once again fortune turned against the Americans. Commodore Yeo hoisted his flag aboard the mighty 120-gun *St. Lawrence* and Chauncey immediately fled to the safety of Sackets Harbor. The lake was again British.

In despair, fearful that his line could easily be turned by amphibious forces if he ventured anywhere near Lake Ontario, Izard straggled back to Fort Erie. On November 5, he blew up the fort and crossed to Buffalo. From there he wrote Armstrong that his health was failing and to endure a northern winter might be his death. He headed south to recuperate. America's last campaign against Canada was over.[23]

It had been Armstrong's ill-advised decision to send Izard from Lake Champlain. His fixation on the Niagara region led him to disregard Izard's warning that the Champlain corridor was being left open, a route used over hundreds of years by native, French, British, and American forces to attack either the St. Lawrence region or upstate New York. "I will make the movement you direct," Izard wrote on July 27, "but the lately erected works at Plattsburg and Cumberland Head will, in less than three days after my departure, be in the possession of the enemy." Izard had offered a spoiling attack on Montreal to pin British forces that might otherwise be transferred to Niagara, but Armstrong dismissed his fears. On August 29, Izard had dutifully marched off at the head of 4,000 men. Left behind were 1,500 regulars and a matching number of militia and volunteers commanded by Brig. Gen. Alexander Macomb.[24]

It seemed incomprehensible that Armstrong would order the Champlain garrison reduced by more than half its strength when July had seen the British take the offensive along the American coast and from Nova Scotia into Maine. First there had been the expedition early in the month from Halifax against the long-disputed Passamaquoddy

Bay that resulted in Eastport on Moose Island being quickly captured and the eighty-eight-man garrison there taken prisoner. The bay was declared annexed to New Brunswick.

More astounding was Armstrong's failure to countermand his orders after August 18, when a large British fleet entered Chesapeake Bay with about 4,000 troops aboard. Half of these men were Peninsular veterans, and their commander, Maj. Gen. Robert Ross, had been one of Wellington's best officers. During July this force had gathered in Bermuda. On August 3, they boarded ships commanded by Vice-Admiral Sir Alexander Cochrane. Ross's instructions from Lord Bathurst had been simple: he was to "effect a diversion on the coasts of the United States of America in favour of the army employed in the defence of Upper and Lower Canada."[25]

While Cochrane was in overall command, he left coordination of the naval and army units to Rear Admiral Sir George Cockburn. The forty-two-year-old Cockburn had garnered much experience raiding the American coast and was Cochrane's favourite for such ventures. Five years older than Cockburn, Ross had never served in North America. He had little idea what resistance to expect or how the landscape would influence events, so he relied on Cockburn's strategic and tactical advice. Cockburn's plan was audacious. He would deliver a blow that would realize the very worst of President James Madison's fears—a dual attack against Washington and Baltimore.[26]

Neither Cockburn nor Cochrane intended to spare these cities from destruction. They well remembered the winter devastation of the Niagara Peninsula, and in late May an American force had crossed Lake Erie to burn the village of Port Dover. Even though an American court of enquiry had disavowed this destruction of private property and the government was at pains to deny that the burning of villages on the Niagara Peninsula had been officially sanctioned, the British Admiralty formally approved a general order from Cochrane to "lay waste" to towns whenever possible. Unarmed civilians were to be spared, but anyone resisting was fair game. Cochrane hoped to frighten the coastal populace into neutrality, but it cleared the decks for Cockburn and other naval commanders to do their worst.[27]

Attacking Washington was bold, but also politically and militarily sound. Politically, capturing the American capital would affirm British control of the American coast—proving that the Royal Navy could do as it pleased. Cockburn knew the city was poorly defended, literally defenceless, so victory was virtually assured.

Brig. Gen. William Winder had not enthusiastically assumed responsibility for defending the city. Chesapeake Bay and the Potomac River provided ample spots for troops to land and then march on Washington. Both were winding watercourses riddled with inlets. The Patuxent River pointed like the tip of a bayonet from the bay toward the capital. With hundreds of miles of confused shoreline to guard, where was he to begin? Having no idea, Winder spent much of July riding about surveying the coast in hopes of divining where the British would put ashore.[28] His movements were so frantic that mail seldom caught up to him and he remained almost continually out of communication with superiors and subordinates alike. No sooner did someone catch wind of his location than he was already gone elsewhere. While industriously carried out, the effort was fruitless. Winder's command was a chimera. He had no troops to construct fortifications.

Armstrong had refused to authorize calling out the militia in July to prepare for possible attack. The secretary of war instead allowed the general to deploy the militia only once it was clear a British attack was under way. Winder thought this madness, but was unable to change Armstrong's mind. Complacently waiting until a British attack to "disseminate through the intricate and winding channels the various orders to the militia" would ensure he would be able to meet the crisis only with "a disorderly crowd without arms, ammunition or organization."[29]

There was also the problem of Baltimore, which lay up Chesapeake Bay to the north of Washington. Winder was supposed to defend it as well. If he concentrated what regular troops he had to cover approaches to the capital, Baltimore would be unprotected. In the end Winder scattered his troops ineffectually about, trying to defend everything while actually defending nothing.

Consequently, when the British fleet appeared in the bay on August 18, Winder and Armstrong were caught flat-footed. Both men had gone out of their way to persuade authorities in Washington, Baltimore, and Maryland's state government that the probability of attack was remote, so when the British did appear there was not only no military readiness but also a lack of psychological preparedness. Typifying the overall lassitude was the fact that Madison did not become aware that Washington faced danger until August 20. Two days later he was preparing to evacuate the government from the city, which was swept by panic.[30] The disorderly crowd Winder had feared was exactly what he now had to try to stave off the British with. That task was beyond him.

TWENTY-TWO

A Sine Qua Non

*T*hree days after the British fleet sailed from Bermuda, coaches bearing the British commissioners clattered through the streets of Ghent and delivered the three men and their entourage to the doorstep of the Hôtel Lion d'Or. Unlike the Americans, who each had at least one private secretary, the British brought only Anthony St. John Baker, the former attaché to Washington. Also amid their number was Henry Goulburn's wife, Jane, and fifteen-month-old child, Harry, plagued with infantile fever since birth. Desiring not to be separated from his wife for what could be months and worried by the child's frail condition, Goulburn had insisted he would go to Ghent only if his family accompanied him. Knowing that the young man would not unreasonably put family ahead of duty, Bathurst consented.[1]

Barely a week had passed between Viscount Castlereagh's providing instructions to the commissioners and their arrival in Ghent. The foreign secretary's challenge had been to write clear directions for topics not yet determined. The war declaration had cited several offences as justifying resort to arms, but were these the only issues at play? And which issues really mattered?

There were four overarching headings under which all the possible issues at hand could be categorized. Firstly, maritime rights, of which the most important in His Majesty's eyes was the right to "enforce in war the allegiance and service of his subjects; [seco]ndly, the protection which the Indians, as allies, are entitled to claim at our hands; [third]ly, the regulation of the frontier to prevent hereafter, as far as possible, jealousy or collision; and [fourt]hly, the question of the Fishery."[2]

Castlereagh knew the American commissioners might not be empowered to agree to terms on all aspects of these issues, so Gambier, Goulburn, and Adams were to draw out what they were able to treat on without committing Britain to anything. While conceding little, Castlereagh wanted his commissioners to assert an array of non-negotiable stipulations.

The Americans wanted an end to impressment and searching of ships. Britain, he emphasized, "can never recede from the principle of holding their own subjects to their duty to allegiance." At best he might consider some system of indulgences to individuals naturalized as United States citizens. As for right of search and withdrawal of British seamen, this could "never be given up." However, Britain could agree to limits to "check abuse." Castlereagh acknowledged that the whole issue was complex and messy, so perhaps it might be better to "waive this discussion altogether" given the issue had been laid to rest "by the return of peace." The threesome was, therefore, to deny having authority to discuss it without reference to Castlereagh.

The foreign secretary considered that Indian and border issues surpassed maritime matters in importance. It would be an absolute, or, as he phrased it, a *sine qua non*, that the treaty secure the boundaries of Indian territory. Britain and the United States must "place their mutual relationships with each other, as well as with several Indian nations, upon a footing of less jealousy and irritation." This could be accomplished by "a mutual guarantee of the Indian possessions, as they shall be established upon the peace, against encroachment on the part of either State." If both governments regarded "Indian territory as a useful barrier between both States" each would "have a common interest to render these people . . . peaceful neighbours." America could end the costly and bloody Indian wars while its seemingly insatiable desire for expansion would be checked to the satisfaction of the Indians and Britain. Given that the United States already controlled vast parts of North America, this need for continued expansion baffled Castlereagh. It was more logical to accept limits and avert further Indian wars.

America's seizure of much of the Floridas and repeated invasions of Canada led Castlereagh to seek revision of the frontier boundaries between the United States and British North America. He did not, however, detail how those boundaries were to be configured. Rather, Castlereagh merely stated that the Treaty of 1783 determining the present boundaries had been "very hastily and improvidently framed in this respect."

That same treaty regulated fishery rights between the two nations in an article consisting of two parts. The first clause had related to open-sea fishing and merely recognized rights of all nations to fish international waters. The second part, which allowed American fishing vessels to fish inside British waters and dry catch ashore, Castlereagh considered annulled by the war.

His final admonition was that the commissioners should determine what the Americans were empowered to negotiate and "the spirit in which they appear to you disposed to conduct the negotiation." Castlereagh would then provide more detailed instructions to guide their forthcoming discussions.[3]

August 7, the morning after their arrival, Baker reported the commissioners' arrival to the Americans. At Hôtel des Pays-Bas, he found only James Bayard's secretary, Col. George Milligan, who escorted Baker to the house on the Rue des Champs. Greeted by Bayard, Baker proposed meeting at one o'clock the next afternoon at the Hôtel Lion d'Or to exchange credentials and decide on the conduct of proceedings. Remaining noncommittal, Bayard promised an answer that evening.[4]

Having given up on waiting for the British and sick of "this dull hole" of a city, Jonathan Russell had gone to Dunkirk.[5] In his absence, the other four commissioners met at noon to consider the British invitation. John Quincy Adams was incensed at this "offensive pretension to superiority." When excited, he paced or flailed his arms about, sometimes pointing a blunt finger at the subject of his attention. He did all of this now, before grabbing from a shelf in his room the seventh and final volume of Hanoverian diplomat Georg Friedrich von Martens's *Recueil des traits*—the definitive collection of world treaties. Riffling to the summary section outlining international protocols, Adams cited chapter 4, section 3. According to this authoritative source, he declared, the British proposal cast them in the role of ambassadors receiving diplomats of inferior rank. Not to be outdone, Bayard hauled out R. Ward's *An Enquiry into the Foundations and History of the Law of Nations in Europe* and cited a case from the 1600s when the British commissioners negotiating with Spain resisted the very "pretension now advanced by the English." But Bayard and Albert Gallatin cautioned against clogging "the negotiation with any question of mere ceremony." Henry Clay was little concerned. When you sat down to cards it was the game that mattered, not the locale. After two hours of heated discussion that frayed nerves, they adjourned for dinner. Over cigars and drinks, they finally agreed to send Christopher Hughes—the mission's senior secretary—to decline the British invitation and propose the Hôtel des Pays-Bas, which, with the Americans gone, could be considered neutral ground.

Now it was the British who needed time to consider. When Baker arrived, Bayard, "to sound and ascertain their feelings," spontaneously proposed holding the meeting at the American residence and offered to show the secretary an excellent room for it. Baker declined to even look. It would be the Pays-Bas or start over.

At one o'clock the next afternoon, the Americans found the British already seated on one side of a long table in a room the hotelier had set aside. Gambier was as resplendent as a peacock in his admiral's uniform, Goulburn and Adams like dour starlings in dark suits on either side of him. Everyone stood. Hands were shaken, courteous bows exchanged, copies of credentials examined and appropriately added to the formal files each commission began to accumulate. Then the Americans sat across from the British.

Gambier opened, assuring the Americans of his government's "sincere and earnest desire that this negotiation might terminate in a successful issue, and the ardent hope of the British commissioners that we might all have the satisfaction of restoring the blessings of peace to our respective countries."

As head of the American commission, Adams offered similar assurances "to bring to these discussions the disposition to meet every sentiment of candor and conciliation with the most cordial reciprocity, concurring, as we did, with the utmost earnestness and sincerity, in the hope that we might eventually have the happiness of reconciling the two nations whose true interests could best be promoted by peace and amity with each other."[6]

Goulburn then said "that his colleagues had devolved upon him the task of opening on their part."[7] It quickly became apparent that this intense, dark-haired young man, seeming irritated at times by every American response or proposal, was the key British player. Goulburn offered "the most explicit declaration that nothing that had occurred since the first proposal for this negotiation would have the slightest effect on the disposition of Great Britain with regard to the terms upon which the pacification might be concluded." Not a man in the room could fail to heed this reminder that since Castlereagh's offer of negotiations the previous fall, peace had returned to Europe, the British army was free for North American service, the Royal Navy sailed the American coastline at will and blockaded the nation's ports. The dark spectre of defeat hung over the United States. Goulburn added that "it would be most conducive to . . . discard all retrospective considerations with regard to anything that had taken place."[8] Instead they should all look to the root causes of the war, and therein he was instructed to raise four points for discussion. After outlining these, Goulburn asked the Americans to advise whether they could discuss each point and to also raise any issues they wished negotiated.

Each of Castlereagh's four points was advanced and detailed. Goulburn made clear that impressment was included only because it was expected that the Americans would wish this discussed. There was no British desire to resolve this matter by treaty between the two nations. The treaty must include the Indians, and fixing boundaries for Indian territory was a *sine qua non* that must be "definitively marked out, as a permanent barrier between the dominions of Great Britain and the United States."[9] Britain also sought to revise the boundary line between America and British North America. Responding to a question from Bayard, Goulburn assured the Americans that Britain "did not contemplate an acquisition of territory."[10] As Castlereagh had provided no instructions, Goulburn did not define the proposed Indian boundary or Canadian border revision. In fact, Goulburn—more familiar with the geography of North America and its current boundaries than the foreign secretary—pressed this issue more forcefully than Castlereagh's instructions had suggested.[11] He was determined that any treaty stifle further imperialistic designs America might entertain. He did not, however, express this intention. Instead, he closed by adding that the previous "concession" to America permitting her citizens to "land and dry fish within the exclusive jurisdiction" of Britain would not be renewed.[12]

Remarking that he wished to ensure clear understanding of each point, Adams repeated them. He understood that impressment was a "point proper for discussion." No, Goulburn interjected, the British "did not think it a point necessary to be discussed," but thought it an American concern.[13]

When Adams said he needed to confer with his colleagues before providing comment on each point raised, Goulburn urged him to provide "an immediate answer" as to whether they had any instructions on the Indian boundary *sine qua non*. Adams refused to be drawn, and the meeting was set over to the next morning. Future meetings would alternate between respective residences. Gambier suggested the American house be first, as the British were still moving from their hotel to better accommodations.[14]

Gloomily, the Americans considered their response. There was little cause for optimism. Gallatin told his son, James, that the British had demanded that the "Indian tribes should have the whole of the North-Western Territory. This comprises the States of Michigan, Wisconsin, and Illinois—four-fifths of Indiana and the third of Ohio. That an Indian sovereignty should be constituted under the guarantee of Great Britain: this is to protect Canada. . . . The other demands are of little importance. They consist of Sackett's Harbour and Fort Niagara, so as to have control of the lakes. But all this means the dismemberment of the United States." Although Goulburn had not outlined the territory sought, Gallatin was certain that was the British intention.

The British commissioners did not impress Gallatin, according to his son. They were "men who have not made any mark and have no influence or weight. He attaches but little importance to them as they are but the puppets of Lord Castlereagh and Liverpool. Father feels he is quite capable of dealing with them."[15]

Through the rest of the afternoon, over dinner, and into the evening, the Americans talked and argued. At issue were the Indians. Impressment could be let lie. Their instructions from Monroe had been explicit that the fishery could await a commercial treaty. Boundaries between America and Canada could be discussed. But they had no instructions on the Indians. Who could have conceived the need? Who could think that the British would make *sine qua non* that America should surrender vast amounts of its sovereign territory to the Indians? It was incomprehensible. Finally, with Gallatin acting as secretary, they drafted a response.

No sooner was this document complete than a package of dispatches and letters from America arrived, including two letters written by Monroe in late June. Gallatin, Adams, and Hughes spent several hours deciphering the simple number code only to find that the June 25 letter reaffirmed that the fisheries were not to be discussed. If the British insisted, the negotiations were to be terminated. The June 27 message confirmed that impressment could be omitted. It was one in the morning when the three men wearily took to their beds. They had decided that nothing in Monroe's letters affected their response.[16]

The British, Adams wrote Louisa, were "polite and conciliatory. Their professions both with regard to their government and themselves, liberal, and highly pacific. But they have not changed the opinion which I have constantly had of the result. . . . At present I do not think that the negotiation will be of long continuance."[17]

After breakfast the three Englishman took their seats across from the Americans at a table set up in the room that Bayard had earlier offered to show Baker. Adams confirmed that they had instructions to negotiate the issue of impressment and allegiance, no instructions on Indian boundaries, instructions regarding British boundary claims, and nothing relating to fisheries. On the second point Adams said instructions could not have been expected as this "was never contemplated by them as being in dispute. No European power had ever considered the Indian nations as Great Britain appeared now to consider them." He suggested the British government "so modify the instruction as to this point being a sine qua non as not to preclude discussion on the other points in which there might be use."

Goulburn replied that both powers had made treaties with the Indians and some of these nations were British allies, so it was not beyond contemplation that "Britain would stipulate for them in any treaty with the U.S." It would be difficult to proceed without some assurance that the American commissioners could at least agree to a provisional article even if they had no specific instructions. The British government's view in this regard was clearly "to procure to her Allies a peace as permanent as that procured for themselves and to establish the Indian Nations as a sort of barrier between the two States to prevent their future collision."

The same effect would be achieved, Bayard countered, if Britain and America entered into a peace treaty and then the United States independently negotiated peace agreements with the Indians. He understood that commissions for negotiations with the Indians had already been appointed and those agreements would "fix limits to their territories."

It was certainly not lost on the British commissioners that the United States had historically broken one treaty after another with the Indians, but they refrained from any sharp rebuke. In a personal note to Lord Bathurst after the meeting, Goulburn said he and his colleagues "have been particularly careful to say nothing in these preliminary proceedings which could in any degree cause irritation on their part and have therefore rather let any observation of the Americans which gave an opening for a sharp answer to pass without observation than get into a squabble which could lead to no object."

The tension, however, was palpable. Goulburn coolly stated that Britain wanted to assure "the permanence of the Peace made with the Indians."

"Is it intended to restrain the Indians from alienating their own lands?" Bayard asked.

"The restraint need not be on the Indian right of alienation but on the right of the U.S. or Great Britain to acquire those lands by purchase or cession," Dr. William Adams responded. They could still sell to a third party.

Clay snapped that he had "extreme difficulty" believing any article on this subject would be accepted by the American government.[18]

The discussion deadlocked, each side agreed to draft a protocol outlining the points that had been discussed over the first two days. These would be compared the next day and together the commissioners would write a final record of the proceedings to forward to their respective governments for consideration.

As the meeting ended, John Quincy Adams told Gambier that he was impressed by the candour and conciliatory attitude the British commissioners had so far displayed. Clay agreed. In his letter to Bathurst, Goulburn expressed similar regard that the Americans had "conducted themselves with more candor and openness than I had expected. . . . I believe they are sincere in their wish to re-establish peace between the two Countries." But he thought there was "little hope of their concluding anything [with regard to the Indian boundary] without the receipt of instructions from America." As to whether the talks continued, he said, that "must depend upon your decision whether we shall proceed to discuss our other points of difference in the uncertainty in which the Americans are with respect to the Indian boundary or whether we shall suspend our proceedings."[19]

Protocols in hand on August 10, they immediately clashed. The British took offence at how the American protocol, meticulously worked up initially by Adams and then supplemented and corrected by the other three commissioners, contained explanatory notes regarding the reasons the American government had offered no instructions on the Indian boundaries and fisheries. Goulburn grumbled that all explanations should be removed and inserted into a dispatch to the respective government because if matters of "argument were admitted on one side it must also be admitted on the other, and must eventually contain everything said at the conferences."

Bayard thought the British had not disclosed their full meaning the day before and "their proposition respecting the Indian boundary, as put by themselves, was not intelligible. . . . Did they mean to take a portion of our territory and assign it to the Indians? Did they mean, in a word, to alter the condition of the Indians in relation to the United States?"

"It could not be said there was a territory *assigned* to people which was already in their possession," Dr. Adams replied.

In the British protocol the words *dominion* and *territory* had often been used in reference to the Indian nations, a fact Adams found rankling. Finally he remarked "that they must be aware the terms Dominions, Territories, and Possessions, as applied to Indians, were of very different import from the same terms as applied to civilized nations; that this difference was well known and understood . . . by all the European nations."

One or the other of those words was necessary to make any sense, Goulburn replied. He preferred *territory*.

The American draft concluded that the British commissioners declined further discussions unless it was agreed that a provisional article might be drawn up on the Indian question subject to ratification by the U.S. government. In the absence of this, the British proposed suspending talks until they consulted their government.

When the British asked that this statement be removed, the Americans replied that this was "a fact so material to the statement of what had actually taken place, that without it the protocol itself must be imperfect."

Dr. Adams thought it "expressed rather too strongly, to say that they had *declined* entering into the discussion."

Those were his exact words the day before, Clay reminded him. True, Adams confessed, but "those were remarks . . . thrown out rather in the manner of friendly discussion than intimating a fixed purpose to decline it in future."[20]

The Americans agreed to excise the offending words. Essentially, when the final document was signed off, the protocol closely resembled the British original. But the Americans would forward their draft protocol to Washington in the expectation that it would clearly illustrate that the British commissioners had not come to Ghent intending to negotiate in good faith. Rather they had come with intent to use the dispute over Indian boundaries as pretense for breaking off discussions.

In a private letter, Bayard commented that the Indian boundary line issue "seems to me at present to offer serious difficulty to a pacification. The pretension . . . in my opinion is totally inadmissible and possibly has been selected as a designed insuperable obstacle to peace. When first disclosed it was declared to be a sine qua non. One such pretension is as complete a barrier against peace as an hundred. . . . The conferences are in consequence suspended and they have written to their Government for further instructions. The state of things does not augur well."[21]

Adams was beside himself with anxiety that in the absence of a peace agreement, which he doubted was attainable, America must soon face a blow that would "lay us prostrate at the mercy of our foe. God forbid! But either that, or a latent energy must be brought forth, of which we have as yet manifested no sign."[22]

While awaiting reply from London, the British commissioners moved to new lodgings in a former Carthusian monastery on the Fratersplein, about a mile north of the city centre. It was a large, drafty building with a six-storey belfry and a four-storey alcove that had been converted into apartments. The greater portion of the building had been transformed into a textile mill after monasteries and convents were abolished following annexation of the Netherlands by France in 1795. The factory was owned by Lieven Bauwens, who had managed to smuggle the plans for the cotton gin out of England in 1800—a feat that enabled Ghent to become a textile capital. By 1814, Ghent's population stood at about 60,000 people—many impoverished factory workers living in squalor and crammed into ancient buildings that lined narrow alleys running off from the wider boulevards that followed the course of the numerous canals connecting the two rivers running through it.

The elegant and lavishly furnished apartments perfectly suited the upper-class expectations of the three commissioners. But Goulburn's wife complained that the drafty rooms provided an unhealthy atmosphere for Harry, while she contracted a cold that proved impossible to shake. There was also the disappointment that Ghent society had largely decamped to the country for the summer and would not return until November. This meant there were few social or cultural events.[23] Invited to lunch at a local dignitary's villa, the Goulburns were greeted at the door by what the extremely short-sighted Jane took to be a butler. Treating the man in the manner appropriate to a servant, she was embarrassed to discover this was in fact their host. That a gentleman would not employ a butler horrified them both, and they were equally dismayed by the villa's stark and sparse furnishings. Leaving as soon as was polite, they vowed to never "make a longer visit to a house where comfort appears to be so ill understood."[24] That Goulburn expected their stay in Ghent to be short undoubtedly reassured his wife.

The Americans held a dinner for all their compatriots living in the city and ended seating twenty-two at the table.[25] On the 13th, the British commissioners came to dine. Goulburn declined, claiming to be unwell with a burst blood vessel in his throat that rendered him incapable of speech, but Gambier and Dr. Adams attended. Gambier happily recounted boyhood days spent in Boston while his uncle was in command of the naval station, and allowed how he had participated in the blockade of New York during the Revolution. As a vice-president of the English Bible Society, he often still corresponded with the Bible Society of Boston, of which Adams was a member. When Bayard edged the conversation gently toward business, Gambier laughed politely. "We won't talk about that now," he said.[26]

When not entertaining, the Americans dined at four and usually spent two hours over the meal. "We then disperse to our several amusements and avocations," Adams wrote Louisa. "Mine is a solitary walk of two or three hours—solitary, because I find none of the other gentlemen disposed to join me in it, particularly at that hour. They frequent the coffee houses, the Reading Rooms, and the billiard tables. Between eight and nine I return from my walk and immediately betake myself to bed. I rise usually about five in the morning, and from that time until dinner am closely engaged in writing or other business." He longed to return to her in St. Petersburg, lamented the shortening days that hinted at the approach of autumn and forced him to abridge the duration of his walks. "I hope we shall have no winter evenings to dispose of. . . ."[27]

On August 19, the British commissioners requested a three o'clock conference at their house. London had finally replied, but the Americans were surprised to learn that the courier bringing the instructions had been none other than Viscount Castlereagh.

The foreign secretary arrived late at the monastery on the Thursday night of August 18 the same day that the British fleet entered Chesapeake

Bay. His instructions were stuffed in a red dispatch box, one of many swelling the vast amount of luggage he was taking to Vienna, where a congress was to convene in September that would redraw the map of Europe. Also in tow was the full retinue that was accompanying him to Vienna, including his wife, her sister, and a gaggle of secretaries, consultants, and servants. Despite the lateness of the hour, Castlereagh summoned the three commissioners, while arrangements were made to accommodate this large party at hotels throughout the city.

It was clear to Castlereagh that the two matters the Americans claimed to have no instructions on posed the greatest barrier to continuing negotiations. Regarding the fishery, he wanted to determine whether they would acknowledge that the "right of fishing and drying within the British jurisdiction does not thereby of right revive" if they were to sign a treaty of peace that dealt with the other issues. Goulburn and the others must get this clarified.

As for the Indian questions, he could understand that they might not have anticipated that Britain would want to establish secure boundaries for the Indians. But, Castlereagh said, "it appears unaccountable . . . that the American Government should have left the negotiators without instructions, inasmuch as they could have had no reason to suppose that the British Government would for a moment listen to a separate peace, to the exclusion of the Indians, who have acted with them as allies during the war."

He agreed with Goulburn that the whole future of the negotiation turned on the point of "whether the Commissioners will or will not take upon themselves to sign a Provisional Agreement upon the points on which they have no instructions. If they decline this, the British Government sees no advantage in prosecuting the discussion further, until the American negotiators shall have received instructions upon these points." If they agreed that they could enter into provisional agreements, he believed the negotiation could continue and the treaty be sent after British ratification to the United States for that government to either confirm or not.

As to the additional American points, Castlereagh rejected any need to discuss blockades and advised the commissioners they could not "be too peremptory in discouraging, at the outset, the smallest expectation of any restitution of captures made under the Orders in Council." On the desire for a commercial treaty, the foreign secretary said the government was willing to enter into one after conclusion of the peace.

On the issue of Canada's boundaries, Castlereagh offered some clarification of the British position, which was to be understood as "strictly defensive." The Great Lakes from Lake Ontario to Lake Superior were to form the "natural military frontier" of the Canadas, and as "the weaker power on the North American continent, the least capable of acting offensively, and the most exposed to sudden invasion, Great Britain considers itself entitled to claim the use of the lakes as a military barrier." If both powers claimed a right to put ships onto the lakes, Castlereagh foresaw a "perpetual contest for naval ascendancy, in peace as well as war," that would only guarantee future conflict. Control of the lakes should be given to Britain and with that went "military command of both shores . . . with a suitable frontier."

But the foreign secretary declared such a conclusion would mean that Britain gained territory from America, and that was not intended. Therefore he proposed that the United States retain control of the southern shores and carry on using the lakes for commercial traffic if it agreed to destroy existing forts, construct no new ones, and withdraw naval vessels from the lakes and rivers that emptied into them. While not wanting territorial concessions from the Americans, the British did want the southern border of Lower Canada adjusted in order to "establish a direct [line] of communication between Quebec and Halifax." The British would also have the right to free navigation of the Mississippi, and the northwestern boundary between Lake Superior and that river must be negotiated.

Castlereagh reiterated that inclusion of the Indians in the peace remained a *sine qua non* and suggested that the Treaty of Greenville imposed by William Henry Harrison, wherein Indians had surrendered the Ohio Valley to America, could serve as the basis for negotiation. The boundaries once agreed were not to be open to acquisition through purchase by either side.

An added instruction was the admonition that the commissioners must take great care "to remove all doubt as to the islands in

Passamaquoddy Bay being considered as falling within the British boundary there."²⁸

Reflecting on the instructions, Goulburn found them overall "more agreeable to my own feelings than the one with which we were provided on leaving London as I confess I did not then understand that it was contemplated to make America disarm on the Lakes and the shores of them." This made sense to him. That said, however, Goulburn was perplexed that Castlereagh had worded the prohibition on either power gaining Indian territory so that it denied acquisition only by purchase. During the first negotiating round, Goulburn had explained that this prohibition would mean that neither party could acquire territory inside the Indian boundaries by purchase "or *otherwise.*"

Castlereagh replied that he objected to Goulburn's inserting this additional word. It was not, he said, Britain's intent "to preclude the Americans from conquering the Indians who might be at war with them and acquiring territory by conquest as a restriction of this nature would expose them to invasion from the Indians from which there would be no redress." If the point was discussed, he instructed Goulburn to "disclaim such a view of the subject."

Goulburn was infuriated by this order and poured out his thoughts in a letter to Lord Bathurst. If the Americans were to be allowed to conquer Indian territory at will, he said, the question should be easily settled. "The Americans will I am sure be ready to assign a boundary if they are told that they may conquer though they may not purchase the Territory within.... Causes of War will always be found for they almost always exist and the only difference in the situation of Canada will be that its frontier will be laid open by a conquering American Army under General Harrison instead of by Treaties for Sale as heretofore.... I do not quite see the justice of Lord Castlereagh's distinction. . . . In other instances in which Barriers of a similar kind have been created (in the low countries for instance) it was never conceived that either country could destroy that Barrier by conquest whatever injuries she might sustain from the inhabitants within it and surely if the Indian Territory is made a barrier it ought to have a similar exemption. America has modes of punishing the Indians more effective than the occupation of their Territory: indeed the occupation of territory is no punishment: for an Indian nation has always heretofore been in the habit of indemnifying itself for an encroachment of this nature by invading a neighbouring nation more remote from the original encroacher—The arrangement too will operate unfairly against us—If an American Indian nation injures us we cannot attack them because they are within the limits of the United States and remonstrance is our only mode of obtaining redress." All this would provide the Americans excuse to eliminate these Indians and thus come up against the Canadian frontier. While cautioning Bathurst to keep his letter quite *private,* he implored the secretary for war and the colonies to get the cabinet—which Castlereagh indicated had approved this idea—to reconsider. He also wondered, since the Americans had not yet objected to Goulburn's original definition of the limits on expansion, how "far ought we to reduce our demand if they do not make the objection?"[29]

TWENTY-THREE

A Capital Burned, a Campaign Lost

The August 19 meeting in the monastery lasted barely an hour, ending in a shouting match. Henry Goulburn alternately read or summarized Castlereagh's instructions. Between Quebec and Halifax, Goulburn said the British had in mind "a mere road . . . which would take off a small corner of the province of Maine." The British demands were really moderate, he noted.

Better able to check his temper than the others, Albert Gallatin jumped in before either John Quincy Adams or Henry Clay could speak. What did the British intend for the American citizens living west of the Treaty of Greenville boundary? Perhaps 100,000 in the territories of Michigan, Illinois, and part of Ohio State would be affected. The treaty, Goulburn replied, was a basis for discussion. The greater populations might warrant an adjustment of the line, but if that could not be agreed, they might have to leave.

"Undoubtedly they must shift for themselves," Dr. William Adams snorted.

James Bayard asked whether the Indian clauses remained a *sine qua non*, which the British affirmed. Was the Great Lakes proposal also a *sine qua non*? Dr. Adams responded, "One *sine qua non* at a time is enough. It will be time enough to answer your question when you have disposed of that we have given you."

Gallatin mentioned English newspaper reports that the British had occupied Moose Island in Passamaquoddy Bay. Was their government intending to keep it? Goulburn said "it was a part of the province of Nova Scotia; that they did not even consider it a subject for discussion" and that he could "demonstrate in the most unanswerable manner that it belonged to them."

"Might as well contest [our] right to Northamptonshire," Dr. Adams barked.

If America was denied the right to militarize the Great Lakes, did the British intend to exercise that right? The British commissioners told Gallatin that "they certainly did."

John Quincy Adams, seething, curtly stated that he did not want to conference further until the British set their proposal in writing. This was agreed, and the Americans committed to provide a written response before the next meeting. Bayard, surprised by the hard British line, wondered, if the conference were suspended, whether Goulburn would return immediately to England. "Yes," the young man replied, "and I suppose you will take a trip to America." As the meeting ended, the Americans learned that Castlereagh was in the city.[1]

No sooner had the Americans departed than Castlereagh strode into the room. He and the commissioners thought the session had gone surprisingly well. Rather than challenging the British demands, the Americans had merely sought clarification. Goulburn had avoided mentioning Castlereagh's point that the Americans could gain by conquest what they would be prohibited from purchasing. The Americans had failed to press for details, apparently believing they were to be denied any avenue to acquire territory.[2]

The news from North America's western frontier was, from the British perspective, favourable. Although the Americans had established forts on the upper Mississippi in 1813 that challenged British dominance, by the summer of 1814 most had either been abandoned or captured. Prairie du Chien, at the junction of the Wisconsin and Mississippi, had come back under British control in early July. This, combined with the British resurgence on Lake Huron, ensured the strong allegiance of the still potent Indian allies. As the man in the government most familiar with the political and military complexities of the war in North America, the undersecretary for war and the colonies was determined not to undermine this alliance. Hence, he would not raise Castlereagh's compromise unless the foreign secretary insisted.

Goulburn assured Castlereagh that the Americans "were disposed both to treat and sign on these arrangements" and the slight expansions of British North America's border. Having voiced "no surprise or repugnance . . . to any of the Suggestions," if the British stood firm, the Americans would acquiesce.[3]

Castlereagh was less optimistic, worried that the war drifted toward a purely territorial conflict for parts of North America that Britain little needed. Adding more trackless wilderness to the empire hardly warranted the inherent costs. There was also the nagging fear that they engaged in a war unlikely to be lost but equally impossible to win.

Writing Prime Minister Liverpool, Castlereagh pondered compromises that might lead the American commissioners to enter into a provisional agreement that included an Indian peace and surrendered Passamaquoddy Bay and the road link between Quebec and Halifax but left Indian boundaries for later discussion. While the American commissioners might agree to that, Castlereagh very much doubted President Madison and his executive would concur. The negotiation process was all a muddle, because the Atlantic Ocean's breadth prevented the American government responding in a timely manner.

The foreign secretary briefly considered meeting the Americans directly and would likely have done so had they requested it. But, he informed Liverpool, "they did not call upon or desire to see me, and I thought my originating an interview would be considered objectionable by our own Commissioners."[4]

But the Americans had never considered that Castlereagh desired direct contact. "We did not see him," Adams wrote Louisa, "but at the conference it is scarcely a figure of speech to say that we felt him. Our opponents were not only charged fourfold with obnoxious substance, they threw off much of the suavity of form which they had observed before."[5]

The British commissioners were deluded in thinking their American counterparts could be bullied into submission. Interrupted in the middle of a private letter to James Monroe by the meeting, Clay immediately afterward added a postscript. It would "be an unpardonable insult" to present the British proposals to the government. "The pretensions of . . . Britain do not admit of deliberation." Clay thought the British unlikely to terminate the conference, instead hoping the Americans would make the definitive break. Failing that, the talks could probably be protracted, but to what purpose? He suspected the British desired merely to keep the Americans at the table until some major defeat pushed them into accepting these outrageous demands. "The reliance will be much better on the firmness and energy of the American people, to conquer again their Independence," he closed.[6]

Gallatin also wrote to Monroe. Supposing that the British cabinet continued the war only to assuage popular opinion and secretly desired peace had been a miscalculation. They could win everything proposed at the table from the barrel of a gun. He predicted a major offensive to gain control of the Great Lakes, a widened Indian war that must be met vigorously by America to expel the adjacent tribes or force them to sue for peace and thus eliminate the *sine qua non* pretext. Gallatin understood that an army of about 14,000 troops was to sail from England in September toward New Orleans. Attacks against the east coast would attempt to draw American forces away from these other objectives. "It is now evident that Great Britain intends to strengthen and aggrandize herself in North America. . . . It is highly probable that our struggle will be longer and more arduous than I had anticipated."[7]

The very day that the commissioners held their stormy meeting, the British began the assault on America's capital. For several days about twenty warships and several unarmed transport vessels had stood in Chesapeake Bay, throwing Washington and all of coastal Maryland into a panic second-guessing where the troops would land. On August 19, a British flotilla forged up the Patuxent River, and Maj. Gen. Robert Ross landed with 4,000 seasoned British regulars at Benedict.

Impeded only by the withering August heat that caused many troops to fall out of line during the march, Ross followed the river to Upper Marlboro. There he paused on August 23 to confer with Rear Admiral Sir George Cockburn, who urged him to press on to the capital. Reinforced with a battery of marine artillery, some sailors, and marines, on August 24, Ross reached Bladensburg on the East Branch, a tributary of the Potomac River, within five miles of Washington. Here, the British faced a hasty defensive line consisting of 7,000 men. Although outnumbering the British, only 1,000 were regulars and another 400 sailors.

Set on commanding heights and concentrated alongside a fortified house, the American position appeared formidable. Approaching the heights required crossing a bridge over the East Branch covered by several artillery pieces.[8]

President James Madison and his entire executive arrived on horseback at eleven o'clock. It was more than a hundred degrees Fahrenheit; sweat drenched their riding clothes. Winder was not on the field. Gen. Tobias Stansbury, who had brought 3,500 Maryland militiamen into the line, commanded in his absence, but Brig. Gen. Walter Smith of the Georgetown militia angrily contested his right. While the two men argued points of seniority, Monroe tried to reorganize a point in the defensive line while, encouraged by Madison, Armstrong made similar martial gestures. Winder appeared about noon, too late to influence events. An hour later cannon on both sides began an exchange. Madison suggested the civilians depart the field so the officers could see to the battle unworried about their safety.[9]

In fact, neither Winder nor any other general further influenced events. As the British advanced, a volley of Congreve rockets was fired at the American line. Iron cylinders 42 inches long and 4 inches in diameter to which a 32-pound explosive charge was fixed, these rockets emitted a loud shriek and trailed a stream of flame as they raced out to a maximum range of 3,000 yards. Though causing visual fireworks and much racket, they were fairly harmless. None of the militia had ever been exposed to them, however, and a shudder rolled through the ranks as the rockets *whish*ed overhead. With the British infantry closing, the first line fell back into the troops behind, causing general panic. Thirty minutes after the attack began, the militia were on the run. Only Commodore Joshua Barney's 400 sailors held fast, manning a battery of guns stripped from gunboats. For two hours they impeded the British until finally the position was turned and the badly wounded Barney sent them back.[10]

Not so the militia and regular troops. They outran the president and his party, scurrying by without pause. The British, who had expected a stiff fight, watched with wonder. "Never did men with arms in their hands make better use of their legs," observed Lt. George R. Gleig.[11] They quickly dubbed the affair the Bladensburg Races. Not that the battle was bloodless. The British counted 64 dead and 185 wounded— mostly due to Barney's work—while American losses were only 10 to 12 killed and about 40 wounded.[12] If the Americans had not bolted, their weight of numbers might have prevailed.

Winder hoped to regroup in the capital, but could not bring his men under control. Most fled to their homes. Those from Washington gathered up their families and a few belongings and joined long lines of civilians abandoning the city. Madison arrived at the White House to find supper growing cold on the table and Dolley gone. She had stuffed a wagon with the silverware, prized velvet curtains, boxes of official papers, books, and a full-length portrait of George Washington that had been painted by Gilbert Stuart and which she had ordered cut from its frame. Everything else was abandoned. Madison could do nothing more to save personal or state possessions. He had only a horse. Calmly mounting it, he rode for Virginia, where the government was instructed to rally to determine its next move. After nightfall, Madison's party rode up to the ferry that would carry them across the Potomac.[13] Looking toward Washington, they saw "columns of flame and smoke ascending through the night . . . from the Capitol, the President's house, and other public edifices, as the whole were on fire, some burning slowly, others with bursts of flame and sparks mounting high up in the horizon . . . If at intervals the dismal sight was lost to our view, we got it again from some hilltop or eminence where we paused to look at it."[14]

The British burned only government buildings. In addition to the Capitol and the president's house, the Treasury, the War Office, and the government propaganda newspaper *National Intelligencer* were torched. Before fleeing the capital, naval secretary William Jones ordered the dockyard burned, including a sloop and recently completed frigate. Two bridges over the East Branch had also been destroyed by the Americans, and the British wrecked the main Potomac crossing. Thousands of tons of military stores were destroyed, including more than 200 artillery pieces. Resistance to the destruction was minimal, but the British suffered some casualties when a dockyard munitions dump exploded massively. Ross led his men out of Washington on the morning of August 25. Four days later, the British boarded their ships at Benedict.[15]

Burning Washington was roundly decried by most Americans as an act of barbarism, but largely the British troops had shown restraint. Even the *Intelligencer* editor admitted that few private buildings were molested.[16] Albert Gallatin was among the unlucky few. His house on Capitol Hill was burned, although all possessions there, save a valuable map collection, were removed before the fire was kindled.[17] More important, the fires, whether through fortune or design, failed to spread to residential areas. Certainly the raid and the destruction wrought by the British fell within the well-established pattern set by both sides over the past two years.

President Madison returned to Washington on August 28, morosely picked through the ashes of the White House, and examined the shell of the Capitol. The pillars in Representatives Hall were badly cracked; the still-smoking great hand-painted dome had collapsed into the cellar. A delegation of Washingtonians and citizens of Georgetown demanded he send a deputation to Admiral Cochrane to capitulate. Madison urged citizens and troops alike not to despair. His rapid return to the city was soon credited with stiffening the nation's backbone.[18] Madison ordered the unharmed post and patent offices converted into halls that could respectively seat the Senate and House of Representatives. The presidential residence was established in the eccentric Octagon House, which had formerly housed the French minister to America. In this manner, the government quickly regained its feet.[19]

Armstrong slunk into the city forty-eight hours after Madison to face a virtual mutiny of regular officers. They bluntly warned Madison that they would tear off their epaulettes if Armstrong remained in charge. Madison charged Armstrong with doing nothing to prepare the city's defence and actively impeding the efforts of others. He cited Armstrong's long-standing insubordinate ways and ordered him to leave town.[20] From

Baltimore, Armstrong submitted his resignation and Monroe was formally appointed secretary of war, also retaining the State Department.

Elsewhere the British were on the offensive. Alexandria, Virginia, endured an August 28 raid by a British squadron. Occupying the town without a fight, Capt. James Gordon agreed to not burn the place if all public works, ordnance and naval stores, and shipping—whether private or public—were surrendered. Twenty-one small vessels were seized and large quantities of military stores destroyed or carried off.[21]

Meanwhile, the British fleet carrying Ross's troops headed for Baltimore intending a demonstration that might turn into an attack if circumstances proved favourable. Cochrane was skeptical. Baltimore was no defenceless Washington. The nation's third-largest city lay 12 miles up Patapsco River from Chesapeake Bay and its very narrow harbour entrance was guarded by Fort McHenry. Senator and militia major general Samuel Smith commanded its defence. Since early 1813 this veteran of the Revolution and renowned political intriguer had been preparing to defend the city. As the British approached Baltimore, Smith deployed almost 15,000 men in its defensive works. More than 1,000 were packed into the small confines of Fort McHenry. When Major General Winder arrived to assume command, Smith curtly refused.[22]

The British disembarked about 4,500 men on September 11 to march overland along the peninsula formed by the Patapsco and Back rivers while a squadron of frigates, bomb and rocket ships, and sloops commanded by Cochrane pushed up the Patapsco to bombard the fort. As during the Washington raid, Cockburn accompanied Ross's troops.

Instead of waiting to be attacked, Smith sent 3,200 men with six small cannon to meet the British halfway along the peninsula. A sharp action followed the next morning in which Ross was struck in the chest by a musket ball and mortally wounded. Col. Arthur Brooke assumed command and broke the American line. The Americans lost 24 killed, 139 wounded, and 50 taken prisoner, while the British counted 46 dead and 295 wounded.

On September 13, Brooke closed to within a mile and a half of Baltimore and sent messengers to Cochrane proposing a joint night attack. After examining the American harbour defences, Cochrane deemed the idea impracticable. He had sixteen fighting ships, of which five were bomb or rocket vessels. The former mounted large mortars that could breach fortress walls, but the rocket ships were largely just for show.

In addition to the fort, the Americans had clogged the harbour entrance by sinking twenty-four vessels of various sizes. Standing behind these wrecks was a line of gunboats. Guarding the Patapsco main channel where the British might land troops behind Fort McHenry stood the smaller Fort Covington and a nearby artillery battery. The best Cochrane could hope for was to batter the two forts into submission, but he saw no utility in throwing Brooke's redcoats against the American defences. Brooke was ordered to remain in place to keep the enemy guessing his intention and then withdraw in the early morning hours of September 14. By then the forts would have been either subdued or not.[23]

The bombardment lasted slightly more than twenty-four hours and 1,500 rounds were fired, of which 400 struck home. Aboard one ship was American lawyer Francis Scott Key, who was trying to arrange the release of a physician captured in Washington and pressed into treating British wounded. Key watched the shelling and scribbled out a little poem entitled "The Star Spangled Banner," which vividly depicted the flag continuing to fly over Fort McHenry even as Congreve rockets whizzed overhead and mortar bombs exploded in airbursts that spewed shrapnel into the fort. In 1931, Congress would declare the poem America's national anthem.[24]

Shortly after dawn, Cochrane ordered the bombardment ceased, and the fleet and troops withdrew. Lingering in the Chesapeake well into October, this force took no further major action. It finally sailed to Jamaica, while Cochrane returned to Halifax.

In American eyes, Baltimore's stand offset the Washington calamity. The British deemed it a modest setback. Far graver was the Lake Champlain failure, where the British suffered a defeat that frustrated London's hopes for the 1814 campaign.

Fortune in war is fickle. The campaign that the British launched in the Lake Champlain region in early September logically should have yielded a success, enabling entrance into the Hudson Valley to cut New England off from the rest of the United States. Combined with the victories that

Lt. Gen. Sir John Sherbrooke's forces were racking up on its coast, New England might have capitulated.

On July 11, a small force out of Halifax had captured Eastport on Moose Island and gained control of Passamaquoddy Bay. Sherbrooke then moved to seize control of all of Maine from New Brunswick to Penobscot Bay, initiating a British strategy to declare the Penobscot River as the new boundary between America and their colonies.[25]

The British entered the bay on August 31. Quickly overcoming a garrison of about fifty men at Castine, they next captured Belfast on the opposite side of the bay and then pushed upriver to Hampden. On September 2, they drove off the defenders, pillaged the town and burned the disabled American corvette *Adams*, which had earlier run aground during a storm. Marching overland halfway back to Passamaquoddy Bay, the redcoats seized the village of Machias on September 10. By September 27, all of Maine between the two bays was subdued.[26]

Canadian governor Sir George Prevost's operation on Lake Champlain could have achieved much the same result in southern New England. But the aggressiveness required to take an army into enemy territory did not come easily to Prevost—not even when the gates were left unguarded. On August 29, Maj. Gen. George Izard had, in accordance with instructions from Armstrong, reluctantly marched 4,000 men to reinforce the Americans on the Niagara Peninsula. Left behind were just 3,000 regulars and militia under Brig. Gen. Alexander Macomb. Only half of these were considered fit for duty. The rest were sick, raw recruits, or New York militia in whom the general had little faith.[27]

Five days after Izard's departure, Prevost crossed into America with 10,000 men. Two-thirds were Peninsular War veterans. What Prevost lacked, however, was naval control of Lake Champlain. This lay in the hands of Capt. Thomas Macdonough and his 26-gun flagship *Saratoga*, the 20-gun *Eagle*, and supporting fleet of a schooner, two sloops, and twelve gunboats. The British, however, were ready to challenge his mastery with a new flagship, the 36-gun *Confiance*, a captured French ship. Still, the overwhelming force Prevost brought to the field seemed substantial enough regardless of who ultimately won the lake contest.

By September 5 the British were camped 8 miles from Plattsburgh, where Macomb's men were throwing up redoubts to meet Prevost's juggernaut. Plattsburgh was a complicated village cut into uneven chunks by the Saranac River, which emptied into Lake Champlain from its midst. The next day the British probed into the outskirts, but Prevost cautiously refrained from pressing the attack. He had no idea where the river crossings were and could not locate the American fortifications. The American naval vessels lurked offshore. Several British gunboats had paralleled the army's advance, but they were insufficient to tackle the U.S. boats. Prevost demanded that the British naval commander, Capt. George Downie, clear away the American vessels. At first, Downie resisted. *Confiance* was not ready for action; most of her crew were soldiers untrained in operating ship-borne guns. But Prevost insisted.

On September 11, Downie sailed directly into the bay in an attempt to bring *Confiance* alongside *Saratoga* before the Americans could react. With him was the 16-gun brig *Linnet*, which dropped anchor beside *Eagle* with 11-gun *Chubb* supporting. The 10-gun *Finch* and most of the British gunboats sawed off against the 17-gun *Ticonderoga* and 7-gun *Preble*. At first things looked good as *Confiance* slammed *Saratoga* with a heavy broadside. But return fire killed Downie, and *Finch* was disabled and forced to strike her colours after running aground. *Chubb*, too, was sent drifting out of control by devastating fire from *Eagle* and was soon captured.

The battle turned on whether *Confiance* could prevail over *Saratoga*. Both vessels were badly damaged, *Saratoga's* starboard guns reduced to a shambles. Using an anchor and hawsers, Macdonough quickly winched his ship around to bring the port guns to bear. This feat of seamanship carried the day. Battered by the fresh broadsides, *Confiance's* colours were soon struck. *Linnet*, no match for *Saratoga*, followed suit. American control of the lake was indisputable. The Americans lost 52 killed and 58 wounded, the British 80 dead and 100 wounded.[28]

Prevost had organized an attack to begin in concert with the naval assault, but his troops had only just begun to move when the battle on the lake abruptly ended. Seeing the British vessels surrendered or wrecked, Prevost's always tremulous nerve failed completely. He cancelled the attack. Demoralized, his army trailed back to Canada, crossing the border on September 14. They reported 35 killed, 47 wounded, and 72 lost as prisoners in the entire campaign, while the Americans suffered just 37 killed and 62 wounded.[29]

An incredulous Macdonough reported to Washington: "The Almighty has been pleased to grant us a signal victory on Lake Champlain." To which Macomb added that Prevost's great army was "now retreating precipitately."[30]

As Prevost drew away, the last hopes of an overwhelming victory cowing the Americans into peace on British terms were dashed. The season of campaigning was through. Whether the war continued into 1815 now rested on discussions between eight men in Ghent.

TWENTY-FOUR

Breaking Points

AUGUST–SEPTEMBER 1814

ow the North American battlefront influenced the faltering discussions at Ghent depended entirely on the vagaries of Atlantic winds, currents, and weather. For the Americans there was the added complication of deciding the best moment for releasing *John Adams*, which stood in port at Helder awaiting orders to bear their final dispatch to Washington. It was already late August. If they delayed longer there would be scarce chance of receiving a reply before winter storms prohibited cross-Atlantic travel. It was therefore decided after the August 19 debacle that secretary George Dallas would return to Washington with the expected British document and various public and private reports they had written either collectively or individually to James Monroe. Only if their response to the British proved quickly written would they delay his departure until it was finished.

Aware of the urgent need to submit the written position, during a marathon session that carried on far into the night, Henry Goulburn scribbled a precisely worded summary of Castlereagh's instructions to the British commissioners. In the morning, the other commissioners and the foreign secretary studied the result. Although the tone was more confrontational than Castlereagh liked, he approved the document, while perhaps not reading it carefully. He and his retinue then boarded a caravan of coaches and continued their journey to Vienna.

Goulburn's note reiterated Britain's dismay that the Americans lacked instructions regarding including the Indians in the peace and setting boundaries for their territories. If they had a "sincere desire for the restoration of peace," then surely they would enter into a provisional agreement subject to the United States government's approval. Despite Castlereagh's admonitions against prohibiting the right to acquire territory through conquest, Goulburn inserted the requirement that neither Britain nor the United States would "acquire by purchase, or otherwise, any territory." The natural military frontier should run from Lake Ontario to Lake Superior, and the Americans must maintain no military presence along the shores of the lakes or on their waters. Finally, Goulburn warned that if the Americans decided they could not consent to provisional agreements, Britain could not "be precluded, by anything that has passed, from varying the terms now proposed, in such a manner, as the state of the war, at the time of resuming the conference, may, in their judgement, render advisable." The ultimatum was clear. Treat now, or face tougher terms later.

While waiting for delivery of the British note, Albert Gallatin had drafted a joint communiqué detailing the concessions demanded and remarking upon "the forcible manner" of their delivery. "We need hardly say, that the demands . . . will receive from us an unanimous and decided negative. We do not deem it necessary to detain the *John Adams*, for the purpose of transiting to you the official notes which may pass on the subject, and close the negotiation; and we felt it our duty immediately to apprise you, by this hasty but correct sketch of our last conference that there is not, at present, any hope of peace."[2]

The British note delivered later that morning contained nothing that dispelled this conclusion. That evening, Dallas left for Washington.

With grim resolve the Americans began responding to the British note. John Quincy Adams prepared a first draft. "I found, as usual," Adams confided to his diary, "the draft was not satisfactory to my colleagues. On the general view . . . we are unanimous, but in my exposition of it, one objects to the form and another to the substance of almost every paragraph." Ever moderate, Gallatin sought to strike anything that might offend. Henry Clay thought the language too figurative and unsuitable to a state paper. Jonathan Russell proposed amendments to virtually every sentence. While agreeing with Adams on what needed to be said, James Bayard chose "to say it only in his own language." Everyone but Adams thought the draft overly long and argumentative regarding the Indian issues. He was to try again.

Two days later the document was still in contention. Gallatin had shredded Adams's second draft, inserting dozens of corrections and alterations. Clay added a couple of paragraphs. Bayard started his own version but failed to complete it. Unable to agree, they finally threw "the shreds and patches" in secretary Christopher Hughes's lap to fashion into something workable.[3] That evening they ended sitting at a Ghent dignitary's table with their British counterparts. Adams found Goulburn's wife charming company, but could not say the same for her husband.

The next day, while the Americans continued labouring over their response, Goulburn wrote to Lord Bathurst. His discussions with various American commissioners had convinced him "that they do not mean to continue the negotiations." Sitting next to him the night before, Clay had bluntly stated that they would seek instructions from Washington because the British demands were equivalent to asking "for the cession of Boston or New York." After dinner, Bayard had taken him aside and warned at length that the negotiations "could not end in peace" because the British terms not only ruined such prospects "but were sacrificing the Party of which he was a member to their political adversaries." He then plunged into a long lesson in American party politics intended to convince Goulburn that Britain's hopes rested with the Federalists, and a peace treaty on less onerous terms would assure that party ascended to power. Goulburn could think of nothing to say to this, so barely offered Bayard the courtesy of a reply. In a postscript, Goulburn noted that "the question of acquiring Indian Territory by conquest can hardly come under discussion."[4]

On August 24, four days after receipt of the British note, the Americans finalized a reply shortly before midnight. All were weary and irritable, displeased with the result. Two-thirds of what Adams had written was jettisoned. "The remnant left," Adams grumbled, "is patched with scraps from Mr. Gallatin, and scraps from Mr. Bayard, and scraps from Mr. Clay, all of who are dissatisfied with the paper as finally constructed." Next morning, the document was signed and Hughes delivered it. Expecting the result to be a rapid closure of the negotiations, Adams began to make plans to return to St. Petersburg, possibly by way of Vienna, where he might attempt a direct discussion with Viscount Castlereagh.[5]

Although only a fifth the length of Adams's original draft, the document set in Hughes's fluid script ran to fifteen pages. The war, it declared, was rooted entirely in maritime issues, so the demand that America surrender "one-third of the territorial dominions of the United States" to "perhaps 20,000 Indians" was both unforeseeable and certain to be rejected. As for unilaterally demilitarizing the Great Lakes and surrendering territory to enable a British road link from Quebec to Halifax, the commissioners said they had no authority "to cede any part of the United States." The terms proposed by Britain "would inflict the most vital injury on the United States, by dismembering their territory, by arresting their natural growth and increase of population, by leaving their northern and western frontier equally exposed to British invasion, and to Indian aggression; they are, above all, DISHONORABLE to the United States, in demanding from them to abandon territory and a portion of their citizens, to admit a foreign interference in their domestic concerns, and to cease to exercise their natural rights on their own shores, and in their own waters."

America no longer desired "to continue [the war] in defence of abstract principles, which have, for the present, ceased to have any practical effect." The commissioners had been instructed "to agree to its termination, both parties restoring whatever territory they may have taken, and both reserving all their rights, in relation to their respective seamen." To ensure lasting peace, they were empowered to discuss all issues over which either nation felt "differences or uncertainty had existed" and might "interrupt the harmony of the two countries." But concluding the peace should not depend on these issues being settled. The demands made by Britain were "NEW and unexpected pretensions" that raised "an insuperable obstacle to a pacification." In conclusion, the commissioners did not need to look to their government for instruction on these points because they would only be "a fit subject of deliberation, when it becomes necessary to decide upon the expediency of an absolute surrender of national independence."[6]

On reading the American response, the British commissioners concluded they required instruction from London. Goulburn advised Bathurst that the Americans' refusal to enter into any provisional agreements was an outcome "not provided for in our instructions" and wanted to ensure cabinet agreed that the negotiations should be broken off. He suggested replying "that their proceeding throughout this part of the negotiation has been nothing more nor less than a dictation to Great Britain that Although America declared War for the sake of annexing our dominions yet she will cede nothing which can contribute to increase their security or difficulty of annexation at a future time." Goulburn thought the Americans sought to blame the rupture of negotiations on Britain. All he desired from Bathurst was a "single line informing us whether [to] break off or not."[7]

The American response startled the British cabinet. From Paris, Castlereagh warned Goulburn against any written reply until briefed by the government on its intention. Writing to Lord Liverpool, the foreign secretary suggested the commissioners had stated the proposition regarding Indian boundaries too "peremptorily." In more muddied language than in previous written instructions, he again argued against Britain being drawn into a territorial war over the Indian question. Against all reason, he suggested, the Americans could be drawn into provisional agreement to the British demands before confessing that the result would just be rejection by Madison's government. As he was leaving Paris within the hour and so lacked time to generate anything but this hasty note, Castlereagh left it up to Liverpool, Bathurst, and the foreign secretary's staff to decide the ultimate response.[8]

Along with the American reply and his personal letter to Bathurst, Goulburn had included a draft response for consideration. While approving its general outline, Liverpool thought the commissioners "had certainly taken a very erroneous view of our policy. If the negotiation had been allowed to break off upon the two notes already presented, or upon such an answer as they were disposed to return, I am satisfied the war would have become quite popular in America." If there was to be a rupture in the negotiations, blame for it "should be thrown upon the American commissioners, and not upon us."

He therefore wanted a more conciliatory tone adopted while offering no significant change of course because there remained no military justification for compromise. "If the campaign in Canada should be as successful as our military preparations would lead us to expect, I do not think we should be justified in conceding more at present than we have done, especially after the demands already made," Liverpool wrote Castlereagh. He expected that the negotiation was unlikely to proceed further; the Americans would likely consult their government and that would necessitate a long adjournment during which time "the result of the campaign" would become known. "If our commander does his duty, I am persuaded we shall have acquired by our arms every point on the Canadian frontier which we ought to insist on keeping."[9] So the British would soften their language while maintaining a tough stance.

As Liverpool and Bathurst massaged Goulburn's reply into something deemed more palatable for American consumption, relations between the commissioners in Ghent remained tense. Despite this they went through the pretense of civility, even dining again at the monastery. Everyone but William Adams and James Bayard made a show of being overly polite and courteous. Under the guise of rough joviality, the naval lawyer and Delaware senator exchanged veiled insults over the value and quality of their respective fowling guns. John Quincy Adams noted how pleased Gallatin was to see Bayard, the Federalist, mocked by the pompous, coarse Englishman. Bayard proclaimed to the other Americans that his adversary was "a man of no breeding."[10]

At every turn Bayard privately cornered Goulburn, determined to convince the young man that a generous treaty would ensure Federalist power, which would be to Britain's advantage. Goulburn declined comment, thinking anything he said would be "liable to much misrepresentation and cannot lead to any good purpose." He advised Bathurst that all he had learned was "that the Federalists are quite as inveterate enemies to us as the Madisonians."[11]

On September 1, Adams, hoping to chat with the British commissioners and Jane Goulburn, called on the monastery. Her husband received him. Lady Goulburn was indisposed and the other commissioners, along with Baker, had gone to Brussels for a couple of days. The ensuing discussion quickly degenerated into a heated argument that Adams thought unmasked "the violence and bitterness of his passion against the United States." Conquering Canada had been the war's only object, the intense Englishman declared, and it was to "the astonishment of the whole world that Canada had not been conquered at the very outset." This was why the Great Lakes must be secured and a barrier nation created for the Indians—to preclude America's embarking on another war of conquest.

Adams denied America had sought to conquer Canada. That was an effect of the war, not a cause. By circuitous turns the argument led to Vice-Admiral Sir Alexander Cochrane's encouraging slaves to take refuge aboard British ships. It was widely known, Adams charged, that many naval commanders had subsequently sold these slaves to plantation owners in the West Indies. Goulburn, personally embarrassed by the use of slaves on his Jamaican plantation, with "apparent agitation" dismissed this allegation as "originating only in the spirit of hostility, and totally destitute of foundation."

Feeling he was gaining advantage, Adams suggested both sides grant amnesty to those Indians living inside their existing boundaries that had fought for the other nation. They must be considered independent nations, Goulburn insisted. America had entered into treaties with them in the past. Did that not reflect acceptance that these peoples enjoyed nationhood?

Where the Indians formed settlements and cultivated land, Adams said, such civilized behaviour resulted in respect of their property by the United States. But most Indians were "wandering hunters" with "habits and attachments and prejudices . . . so averse to any settlement . . . it was impossible for such people ever to be said to have possessions. Their only right upon land was a right to use it as hunting-grounds, and when those lands where they hunted became necessary or convenient for the purposes of settlement," the U.S. would acquire it by treaty. This approach was fair and just. The proposal that the Indians have a nation with inviolable borders was bound to fail. "It was opposing a feather to a torrent." The United States numbered eight million; its boundaries must expand as the population grew.

"What!" cried Goulburn. "Is it, then, in the inevitable nature of things that the United States must conquer Canada?"

"No."

"But what security, then, can Great Britain have for her possession of it?"

A "liberal and amicable course of policy toward America," Adams replied. Or in the absence of that Britain must deploy her great military superiority to secure Canada's borders.

Goulburn rejected this, pointing out that the United States—by sheer dint of proximity and weight of its great populace—must always enjoy military dominance in North America. Canada could have no security. There were also many civilized Indians, and the American policy of pushing them back from their lands only drove these people into the British provinces where they encroached on the boundaries of Indians already dwelling there.

Adams claimed to have "never heard any complaint of this kind before." If true, he dismissed it as something easily solved.

Goulburn offered no reply and Adams sensed, "in the pressure for an argument, he had advanced more than he was inclined to maintain." Nor would he agree that the demand that the Americans remove their military from the Great Lakes was "humiliating or unusual," even when asked if Britain would ever accede to such a stipulation. Adams finally said that if Goulburn saw nothing "dishonourable" in this then there was hardly any point in continuing the argument. "We and our nation would feel it to be such; that such stipulations were indeed often exhorted from the weakness of a vanquished enemy, but they were always felt to be dishonourable, and had certainly occasioned more wars than they had ever prevented."

Having gained the last word, Adams took his leave. Goulburn, he concluded, was "personally the most inveterate of the three . . . and the most in the confidence of his Government."[12] The British commissioner, for his part, thought Adams "a very bad arguer" and a bully.[13]

Everyone believed negotiations were at an end. They merely awaited confirmation by the British cabinet. The Americans renewed their lease only to mid-September; by then they would surely be gone. Goulburn chanced upon Gallatin on September 3 and was in no mood for normal niceties. "I don't think you have the slightest intention of making peace," he challenged.

"Surely you cannot mean this! Why should I have taken the long journey to Russia in 1813 and given up everything else in the one hope of making peace?" To James he suggested that Goulburn's bilious accusations stemmed from his having made "serious mistakes" during the negotiation that had resulted in a stern reprimand from his superiors.[14]

On September 4, the British cabinet's response arrived. Goulburn and William Adams took immediate advantage of the permission granted to "make some alterations in its style" before passing a copy to the Americans. These changes, Goulburn assured Bathurst, were intended "with a view of rendering the note more consistent with what had been before expressed by us." He expected the Americans to remain inflexible, more convinced than ever "that their government had no real intention of making Peace but had acceded to the proposal of negotiating with the sole view of deriving from the negotiation some means of reconciling the People of America to the continuance of the War—The Indian Boundary appears to them calculated to answer this object, and their desire of negotiating is therefore at an end."[15]

The British reply, combative as ever, opened with "unfeigned regret" that the Americans demonstrated so little interest in negotiating a peace while their British counterparts had "departed from the usual course of negotiating, by disclosing all the objects of their Government." While the Americans might claim the war had been declared over maritime issues, "it is notorious to the whole world that the conquest of Canada, and its permanent annexation to the United States, was the declared object. . . . If, in consequence of a different course of events on the continent of Europe, his Majesty's Government had been unable to reinforce the British armies in Canada, and the United States had obtained a decided superiority in that quarter, is there any person who doubts that they would have availed themselves of the situation to obtain on the side of Canada important cessions of territory, if not the entire abandonment of that country by Great Britain?"

A decade of American frontier expansionism and in the Spanish Florida and Louisiana colonies was detailed. While America boasted a population exceeding seven million, British North America numbered merely 500,000. Those colonists posed no threat to America, while, given past attempts to conquer Canada, the same could not be said for the United States. Yet the reasonable proposal that America remove itself militarily from the Great Lakes and accede to an Indian nation whose boundaries provided a protective buffer between British and American territory had been rejected. A vigorous defence of the proposition that America should return to the Indians all territory acquired that lay beyond the Treaty of Greenville boundaries was offered. In closing, the British demanded to know whether the Americans "will take upon themselves the responsibility of breaking off the negotiation altogether."[16]

Bayard declared the response "a very stupid production." Through a long afternoon the five men discussed the sixteen-folio-length-page document, each seemingly bent on outdoing the others in expressing outrage. That the conquest of Canada should be held up as "the declared object" was ridiculous. Never had the American government officially stated that intention—it had always remained a topic to be discussed or articulated in informal ways by senators and congressmen, such as Henry Clay, during speeches or in the pages of the party and unofficial government newspapers, or occasionally in secret memoranda penned by the likes of James Monroe. Clay, who often claimed Canada ripe for the picking if only military competency were to be had, declared that their reply should warrant no more than a terse half-page to finish the matter. Ever inclined to be contrary, the prickly Adams calmly announced that he thought the British response was "neither . . . stupid nor proper to be answered in half a page." Gallatin suggested that he dissect the document and minute whatever warranted notice. With relief the others, due at the theatre for a production of *La Rhétorique*, consented. When the curtain went up, the actors delivered lines in Flemish. Mystified, Adams kept drifting off. Finally he slipped out an exit and spent the remaining evening walking on the Place d'Armes.[17]

The following afternoon, Gallatin met the others armed with a detailed analysis of the British response and minutes regarding what warranted comment. Pessimistic and depressed, Bayard suggested compromise. The Americans could agree that the Treaty of Greenville should stand despite subsequent settlement beyond its borders. Adams and Clay denounced any stipulations regarding the Indians. Perhaps referring disarmament on the Great Lakes to Washington would sustain the negotiation, Gallatin offered. Dismissing this, Adams dragged out Monroe's initial instructions, which sanctioned no military or territorial concessions. Ever since his argument with Goulburn, Adams had been churning the Indian question about. The "very employment of Indians by Great Britain was contrary to the laws of war," he announced. So far as the avowed concern about Canada's security, the threat of American invasion was offset by the vulnerability of the nation's vast commercial fleets to capture by the Royal Navy. These points must be made.

To his chagrin, the others thought use of Indians in war an issue best left alone. After all, the Americans employed them whenever possible. But they agreed to employ the naval argument. That their response would likely end the negotiation charade was much on everyone's mind. Gallatin suggested that once the rupture was final, Washington might consent to retain several ministers in Europe who could renew discussions in the future.

The next day Adams doggedly pursued insertion of a paragraph condemning "employment of savages as contrary to the laws of war." To mollify him, it was agreed Adams should draft a paragraph for consideration. That night, he laboured over the paragraph and examined Gallatin's draft reply. From Clay's room, Adams could hear a card game going on; Jonathan Russell and two others were present. He went to bed to the sounds of their voices. Awakening at 3:45 the next morning, Adams heard the men finally retiring. Long before daybreak, Adams washed and dressed, then sat at his desk waiting for the sky to lighten sufficient to enable reading or writing. He wrote a long draft to replace Gallatin's, only to strike most of it out when he decided the other man's was preferable except in regard to the Indian boundary.

That afternoon the commissioners accepted Gallatin's draft as amended by Adams with respect to the Indian boundaries. They also adopted the essence of his paragraph against employing Indians in war, but made a multitude of amendments that little satisfied him. There followed the laborious task of having Christopher Hughes pen the response under the careful eye of the others to ensure no changes slipped in. Not until the afternoon of September 9 was the reply delivered.[18]

In the main there was little new. The response largely refuted the need for an Indian boundary and decried any limit on American expansion as "arresting the natural growth of their population and strength" and dooming the Indians "to perpetual barbarism." Untrue was the contention that America bore hostile intentions toward the Indians. They sought only peaceful coexistence. But the British "employment of savages, whose known rule of warfare is the indiscriminate torture and butchery of women, children, and prisoners, is itself a departure from the principles of humanity observed between all civilized and Christian Nations, even in war" and led to "unjustifiable aggravation of the calamities and horrors of war." Without offering specific incidents, they accused British officers of watching over massacres and despoiling of the dead by Indian warriors. They proposed that each nation disavow using Indians in warfare.

Again they rejected an independent Indian nation, as well as disarmament of the Great Lakes. Referring either idea to Washington would be useless, doomed to immediate rejection. The Americans closed by saying they remained ready as always to continue the negotiation.[19]

Illogical, emotional, full of unsubstantiated ravings, this American response seemed certain to break the negotiation. Adams expected word that very day, but there came only silence. He realized that the test of wills might continue as each side tried to force the other to make the break. But he remained certain that further discussion could not bear fruit.[20]

The British commissioners agreed. While they forwarded the document to London with a covering note requesting "instructions as to the line of conduct which it may be proper to adopt with respect to the continuance of the negotiation," it was plain they considered matters at an end.[21] On September 15, the Americans hosted what they thought would be the last dinner taken together. Before the sitting, Gambier asked Adams if he planned to immediately return to St. Petersburg. "Yes, that is, if you send us away," Adams replied. Gambier deeply lamented the outcome and hoped they should be friends some day.[22]

Goulburn and Clay had an almost civil conversation during which the Kentuckian explained that even if America acceded to the Indian boundary proposition and the eastern states and Great Britain tried to enforce such an agreement, they would not be able to "restrain that part of the American population which is to the Westward of the Alleghany, from encroaching upon the Indian Territory and gradually expelling the aboriginal inhabitants." Goulburn, as usual, listened and said little. But he then wrote Bathurst that under "these circumstances I do not deem it possible to conclude a *good peace* now—as I cannot consider that a good peace . . . leaves the Indians to a dependence on the *liberal policy* of the United States."²³

But even as Goulburn wrote his mentor in London, the foundation of this position was weakening, indeed crumbling to dust, as, independent of the other, Lord Liverpool and Viscount Castlereagh each succumbed to second thoughts.

Moving slowly from one seat of European power to another on a winding path that would end in Vienna, the foreign secretary found the American war ever less important. The puzzle of reconstructing the stability of the continental European empires was a heady, demanding challenge, one that perforce required his full attention. Yet this unnecessary and costly war across the Atlantic continued to impinge upon his time. He fretted that the commissioners had taken too hard a line and that, when the record of the discussions was disclosed, the opposition in the House of Commons would hold the government accountable for failing to negotiate a treaty. Perhaps the British position should be softened some way to conciliate the Americans.

Liverpool reached the same conclusion for similar reasons. "I quite agree with you," he wrote Bathurst on the 11th, "in the *Absolute Necessity*, of including the Indians in the Treaty of Peace. . . . but I would not make a sine qua non of more." He thought that the Great Lakes demands could be modified. Perhaps Sackets Harbor could be left to the Americans.²⁴ Four days later he complained to Bathurst that the commissioners "evidently do not feel the inconveniences of the war. I feel it strongly, but I feel it is nothing now compared with what it may be a twelve-month hence, and I am particularly anxious therefore, that we should avoid anything . . . which may increase our difficulties concluding it."²⁵ Thus, a chink in the British armour now opened.

TWENTY-FIVE

Shifting Stances

FALL 1814

enry Goulburn registered the softening British stance with dismay. The earnest undersecretary for war and the colonies detected a weakening resolve to decide the issue on the battlefield. He was disappointed by the haphazard campaign arrangements for the attack on New Orleans.[1] As originally conceived, 15,000 Peninsular veterans were to sail from southern France on this mission. The British had long realized the city's strategic importance. Whoever held it controlled the mouth of the Mississippi River and could effectively cork the most essential line of communication for every American west of the Appalachians, for it was down this waterway their exports flowed. Until the victory over France, there had never been enough soldiers to undertake this operation.

But no sooner was the decision made to assemble the great invasion force than Lord Liverpool's cabinet cancelled its creation. Mild strains between Russia and Great Britain over dominance in Europe posed sufficient concern to warrant maintaining a sizable army on the continent. Only 2,600 would be sent to North America, where they would unite with 3,400 men under Maj. Gen. Robert Ross. When these instructions were issued on September 6, Ross was already a week dead at Baltimore.

Lord Bathurst believed the British in North America were everywhere triumphant—or hoped that was the case. Vice-Admiral Sir Alexander Cochrane had certainly expressed only optimism for the summer operations. It was mainly his assurance that New Orleans and Louisiana could be easily won that led cabinet to scrap the large-scale operation. A couple of thousand men could do the job, he had written. The Admiralty tripled that number for insurance and delayed the operation until December because of the harsh tropical Gulf of Mexico climate. Command the mouth of the Mississippi and seize some important possession that could be used as a bargaining chip in the negotiations, Bathurst instructed Cochrane and the dead Ross. Whether that chip was New Orleans or some chunk of Georgia, where it was believed friendly Indians waited to greet the British with open arms, was left to the two officers on the scene.[2]

Goulburn considered the scheme fatally flawed, doomed by the ravages of malaria and cholera as much as possible enemy action. "Though a small force might gain possession of the point which they are destined to occupy," he advised, "yet it will be difficult . . . to retain it under the disadvantages of an unhealthy climate and a constant reduction of numbers incident to its defence against the Enemy."[3]

But Goulburn was in Ghent, his absence from No. 14 Downing Street denying him influence over the war's prosecution. And Bathurst was not a man to second-guess the military men. If Cochrane thought 2,000 sufficient, surely 6,000 would ensure success.

Too little, Goulburn reiterated, but then that was also true of the efforts made by Governor Sir George Prevost in Canada. That he could not gain supremacy on the Great Lakes was incomprehensible, his "indisposition to attempt any thing" almost treasonable. "It appears to me as it has always done that the ascendancy on the lakes must be attained by military operations against the land side of the Enemy's harbours. It is impossible for us to outbuild the Americans whatever exertions we might make for the purpose of increasing our fleets and unless Prevost will attempt something of this kind while the Enemy's troops are raw and their ports not completely fortified Canada will always be kept in a state of anxiety."[4]

Goulburn saw the initiative in North America being surrendered through Prevost's incompetence. A burdensome sense of futility weighed on his slight shoulders as he witnessed the cabinet soften its stance at the negotiating table. He had sought to win the battle for the lakeshore that Prevost refused to fight. Looking at the new instructions from London, Goulburn sensed the Indians might be completely abandoned. Gone was insistence on a distinct Indian nation with guaranteed boundaries based on the Treaty of Greenville. In its stead the Indians should be included in the treaty and "restored to all the rights, privileges, and territories which they enjoyed in the year 1811 previous to the commencement of the war." Boundaries were open to discussion and a reciprocal agreement proposed that neither side purchase lands lying within these "lines of demarcation." No longer did the word *otherwise* appear; nor did the phrase *sine qua non*. Further, the boundaries could be revised on agreement. As for the Great Lakes and other territorial alignments between the United States and Canada, those could be set aside in order to concentrate on the Indian question. These essential points were buried at the end of a document that contained a long, tortuous preamble setting out the reasons Britain had to fear America's expansionist tendencies, given a long history of past conduct that was meticulously, often inaccurately, outlined.[5]

Receiving the note on September 20, the Americans quickly recognized the shift it represented. But that little lifted their spirits. John Quincy Adams noticed that when each note arrived its immediate effect was "to deject us all. We so fondly cling to the vain hope of peace, that every new proof of its impossibility operates upon us as a disappointment." Albert Gallatin and James Bayard were openly despondent, a fact that increased Adams's irritability. Bayard no longer rose to the bait when Adams scolded them like some schoolmaster disappointed in his students, while Gallatin playfully brushed these displays of temper aside with a well-delivered joke. Clay and Russell grimly kept to the business at hand, carefully reading the British note and expressing their thoughts on how it should be received.

Despite the significant movement, Gallatin cautioned that Washington would still never agree to include any articles regarding the Indians. However, it would be "a bad point for us to break off the negotiations upon; that the difficulty of carrying on the war might compel us to admit the principle at least, for now the British had so committed themselves with regard to the Indians that it was impossible for them to further retreat."

Bayard concurred. If the negotiation was to end, best to find a point that would unite Americans in support of the war. Everyone agreed, but Adams counselled them to not let this knowledge lead them into complying with British claims. That the *sine qua non* had been discarded should not preclude the British later abandoning their new position. And surely if the

Indian question would not serve to rally America behind the war, its entire pursuit was "hopeless."

Earnestly, Gallatin repeated that breaking off over the Indians was a bad idea.

Pointing a blunt finger at him, Adams snapped, "Then it is a good point to admit the British as the sovereigns and protectors of our Indians."

Gallatin shook his head and said with a smile, "That's a non sequitur." No, it's a sequitur, Adams laughed, and the mood lifted noticeably. As previously, Gallatin analyzed the note to frame the basis for their draft response.

At 4:30 the following morning Adams was at his desk writing proposals for consideration. It was the autumnal equinox and he noted that for the next half-year it would be necessary "to rise by the light of the morning stars."[6] With each British note, it seemed the need to respond by committee dragged out the time needed. Six days this time, the arguments intense and far ranging. Gallatin typically desired to respond only to the proposals offered, which he then did in great detail. Equally to type, Adams dealt with the proposals tersely and then waded into a polemical reply to all the allegations raised in the long British preamble. In the midst of their discussions a packet of English newspapers was delivered that contained an account of the American defeat at Lundy's Lane in July. The mood grew increasingly sombre, Adams confiding to his diary that this was likely the first of "a long and heavy series before us."

Adams noticed a distasteful trend. Should Gallatin disagree with any suggestion Adams made for revision of the proposal, inevitably the other three commissioners would back him. The simple fact was that Gallatin, rather than Adams, to whom the position had been given by the president, had emerged as the commission's leader. And Adams feared this worldly European-turned-American was overly inclined toward compromise to achieve peace.

Goulburn, too, seemed to entertain this possibility. After the American note was delivered, he visited Gallatin alone. Dropping his normal brusque and superior manner, Goulburn was unusually gracious during their conversation. "I rely on your tact and good sense," the young man confided. "You're a man I can treat with. In fact, you're not the least like an American." Gallatin's son was unable to read whether his father was pleased by this or not. With a bemused smile Gallatin told James that the "only Americans are the Red Indians."[7]

Goulburn's reading of Gallatin might have been different had he realized that most of the current reply emanated from his hand. It contained no concessions. The Americans rigidly held their ground, recasting the previous long arguments into slightly more strident language that circled with much repetition back upon itself. Several times within adjoining paragraphs they hammered home the point that America would always treat the Indians fairly but that the nation must be free, "in proportion as their growing population may require, to reclaim from a state of nature, and to bring into cultivation" territory as needed. Yet in doing so "they will not violate any dictate of justice or humanity; for they will not only give to the few thousand savages, scattered over that territory, an ample equivalent for any right they may surrender, but will always leave them the possession of lands more than they can cultivate, and more than adequate to their subsistence, comfort, and enjoyment by cultivation."

As far as the Americans were concerned, "peace would long since have been concluded, had not an INSUPERABLE BAR against it been raised by the NEW and unprecedented demands of the British government."[8] That said, they delivered their note on September 26 and tried to calmly await a response.

All was not going well in the house dubbed Bachelors' Hall. Russell was increasingly unhappy with lodging among men whose company he did not enjoy. Although he idolized Clay, his attitude toward the others was completely different. Every suggestion he offered regarding the replies to the British was, in his estimation, ignored. Not given to outbursts like Adams, or gifted with Bayard's oratorical skill, or possessed of the certitude of America's position evinced by Clay, or blessed with Gallatin's keen intelligence, Russell monitored proceedings in sulky silence. At month's end, he moved back to the Hôtel des Pays-Bas. None of the others objected. Indeed, they barely noted his departure.[9]

October 1 dawned cold and wet. Rain spattered the windows of Adams's room. This fall was proving Belgium's wettest on record, a fact that made all the commissioners more miserable. Clay, Russell, and Hughes were sightseeing in Brussels. The house seemed hollow, bitterly cold before the servants lit the fires. Adams found it too chill and damp to rise before dawn to see to his writing. The journal entries shortened, dashed off in the midst of the day's other duties. Midday, he ventured out on a walk and upon returning was met by a much-distressed Gallatin. Washington taken, the man reported, the navy yard and public buildings burned on August 25. The word was unofficial, delivered by a passing American who had read of it in a British newspaper.[10]

Gallatin raged that burning the Capitol and presidential residence was purely "an act of vandalism" with no compare in the twenty-year European war. Paris had been spared by the Russians, Naples by Napoleon. The British had acted out of petty envy because, except for a few cathedrals, they had no public buildings to compare with the grandeur of those in Washington.[11]

This is "only the beginning of sorrows; the lightest of a succession of calamities through which our country must pass, and by which all the infirmities and all the energies of its character will be brought to light," Adams wrote Louisa. "In itself the misfortune of Washington is a trifle." The British success, he predicted, would result in their commissioners finally breaking up this "idle and hopeless farce of . . . negotiation. There can be no possible advantage to us in continuing it any longer."[12]

Perhaps because Clay had always espoused America's military prowess more than the others, Goulburn took it upon himself to forward to him in Brussels a packet of newspapers detailing Washington's destruction. "If you find Brussels as little interesting as I have done you will not be sorry to have the occupation of reading the latest Newspapers which I have received," his covering note observed.[13]

Having only just received the news themselves, the British were uncertain how best to exploit it. Bathurst, who like Goulburn preferred a tough stance, instructed the commissioners to put the Indian nation proposal back on the table with the old statement of willingness to accept a provisional agreement subject to U.S. government approval. If the Americans claimed lack of authority, Bathurst was ready to "suggest that the talks shall be suspended" until they received instructions.[14] In a private letter to Goulburn, he urged his young protégé "to put on a face of compress'd joy . . . in communicating the news to the American ministers."[15] Except for forwarding newspapers to Clay, Goulburn restrained his elation. The British commissioners instead did nothing until receiving instructions from London.

This was just as well, because Bathurst's position was unsupported by either Liverpool or Castlereagh. While the prime minister considered the destruction of Washington "very satisfactory," he assured the foreign secretary and the Duke of Wellington—the latter serving as ambassador to the restored Bourbon court in Paris—that it made "no difference in our anxious desire to put an end to the war if it can be done consistently with our honour." The terms being offered the Americans, Liverpool believed, were so conciliatory that were they accepted it was inevitable the government would face censure domestically. "But I feel too strongly the inconvenience of a continuance of the war not to make me desirous of concluding it at the expense of some popularity; and it is a satisfaction to reflect that our military success will at least divest the peace of anything which could affect our national character." Whether peace was possible remained to be seen, however, as Liverpool thought the American "tone in the negotiation very different from what their situation appears to warrant."[16]

Yet his October 1 instruction to Bathurst advocated a less conciliatory tone. The response, he advised, should condemn the "spirit of acquisition and aggrandizement" demonstrated by America's seizure of parts of the Floridas. It should also make clear that whatever the commissioners and their government claimed, Britain knew the war was motivated by desire to conquer Canada. If the Americans refused serious negotiation "we might as well suspend or break off the negotiations at Ghent, and settle our instructions to Sir G. Prevost in the course of the next week."[17]

The British viewed the forthcoming exchange as the make-or-break point. On October 5, Bathurst appended a note to the draft reply that instructed the commissioners to feel free to alter it if doing so would render it more palatable to the Americans. But the proposed Indian article was not to be modified or expanded upon, as its substance was too important. If the Americans refused to accept this, he said curtly, "you will return home."[18]

In substance, the British note was moderately less combative but ran to a tedious fifteen pages. Much legal precedence was trotted out to justify the British claims to a right to negotiate on behalf of the Indians. No longer, however, was there any mention of creating an Indian nation. Rather, it alleged that the United States considered all Indians living within lands claimed by it as American subjects and so when these peoples sided with the British in the current war they were exposed to retribution "as rebels, or disaffected persons." The Americans, then, could dispossess them of their lands at will. Such pretensions "Great Britain CAN NEVER RECOGNIZE: however reluctant his Royal Highness, the Prince Regent may be to continue the war, that evil must be preferred, if peace can only be obtained on such conditions."

The British proposed that, immediately upon entering into a treaty, both countries be bound to end all hostilities with Indian tribes they were at war with and "restore to such tribes or nations, respectively, all the possessions, rights, and privileges, which they may have enjoyed or been entitled to in 1811, previous to such hostilities; provided always, that such tribes or nations shall agree to desist from all hostilities" upon being notified of the treaty agreement.

"Whatever may be the result of the proposition thus offered," this was "their ultimatum." They awaited a response "with anxiety" because on this "their continuance in this place will depend."[19] A gauntlet had been dropped.

The Americans received the British note while having dinner on the evening of October 8. Everyone was in a foul mood. They had spent the day arguing over the protocol by which a report on the negotiations should be sent to Tsar Alexander I. Adams, Russell, and Clay ended up shouting at each other about which of their secretaries should carry the report to the emperor in Vienna. Although the issue was insignificant, their display of temper worried them all. Until now strained harmony had been maintained between these five men of very different temperaments. But the stress of months together and the likelihood of failure was wearing them down. Tempers simmering, they agreed to not discuss the proposal until the next afternoon.

At first blush, the Americans found the note "domineering and insulting" as ever. The ultimatum forced them into a corner. Even though it was couched in relatively moderate language and signified a substantial retreat on earlier demands relative to the Indians, rejecting it would be politically damning. When the record of the negotiations was made public, which would certainly happen, President Madison's government would face the outrage of New England and probably other parts of the nation for turning its back on peace by rejecting such a seemingly moderate proposal. As for the five commissioners, they would be saddled with full blame for mishandling the negotiations. If they could not reject the article, though, how were they to accept it without appearing to have meekly given in?

Bayard suggested a face-to-face conference where they would demand to see a draft of the entire proposed treaty. It was unreasonable of the British to present them with just one article with an attached ultimatum. But if the British refused his request, Bayard still opposed ending the negotiation. Clay favoured accepting the article, but insisted they must reject any demand that America disarm on the lakes. The two things taken together, he said, "would deliver the whole western country up to the mercy of the Indians." Trouble was, they had no idea of knowing whether the British continued to want disarmament or not. They were being forced to accept one article blind to what other treaty terms would then be presented.

For days they argued. Clearly they had no choice but to accept the article, but how? Clay and Gallatin favoured a short response of no more than four pages. Adams wanted to match the British word for word. Gallatin proposed usurping the article as representing precisely the view the Americans had expressed on the Indian subject. Taking entirely the opposite tack, Adams was for representing "it as a very great concession, made for the sake of securing the peace." He wanted to include a paragraph arguing for the cession of Canada to the United States as being in the interest of all. The others rejected that notion out of hand, as they did his concession idea. Finally it fell to Clay to merge both men's drafts into something everyone could accept.

Clay's response, much edited by the group, followed Gallatin's idea of portraying the article as essentially being what the Americans had always proposed. It would place "these tribes PRECISELY and in EVERY RESPECT, in the same situation as that in which they stood BEFORE the commencement of hostilities."

In accepting the article, they then requested that the British provide the *projet* of a treaty "embracing ALL the points deemed material by Great Britain" to which they would then present "a *counter projet* with respect to *all* the articles, to which they may not agree and on subjects deemed material by the United States, and which may be admitted in the British *projet*."[20]

On the 14th the response was finally ready, Hughes busy writing it up in final form, when the British commissioners delivered copies of more London papers. The Americans read about Passamaquoddy Bay being taken, the frigate *Adams* burned, British successes on Lake Huron and in the northern Mississippi. Plattsburgh, too, was reported captured.

It was a defeated five who signed their response at noon for delivery. Adams disliked the response "very much in all its parts," but had little luck in any of his proposed amendments. Clay, who had always predicted the war would carry no public losses for America, railed "at commerce and the people of Massachusetts, and [told] what wonders the people of Kentucky would do if they should be attacked."[21]

The note was delivered that afternoon with the expectation that it would be at least ten days before the British responded. In the ensuing days Russell confronted Adams. He was dissatisfied with the note sent to the British. Adams concurred and asked why Russell had not supported him in opposition. Because, Russell answered, he had thought Clay "would have been the most stubborn . . . upon the point relative to the Indians, and, finding him give way, and being himself the youngest member of the mission, and being from a State that cared nothing about Indian affairs, he had not thought it was his business to be more stiff about it than others." Bayard, Adams pointed out, had argued against the article. If three of them had upheld this view, Gallatin and Clay would have been forced to come around. Russell sniffed off this conjecture. "Bayard always talked about keeping a high tone," he said, "but when it came to the point he was always on the conceding side."[22]

Two days before the American commissioners agreed to the Indian article, their report on the negotiations and record of dispatches up to the date of George Dallas's sailing home aboard *John Adams* came under scrutiny during a secret session of the House of Representatives in Washington.

Dallas had hand-delivered the materials to James Monroe on October 6. Meeting in the study of Octagon House—the unusual three-storey, octagonal brick building that had been given up by the French minister to provide a suitable residence for the president—James Madison's administration found the packet's contents a mixed blessing. On the one hand, the excessive British demands might help galvanize the nation behind the war effort. Opposed to that was the probability that the negotiations had by now collapsed.

The immediate question was how to exploit the material to advantage. Madison solved that problem by providing its entire contents to the recently reconvened Thirteenth Congress. Three days of secret deliberations resulted in passage of a motion ordering the printing of 10,000 copies of the dispatches and their public distribution. This propaganda ploy proved moderately successful. While Republicans could be expected to decry the British demands as unacceptable, some Federalist newspapers and politicians also condemned them as tantamount to requiring the nation to surrender its freedom.

Privately Madison believed there was no further prospect of a negotiated peace unless the British cabinet was drastically reconstituted so that moderate politicians became ascendant. This he realized was improbable despite young Dallas's assurances that some, including Lord Chancellor David Erskine, who had once been Britain's minister to America, opposed the war. Dallas reported a conversation in which Erskine allegedly declared, "America is right and we are wrong in this war." To this Attorney General Richard Rush commented: "I am not without a hope that the events of Baltimore, Plattsburgh, and Champlain, with the drubbing that my Lord Wellington's heroes have received on the Niagara, will induce many people in England to Lord Erskine's way of thinking."[23]

Monroe, meanwhile, drafted further instructions for the commissioners in Ghent in the faintest hope that the talks might not yet have irreparably ruptured. He authorized them to drop all previous demands if the "*status quo ante bellum*" could be restored. They were empowered to follow their own judgment in agreeing to treaty articles, subject, of course, to ratification by the government.[24]

Madison remained dubious that peace was possible, but took consolation in the hope that, "if the English force us to continue the war, they will make us do in ten years what we perhaps would not do in half a century." The struggle of arms, the president believed, would hasten the country's political and economic development, ultimately uniting its disparate peoples and interest groups in a common national purpose that would be sustained after war's end.[25]

Unity of purpose was more easily forecast than achieved in the present. In New England illicit trade with Canada thrived, as did the refusals of financiers to issue war loans to the federal government and of the states to fill militia requests. The government in October skated perilously along the knife-edge of bankruptcy, with the navy unable to meet its payroll. Secretary of the Navy William Jones, near ruin from spiralling personal debts occasioned by bad investments in questionable Asian merchandise, pleaded for Madison to accept his resignation. Treasury Secretary George Campbell's health was broken. After tabling a report that forthcoming federal expenses would run to $24.8 million while revenues delivered barely $13 million, he resigned. Alexander Dallas, father of young George, stepped into his shoes.[26] He could offer no solution to cover the gap other than the dreaded political deathtrap of direct taxation. The House and the Senate would have none of it. The treasury must lurch along as before. So, too, the army. Conscription was jettisoned in favour of greater bounties and call-ups of phantom militias who might or might not make an appearance in the moment of necessity.

Fluctuating between resolution and despair, Madison soldiered on with tempered patience. New England was the problem, he quietly told friends, and its lack of patriotic fervour served to encourage Britain's continuing hostilities. Madison hoped for a turn in fortune, but braced for the worst. "In the meantime," he wrote, "the course to be taken by the Government is full of delicacy and perplexity, and the more so under the pinch which exists in our fiscal affairs, and the lamentable tardiness of the Legislature in applying some relief."[27]

In the absence of action, Congress turned to prayer. A day of "Public Humiliation, and Fasting, and of Praying to Almighty God, for the safety and welfare of these states" was proclaimed. Opposed to religious proclamations on principle, Madison kept his personal opinion quiet, and, on November 16, signed the bill to set aside January 12, 1815, as a national fast and prayer day.[28]

British resolve rather than divine intervention was more at work on America's behalf in the autumn of 1814. Mid-October brought to London official reports of the string of misfortunes on the North American battlefields. Lord Liverpool summed up the cabinet's feelings in an October 21 letter to Castlereagh. The news was "chequered." While the failed raid on Baltimore could be considered somewhat successful in its having "done them as much mischief as the capture of Washington," it had come at the price of Maj. Gen. Robert Ross's death. That left the Gulf of Mexico expedition without a commander until Maj. Gen. Sir Edward Pakenham, Wellington's brother-in-law, could cross the ocean to replace him. That was one setback, but not in itself critical. The truly devastating news was the complete failure of Prevost's offensive at Lake Champlain. "He has . . . managed the campaign in that quarter as ill as possible, and if he cannot redeem himself by some brilliant success . . . must be recalled at the end of the campaign." Liverpool regretted sending the majority of reinforcements to Canada. Had they been given to Ross, who knew what might have been achieved? "We thought, however, we were acting for the best, and so we were if we had had a competent officer in the command in Canada."

However, Liverpool took heart in the news gleaned from American papers that showed the populace failing to rally around Madison's government despite Washington's having been burned. Having Madison remain president, he felt, was "the best thing for us. . . . His government must be a weak one, and feeling that it has not the confidence of a great part of the nation, will perhaps be ready to make peace for the purpose of getting out of its difficulties."

As for the negotiations, he reported that the Americans had accepted the Indian article and so the talks continued "with more prospect of success than has hitherto existed." The negotiations should come to a head in ten days, after which it would be clear whether a treaty could be agreed upon.[29]

Goulburn warned Bathurst that Prevost's defeat at Plattsburgh seriously handicapped Britain's ability to negotiate from strength. "Even our brilliant success at Baltimore as it did not terminate in the capture of the town will be considered by the Americans as a victory. ... We owed the acceptance of our article respecting the Indians to the capture of Washington and if we had either burnt Baltimore or held Platsburg I believe we should have had peace on the terms which you have sent to us in a month at latest. As things appear to be going on in America the result of our negotiation may be very different." Only New England's lack of support for the war kept him from "despair."[30]

Goulburn was responding to a covering letter from Bathurst that contained the next set of instructions for the British commissioners, received on the 21st. Duly informed, they presented another note to the Americans the following day. Adams thought it presented "the same dilatory and insidious character as their preceding notes," but appreciated its being shorter.[31] While not containing the requested *projet* of a treaty, it did outline what Britain considered should and should not be included. Forcible seizure of mariners was an issue that could be let lie to some other time; same with the fisheries. Regarding boundaries, it seemed the northwest boundary could be agreed as running from Lake of the Woods to the Mississippi, and the others could be negotiated.

Over the ensuing week the American and British commissioners exchanged several terse notes that inched the negotiations slowly toward the next step—which side would table a draft treaty. On the 31st, the British played a trump card that decided the issue. The article concerning the Indians accepted, and everything Britain desired having been outlined in their note of October 21, they had "no further demands to make, no other stipulations on which they are instructed to insist, and they are empowered to sign a treaty of peace forthwith in conformity with those stated in their former note." They urged the Americans to "no longer hesitate to bring forward, in the form of articles or otherwise ... those specific propositions, upon which they are empowered to sign a treaty of peace between the two countries."[32] If America truly wanted peace, her commissioners were going to have to frame a treaty that could secure it.

TWENTY-SIX

A Game of Brag

Not surprisingly, preparing the *projet* fell to Albert Gallatin and John Quincy Adams, the two men working independently according to their own designs. Each day some of the commissioners gathered to discuss the work so far completed. James Bayard assumed a moderating role, counselling compromises that would advance matters. Henry Clay attended sporadically, Jonathan Russell rarely. The latter, increasingly complaining that his opinions were ignored, his presence unwanted, spent most of his time shut away at his hotel.

When Gallatin presented clauses that restored the rights of Americans to fish and dry catch in British waters in exchange for navigational rights on the Mississippi, Clay went into a rage. Say nothing about the "trifling" fisheries, he said. Who cared if that right was lost? Clay wanted no Englishmen plying the Mississippi.[1]

No attempt by Adams to explain the fishery issue's importance to New England could reach the Kentuckian. He disagreed, as if on principle, with anything Adams advocated. Clay was routinely "losing his temper and growing peevish and fractious." A gulf was developing between the two men that extended beyond clashes of ideas. Each man sharing as he did quarters that adjoined the other, lifestyles created equal friction. Clay, the gambler, cigar smoker, heavy wine drinker, almost nightly saw his guests off as Adams was rising between five and six in the morning. "I light my candle and my fire immediately on rising," Adams wrote, "and now read and write about an hour by candle-light every morning." The first book opened was the Bible. He breakfasted at nine, maintained his nightly walk regimen whenever the rains relented. Tuesdays and Fridays he wrote to Louisa. Evenings were longer than customary, as he tended to partake of the theatre once a week and did not take his walk until after dark because the hours before were spent writing or in meetings. But the rains discouraged venturing out for long. "My chief fault now is a great relaxation of my customary exercise. This must be corrected," he confided to his diary.[2]

Occasionally, the Americans dined with their British counterparts, but the atmosphere was increasingly strained. Etiquette prevented discussion of either treaty or war, but after months together most polite, general topics were exhausted. The Americans found the British dull, while their counterparts scorned these colonials' lack of refinement. "As an instance of their vulgarity what think you of their turning up their coat sleeves at the commencement of dinner as if they intended to act the part of the cooks rather than guests?" Henry Goulburn asked.[3] The British were bored, stuck in Ghent until the Americans presented a draft treaty.

From London notes urgently enquired when the treaty would be ready for consideration. Goulburn could offer no prediction. Lord Liverpool knew the negotiation would determine whether the war effort must be escalated or terminated. Lord Bathurst urged the recall of Sir George Prevost, but who was to replace him? One choice, obviously the best, was Wellington—the fabled Iron Duke whose star had so risen he could dictate whatever terms of service to the country suited his personal ambition. Wellington's influence was such that he could be ordered nowhere, so Liverpool extended an invitation.

To Viscount Castlereagh, Liverpool wrote, "I feel most anxious, under all circumstances, that he should accept the command in America. There is no other person we can send there really equal to the situation. . . . The Duke of Wellington would restore confidence to the army, place the military operations on a proper footing, and give us the best chance of peace. I know he is very anxious for the restoration of peace with America if it can be made upon terms at all honourable. It is a material consideration, likewise, that if we shall be disposed for the sake of peace to give up something of our just pretensions, we can do this more cred-itably through him than through any other person."[4]

Wellington replied on November 9. "I have already told you and Lord Bathurst that I feel no objection to going to America, though I don't promise . . . much success there. I believe there are troops enough there for the defence of Canada for ever." Even limited offensive action seemed possible. He dismissed the American army as incapable of beating Peninsular veterans, "if common precautions and care were taken."

The problem, he said, was not command incompetence but lack of "naval superiority on the Lakes. Till that superiority is acquired, it is impossible . . . to keep the enemy out of the whole frontier, much less to make any conquest from the enemy. . . . The question is, whether we can acquire this naval superiority on the Lakes. If we can't I shall do you but little good in America; and I shall go there only to prove the truth of Prevost's defence, and to sign a peace which might as well be signed now."

Wellington told Liverpool, "You have no right from the state of the war to demand any concession of territory from America." Having failed to carry the war effectively onto American soil, the cabinet could not "on any principle of equality in negotiation, claim a cession of ter-ritory excepting in exchange for other advantages which you have in your power."

Wellington dismissed any notion that the British could maintain the occupation between Penobscot and Passamaquoddy Bay if attacked by a determined American force. Only if significant ground was captured at New Orleans could cession of land be demanded.

The day after Wellington's scathing analysis of Britain's military prospects in America and their ramifications for the negotiation, the American draft treaty was delivered to the monastery. Coming to agreement on the articles and their wording had fractured the previously united front that the Americans had maintained by treating each other with careful consid-eration. Most stubborn and angrily outspoken, Clay almost deadlocked the undertaking by opposing the clauses retaining the fishery rights in exchange for Mississippi navigation rights.

On November 4, he retracted his earlier agreement to leave impressment to future negotiations, insisting the matter be resolved in this treaty.
It was put to a vote, and Clay, Russell, and Adams favoured such an article, so a clause was included. The precedent of resolving sticking points
through ballots established, prospects for concluding the discussion
looked good until Monday, November 7, when the fishery issue was
voted on. Adams backed Bayard and Gallatin in supporting inclusion
of articles, with Russell—choosing friendship over regional loyalty—and
Clay in opposition. If the articles were included, Clay declared, he would
not sign the treaty.

Tuesday afternoon Clay offered to compromise: instead of treaty
articles, merely mention the fisheries in the covering note as a subject
for possible inclusion. Adams submitted an article that would return
fishery rights and British navigation rights to their original status before
hostilities. Gallatin worried that the tack Clay and Adams were taking
would result in the British not replying on the fisheries and declaring the
earlier liberty to fish and dry catch within British jurisdiction abrogated
by the war. The debate stalemated until Bayard backed substituting
Clay's paragraph for the proposed article. Slowly, patiently, he cajoled
the others into this course.

While finalizing the documents, Adams inserted a new idea on the
morning of the 10th. When he met with the others later, Adams saw
that virtually his entire draft had been erased in favour of Gallatin's
version. Adams had expected this—his language was always considered
inflammatory and discursive—but he was dismayed to see his new
paragraph deleted.

This idea was one Adams had been considering for some time.
Their own discussions proved that negotiating terms upon which a
new state of peace between Britain and the United States was going to
be difficult. Each side naturally wanted gains that generally represented
losses to the other.

In the past, relations had been uneasy but not intolerable—especially if one considered that impressment and order-in-council trade
restrictions were no longer at issue. So why not simply "conclude the
peace on the footing of the state before the war, applied to all the subjects

of dispute between the two countries, leaving all the rest for future and pacific negotiation?"

Adams insisted the paragraph to this effect be resurrected. Clay objected that their instructions forbade renewing the Treaty of 1794 terms allowing British trade with Indians inside American territory. Gallatin temporized that the proposal did not necessarily mean renewal of that treaty as "it only offers the state before the war with regard to the objects in dispute. The Indian trade had never been in dispute." Clay forced him to concede that if the British accepted the proposal and suggested renewing all treaties then in force, then the Americans would not be able to refuse.

Sensing he was gaining ground, Adams pressed the issue. Yes, they would be exceeding their instructions. But those had been written in April 1813. The government had since revoked some points in favour of new propositions. Surely they would revoke this point if it were realized that it posed a final obstacle to peace. Adams declared he would personally "take on . . . the responsibility of trespassing upon their instruction thus far. Not only so, but I would at this moment cheerfully give my life for a peace on this basis. If peace was possible, it would be on no other." And, if Britain refused, it "would put the continuance of the war entirely at the door of England."

Clay argued that the timing was wrong. The proposal should be offered only as a last recourse, if at all.

Weighing in on Adams's side, Bayard thought the moment ripe. Delay a couple more months and the war might have turned further against America.

"How does the proposal offer more than the [treaty] itself?" Russell asked.

The treaty, Adams answered, "offered all the knots of the negotiation for solution now; and the proposal was to make peace first, and leave them to be solved hereafter."

Clay relented to the proposal being part of the covering note, but warned he might still not sign the treaty. Upon examining the covering note, he snorted that the British "would laugh at us for it. They would say, 'Ay, ay! pretty fellows you, to think of getting out of the war as well as you got into it!'"

Secretly Adams feared this precise response, but he hoped that Britain would hesitate to protract the war by refusing such terms.[5]

Goulburn's reaction accorded with Clay's expectation and Adams's fears. "The greater part of their *projet*," he wrote Bathurst, "is by far too extravagant to leave any doubts upon our minds as to the mode in which it could be combated." But to respond with reasons why each clause was objectionable "would be voluminous." Goulburn, however, was in such haste to get the American materials off to London that he failed to comment on the proposal offered in the note. His main concern regarded clauses that would recognize America's right to Louisiana and vague wording of the northern boundary that opened the door to encroachment all the way to the northwest coast. With the American papers, Goulburn included a proposed British counter-*projet* that he, Gambier, and Dr. Adams had drawn up.[6]

Four days later Goulburn wrote to Bathurst again. The American scheme was clear to him now. "We shall have no peace with America unless we accede to their proposition of placing things upon the same footing in point of privileges as well as rights as they stood when war was declared to which I presume we are not ready to accede." He doubted that the Americans would give up Fort Niagara and Michilimackinac on Lake Huron or agree that their right to fisheries within British jurisdiction had been abrogated by the war. "If you agree with me in opinion that our insisting on either of these propositions will break off the negotiation, the question to be decided will be merely upon which of the two it would be most advantageous to us to break off." Goulburn inclined toward the fishery issue. He then detailed various negotiating ploys that might gain Britain advantage on precise treaty clauses, assuming by some miracle the negotiation continued.[7]

Even as the young hard-liner was outlining his plan to defeat the Americans at the bargaining table, the mood at No. 10 Downing Street favoured peace at any price. Wellington's harsh assessment had badly rattled Liverpool. On every horizon dark clouds formed. From Vienna, Castlereagh warned that the war with America weakened Britain's position in negotiations. The war was a liability from which little of worth could be won. Equally worrisome, pro-Bonaparte movements in

France were gaining support. Should there be a rising against the imposed monarchy, Europe might again plunge into war. Having Wellington and a large share of the British army overseas would be disastrous. The political opposition at home was also reaping much hay from the publication of the Ghent negotiation papers up to the end of August. Cast in a certain light, the papers exposed a British government making war for little purpose other than territorial acquisition. Finances were even more of a concern. With the European war at an end, continuing the property tax courted political ruin, yet that tax was necessary to fund the war with America.

Cabinet mulled all these issues, read and reread the American *projet* and accompanying note and considered their own previous position. Then, as Liverpool explained to Castlereagh, "we . . . determined, if all other points can be satisfactorily settled, not to continue the war for the purpose of obtaining or securing any acquisition of territory."[8]

It fell to Bathurst to break the news to the commissioners in Ghent. He did so reluctantly, with a hand that trembled so that ink drops spattered among the words on the page like so many shed tears. Struggling to explain reasons he little agreed with, the secretary for war and the colonies wrote three separate letters to Goulburn over the course of November 21 and 22.

Three days later, Goulburn received them in a scattershot of deliveries over several hours. His reply was taut with barely contained anger and deep regret. "You know that I was never much inclined to give way to the Americans. I am still less inclined to do so after the statement of our demands with which the negotiation opened and which has in every point of view proved most unfortunate. Believing however in the necessity of the measure you may rely upon our doing the utmost to bring the negotiation to a speedy issue; but I confess I shall be much surprised if the Americans do not by cavilling and long debate upon every alteration proposed by us contrive to keep us in suspense for a longer time than under present circumstances desirable."

Goulburn agreed with Bathurst's instruction that Britain must "practically admit the Americans to the Fisheries as they enjoyed them before the War and shall not without a new war be able to exclude them." Dr. Adams and Gambier, however, did not consent to this, so for now the commissioners would hold out against such articles unless ordered to do otherwise.

Retention of Passamaquoddy Bay would be attempted, but Goulburn expected "the Americans will . . . fight hard to get possession in the first instance." Again, he sought clarification on how hard this acquisition should be pushed. In closing, Goulburn's bitterness at the virtual abandonment of the Indians spilled forth. "I had till I came here no idea of the fixed determination which prevails in the breast of every American to extirpate the Indians and appropriate their Territory; but I am now sure that there is nothing which the people of America would so reluctantly abandon as what they are pleased to call their natural right to do so."[9]

Some men might have resigned rather than continue a negotiation considered as good as lost. But Goulburn was too dutiful a public servant to turn his back on the government he served. So he joined the other two commissioners at a long table in the monastery and for two days they carefully worked through the American treaty, noting their comments and proposed rewordings in the margins. They would not submit the draft they had earlier prepared. If there was to be a treaty, the base for it would be that drawn by the Americans.

On November 27, they sent their work to the Americans for consideration. Adams was initially unsure what to make of it all. "They have rejected all the articles . . . on impressment, blockade, indemnities, amnesty, and Indians. They have definitively abandoned the Indian boundary, the exclusive military possession of the Lakes . . . but with a protestation that they will not be bound to adhere to these terms hereafter, if the peace should not be made now. . . . All the difficulties to the conclusion of a peace appear to be now so nearly removed, that my colleagues all considered it as certain. I think it myself probable. But unless we take it precisely as it is now offered, to which I strongly incline, I distrust so much the intentions of the British Government, that I still consider the conclusion as doubtful and precarious."[10]

It was not the nature of the American commissioners to act precipitously. Instead they moved cautiously. The group caucused after Gallatin and

Adams prepared separate minutes. "There are still some things . . . so objectionable that they ought on no consideration to be admitted," Gallatin advised. The main disagreement regarded a northwest boundary and Britain's related claim to Mississippi navigation rights.

Clay vehemently opposed the latter, while Gallatin favoured its acceptance contingent on restoration of American fishery rights. Typically, Clay lost his temper, declaring the fishery "of little or no value." No amount of reasoning would sway him, not even Gallatin's impassioned argument that abandoning the fishery issue and potentially America's claim of sovereignty over Moose Island in Passamaquoddy Bay could create a national schism that caused New England's separation from the Union. "No use in attempting to conciliate people who would never be conciliated," Clay retorted. The government was too willing "to sacrifice the interests of its best friends for those of its bitterest enemies . . . there might be a party for separation at some future day in the Western States too."

"You speak under the impulse of passion," Adams protested. As a man of Massachusetts, he "should be ashamed to show my face among my countrymen" if the commissioners agreed to surrender Moose Island or failed to rigorously pursue restoration of fishery rights. British navigation on the Mississippi was the trivial concession, of no particular commercial value as Britain was ceding any claim to territorial acquisition bordering the river itself.

Exhausted, tempers frayed, the three men consented when Bayard proposed a vote. Gallatin would draft for consideration an article swapping fishery rights for Mississippi navigation. Hoping to speed the negotiation's conclusion, he also wanted a direct conference with the British commissioners so they could together draft a final treaty. It was agreed to sleep on these matters.[11]

"A dreadful day," James Gallatin confided to his diary. The argument had echoed through the large house, leaving all the secretaries and servants shaken and nervous. That afternoon, an unusual letter had been delivered for his father. Intrigued, James noted that it was from the Duke of Wellington and marked "Strictly confidential." After reading it, Gallatin set the letter on a table and walked out of the room. Impulsively, James picked it up. Wellington reported that he had "brought all his weight to bear to ensure peace." James was even more surprised by the next paragraph. "I gather, Mr. Madison, as well as Mr. Monroe gave you full power to act, without even consulting your colleagues on points you considered of importance. I now feel that peace is shortly in view. Mr. Goulburn has made grave errors and Lord Castlereagh has read him a sharp lesson." Hurriedly he began copying the letter, as he normally did with important correspondence to ensure their preservation, but stopped when his father burst in. Without noting that James had recorded a small part of it, Gallatin snatched up the letter "and burned it."[12] That Wellington, Britain's senior general and a serving ambassador, would correspond privately with a commissioner representing a belliger-ent nation startled young James, and clearly his father had realized the potentially treasonous import. But what was Wellington hinting? That Goulburn was on such a tight leash that the Americans could insist on almost anything and have it acceded to? Some on the commission—Clay particularly—might read this intelligence thusly. Best if Gallatin kept the entire thing secret, knowledge to use only with greatest care.

The morning brought a return to the same arguments. In the heat of discussion that followed, Gallatin sought to lighten the mood. "Mr. Adams," he noted, "cared nothing at all about the navigation of the Mississippi, and thought of nothing but the fisheries. Mr. Clay cared nothing at all about the fisheries, and thought of nothing but the Mississippi. The East was perfectly willing to sacrifice the West and the West was equally ready to sacrifice the East. Now he was a Western man, and would give the navigation of the river for the fisheries. Mr. Russell was an Eastern man, and was ready to do the same."

Taking the hint, Adams proposed a coalition of east and west whereby he and Clay agreed that if the British refused the fishery renewal he would deny them access to the Mississippi. "The conse-quence of our making the offer would be that we should lose both," Clay replied, and the argument resumed, though, not so heatedly.[13]

On the last day of November, the commissioners reached a series of compromises to send to their British counterparts. By a three–two vote, Clay and Russell dissenting, the fisheries and navigation rights would be united in a single article.[14] The British were invited to conference the following day. They responded a few hours later that they would host the meeting.

Adams was uneasy about the conference, "while we were so far from being agreed among ourselves." For the past three months all negotiation had been via exchanged notes. He feared the British would see that the Americans were far from united. He could not imagine Clay presenting a position in a way agreeable to him or that anything he said would accord with the Kentuckian's opinion. But Gallatin insisted this was the only way to conclude matters, so Adams acquiesced.[15]

At noon the next day, Gambier expressed happiness that they met now "with much fairer prospects of success than when we had last met," in late August.[16] This cordial opening represented the last pleasantry during the long afternoon of argument that followed. Most of the debate revolved around two issues. The first part of the treaty attempted to restore the boundaries of each nation to their pre-war condition and established a dispute-resolution mechanism whereby a commissioner from each nation would be appointed to examine each case. If agreement could not be reached, disputes would be referred to an agreed third-party nation. Here, the Americans butted up against British resolve to keep Moose Island, which they claimed historically fell within the boundaries of Nova Scotia despite its having been part of the District of Maine prior to the war.

Equally contentious was the fishery–Mississippi issue. Clay might dismiss the relevance of having the right to fish and dry catch in British waters, but everybody else comprehended its economic value. The year before the war 1,200 American ships totalling 43,000 tons of shipping had landed catches worth $1.4 million in those waters. Loss of that right would cost New England mightily while certainly expanding British North America's fishing fleet as it moved to fill the commercial gap.[17] Accordingly, the British commissioners argued their right to access the Mississippi while declaring the fishery rights abrogated by the war.

After much argument, Goulburn agreed to refer both issues to his government. "But, gentlemen, we cannot say that our Government will not require something else. We had hoped we could have concluded without referring again to our Government. We mean to say, that we were now authorized to sign the treaty as we sent it to you."

"We made no question," Clay snapped, "that you would sign the treaty if we agreed to it in your own terms."

Goulburn, seemingly awkward at this blunt reply, responded: "Yes, but we only regret the *delay*, and should have wished to have concluded now. We wish the delay may not be imputed to us."[18]

Immediately after seeing the Americans out the door, Goulburn scribbled a hasty letter to Bathurst. "Knowing . . . the anxiety of the Government to have an early and favourable termination of this negotiation we felt ourselves . . . inclined to give up . . . the free navigation of the Mississippi . . . as we had obtained . . . the important admission that our right to [that] and their right to the Fisheries both rest on the footing of a stipulation in a Treaty and consequently if we give up the Mississippi we have a full right to exclude them from the use of our Territory for purposes connected with the Fishery."

Goulburn reported surprise that the Americans seemed in no haste to sign the treaty even when told that if they declined the British commissioners would not feel "bound to accede to the articles already agreed" later on. "This however produced no effect."

He urged Bathurst to secure a response from cabinet quickly because more delay might mean the treaty would fail to reach America for ratification before the House of Representatives dissolved on March 2. "There is not much time to lose," he warned.[19]

It was December 10 when the eight commissioners next met, this time at Bachelors' Hall. Gambier explained each British proposition. Regarding return of territory, the British insisted that "belonging to" be embedded into the clause—an obvious sally to prevent Moose Island having to be restored. John Quincy Adams curtly replied that the Americans would have to consider their response.

Proceeding to the eighth article, Gambier said his government considered the 49th parallel serving as the boundary gave America more territory than before and therefore a British right to the Mississippi would serve as a compensatory measure. The British offered a new clause setting aside for future negotiation both the right of fishery and navigation of the Mississippi. After two hours of discussion, the meeting ended and the Americans returned home to discuss the proposals. In less than an hour they agreed to reject all the British proposals.

Bayard said the British had neatly inverted the American eighth article. Where the Americans had offered Mississippi navigation in exchange for fishery rights, the British were willing to abandon navigation rights if the Americans gave up the fishery claim. This Gallatin argued was inescapable, the American ground for claiming fishery rights "untenable." He was ready to abandon the demand.

"I pledged to it as mine," Adams stated. Further, he believed the British willingness to abandon the Mississippi claim in return for their giving up the fishery indicated they knew the American case was strong and that this was more valuable than the Mississippi right.

"It was an extraordinary thing," Gallatin allowed, "that the question of peace or war now depended solely upon two points in which the people of the State of Massachusetts alone were interested"—Moose Island, and the fisheries within British jurisdiction. Adams sensed in this evidence of "the very perfidious character of the British propositions." They hoped to foment separatist sentiment in New England by forcing the American government to sacrifice interests there for gains in the west. When Russell bemoaned the fact that the issues centred on "a disaffected part of the country," Clay retorted that he "would do nothing to satisfy disaffection and treason; he would not yield anything for the sake of them."

Better, Clay claimed, to continue the war three years longer. "He had no doubt but three years more of war would make us a warlike people, and that then we should come out of the war with honor. . . . He was for playing *brag* with the British . . . they had been playing *brag* with us throughout the whole negotiation." Clay asked if Adams knew how to play *brag*. Adams confessed to having forgotten. "The art of it," Clay said, is "to beat your adversary by holding your hand with a solemn and confident phiz, and outbragging him."

"Ay," said Bayard, "but you may lose the game by bragging until the adversary sees the weakness of your hand." *Sotto voce* to Adams, Bayard said, "Mr. Clay is for bragging a million against a cent."

Perhaps, Gallatin suggested, now was the time to raise the idea of settling the entire treaty by agreeing to the *status quo ante bellum* upon all subjects of difference. Clay flew into a tirade, proclaiming that he "would never sign a treaty on the general status ante bellum, including the British right to trade with the Indian, so help him God to keep him steady to his purpose." Shaking with rage, Clay "stalked to and fro across the chamber, repeating five or six times, 'I will never sign a treaty upon the status ante bellum with the Indian article, so help me God!'" In the face of this ultimatum, all but Adams quickly backed down.

"Clay actually beat again a majority," Adams reflected, "by outbragging us."

But Clay was not yet done. The peace as currently proposed was a bad one. Signing it "would break him down entirely, and we should all be subject to much reproach."

"On the contrary," Bayard said, "it would be highly creditable to us. It would relieve the country from such an immense pressure—twenty-one millions of taxes, commerce restored, and substantially nothing given up."

"When the people were secure in the enjoyment of all we should obtain," Adams replied, "they will count it for nothing, and only look at what we yielded; and the very people now the most clamorous against the war will then be equally clamorous against the concessions made by us for peace."

"Most all treaties are unpopular," Gallatin counselled. "Ours, if we make one, will share the common fate."[20]

Tempers still festering, the Americans entered the monastery meeting hall the next day to find a similar mood prevailed among their counterparts. Goulburn's every comment was combative. Gambier's attempts to float a sense of joviality and camaraderie about the table were wrecked on shoals of stony indifference projected by the seven others.

John Quincy Adams got to the point. Two differences remained. America could not cede Moose Island either temporarily or permanently because the federal government had no authority to do so without consent of the State of Massachusetts of which the island was a part.

"Goulburn lost all control of his temper. He has always in such cases," Adams observed, "a sort of convulsive agitation about him, and the tone in which he speaks is more insulting than the language that he uses." It was merely a desire to avoid hostilities with the United States that had prevented Great Britain from occupying these rightful possessions of British North America in the past, he argued. If this was refused on grounds that there was no consent from a particular state, "there could be no safety for Great Britain in treating with the United States at all," for this excuse would be proffered whenever a decision to return territory to Britain was agreed by the commission that the treaty would create. Deadlocked, everyone agreed to move on to the equally contentious eighth article.

The Americans declined the British substitute clause as amounting to nothing. Although the two sides made various attempts to write a clause acceptable to them all, no progress was made. Finally the British left the room to talk privately. They returned with a request that the Americans give them a written ultimatum upon these two points that could then be submitted to their cabinet.

Adams believed the British were setting up an excuse to rupture the negotiations. Clay, however, was in a grand mood, "so confident that the British Government had resolved upon peace that . . . he would give himself as a hostage and a victim to be sacrificed if they broke off on these points."[21]

Two days passed as the Americans wrangled over the content of the ultimatum, and the final draft written by Gallatin was surprisingly conciliatory. The Americans would exempt the islands in Passamaquoddy Bay from the restoration of territory required by the first article so long as their claim was not sacrificed. If no agreement on possession was settled within a given time, the island would revert to whoever had held it before the war.

As for article eight, they proposed inserting "an article which should recognize the right of Great Britain to the navigation of that river, and that of the United States to a liberty in certain fisheries, which the British Government considered as abrogated by the war." They would not subscribe to any clause indicating an abandonment of this right.[22]

Goulburn forwarded the American note to Bathurst with a covering letter. He recommended accepting the Passamaquoddy proposal providing the time limit was dropped, as that gave them "inducement to decline acting or to practice some fraud in order to delay the decision of the Commissioners." The possibility of leaving out the eighth article entirely was broached as likely to succeed.[23]

Each side passed the ensuing days restlessly waiting for Bathurst's instructions. On the 22nd, Adams was intercepted by Bayard while on a walk. The British note had been delivered. The two men hurried back to the house. Instead of the timeline on restoration of islands in Passamaquoddy Bay, the British proposed "that no unnecessary delay of the settlement should be interposed."

Clay, upon seeing that the eighth article was to be struck, took exception, for he had expected the rights of navigation and fisheries would both be maintained by the British as abrogated and preferred that outcome. He threatened again not to sign the treaty. That evening Clay argued that they should delay their response, that doing so would gain more concessions. Russell appeared to support him. Gallatin and Bayard were too eager for peace, Clay said. Adams later wrote that Clay then turned to him and asked "whether I would not join him now and break off the negotiation. I told him no; it was now too late. I had offered to break off on the Indian article, which he had chosen not to do. There was nothing now to break off upon." Finally they agreed to meet the British the next day.

When the three British commissioners arrived at the American residence, they were quickly apprised that their proposals were acceptable. The conference this day was "to make final arrangements for the conclusion of the treaty . . . and to sign it whenever it would be agreeable to them." Peace suddenly at hand, everyone grasped hold. Final wording was agreed with relative ease and only a small amount of face-saving argument. Clay permitted the Indian article to pass without protest. The British commissioners consented to a significant departure from standard treaty protocol—instead of hostilities considered ended once the eight men signed and exchanged the documents, the war would cease only upon ratification by each government. But in exchange, the British insisted the clause require each government to accept the whole without any modification or reject it. It then fell to the two secretaries to each draft three exact copies for signing the following day.

Late on the afternoon of Christmas Eve, the Americans crowded into a carriage, spread blankets over their knees against the bitter chill, and were carried to the monastery. The British greeted them in the grand refectory, where the documents were laid out on the long table over which they had so often haggled. For two hours the men and their secretaries meticulously compared the drafts. Some commas were inserted, but everyone decided to turn a blind eye to a discrepancy in how the secretaries had spelled out the dates in order to avoid having to redo the whole. Then came the signing, an event that took thirty minutes. The British inscribed their signatures first, then the Americans. Gambier then handed the British copies to Adams in exchange for the American ones. The old naval officer proclaimed a fervent wish that the peace be permanent, to which Adams expressed his hope that it be the last treaty of peace Great Britain and the United States should make.

Outside a carriage waited to speed Anthony St. John Baker and the treaties to London. In the late afternoon, giving the commissioners time to write covering letters, Christopher Hughes would depart for Bordeaux, where the U.S. ship *Transit* waited to carry him to Washington. As Baker's carriage clattered down the darkened streets, the Americans boarded their own and clip-clopped home. It was 6:30, and throughout the city pealing church bells signalled the commencement of the celebration of Christ's birth.

That night, by candlelight, Adams closed his journal entry for the day with "a humble offering to God for the conclusion to which it has pleased him to bring the negotiation for peace at this place, and a fervent prayer that its result may be propitious to the welfare, the best interests, and the union of my country."[24]

In a private letter to James Monroe written on Christmas Day, Gallatin stated with reserve that the treaty was "as favourable as could be expected under existing circumstances, so far as they were known to us." The European powers, he believed, desired the war to continue in order to weaken Britain. But none would assist America in it. With peace those same powers could be expected to desire more formal relations with the United States, due to its having not been beaten. As for the treaty itself, he believed they had surrendered nothing of consequence, but claimed no significant gain besides peace. To Gallatin that was sufficient.[25]

Surprisingly, the man who had threatened to break the negotiation at the last moment put the most favourable interpretation on the treaty's signing. While the terms were not what he and America had expected to gain, Clay wrote, "they cannot be pronounced unfavorable. We lose no territory, I think no honor. If we lost a particular liberty in the Fisheries, on the one hand . . . we gain, on the other the exemption of the Navigation of the Mississippi from British claims. We gain also the right of exemption from the practice of trading with the Indians.

"Judged by another standard, the pretensions of the enemy at the opening of the negotiation, the conditions of the peace certainly reflect no dishonour on us."[26] In this way the man who had led a nation and its president to war explained away the fact that none of the war's goals, officially stated or not, had been won. Honour had been preserved. That sufficed.

TWENTY-SEVEN

The Blessing of Peace

*A*s the American commissioners wrote to James Monroe, Anthony St. John Baker's carriage rumbled toward Ostend, where a ship waited. Sweat steamed off the hides of the straining, tiring horses, but the secretary allowed few pauses for rest, food, or water. He slept as possible in the rocking, swaying carriage. Then, in the early morning of Christmas Day, came the sharp, splintering crack of a wheel spoke breaking. For hours the secretary paced impatiently by the roadside in the damp cold while repairs were made. Even with this delay, he delivered the treaties to Lord Liverpool forty-three hours after their signing.

Within hours Liverpool presented the treaty to the Prince Regent, who ratified it after the most cursory glance. Baker, accompanied by Clay's secretary, Henry Carroll, quickly boarded HMS *Favourite* and sailed for America. Christopher Hughes was already at sea aboard *Transit*, each man serving as insurance in case the other and his precious documents were lost to storm or brigands.[1] Originally, Carroll was to have provided a third assurance that the treaty reached America by travelling on another ship from Amsterdam, but that vessel was already locked in ice as winter crushed down upon Europe.[2]

Until the United States ratified the treaty, peace was not final, and the treaty set a deadline of four months from December 24, 1814, for that to occur or it was nullified. Even after ratification, there was the complicated problem of getting the word out to ships at sea. Both nations had naval forces scattered far across the world's oceans, many of them hunting each other. It would take weeks for messenger ships to bear the news to the many ports where they must eventually call for supplies. Realizing the time required to get word to the Indian Ocean must be longer than to a port close to North America, such as the Bahamas, a schedule was drafted that allotted twelve days for the news to be spread to ships closest to the North American coast and up to 120 days for those in the southern Pacific or Indian oceans. Prizes taken in this time would be returned.

But not only ships would receive the news belatedly. Across the ocean, in the malarial bayous, swamps, and waterways surrounding New Orleans, two armies gathered for battle. A peace was signed, but the killing not yet done.

The British intention to attack New Orleans was one of the war's worst-kept secrets. Gallatin had warned Monroe of the operation months before, and British newspapers had reported the departure of the troops to West India and later Maj. Gen. Sir Edward Pakenham's sailing to join them. Maj. Gen. Andrew Jackson—given command over Gulf Coast operations in May 1814—had dismissed all this forewarning. Pensacola, with its better harbour, seemed a more logical target to the Tennessean. A Spanish possession garrisoned by only 500 troops, it was ripe for conquest. On November 7, 1814, Jackson had drawn up 4,100 men before it only to find the Spanish flown, the city gates open. Unbeknown to Jackson, however, a small force of British marines had occupied the vital forts that guarded the harbour's mouth. Outnumbered, they set off huge explosive charges that destroyed the forts, rendering the harbour indefensible from seaborne assault, and then withdrew to waiting ships. Pensacola was neutralized.[3]

Unsure which way to turn to meet the forthcoming British assault, Jackson marched to Mobile, where no sign of a British fleet was to be seen. Belatedly, Jackson adhered to frantic signals from Washington urging that he establish a defence around New Orleans. Jackson entered the city on December 1—beating the British by just a week.

New Orleans was, however, more easily defended than attacked. Lying 100 miles up the Mississippi, it was surrounded by water. Lake Pontchartrain stood to the north, Lake Borgne to the east, and the ground west and south was webbed with bayous, creeks, and festering swamps. Marching on the city from the coast with a European-trained army posed a formidable challenge. About sixty-five miles down the Mississippi from the city, the twenty-eight guns of Fort St. Philip effectively blocked the river. Although those guns were probably sufficient, Jackson put 200 slaves to work digging a battery on the adjacent riverbank.

Having denied the British use of the river, Jackson examined likely overland approaches from the east. Five small gunboats under Lt. Thomas Ap Catesby Jones were deployed on Lake Borgne, truly a bay that opened into Mississippi Sound but barred to deep-draft ocean ships by a shoal across its mouth. Anchored behind this protective shoal, Jones kept a wary eye seaward. On December 8, Vice-Admiral Sir Alexander Cochrane's ships dropped anchor off Ship Island at the eastern entrance to Mississippi Sound. The ship bearing Pakenham having not yet caught up, general command rested with Maj. Gen. John Keane, but it fell to Cochrane to devise a means to put 6,000 men in a position to carry New Orleans.

As he examined the thorny problem, Cochrane's earlier boasts that he could take the city with just 2,000 troops haunted the admiral. Closing on it with warships was impossible, so all their great guns were rendered useless. After studying the terrain for several days, Cochrane and Keane decided the troops must move by shallow-draft craft to the western shore of Lake Borgne. Here, they would land at the mouth of Bayou des Pêcheurs and follow an 8-mile winding course of bayous and canals through swaths of cypress swamps to gain a road 7 miles south of New Orleans that bordered the Mississippi. This would place them well above the American forts guarding the river.[4]

First the gunboats had to be eliminated. On the night of December 12, a flotilla of forty-five launches, barges, and pinnaces under oars entered the lake. Aboard were 1,000 seamen and marines. Soon after daybreak, Jones spotted the British and attempted to escape under sail. But the winds were fickle and scant, so he could put little distance between his boats and the patient, seemingly tireless oarsmen. For thirty-six hours the British rowed and the Americans tried to fill sails. Then, at mid-morning on December 14, the British dropped anchor just out of gunshot range and took breakfast.

The American gunboats were spread out in a line. Barely a breeze lifted the sails, so each ship would fight where it stood. After an hour anchors were weighed and the oarsmen pulled hard as they came into range. The American guns opened with a fierce fire, Jones's only hope being to smash the British craft before they got alongside. Despite the heavy rain of round and grapeshot, the British oarsmen prevailed.[5] About 11:30 several craft swarmed around his flagship and marines clambered over the gunwales to fight his crew hand-to-hand. Jones and the British flotilla commander, Capt. Nicholas Lockyer, were severely wounded. After a twenty-minute melee the boat was in British hands, its guns turned against the others. Thirty-minutes later the battle was over, all the American vessels captured.[6] The British dash through cannon fire had been costly, most of their casualties resulting from it. Nineteen men were dead, 75 wounded, while the Americans had 6 killed and 35 wounded.[7]

With Lake Borgne in British hands, Cochrane shuttled the redcoats and supplies across the lake's 60-mile span in open boats—an operation that took six days to complete. Rather than landing the troops directly at Bayou des Pêcheurs, a staging ground was established on a swampy, uninhabited islet called Isle aux Poix, near the mouth of the Pearl River and about halfway to the final landing point. While this movement was under way, an advance guard of 1,600 men moved into the bayou on December 23. They slipped undiscovered about 5 miles up the waterways in boats before having to disembark. From there, the force cut a crude road through a cypress swamp that followed a canal supplying water to a plantation. Astride the road bordering the Mississippi River, Keane allowed the exhausted troops to camp rather than exploiting the complete surprise to be gained by pressing on to New Orleans.[8]

Jackson learned of the British whereabouts late in the day, yet had no idea if this was the main attack.[9] But always aggressive, Jackson was not going to let the British presence go unchallenged. That night, 900 regulars, 550 Tennessee riflemen, and 650 Louisiana and Mississippi militiamen—200 of whom were freed slaves—attacked the British troops. Although many redcoats were already asleep when the attack came in, they quickly rallied. A fierce, confused night-time brawl ensued, with men discharging muskets at point-blank range, stabbing with bayonets, and using empty muskets as clubs. After four hours the Americans were driven off at about midnight, when British reinforcements appeared. British losses numbered 46 dead, 167 wounded, and 64 missing. The Americans reported 24 killed, 115 wounded, and 74 missing.

Retreating two miles, Jackson placed his men behind Rodriguez Canal on the southern boundary of Chalmette Plantation, where a three-quarter-mile wide swath of dry ground was flanked by the river on one side and impenetrable cypress swamp on the other. Across the canal lay a recently harvested sugar-beet field. Now convinced he faced the main British force, Jackson decided to make this his last stand.

The British proceeded with deliberation rather than haste. While they slowly advanced the rest of the army into place, Jackson's men breached nearby levees and flooded the previously dry canal with muddy water. Behind its northern bank they erected a shoulder-high rampart thick enough to withstand cannon shot by packing mud around sugar barrels. On the opposite bank of the Mississippi a battery of naval guns guarded by 800 Kentucky militiamen protected his flank.

On Christmas Day, Maj. Gen. Pakenham arrived. The British now had about 4,000 men drawn up alongside the Mississippi. Jackson faced them with about the same number. Although the thirty-six-year-old Pakenham had served as his brother-in-law's adjutant during the Peninsular War, his reputation was largely self-made. He had fought with distinction at Salamanca. But the present situation discouraged him. Across the river was a strong gun line; on the river itself two gunboats, *Caroline* and *Louisiana*, could bring guns to bear on any attack. The Americans were heavily entrenched.[10]

His first move was against the gunboats. After constructing a furnace in which round shot was transformed into hot shot, British cannon brought the two boats under fire on December 27. Badly stricken, *Caroline* caught fire and exploded. *Louisiana*, however, was winched out of range upstream.

At dawn the next day Pakenham ordered an infantry assault against the American works. Two columns marched toward Jackson's men only to be raked by intense, accurate fire. Floated back into range, *Louisiana* loosed 800 rounds. Pakenham broke off the attack before his troops suffered significant loss. Later estimates reported 35 American casualties and 55 British.[11]

It was obvious that the American works could not be carried without aid of artillery. Laboriously, the British dragged and floated boats bearing ten 18-pound guns, four carronades, and a minimal amount of ammunition from Lake Borgne through the swamps. Not until New Year's Day were the batteries ready, and a two-hour artillery duel ensued. The British had naively placed their cannon behind breastworks constructed from barrels of sugar, thinking this would substitute for ones filled with sand. The American shot ripped through the barrels with ease, killing and wounding more than 75 British gunners. That night the guns were dragged out of range.

Pakenham could only wait until all his infantry were gathered and then throw an all-out assault against the American line. Not until January 7 was everyone in place. That night 1,200 men under Col. William Thornton crossed the river to capture the American naval guns and turn Jackson's flank. To enable the crossing, levees had to be breached to flood Villeré Canal in order to pass boats from the canal into the river. Once the assault on the opposite shore began, Pakenham would advance two columns, one of 2,200 men under Maj. Gen. Sir Samuel Gibbs, the other 1,200 strong led by Keane. Another 1,200 men commanded by Maj. Gen. John Lambert stood in reserve.[12]

Facing them was a melange numbering about 3,500 with another 1,000 in reserve. Regulars, Kentucky and Tennessee volunteers, Creoles, freed slaves, and a motley crew of Baratarian pirates led by Jean Laffite jammed the front line. Jackson had once declared the pirates "hellish Banditti," but he had promised to seek a blanket presidential pardon in return for their joining the Americans.[13] Jackson's weakest point lay across the river, where just 450 Louisiana militiamen guarded the naval guns.

At daybreak on January 8, mist lay heavy over the ground between the two forces. Cut to stubble, the sugar-beet fields offered no cover. As the British advance began there was no sign that the naval guns had been carried. Cannon on both sides opened with a heavy thunder. From behind the American barricades drummers pounded out "Yankee Doodle." The British soldiers were veterans of seven years of war, but they were bitter, too. Most had expected discharge after the Peninsula. Instead they had been shipped to a new battlefield. Many had complained of this to officers during the night, but to no avail.

Gibbs led his column directly into the fire of an 18-pound battery. The naval guns were slamming heavy shot from across the river. Musket fire lashed out from the breastworks. Twice the column shuddered to a halt, the lines had to be redressed, the men stiffened with bellowed orders by officers and sergeants before they continued into the hellish rain. Almost at the American line, Gibbs fell mortally wounded. Pakenham galloped forward to take command and was killed by grapeshot. Those who managed to cross the canal discovered that the fascines and scaling ladders for getting over the breastworks had been forgotten. Lambert was rushing up, within 250 yards of the canal, when the column broke and streamed through the ranks of his men. On the other side of the line, Keane's column had almost gained the American position before being driven back by the same intense fire. Keane was severely wounded. Only across the river, although badly delayed, did the British achieve any success when Thornton carried and spiked the naval guns. Having driven the Kentucky militia from the field, he was ready to turn Jackson's position if reinforced. But the only general left standing, Lambert, had had enough. A Peninsular veteran, he considered the fighting this day "arduous beyond anything I have ever witnessed."

The British withdrew about 2 miles. Their losses had been staggering, 291 dead, 1,262 wounded, 484 missing, and almost all from the 3,400 men in the two columns. Jackson's casualties were trifling, 13 dead, 39 wounded, and 19 missing.[14] The Americans had finally won a decisive and major victory. But it was also bittersweet, for it could not affect the outcome of a war already settled by treaty.

Although urged to take the offensive, Jackson recognized that while he could exert sufficient discipline over his unruly troops while on the defensive, sending them into an attack was another matter. The British had established a defensive line mirroring his own in strength and narrowness of front. An attack would end in his men being slaughtered as the British had been.

A two-day truce enabled the British to clear their dead and wounded from the field. Then the two sides waited, each hoping the other would make a foolish charge. Finally, on January 18, Lambert led his men back to the ships.

In Ghent, three days before the Chalmette Plantation bloodbath, the mayor hosted a lavish banquet at the grand Hôtel de Ville attended "by the principal gentlemen of the city" to fête the commissioners.[15] Since the announcement of the treaty at noon on Christmas Day, the city had swept the Americans and British up in a swirl of celebration, gentility competing fiercely to gather as many of the men into their drawing rooms at once. Bored and restless, it proved not uncommon for all to be in attendance most nights. Early in the month, the Americans had given up their lease on the Rue des Champs and moved back to the Hôtel des Pays-Bas but found the accommodation cramped compared to the apartments they had earlier enjoyed.

With the treaty signed, the gulf between them and the British had diminished. The Americans cheerfully saw Vice-Admiral James Gambier and Dr. William Adams off when they departed the city on January 3. Henry Goulburn remained so at least one British commissioner could attend the mayor's event. John Quincy Adams found this intense young man easier to take now than most of his own colleagues.

A nasty dispute between Adams and Henry Clay—loyally supported by the sycophantic Jonathan Russell—had erupted within days of the signing, over handling of the vast library of documents, maps, letters, ledgers, and other materials accumulated during the lengthy search for peace that had begun in St. Petersburg more than two years before. By chance rather than design, Adams maintained this archive in his room. Clay wanted it packed up and loaded aboard *Neptune*, on which he expected to soon sail to America, whereupon he would deliver it to the State Department. Rather than proposing this as a request, Clay turned it into a demand. Instinctively balking at being bullied, Adams refused on grounds that convention held that the commission head should maintain possession of the archive and be responsible for its delivery. The increasingly bitter argument, its resolution all the more pressing as Clay and James Bayard were to depart the next day for Paris, was still in full heat when the commissioners attended the January 5 banquet.

Having been earlier advised that Goulburn planned to wear a ceremonial uniform, the Americans did likewise. The white cotton hangings that covered all the walls and windows of the hotel's large hall sharply highlighted the scarlet or blue worn by the commissioners. Behind the head table American and British flags were intertwined under an assemblage of olive trees. Adams found himself seated next to Goulburn at the very centre of the head table, the two men between the mayor and provincial intendant. The hall was crowded with about ninety people. A band played first "Hail, Columbia" followed by "God Save the King," then proceeded to repeat both endlessly as the night progressed. After several airings Goulburn whispered that the whole thing was becoming "tiresome," to which Adams quietly agreed.

As relentlessly alternating as the music, mayor and intendant raised repeated toasts to "His Britannic Majesty" and "the United States," then "the Negotiators" and "the Peace." Finally Adams urged Goulburn to interject with a toast, so he rose and raised a glass to "the Intendant and the Mayor; the City of Ghent, its prosperity; and our gratitude for their loyal hospitality and the many acts of kindness that we have received from them." Able to cap that with one that would ensure it be the last, Adams toasted, "Ghent, the city of peace; may the gates of the temple of Janus, here closed, not be opened again for a century."[16]

Having tarried only for this final banquet, Goulburn and his family departed for London two days later. He was relieved to go. The celebrations had grated, for he did not believe the peace negotiated good for Britain, Canada, or the Indians to whom he had tried to remain loyal only in the end to sacrifice them in accordance with Liverpool's instructions.

Adams ended the dispute over the archive by threatening to reveal the entire argument in a letter to Monroe. Caught for once short in brag, Clay capitulated, acknowledging that such a letter would dishonour them all by making it "look as if we had fallen to a scramble after a few books and papers." Everyone agreed to keep the dispute secret. Adams retained the documents, while the books, maps, and other less sensitive material were to be stored with the American agent in London until instructions for their return were sent by Washington.

On January 7, Clay and Bayard caught a public stagecoach to Lille en route to Paris. Bayard was unwell, having developed a harsh, phlegmy cough he seemed unable to shed. Russell followed shortly thereafter, neither Adams nor Gallatin bothering to note his departure. On January 12, Albert Gallatin and his son left for Geneva, which Gallatin had not seen in years and James ever. Before going, Gallatin assured Adams he would return when necessary to participate in the expected next stage of normalizing relations with Britain by way of negotiation of a commercial treaty. Of them all, Adams reflected, Gallatin had "contributed the largest and most important share to the conclusion of peace, and there has been a more constant concurrence of opinion between him and me upon every point of our deliberations, than perhaps between any two other members of the mission."[17]

In the meantime the landlords of the monastery and Bachelors' Hall put up for auction all the furniture alleged to have been used by the commissioners. The sale lasted ten days, and Adams was amused to see many unrecognizable items offered. "Under the name of effects having belonged to us they have emptied all the upholsterers' shops in the city . . . the good people of the place consider the Congress of Ghent as an epoch of so much importance in the history of their city, that they have given extravagant prices for some of our relics. I am told that an old inkstand, which was used at the conference, was sold for thirty francs, though it was not worth as many sous. . . . The worst part of the joke was that they put off quantities of bad wine, as if it had been ours. We did not leave a bottle for sale."[18]

Adams lingered in Ghent, pottering over the papers and records, putting them in order, reluctant now to leave a city he admitted to having grown fond of. On January 26, after seven months and two days in what he deemed "the most memorable period of my life," Adams climbed into a carriage loaded with many trunks of papers and effects for the journey to Paris.[19] None of the men would ever return.

In North America, President Madison fretted for news. No word from New Orleans, nothing from Ghent. The government was in crisis, near bankrupt, and only feeble preparations were under way for a spring campaign against Canada. He had no reason to believe it would succeed where the others had failed. An attempt by Capt. Stephen Decatur to slip the frigate *President* out of New York harbour on January 14 had ended in disaster, proving the effectiveness of the British blockade. Intercepted, *President* had fought a long engagement that ended with Decatur striking her colours after one-fifth of his crew were killed and wounded and the ship badly holed.[20] That other frigates had eluded the blockade and were on the rampage was scant consolation, and the symbolism of the captured ship's name was not lost on the anti-war press.

Federalists in New England were dangerously close to insurrection. On January 9, Madison had instructed Monroe to draw secret plans to raise an army of New York volunteers to "put rebellion down" in the northern states.[21] Three days later his fears seemed warranted when a series of constitutional amendments was released by twenty-six delegates who had held a secret conference in Hartford, Connecticut. The Hartford Convention demanded a two-thirds vote by Congress be required to declare war, curb commerce, or admit new states; denied foreign-born citizens from holding federal office; limited presidents to one term; and prohibited the immediate predecessor coming from the same state.

Rumours swirled on the windy Washington streets that Jackson had surrendered, the negotiations failed. Predictions were high that Madison would resign. Better that than the disgrace of impeachment. Even friends thought it unlikely his presidency could survive more defeats. Some worried for the man himself. The last year he had been ill as often as not and looked weak and tired, older than his sixty-three years.

Madison's demeanour would have been grimmer still had he learned that the British had carried out two landings on American soil other than at New Orleans. On January 13, troops off a small fleet commanded by Capt. Robert Barrie had assaulted and captured a fort on Point Peter, on the southern Georgia coast. From there they marched inland and occupied the town of St. Marys. Then, on the night of February 7–8, the force from New Orleans forced the surrender of Fort Bowyer and opened the way for occupation of Mobile. Only the arrival of a ship bringing news of the treaty prevented the troops at both St. Marys and Fort Bowyer from conducting further operations. They each withdrew on February 13.

It was at this bleakest hour in Madison's presidency that a courier galloped into Washington on February 5 and in minutes jubilation reigned. Jackson victorious! New Orleans saved! Nine days later the celebrations verged on delirium as word spread that two men from Ghent had landed in New York and even now the president had in hand a peace treaty. Unable to contain his curiosity, Pennsylvania senator Jonathan Roberts raced to Octagon House, where he found Madison sitting alone in his parlour, the room "still and dark." Roberts apologized for bursting in on the basis of what must have been an unfounded rumour. "I believe there is peace," Madison told his friend in a soft voice.[22]

The next day the treaty went to the Senate, where it was ratified on February 16 without a dissenting vote. On February 17, in his curious Octagon House study that occupied a room above the turret-like portico, Madison ratified the treaty and sent it to Congress with a covering note stating that the conclusion of the war was highly honourable to America. It was, he declared, "the natural result of the wisdom of the legislative councils, of the patriotism of the people, of the public spirit of the militia, and of the valor of the military and naval forces of the country. Peace, at all times a blessing, is peculiarly welcome, therefore, at a period when the causes of the war have ceased to operate, when the Government has demonstrated the efficiency of its power of defense, and when the nation can review its conduct without regret and without reproach."[23]

Two years and eight months after it began, the War of 1812 was at an end.

Honour Preserved

*O*nce the war concluded, the primary question became whether the Treaty of Ghent provided a good peace. Response in the United States was largely favourable—nothing much given up and no penalty incurred for starting the war. Specific clauses and their import were hardly examined by the popular press or federal politicians of either stripe. Federalists tried to tarnish it. A "Treaty, which gives us peace, is represented as glorious, when it has given us nothing else. And it is attempted to make us believe that all the objects of the war have been obtained, when every thing, for which it was declared has been abandoned."[1]

True, but most Americans cared not. The influence of the Federalists was on the wane, the party destined to oblivion and few sorry to see its passing. America faced one-party rule as Republicans realized a "glorious opportunity . . . to place themselves permanently in power" for decades to come.[2] In reality, the Republican Party largely ceased to be, too, as interest groups rallied behind one or another presidential candidate claiming to be *the* true Republican. A decade passed before a semblance of party politics re-emerged, with the rise of Andrew Jackson's Democratic Party met by the National Republicans led by John Quincy Adams and Henry Clay. Later, the Whigs emerged with an anti-Jacksonian platform opposed to anything Old Hickory favoured.

Jackson's victory at New Orleans captured the popular imagination far more than dry pages of a treaty. Overnight, savage Indian fighter became national celebrity—the country's most legendary war hero. Soon all the failed campaigns were forgotten, the myth emerging that out of one victory the United States won the war. Nationalism ran rampant; even New Englanders climbed aboard the Union fidelity wagon. Anglophobia was at least as strong in the years immediately following the war as had been the case after independence.

Nationalism marched hand in hand with vigorous expansionism. Spanish West Florida, annexed in 1813, was retained without apology to the neutral power from which it was wrested. The Indian confederacy, hopelessly fragmented by the war and Tecumseh's death, was doomed. Within three years all the continent south of the 49th parallel and east of the Mississippi, save what remained of Spanish Florida, had been granted statehood or territorial status. Growing numbers of settlers, gold prospectors, buffalo hunters, fortune seekers, and freebooters of all kinds had pushed outward to the Missouri River and well beyond by the end of the decade. The Indian nations in their path fled westward as refugees, moved to assigned reservations, or faced slaughter by the army. This pattern would continue until Americans declared the west won. Only a remnant of the peoples from whom a continent was taken survived.

As the nation expanded, as the north's commercial and industrial wealth increased and the agrarian south found vibrant markets for its cotton and other crops, America enjoyed a rare period of unity dubbed the "era of good feelings." The role of the federal government increased, bringing limited taxation and an enlarged army and navy. This fed the myth that the lasting consequence of the war was an America with a clear vision of itself as the one nation, indivisible under God, intended by its forefathers. This myth prevailed even after the lie of it was exposed by a civil war from 1861 to 1865 that pitted American against American in the ranks of armies larger than those fielded in any European war, the butchery on the battlefields also far greater due to advances in the means of killing that outpaced the tactics of generals. In the aftermath of such a cataclysm, the War of 1812 receded into the shadows of history to almost disappear from the American conscience.

Not so for British North America. At first, public reaction to the peace was mainly negative. Although cessation of war was desirable, the treaty failed to secure the colonies from future American aggression. On the southern shores of the Great Lakes, U.S. troops still manned fort ramparts and American warships plied the waters. It seemed the hostilities could begin anew on the slightest excuse.

There was also the Indian issue. The fur trade was still important to the economy of the Canadas, and abandonment of the Indian confederacy at Ghent could only spell the gradual demise of this vibrant industry. Yet even in 1815, that economy was being displaced in importance by agriculture, timber harvesting, and fishing. People pursuing these ways of life had little in common with the Indians and were often at odds with them, so appeals for protection of native peoples from American displacement were subdued. Soon enough the frontier would be pushed back in British North America as well, although with minimal bloodshed. Disease, famine, and less-than-voluntary consignment to reserves more efficiently cleared the way at less economic cost than war.

At the war's outset the British colonies had consisted of an uneasy mix of French Canadians, native-born British subjects, Empire Loyalists who had fled the Revolution to the south, and American migrants who had crossed a border seeking economic gain. During the course of the war these groups developed a vague sense of commonality based more on an exclusionary definition of identity. If they were not yet Canadian, they were not American. Had they desired to be so, the war provided ample opportunity to align themselves with the invading forces, and against insurgency the British could not have prevailed. They had not done so. Instead, a majority had supported the British resistance to American invasion. The myth that the militia almost single-handedly saved Canada from conquest was born. After the war, a wary eye was kept on America lest she try again. In the century that followed the war, Canadians did not look southward for inspiration, institutions, or forms of government. They looked instead across the Atlantic to Britain. So it was natural that the federal government created in 1867 when the colonies confederated into the Dominion of Canada hove to the British parliamentary model.

The War of 1812, of course, never held much importance to Great Britain. Yet, when its details were released by Lord Liverpool, the treaty was subject to much criticism. It was, the London *Times* accused, a "deadly instrument," a "degrading manner of terminating the war" by imposing a "premature and inglorious peace."³ Most of the nation's newspapers issued similar pronouncements. The peace enabled America to escape rightful punishment for its temerity in challenging British might and for serving as lackey to Napoleon. The outpouring of rage was, however, short-lived.

While the House of Commons opposition openly criticized the cabinet and, more vehemently, the three commissioners for incompetently negotiating the treaty, they were not adverse to its outcome. Nobody had wanted a war with the United States, few cared about the Indians, and the peace seemed to have secured British North America from future American incursion. During the sputtering debates on the matter, the House benches were largely empty.

No doubt the treaty might have incurred greater scrutiny had it not been for the crisis brought on by Napoleon's return from exile on March 1. Who could think of matters in North America when the French were mobilizing? The Hundred Days were upon Europe, and more than a few wondered what might have happened had Britain sent thousands of its troops and also Wellington overseas. When the Iron Duke faced Napoleon and broke the French army at Waterloo on June 18, the wisdom of his being retained at home rather than sent to the colonies seemed divinely inspired. By the time of Napoleon's abdication four days later, the ramifications of the Treaty of Ghent had ceased to be of importance to all but the commissioners tasked to carry out the resolution of issues left outstanding.

These took years to resolve. After some rancorous negotiation, in late 1815 the British withdrew from the forts on the Mississippi and Fort Michilimackinac on Lake Huron. Congress moved to cement this victory by passing legislation in 1816 that barred British trade with American Indians. In 1817, the Passamaquoddy islands were divided. Britain got most of them, but not Moose Island. The British garrison there left the following year. Potential for a naval rearmament race on the strategically vital lakes was defused by the Rush–Bagot Agreement in April 1817 that limited each side to one warship on Lake Ontario, two on the upper lakes, and one on Lake Champlain. Albert Gallatin was among a team of commissioners who negotiated and ratified the Convention of 1818, which renewed commercial agreements that he, John Quincy Adams, and Henry Clay had negotiated in 1815 with, among other British representatives, Henry Goulburn and Dr. William Adams. The 1818 agreement went further than the first. It settled the 49th parallel from Lake of the Woods to Stony Mountain, with the area west of the Rockies jointly shared for ten years and a boundary settled then. America gained rights to fish and dry catch along limited Canadian coastlines, while the British gave up any right to Mississippi navigation.

It is doubtful any of the Ghent commissioners saw the negotiation as a crowning achievement in their careers. Vice-Admiral James Gambier was so distraught over the allegations that the British commissioners had failed in their duties that he applied to Lord Liverpool for compensation. Cabinet quietly awarded him a handsome £2,250 and William Adams £2,000. Henry Goulburn declined similar compensation.

Gambier retired to his estate and pansy-propagation pursuits. On July 22, 1830, at age seventy-three, by right of seniority he was raised to the just-emptied position of Admiral of the Fleet. As per custom it was not expected he would actually raise his flag and assume the duty. On April 19, 1833, he died.

William Adams was among the lawyers involved in preparing the government's defence of a bill in 1820 aimed at dissolving the marriage between Queen Caroline and King George IV—the former Prince Regent—that after a four-month hearing was abandoned by the House of Lords. His health broken from the long hours, Adams resigned his profession in 1825. Retiring to Thorpe in Surrey, he lived to the age of seventy-nine, dying on June 11, 1851.

Henry Goulburn's public career was long and distinguished. In 1821 he became a member of the Privy Council and chief secretary to the lord lieutenant of Ireland, then chancellor of the exchequer in 1828. He held this position until the government's fall in 1830. Apart from a brief interlude in 1827, Goulburn had been a member of every government since 1810. Dogged by poor health, his time in opposition was little more restful, and in 1834 he returned to cabinet as part of a resurgent Tory Party and assumed the post of home secretary—the very office where his public service career had begun. In 1841, he was again chancellor of the exchequer, under the third prime minister that he loyally served. Still on the government side of the House in 1856 but out of cabinet because of his age and uncompromising conservative values, Goulburn contracted pleurisy and died on January 12, 1856, at age seventy-one.

Goulburn's early mentor, the Earl of Bathurst, continued as secretary for war and the colonies until 1827, when Lord Liverpool resigned. He then served as lord president of the council in the Duke of Wellington's government to 1830. Four years later he died at seventy-two years old.

The mercurial Viscount Castlereagh was both celebrated and impugned by his countrymen after 1815. His brilliant diplomacy at the Congress of Vienna and later conferences checked Russian ambitions in Europe while strengthening the then weak central powers of Germany and Italy. For this and other achievements in international affairs he was hailed. But as leader of the House of Commons he could not escape being tarnished as chief architect behind repressive policies introduced at home between 1815 and 1819 to which he was largely opposed. After a failed plot to assassinate the cabinet, Castlereagh carried a pistol at all times and claimed that his life was in jeopardy. Excessive suspicion gave way to open paranoia that manifested itself in unsupported belief that he faced blackmail from unidentified conspirators holding fraudulent evidence that he was homosexual. Just before Castlereagh was to have departed for a major conference in Verona, his doctors confined him to his country home. His razor confiscated, the fifty-three-year-old Castlereagh slit his throat with a penknife on August 12, 1822. Castlereagh was entombed in Westminster Abbey, but he was also scorned in verse by Romantic poets Shelley and Byron.

Expected to preside over merely a caretaker government, Lord Liverpool served continuously as Britain's prime minister for almost fifteen years. Had not a paralytic stroke forced his retirement on February 17, 1827, at age fifty-six, Liverpool might have continued in office until he deigned to leave it. In part, his long tenure was due to a lack of charisma that rendered him dogged administrator rather than dynamic leader. Less than two years after the stroke, Liverpool died in London on December 4, 1828.

President James Madison was constitutionally limited to two terms in office and so took his leave on April 6, 1817. He retired to his Virginia estate,

Montpelier, closing a political career that spanned forty-one years and dated back to the birth of America. He died at age eighty-five on June 28, 1836. His loyal secretary of state, James Monroe, succeeded him as the nation's fifth president—fulfilling by fact rather than design the Federalist gibe that Virginia had imposed on America a dynasty of three Jameses.

When Monroe's presidency ended in 1824, John Quincy Adams, Henry Clay, and Andrew Jackson threw their hats into the ring. William Crawford, the American minister to France during the war, also ran, with Albert Gallatin his vice-presidential running mate. In a close contest, Jackson carried the popular vote but failed to win a majority. Adams was next in line, with Clay trailing at the tail end. It fell to Congress to decide the winner. While Clay still carried a grudge against Adams, he despised Jackson. His weight in Congress carried sufficient sway to tip the decision in Adams's favour, and Clay was rewarded with the secretary of state post.

Adams survived only one term, being swept from office by Jackson in 1828 after a particularly bitter campaign marked by personal slanders. Returning to Congress in 1831, Adams played the role of the nation's conscience by recalling its puritanical roots but was equally renowned for his inability to control his temper. After sixteen consecutive years in the House, Adams died at age eighty on February 23, 1848, just two days after a stroke left him slumped over his desk on the congressional floor.

Clay's naked presidential ambitions were to go unrealized. Upon returning from Ghent he had been re-elected House Speaker and confidently expected that he was bound for a rebuilt White House. Three times he announced his candidacy and as often stood back waiting for an expected call from supporters, who kept their silence. Moving up to the Senate in 1831 to better oppose Jackson, Clay became the leader of the Whig Party. He was still aspiring to the presidency when carried off by death at seventy-five in 1852.

Of the Americans at Ghent, James Bayard had been liked and respected by all the others. Upon leaving the city he had gone to Paris to await passage to America. But he was ill, suffering severe chest congestion that left him incapacitated for weeks at a time, and his stay there was a trial of endurance. He longed for home, feared he would die before reaching it. *Neptune* sailed with Bayard and William Crawford aboard on June 18,

1815, and entered Delaware harbour on August 1 after forty-three days at sea. Bayard, bedridden the entire voyage, was taken ashore on a stretcher carried by twelve sailors. They refused to surrender him to the crowd of well-wishers who had gathered at news of his illness, insisting on bearing him home. Bayard told his family he would not survive. Five days later the forty-eight-year-old Federalist was dead.

If Bayard was the most respected among the Ghent commissioners, Jonathan Russell was the least so. Having assumed his post as minister to Sweden, he remained there until 1818. In 1821, he was elected to Congress as a Massachusetts representative for what proved his only term. Russell's mediocrity would have earned him a moderate, not unfavourable niche in American history for his various roles in diplomacy. But, longing for more influence, Russell embarked on a vile and largely fraudulent campaign against his fellow negotiators Adams and Gallatin. Casting Adams as the chief villain and Gallatin as an appeaser seeking peace, Russell authored a phoney version of a lost correspondence he had sent to James Monroe that portrayed himself as both defender of New England and champion of the west. Monroe finally found the original letter, which unmasked the lies of Russell's product. Undeterred, Russell produced another version that differed significantly from the previous two. Shunned by Clay, whom he kept trying to draw into his web of deceit, Russell became increasingly unhinged. Finally Adams lashed back with typical erudition and prodigious output by documenting the entire controversy, analyzing in detail Russell's three letter versions, and publishing the entire thing in September 1822. Disgraced, Russell next tried to smear Clay, but with no success. Soon, when a man's reputation was ruined by public disclosure, Americans declared that he had been "jonathanrusselled." When he died at sixty in 1832, Adams wrote: "He is gone to his account and is sufficiently punished in this world for his perfidy."[4]

Albert Gallatin had refused to be drawn by Russell's attacks. After Ghent, Madison had offered Gallatin either secretary of the treasury or the post of minister to France. In 1816 he chose the latter and served in that capacity for seven years, returned home for three years (where he ran unsuccessfully for vice-president alongside Crawford), and then returned to Europe for a year as minister to Britain. Gallatin entered private life and died at eighty-eight on August 12, 1849, preceded three months earlier by his wife. In his later years, Gallatin studied North America's Indian tribes and in 1842 founded the American Ethnological Society of New York, leading to his being called the father of American ethnology. On his deathbed, he had embarked on a rigorous self-examination, "to see whether I am in charity with all mankind. On this retrospect I cannot remember any adversary whom I have not forgiven, or to whom I have failed to make known my forgiveness."[5] Fitting last words for the man who had nudged the Ghent negotiations one small step at a time toward a satisfactory peace where the honour of both sides was preserved.

It is interesting to note that although its future rode on the outcome of the negotiations, no representatives from British North America were invited to join the British delegation at Ghent or to propose terms for the peace. Goulburn was the only commissioner possessing even a scant knowledge of the colony's geography or the circumstances of its people. Perhaps tellingly, he considered the treaty a poor one for Canada, for the Indians, and for Britain. In the event, his concerns that Canadians and Indians were sacrificed for a speedy peace proved true only for the latter. Except for the Fenian raids of 1866, the borders stood inviolable thereafter from American military invasion. Had the commissioners in Ghent failed to reach agreement it is likely that the war would have ground on for years to come. Weary from decades of conflict, Britain might have given up on defending its holdings in North America, which perpetually cost more than they returned in the way of resources and wealth. Ultimately, although most Canadians failed to recognize it at the time, the Treaty of Ghent preserved the future of British North America by establishing a foundation of security from American incursions that ensured its survival. Combined with the new sense of selfhood that was fostered by the performance of the Canadian militia during the war, the conditions of the peace set British North America on the path that would in less than fifty years see the emergence of Canada as a distinct nation.

TREATY OF PEACE AND AMITY,

Between his Britannic Majesty and the United States of America.

His Britannic Majesty and the United States of America, desirous of terminating the war which has unhappily subsisted between the two countries, and of restoring, upon principles of perfect reciprocity, peace, friendship, and good understanding between them, have, for that purpose, appointed their respective plenipotentiaries, that is to say: His Britannic Majesty, on his part, has appointed the right honorable James Lord Gambier, late admiral of the white, now admiral of the red squadron of his Majesty's fleet, Henry Goulburn Esquire, a member of the Imperial Parliament, and under Secretary of State, and William Adams, Esquire, Doctor of Civil Laws:—And the President of the United States, by and with the advice and consent of the Senate thereof, has appointed John Quincy Adams, James A. Bayard, Henry Clay, Jonathan Russell and Albert Gallatin, citizens of the United States, who, after a reciprocal communication of their respective full powers, have agreed upon the following articles:

Dec. 24, 1814. Ratified and confirmed, by and with the advice and consent of the Senate, Feb. 17, 1815.

1821, ch. 40. 1827, ch. 38. 1825, ch. 52.

ARTICLE THE FIRST.

There shall be a firm and universal peace between his Britannic Majesty and the United States, and between their respective countries, territories, cities, towns, and people, of every degree, without exception of places or persons. All hostilities, both

Firm and inviolable peace.

by sea and land, shall cease as soon as this treaty shall have been

Territory, &c.
to be restored,
with exceptions.

ratified by both parties, as hereinafter mentioned. All territory, places, and possessions whatsoever, taken by either party from the other, during the war, or which may be taken after the signing of this treaty, excepting only the islands hereinafter mentioned, shall be restored without delay, and without causing any destruction, or carrying away any of the artillery or other public property originally captured in the said forts or places, and which shall remain therein upon the exchange of the ratifica-

Archives and
records to be
restored.

tions of this treaty, or any slaves or other private property. And all archives, records, deeds, and papers, either of a public nature, or belonging to private persons, which, in the course of the war, may have fallen into the hands of the officers of either party, shall be, as far as may be practicable, forthwith restored and delivered to the proper authorities and persons to whom they respectively belong. Such of the islands in the Bay of Passamaquoddy as are claimed by both parties, shall remain in the possession of the party in whose occupation they may be at the time of the exchange of the ratifications of this treaty, until the decision respecting the title to the said islands shall have been made in conformity with the fourth article of this treaty. No disposition made by this treaty, as to such possession of the islands and territories claimed by both parties, shall, in any manner whatever, be construed to affect the right of either.

ARTICLE THE SECOND.

Immediately
on ratification,
orders to be sent
to armies, &c.
to cease hostil-
ities.

Immediately after the ratifications of this treaty by both parties, as hereinafter mentioned, orders shall be sent to the armies, squadrons, officers, subjects and citizens, of the two powers, to cease from all hostilities. And to prevent all causes of complaint which might arise on account of the prizes which may be taken at sea after the said ratifications of this treaty, it is reciprocally agreed, that all vessels and effects which may be taken after the space of twelve days from the said ratifications, upon all parts of the coast of North America, from the latitude of twenty-three degrees north, to the latitude of fifty degrees north, and as far eastward in the Atlantic ocean, as the thirty-sixth degree of west longitude from the meridian of Greenwich, shall be restored on each side: That the time shall be thirty days in all other parts of the Atlantic ocean, north of the equinoctial line or equator, and the same time for the British and Irish channels, for the Gulf of Mexico and all parts of the West Indies: Forty days for the North seas, for the Baltic, and for all parts of the Mediterranean: Sixty days for the Atlantic ocean south of the equator, as far as the latitude of the Cape of Good Hope; Ninety days for every other part of the world south of the equator: And one hundred and twenty days for all other parts of the world, without exception.

Limitation of time of capture in different latitudes.

ARTICLE THE THIRD.

All prisoners of war taken on either side, as well by land as by sea, shall be restored as soon as practicable after the ratifications of this treaty, as hereinafter mentioned, on their paying the debts which they may have contracted during their captivity. The two contracting parties respectively engage to discharge, in specie, the advances which may have been made by the other for the sustenance and maintenance of such prisoners.

Prisoners of war to be restored.

ARTICLE THE FOURTH.

Whereas it was stipulated by the second article in the treaty of peace, of one thousand seven hundred and eighty-three, between His Britannic Majesty and the United States of America, that the boundary of the United States should comprehend all islands within twenty leagues of any part of the shores of the United States, and lying between lines to be drawn due east from the points where the aforesaid boundaries, between Nova Scotia, on the one part, and East Florida on the other, shall respectively touch the bay of Fundy, and the Atlantic ocean, excepting such islands as now are, or heretofore have been, within the limits of Nova Scotia; and whereas the several islands in the Bay of Passamaquoddy, which is part of the Bay of Fundy, and the island of Grand Menan in the said Bay of Fundy, are claimed by the United States as being comprehended within their aforesaid boundaries, which said islands are claimed as belonging to his Britannic Majesty, as having been at the time of, and previous to, the aforesaid treaty of one thousand seven hundred and eighty-three, within the limits of the province of

Reference of the boundary established by the treaty of 1783.

Nova Scotia: In order, therefore, finally to decide upon these claims, it is agreed that they shall be referred to two commissioners to be appointed in the following manner, viz: one commissioner shall be appointed by his Britannic Majesty, and one by the president of the United States, by and with the advice and consent of the Senate thereof, and the said two commissioners so appointed shall be sworn impartially to examine and decide upon the said claims according to such evidence as shall be laid before them on the part of his Britannic Majesty and of the United States respectively. The said commissioners shall meet at Saint Andrews, in the province of New Brunswick, and shall have power to adjourn to such other place or places as they shall think fit. The said commissioners shall, by a declaration or report under their hands and seals, decide to which of the two contracting parties the several islands aforesaid do respectively belong, in conformity with the true intent of the said treaty of peace of one thousand seven hundred and eighty-three. And if the said commissioners shall agree in their decision, both parties shall consider such decision as final and conclusive. It is further agreed, that in the event of the two commissioners differing upon all or any of the matters so referred to them, or in the event of both or either of the said commissioners refusing, or declining, or wilfully omitting, to act as such, they shall make jointly or separately, a report or reports, as well to the Government of his Britannic majesty as to that of the United States, stating in detail the points on which they differ, and the grounds upon which their respective opinions have been formed, or the grounds upon which they, or either of them, have so refused, declined, or omitted to act. And his Britannic majesty, and the government of the United States, hereby agree to refer the report or reports of the said commissioners, to some friendly sovereign or state, to be then named for that purpose, and who shall be requested to decide on the differences which may be stated in the said report or reports, or upon the report of one commissioner, together with the grounds upon which the other commissioner shall have refused, declined, or omitted to act, as the case may be. And if the commissioner so refusing, declining, or omitting to act, shall also wilfully omit to state the grounds upon which he has so

Mode of the appointment of commissioners.

Meeting of the commissioners.

In cases of disagreement of commissioners.

Reference to a friendly power.

done, in such manner that the said statement may be referred to such friendly sovereign or state, together with the report of such other commissioner, then such sovereign or state shall decide ex parte upon the said report alone. And his Britannic majesty and the government of the United States engage to consider the decision of such friendly sovereign or state to be final and conclusive on all the matters so referred.

ARTICLE THE FIFTH.

Whereas neither that point of the high lands lying due north from the source of the river St. Croix, and designated in the former treaty of peace between the two powers as the northwest angle of Nova-Scotia, nor the northwesternmost head of Connecticut river, has yet been ascertained; and whereas that part of the boundary line between the dominions of the two powers which extends from the source of the river St. Croix directly north to the abovementioned northwest angle of Nova-Scotia, thence along the said highlands which divide those rivers that empty themselves into the river St. Lawrence from those which fall into the Atlantic ocean to the northwesternmost head of Connecticut river, thence down along the middle of that river to the forty-fifth degree of north latitude; thence by a line due west on said latitude until it strikes the river Iroquois or Cataraguy, has not yet been surveyed: it is agreed, that for these several purposes two commissioners shall be appointed, sworn, and authorized to act exactly in the manner directed with respect to those mentioned in the next preceding article, unless otherwise specified in the present article. The said commissioners shall meet at St Andrews, in the province of New-Brunswick, and shall have power to adjourn to such other place or places as they shall think fit. The said commissioners shall have power to ascertain and determine the points abovementioned, in conformity with the provisions of the said treaty of peace of one thousand seven hundred and eighty three, and shall cause the boundary aforesaid, from the source of the river St. Croix to the river Iroquois or Cataraguy, to be surveyed and marked according to the said provisions. The said commissioners shall make a map of the said boundary, and annex to it a declaration under their hands and

Commissioners to settle boundaries.

Meeting and proceedings of commissioners.

seals, certifying it to be the true map of the said boundary, and particularizing the latitude and longitude of the northwest angle of Nova-Scotia, of the northwesternmost head of Connecticut river, and of such other points of the said boundary as they may deem proper. And both parties agree to consider such map and declaration as finally and conclusively fixing the said boundary. And in the event of the said two commissioners differing, or both, or either, of them, refusing, declining, or wilfully omitting to act, such reports, declarations, or statements, shall be made by them, or either of them, and such reference to a friendly sovereign or state, shall be made, in all respects, as in the latter part of the fourth article is contained, and in as full a manner as if the same was herein repeated.

In case of difference, to be referred to a friendly power.

ARTICLE THE SIXTH.

Doubts as to the boundary from a point in the forty-fifth degree of north latitude, to be referred to commissioners.

Whereas, by the former treaty of peace that portion of the boundary of the United States from the point where the forty-fifth degree of north latitude strikes the river Iroquois or Cataraguy to the lake Superior, was declared to be "along the middle of said river into lake Ontario, through the middle of said lake until it strikes the communication by water between that lake and lake Erie, thence along the middle of said communication into lake Erie, through the middle of said lake until it arrives at the water communication into the lake Huron, thence through the middle of said lake to the water communication between that lake and lake Superior." And whereas doubts have arisen what was the middle of the said river, lakes and water communications, and whether certain islands lying in the same were within the dominions of his Britannic majesty or of the United States: In order, therefore, finally to decide these doubts, they shall be referred to two commissioners, to be appointed, sworn, and authorized to act exactly in the manner directed with respect to those mentioned in the next preceding article, unless otherwise specified in this present article. The said commissioners shall meet, in the first instance, at Albany, in the state of New-York, and shall have power to adjourn to such other place or places as they shall think fit: The said commissioners shall, by a report or declaration, under their hands and seals, designate the boundary through the said river, lakes, and water

Meeting and duties of the commissioners.

communications, and decide to which of the two contracting parties the several islands lying within the said rivers, lakes, and water communications, do respectively belong, in conformity with the true intent of the said treaty of one thousand seven hundred and eighty-three. And both parties agree to consider such designation and decision as final and conclusive. And in the event of the said two commissioners differing, or both, or either of them, refusing, declining, or wilfully omitting to act, such reports, declarations or statements, shall be made by them, or either of them, and such reference to a friendly sovereign or state shall be made in all respects as in the latter part of the fourth article is contained, and in as full a manner as if the same was herein repeated.

In case of disagreement of the commissioners, reference to a friendly power.

ARTICLE THE SEVENTH.

It is further agreed that the said two last-mentioned commissioners, after they shall have executed the duties assigned to them in the preceding article, shall be, and they are hereby authorized, upon their oaths impartially to fix and determine, according to the true intent of the said treaty of peace, of one thousand seven hundred and eighty-three, that part of the boundary between the dominions of the two powers, which extends from the water communication between lake Huron, and lake Superior, to the most north-western point of the lake of the Woods, to decide to which of the two parties the several islands lying in the lakes, water communications, and rivers, forming the said boundary, do respectively belong, in conformity with the true intent of the said treaty of peace, of one thousand seven hundred and eighty-three; and to cause such parts of the said boundary, as require it, to be surveyed and marked. The said commissioners shall, by a report or declaration under their hands and seals, designate the boundary aforesaid, state their decision on the points thus referred to them, and particularize the latitude and longitude of the most north-western point of the lake of the Woods, and of such other parts of the said boundary as they may deem proper. And both parties agree to consider such designation and decision as final and conclusive. And, in the event of the said two commissioners differing, or both, or either of them refusing, declining, or wilfully omitting to act, such reports, declarations, or statements, shall be made by them,

Commissioners to fix the boundary to the water communication between the lakes Huron and Superior, and the lake of the Woods.

In case of disagreement of commissioners a reference.

or either of them and such reference to a friendly sovereign or state, shall be made in all respects, as in the latter part of the fourth article is contained, and in as full a manner as if the same was herein repeated.

ARTICLE THE EIGHTH.

The board of commissioners may appoint a secretary, and employ surveyors.

The several boards of two commissioners mentioned in the four preceding articles, shall respectively have power to appoint a secretary, and to employ such surveyors or other persons as they shall judge necessary. Duplicates of all their respective reports, declarations, statements and decisions, and of their accounts, and of the journal of their proceedings, shall be delivered by them to the agents of his Britannic majesty, and to the agents of the United States, who may be respectively appointed and authorized to manage the business on behalf of their respective governments.

Compensation of the commissioners.

The said commissioners shall be respectively paid in such manner as shall be agreed between the two contracting parties, such agreement being to be settled at the time of the exchange of the ratifications of this treaty. And all other expenses attending the said commissions shall be defrayed equally by the two parties. And in the case of death, sickness, resignation, or necessary absence, the place of every such commissioner, respectively, shall be supplied in the same manner as such commissioner was first appointed, and the new commissioner shall take the same oath or affirmation, and do the same

All grants of land prior to the commencement of the war, falling within the dominions of the other party, to be valid.

duties. It is further agreed between the two contracting parties, that in case any of the islands mentioned in any of the preceding articles, which were in the possession of one of the parties prior to the commencement of the present war between the two countries, should, by the decision of any of the boards of commissioners aforesaid, or of the sovereign or state so referred to, as in the four next preceding articles contained, fall within the dominions of the other party, all grants of land made previous to the commencement of the war, by the party having had such possession, shall be as valid as if such island or islands had, by such decision or decisions, been adjudged to be within the dominions of the party having had such possession.

ARTICLE THE NINTH.

The United States of America engage to put an end, immediately after the ratification of the present treaty, to hostilities with all the tribes or nations of Indians with whom they may be at war at the time of such ratification; and forthwith to restore to such tribes or nations, respectively, all the possessions, rights, and privileges, which they may have enjoyed or been entitled to in one thousand eight hundred and eleven, previous to such hostilities: *Provided always,* That such tribes or nations shall agree to desist from all hostilities, against the United States of America, their citizens and subjects, upon the ratification of the present treaty being notified to such tribes or nations, and shall so desist accordingly. And his Britannic majesty engages, on his part, to put an end immediately after the ratification of the present treaty, to hostilities with all the tribes or nations of Indians with whom he may be at war at the time of such ratification, and forthwith to restore to such tribes or nations, respectively, all the possessions, rights, and privileges, which they may have enjoyed or been entitled to, in one thousand eight hundred and eleven, previous to such hostilities: *Provided always,* That such tribes or nations shall agree to desist from all hostilities against his Britannic majesty, and his subjects, upon the ratification of the present treaty being notified to such tribes or nations, and shall so desist accordingly.

Ratification of the Indian treaty.

ARTICLE THE TENTH.

Whereas the traffic in slaves is irreconcileable with the principles of humanity and justice, and whereas both his Majesty and the United States are desirous of continuing their efforts to promote its entire abolition, it is hereby agreed that both the contracting parties shall use their best endeavors to accomplish so desirable an object.

Contracting parties shall use their best endeavors to promote the entire abolition of the slave trade.

Post. p. 572.

ARTICLE THE ELEVENTH.

This treaty, when the same shall have been ratified on both sides, without alteration by either of the contracting parties, and the ratifications mutually exchanged, shall be binding on both parties, and the ratifications shall be exchanged at Washington, in the space of four months from this day, or sooner, if practicable.

This treaty to be binding when ratifications exchanged.

IN FAITH WHEREOF, we, the respective plenipotentiaries, have signed this treaty, and have thereunto affixed our seals.

Done, in triplicate, at Ghent, the twenty-fourth day of December, one thousand eight hundred and fourteen.

GAMBIER,	(L. S.)
HENRY GOULBURN,	(L. S.)
WILLIAM ADAMS,	(L. S.)
JOHN QUINCY ADAMS,	(L. S.)
J. A. BAYARD,	(L. S.)
H. CLAY,	(L. S.)
JONA. RUSSELL,	(L. S.)
ALBERT GALLATIN.	(L. S.)

———

INTRODUCTION

1. Charles William Vane, ed., *Correspondence, Despatches and Other Papers of Viscount Castlereagh, Second Marquess of Londonderry* (London: John Murray, 1853), 67–68.

2. *State Papers, on the Negotiation and Peace with America, 1814* (London: Sherwood, Neely and Jones, 1815), 22–23.

ONE: A REPUBLICAN OF THE FIRST FIRE

1. Bernard Mayo, *Henry Clay: Spokesman of the New West* (Boston: Archon Books, 1966), 403.

2. Ibid., 150–51.

3. Robert V. Remini, *Henry Clay: Statesman for the Union* (New York: W. W. Norton, 1991), 158–68.

4. Mayo, 40–42.

5. James F. Hopkins, ed., *The Papers of Henry Clay: Volume 1—The Rising Statesman, 1797–1814* (Lexington: University of Kentucky Press, 1959), 256.

6. Ibid., 498.

7. Mayo, 270–71.

8. Elizabeth Donnan, ed., "Papers of James A. Bayard, 1796–1815," *Annual Report of the American Historical Association for the Year 1913*, 1915: 6.

9. Ibid., 6–7.

10. Ibid., 110–11.

11. Mayo, 275.

12. Epes Sargent, *The Life and Public Services of Henry Clay, Down to 1848*, ed. Horace Greeley (Philadelphia: Portland Coates, 1852), 29.

13. Hopkins, 396–97.

14. Mayo, 340.

15. Robert Allen Rutland, *The Presidency of James Madison* (Lawrence, KS: University Press of Kansas, 1990), 10.

16. Ibid.

17. Raymond Walters, Jr., *Albert Gallatin: Jeffersonian Financier and Diplomat* (New York: Macmillan, 1957), 198.

18. Ibid., 200–201.

19. James Fulton Zimmerman, *Impressment of American Seamen* (Port Washington, NY: Kennikat Press, 1966), 157.

20. Bradford Perkins, *Prologue to War: England and the United States, 1805–1812* (Berkeley: University of California Press, 1961), 26–27.

21. Ibid., 27.

22. Mayo, 228.

23. Perkins, 55–57.

24. Ibid., 53.

25. Ibid., 54.

26. Ibid., 29.

27. Walters, 146.

28. Perkins, 71.

TWO: INSULT TO THE FLAG

1. James F. Hopkins, ed., *The Papers of Henry Clay: Volume 1—The Rising Statesman, 1797–1814* (Lexington: University of Kentucky Press, 1959), 449.

2. Michael Lewis, *A Social History of the Navy, 1793–1815* (London: George Allen & Unwin, 1960), 98–104.

3. James Fulton Zimmerman, *Impressment of American Seamen* (Port Washington, NY: Kennikat Press, 1966), 13–15.

4. Lewis, 128.

5. Ibid., 434–35.

6. Zimmerman, 30.

7. Hopkins, 449.

8. A. T. Mahan, *Sea Power in its Relation to the War of 1812*, vol. 1 (Boston: Little, Brown, 1905), 155.

9. Pierre Berton, *The Invasion of Canada: 1812–1813* (Toronto: McClelland and Stewart, 1980), 35.

10. Henry Adams, "The Chesapeake and the Orders-in-Council of November 1807," in *The Causes of the War of 1812: National Honor or National Interest?* ed. Bradford Perkins (New York: Holt, Rinehart and Winston, 1962), 23.

11. Berton, 35.

12. Bradford Perkins, *Prologue to War: England and the United States, 1805–1812* (Berkeley: University of California Press, 1961), 140–41.

13. Adams, 23–24.

14. J. Mackay Hitsman, *The Incredible War of 1812: A Military History* (Toronto: Robin Brass Studio, 1999), 16.

15. Perkins, 140.

16. Adams, 24.

17. Ibid., 25.

18. Ibid.

19. Ibid., 26–27.

20. Mahan, 156.

THREE: THE SEARCH FOR SATISFACTION

1. Bradford Perkins, *Prologue to War: England and the United States, 1805–1812* (Berkeley: University of California Press, 1961), 142–43.

2. Robert Allen Rutland, *The Presidency of James Madison* (Lawrence, KS: University Press of Kansas, 1990), 8–18.

3. Ibid.

4. Ibid.

5. Patrick C. T. White, *A Nation on Trial: America and the War of 1812* (New York: John Wiley & Sons, 1965), 41.

6. Perkins, 144.

7. White, 41.

8. Frank A. Updyke, *The Diplomacy of the War of 1812* (Gloucester, MA: Peter Smith, 1965), 43–44.

9. John Austen Stevens, *Albert Gallatin* (Boston: Houghton, Mifflin, 1972), 10.

10. Raymond Walters, Jr., *Albert Gallatin: Jeffersonian Financier and Diplomat* (New York: Macmillan, 1957), 53–54.

11. Ibid., 195.

12. Henry Adams, ed., *The Writings of Albert Gallatin* (New York: Antiquarian Press, 1960), 339.

13. Stevens, 289.

14. Adams, 345–52.

15. Perkins, 145.

16. A. T. Mahan, *Sea Power in its Relation to the War of 1812*, vol. 1 (Boston: Little, Brown, 1905), 164.

17. Ibid., 161.

18. Adams, 338.

19. Perkins, 145–46.

20. Updyke, 44.

21. Ibid., 45.

22. James Fulton Zimmerman, *Impressment of American Seamen* (Port Washington, NY: Kennikat Press, 1966), 137.

23. Updyke, 47.

FOUR: IMPERIOUS NECESSITIES

1. Louis M. Hacker, "The Desire for Canadian Land," in *The Causes of the War of 1812: National Honor or National Interest?* ed. Bradford Perkins (New York: Holt, Rinehart and Winston, 1962), 46–47.

2. R. David Edmunds, *Tecumseh and the Quest for Indian Leadership* (Toronto: Little, Brown, 1984), 17–29.

3. John Sugden, *Tecumseh: A Life* (New York: Henry Holt, 1997), 6–22.

4. Benjamin Drake, *Life of Tecumseh* (Cincinnati: n.p., 1841), n.p.

5. Mary Beacock Fryer and Christopher Dracott, *John Graves Simcoe, 1752–1806: A Biography* (Toronto: Dundurn Press, 1998), 169.

6. J. Mackay Hitsman, *The Incredible War of 1812: A Military History* (Toronto: Robin Brass Studio, 1999), 11.

7. Fryer and Dracott, 169–70.

8. Sugden, 87–90.

9. Fryer and Dracott, 174.

10. Sugden, 90.

11. Ibid., 91–92.

12. Ibid., 106–7.

13. Michael Kraus, *The United States to 1865* (Ann Arbor: University of Michigan Press, 1959), 301.

14. Paul Johnson, *A History of the American People* (London: Phoenix Giant, 1998), 257.

FIVE: BRITISH INTRIGUE

1. James F. Hopkins, ed., *The Papers of Henry Clay: Volume 1—The Rising Statesman, 1797–1814* (Lexington: University of Kentucky Press, 1959), 450.

2. Ibid., 452.

3. John Sugden, *Tecumseh: A Life* (New York: Henry Holt, 1997), 193.

4. Ibid., 113–21.

5. Ibid., 167–68.

6. R. David Edmunds, *Tecumseh and the Quest for Indian Leadership* (Toronto: Little, Brown, 1984), 118.

7. Ibid., 122.

8. Ibid., 125.

9. Julius W. Pratt, *Expansionists of 1812* (New York: Macmillan, 1925), 43.

10. Ibid., 42–44.

11. Ibid., 45–46.

12. Ibid., 46.

13. Pierre Berton, *The Invasion of Canada: 1812–1813* (Toronto: McClelland and Stewart, 1980), 68–69.

14. Sugden, 229–36.

15. Berton, 76.

16. Pratt, 48.

17. Ibid., 55.

18. Ibid., 51.

19. D. B. Read, *Life and Times of Major-General Sir Isaac Brock* (Toronto: William Briggs, 1884), 70–71.

20. Pratt, 53.

SIX: WAR HAWKS

1. Bernard Mayo, *Henry Clay: Spokesman of the New West* (Boston: Archon Books, 1966), 402–3.

2. Irving Brant, *James Madison: The President, 1809–1812* (New York: Bobbs-Merrill, 1956), 358–59.

3. Mayo, 408.

4. Brant, 248.

5. Mayo, 409.

6. Brant, 381.

7. James F. Hopkins, ed., *The Papers of Henry Clay: Volume 1—The Rising Statesman, 1797–1814* (Lexington: University of Kentucky Press, 1959), 604.

8. Ibid., 604–5.

9. Ibid., 605–9.

10. Ibid., 611.

11. Louis M. Hacker, "The Desire for Canadian Land," in *The Causes of the War of 1812: National Honor or National Interest?* ed. Bradford Perkins (New York: Holt, Rinehart and Winston, 1962), 49.

12. Samuel Flagg Bemis, *The American Secretaries of State and their Diplomacy*, vol. 3 (New York: Pageant Book Company, 1958), 246.

13. Paul Johnson, *A History of the American People* (London: Phoenix Giant, 1998), 379.

14. W. T. Easterbrook and Hugh G. J. Aitken, *Canadian Economic History* (Toronto: Macmillan Company of Canada, 1958), 154.

15. Pierre Berton, *The Invasion of Canada: 1812–1813* (Toronto: McClelland and Stewart, 1980), 25.

16. Norman K. Risjord, "1812: Conservatives, War Hawks, and the Nation's Honor," in *National Unity on Trial, 1781–1816*, ed. E. James Ferguson (New York: Random House, 1970), 235.

17. Hacker, 49–50.

18. Brant, 361–64.

19. Ibid., 402–3.

20. Elizabeth Donnan, ed., "Papers of James A. Bayard, 1796–1815," *Annual Report of the American Historical Association for the Year 1913*, 1915: 190.

21. Raymond Walters, Jr., *Albert Gallatin: Jeffersonian Financier and Diplomat* (New York: Macmillan, 1957), 248.

22. Ibid., 247–48.

23. Ibid., 248.

24. Brant, 404–5.

25. Robert Allen Rutland, *The Presidency of James Madison* (Lawrence, KS: University Press of Kansas, 1990), 87–88.

26. Alexander Balinky, *Albert Gallatin: Fiscal Theories and Policies* (New Brunswick, NJ: Rutgers University Press, 1958), 186–89.

27. Hopkins, 637.

28. Brant, 427.

29. Rutland, 92.

30. J. C. A. Stagg, *Mr. Madison's War: Politics, Diplomacy, and Warfare in the Early American Republic, 1783–1830* (Princeton, NJ: Princeton University Press, 1983), 108.

31. Rutland, 91.

32. Stagg, 109.

33. *Annals of Congress*, 12th Cong., 1st sess., June 1812, 288–96.

34. Irving Brant, *James Madison: Commander in Chief, 1812–1836* (New York: Bobbs-Merrill, 1961), 22.

35. Hopkins, 675–76.

SEVEN: WHILE DISUNION PREVAILS

1. Samuel Flagg Bemis, *The American Secretaries of State and their Diplomacy*, vol. 3 (New York: Pageant Book Company, 1958), 250–51.

2. Irving Brant, *James Madison: Commander in Chief, 1812–1836* (New York: Bobbs-Merrill, 1961), 33–34.

3. J. Mackay Hitsman, *The Incredible War of 1812: A Military History* (Toronto: Robin Brass Studio, 1999), 45–46.

4. Robert Allen Rutland, *The Presidency of James Madison* (Lawrence, KS: University Press of Kansas, 1990), 107.

5. Brant, 39.

6. Ibid., 39–40.

7. Henry Adams, ed., *The Writings of Albert Gallatin* (New York: Antiquarian Press, 1960), 521.

8. Brant, 37.

9. Hitsman, 45–46.

10. Brant, 46.

11. Hitsman, 46–47.

12. Rutland, 110.

13. Ibid., 44.

14. Ibid., 286.

15. Francis Gore, "Memorandum: Warlike Tribes of Indians in THE CANADAS," Lord Bathurst Papers, MG 24 A 8, Library and Archives Canada, 50–54.

16. Hitsman, 25–26.

17. Ibid., 286.

18. Isaac Tupper, ed., *The Life and Correspondence of Major-General Sir Isaac Brock, K.B.* (London: Simpkin, Marshall, 1847), 258.

19. Pierre Berton, *The Invasion of Canada: 1812–1813* (Toronto: McClelland and Stewart, 1980), 133.

20. Tupper, 72.

21. Ibid., 200–201.

22. Ibid.

23. Hitsman, 61.

24. Reginald Horsman, *The War of 1812* (New York: Alfred A. Knopf, 1969), 34–35.

25. William Wood, ed., *Select British Documents of the Canadian War of 1812*, vol. 1 (New York: Greenwood Press, 1968), 364–65.

26. George F. G. Stanley, *The War of 1812: Land Operations* (Toronto: Macmillan of Canada, 1983), 91.

27. Ibid., 6.

28. Woodford, Frank B. *Lewis Cass: The Last Jeffersonian* (New York: Octagon Books, 1973), 59.

29. Berton, 126–27.

30. Hitsman, 70.

31. Stanley, 129–30.

32. Ibid., 131.

33. Berton, 135–41.

EIGHT: FAILURES OF COMMUNICATION

1. J. Mackay Hitsman, *The Incredible War of 1812: A Military History* (Toronto: Robin Brass Studio, 1999), 71–72.

2. Bradford Perkins, *Castlereagh and Adams: England and the United States, 1812–1823* (Los Angeles: University of California Press, 1964), 10.

3. William R. Manning, ed., *Diplomatic Correspondence of the United States: Canadian Relations, 1784–1860* (Washington: Carnegie Endowment for International Peace, 1940), 611–12.

4. J. A. R. Marriott, *Castlereagh: The Political Life of Robert, Second Marquess of Londonderry* (London: Methuen, 1936), 181–82.

5. Perkins, 11.

6. Wendy Hinde, *Castlereagh* (London: William Collins Sons, 1981), 180

7. Norman Gash, "The Earl of Liverpool," in *The Prime Ministers, Volume the First: Sir Robert Walpole to Sir Robert Peel*, ed. Herbert Van Thal (London: George Allen & Unwin, 1974), 285.

8. Charles Clive Bigham, *The Prime Ministers of Britain, 1721–1921* (Freeport, NY: Books for Libraries Press, 1924), 184.

9. Ibid., 187.

10. Hinde, 166.

11. Ione Leigh, *Castlereagh* (London: Collins, 1951), 212.

12. Ibid., 213–14.

13. Bigham, 189–90.

14. Gash, 287.

15. Leigh, 244.

16. Hinde, 179.

17. Gash, 290.

18. Frank A. Updyke, *The Diplomacy of the War of 1812* (Gloucester, MA: Peter Smith, 1965), 140.

19. Leigh, 55.

20. Ibid., 57.

21. Ibid.

22. Charles Wibley, *Political Portraits: Second Series* (London: Macmillan, 1923), 72.

23. Sir Herbert Maxwell, ed., *The Creevey Papers: A Selection from the Correspondence & Diaries of the Late Thomas Creevey, M.P.*, vol. 2. (London: J. Murray, 1903), 42.

24. Francis Bamford and the Duke of Wellington, eds., *The Journal of Mrs. Arbuthnot, 1820–1832* (London: Macmillan, 1950), 181–82.

NINE: THE DEMONS OF WAR UNCHAINED

1. Wendy Hinde, *Castlereagh* (London: William Collins Sons, 1981), 173.

2. William R. Manning, ed., *Diplomatic Correspondence of the United States: Canadian Relations, 1784–1860* (Washington: Carnegie Endowment for International Peace, 1940), 615–16.

3. Patrick C. T. White, *A Nation on Trial: America and the War of 1812* (New York: John Wiley & Sons, 1965), 132–33.

4. Ibid., 133–34.

5. Frank A. Updyke, *The Diplomacy of the War of 1812* (Gloucester, MA: Peter Smith, 1965), 137.

6. Ibid., 139.

7. George F. G. Stanley, *The War of 1812: Land Operations* (Toronto: Macmillan of Canada, 1983), 101–2.

8. Pierre Berton, *The Invasion of Canada: 1812–1813* (Toronto: McClelland and Stewart, 1980), 159–60.

9. J. Mackay Hitsman, *The Incredible War of 1812: A Military History* (Toronto: Robin Brass Studio, 1999), 79–80.

10. Ibid., 78.

11. White, 132.

12. Samuel Flagg Bemis, *The American Secretaries of State and their Diplomacy*, vol. 3 (New York: Pageant Book Company, 1958), 255.

13. Berton, 152.

14. Ibid., 152–53.

15. Ibid., 156–57.

16. Irving Brant, *James Madison: Commander in Chief, 1812–1836* (New York: Bobbs-Merrill, 1961), 67.

17. Ibid., 75.

18. Robert Allen Rutland, *The Presidency of James Madison* (Lawrence, KS: University Press of Kansas, 1990), 112.

19. Ibid.

20. Berton, 204.

21. J. C. A. Stagg, *Mr. Madison's War: Politics, Diplomacy, and Warfare in the Early American Republic, 1783–1830* (Princeton, NJ: Princeton University Press, 1983), 246–47.

22. Ibid., 247–48.

23. Ibid., 249.

TEN: THE VALIANT HAVE BLED

1. Pierre Berton, *The Invasion of Canada: 1812–1813* (Toronto: McClelland and Stewart, 1980), 217–19.

2. Reginald Horsman, *The War of 1812* (New York: Alfred A. Knopf, 1969), 44–45.

3. George F. G. Stanley, *The War of 1812: Land Operations* (Toronto: Macmillan of Canada, 1983), 121.

4. Berton, 233–35.

5. Stanley, 124.

6. Ibid., 126–27.

7. Ibid., 127.

8. Berton, 240–41.

9. J. Mackay Hitsman, *The Incredible War of 1812: A Military History* (Toronto: Robin Brass Studio, 1999), 96–98.

10. Stanley, 129–30.

11. Hitsman, 99.

12. Berton, 252.

13. Ibid., 252–53.

14. Hitsman, 100.

15. Stanley, 131–32.

16. Irving Brant, *James Madison: Commander in Chief, 1812–1836* (New York: Bobbs-Merrill, 1961), 92–93.

17. Stanley, 132–33.

18. Ibid., 134.

19. Ibid., 135.

ELEVEN: OPPORTUNITIES FOR USEFULNESS

1. D. M. Young, *The Colonial Office in the Early Nineteenth Century* (London: Longman's, 1961), 124–25.

2. Ibid., 21.

3. Ibid., 1.

4. Ibid.

5. Francis Bamford and the Duke of Wellington, eds., *The Journal of Mrs. Arbuthnot, 1820–1832* (London: Macmillan, 1950), 158–59.

6. Brian Jenkins, *Henry Goulburn, 1784–1856: A Political Biography* (Montreal: McGill-Queen's University Press, 1996), 6–18.

7. Ibid., 21.

8. Ibid., 56–57.

9. Ibid., 64.

10. Young, 276.

11. Jenkins, 19.

12. Ibid., 69.

13. Ibid., 70.

14. Ibid., 77.

15. Ibid.

16. Ibid., 78.

17. Reginald Horsman, *The War of 1812* (New York: Alfred A. Knopf, 1969), 62.

18. Ibid., 61–63.

TWELVE: FAILURES OF COMMAND

1. Robert Allen Rutland, *The Presidency of James Madison* (Lawrence, KS: University Press of Kansas, 1990), 117–18.

2. J. C. A. Stagg, *Mr. Madison's War: Politics, Diplomacy, and Warfare in the Early American Republic, 1783–1830* (Princeton, NJ: Princeton University Press, 1983), 273.

3. J. Mackay Hitsman, *The Incredible War of 1812: A Military History* (Toronto: Robin Brass Studio, 1999), 102.

4. George F. G. Stanley, *The War of 1812: Land Operations* (Toronto: Macmillan of Canada, 1983), 88–89.

5. Hitsman, 110–12.

6. Brock to Liverpool, 29 August 1812, British Colonial Office Papers, class 42, vol. 352, 105.

7. William Wood, ed., *Select British Documents of the Canadian War of 1812*, vol. 1 (New York: Greenwood Press, 1968), 596.

8. Stanley, 115.

9. James F. Hopkins, ed., *The Papers of Henry Clay: Volume 1—The Rising Statesman, 1797–1814* (Lexington: University of Kentucky Press, 1959), 715.

10. Ibid., 720.

11. Stanley, 115.

12. John Sugden, *Tecumseh: A Life* (New York: Henry Holt, 1997), 312–19.

13. Stagg, 275–77.

14. Irving Brant, *James Madison: Commander in Chief, 1812–1836* (New York: Bobbs-Merrill, 1961), 112.

15. Stagg, 277–78.

16. Hopkins, 750–51.

17. Raymond Walters, Jr., *Albert Gallatin: Jeffersonian Financier and Diplomat* (New York: Macmillan, 1957), 255–56.

18. Brant, 133–34.

19. Ibid., 144.

20. Stagg, 278–83.

21. Julius W. Pratt, *Expansionists of 1812* (New York: Macmillan, 1925), 227–29.

22. Ibid., 235.

23. Ibid., 236.

24. Stagg, 280–81.

25. Rutland, 120.

26. Stagg, 282–84.

27. Ibid., 286.

28. Stanley, 143–44.

29. Hitsman, 126–27.

30. Brant, 143.

31. Stagg, 289–92.

32. Rutland, 125.

THIRTEEN: A PEACE SINCERELY DESIRED

1. Charles Francis Adams, ed., *Memoirs of John Quincy Adams*, vol. 2 (Freeport, NY: Books for Libraries Press, 1969), 403–5.
2. Ibid., 400.
3. Ibid., 401.
4. Fred L. Engelman, *The Peace of Christmas Eve* (London: Rupert Hart-Davis, 1962), 26.
5. Pierre Berton, *Flames Across the Border: 1813–1814* (Toronto: McClelland and Stewart, 1981), 272.
6. Engelman, 26.
7. Adams, 409.
8. Ibid., 417.
9. Ibid., 438–39.
10. Irving Brant, *James Madison: Commander in Chief, 1812–1836* (New York: Bobbs-Merrill, 1961), 155.
11. Henry Adams, ed., *The Writings of Albert Gallatin* (New York: Antiquarian Press, 1960), 532–33.
12. Brant, 156–58.
13. Count Gallatin, ed., *The Diary of James Gallatin: Secretary to Albert Gallatin—A Great Peace Maker, 1813–1827* (New York: Charles Scribner's Sons, 1920), 1.
14. J. C. A. Stagg, *Mr. Madison's War: Politics, Diplomacy, and Warfare in the Early American Republic, 1783–1830* (Princeton, NJ: Princeton University Press, 1983), 299–300.
15. Gallatin, 2.
16. Brant, 158.
17. Ibid., 159.
18. Elizabeth Donnan, ed., "Papers of James A. Bayard, 1796–1815," *Annual Report of the American Historical Association for the Year 1913*, 1915: 204.
19. Ibid., 206.
20. Frank A. Updyke, *The Diplomacy of the War of 1812* (Gloucester, MA: Peter Smith, 1965), 149.
21. Donnan, 205.
22. Henry Adams, 539.
23. Ibid., 540.
24. Ibid., 543–44.
25. Ibid., 544–45.
26. Brant, 161–62.
27. Ibid., 161.
28. Donnan, 385–86.

FOURTEEN: AN EXPANDED WAR

1. J. Mackay Hitsman, *The Incredible War of 1812: A Military History* (Toronto: Robin Brass Studio, 1999), 117.
2. Irving Brant, *James Madison: Commander in Chief, 1812–1836* (New York: Bobbs-Merrill, 1961), 112.
3. Ibid., 117.
4. Hitsman, 117.

5. Reginald Horsman, *The War of 1812* (New York: Alfred A. Knopf, 1969), 69.

6. Ibid., 70–71.

7. Ibid., 70–72.

8. James Barnes, *Naval Actions of the War of 1812* (New York: Harper & Brothers Publishers, 1896), 113–35.

9. Horsman, 77–80.

10. Brant, 164–65.

11. Horsman, 86.

12. A. T. Mahan, *Sea Power in its Relation to the War of 1812*, vol. 2 (Boston: Little, Brown, 1905), 30–31.

13. Hitsman, 143–44.

14. Ibid., 132–33.

15. Mahan, 35.

16. Hitsman, 137.

17. George F. G. Stanley, *The War of 1812: Land Operations* (Toronto: Macmillan of Canada, 1983), 169.

18. Pierre Berton, *Flames Across the Border: 1813–1814* (Toronto: McClelland and Stewart, 1981), 40–41.

19. Stanley, 170.

20. Ibid., 172–73.

21. Horsman, 92.

22. Ibid., 93–94.

23. Stanley, 179.

FIFTEEN: A SUCCESSION OF DEFEATS

1. Mary Agnes Fitzgibbon, *A Veteran of 1812: The Life of James Fitzgibbon* (Toronto: Prospero Books, 2000), 67.

2. Pierre Berton, *The Invasion of Canada: 1812–1813* (Toronto: McClelland and Stewart, 1980), 282–83.

3. J. Mackay Hitsman, *The Incredible War of 1812: A Military History* (Toronto: Robin Brass Studio, 1999), 141.

4. Ibid., 141–42.

5. John Sugden, *Tecumseh: A Life* (New York: Henry Holt, 1997), 333–38.

6. Reginald Horsman, *The War of 1812* (New York: Alfred A. Knopf, 1969), 101.

7. George F. G. Stanley, *The War of 1812: Land Operations* (Toronto: Macmillan of Canada, 1983), 182–85.

8. Hitsman, 148–49.

9. Ibid., 185–86.

10. Pierre Berton, *Flames Across the Border: 1813–1814* (Toronto: McClelland and Stewart, 1981), 77–78.

11. Stanley, 187–90.

12. Hitsman, 150–51.

13. Ronald L. Way, "The Day of Crysler's Farm," in *The Defended Border: Upper Canada and the War of 1812*, ed. Morris Zaslow (Toronto: Macmillan Company of Canada, 1964), 63.

14. Berton, *Flames Across the Border*, 70–73.

15. Hitsman, 154–55.

16. Stanley, 198–200.

17. Berton, *Flames Across the Border*, 83–84.

18. Stanley, 197.

19. Irving Brant, *James Madison: Commander in Chief, 1812–1836* (New York: Bobbs-Merrill, 1961), 207.

20. Ibid., 192.

21. Ibid., 181.

22. Ibid., 182.

23. Ibid., 190.

24. Ibid., 193.

25. Berton, *Flames Across the Border*, 211.

SIXTEEN: HAVE MET THE ENEMY

1. George F. G. Stanley, *The War of 1812: Land Operations* (Toronto: Macmillan of Canada, 1983), 163–65.

2. A. T. Mahan, *Sea Power in its Relation to the War of 1812*, vol. 2 (Boston: Little, Brown, 1905), 62–63.

3. Ibid., 68–72.

4. Reginald Horsman, *The War of 1812* (New York: Alfred A. Knopf, 1969), 103–5.

5. Stanley, 156–57.

6. William F. Coffin, *1812—The War and the Moral: A Canadian Chronicle* (Montreal: John Lovell, 1864), 207–13.

7. J. Mackay Hitsman, *The Incredible War of 1812: A Military History* (Toronto: Robin Brass Studio, 1999), 167.

8. Pierre Berton, *Flames Across the Border: 1813–1814* (Toronto: McClelland and Stewart, 1981), 138–39.

9. Ibid., 140.

10. Stanley, 158–60.

11. Hitsman, 168–69.

12. Berton, 145–47.

13. William Wood, ed., *Select British Documents of the Canadian War of 1812*, vol. 2 (New York: Greenwood Press, 1968), 46.

14. Ibid., 49.

15. Mahan, 51–55.

16. Ibid., 58–61.

17. Hitsman, 163.

18. Ibid., 168–171.

19. Mahan, 80–90.

20. Wood, 274–75.

21. Berton, 164.

22. Ibid., 165–69.

23. Wood, 282–83.

24. John Richardson, *War of 1812* (Brockville, ON: n.p., 1842), 118–20.

25. John Sugden, *Tecumseh: A Life* (New York: Henry Holt, 1997), 360.

26. Ibid., 362.

27. Hitsman, 173–74.

SEVENTEEN: FIELDS OF VICTORY, FIELDS OF SHAME

1. J. Mackay Hitsman, *The Incredible War of 1812: A Military History* (Toronto: Robin Brass Studio, 1999), 178.

2. Ibid.

3. J. C. A. Stagg, *Mr. Madison's War: Politics, Diplomacy, and Warfare in the Early American Republic, 1783–1830* (Princeton, NJ: Princeton University Press, 1983), 345.

4. Pierre Berton, *Flames Across the Border: 1813–1814* (Toronto: McClelland and Stewart, 1981), 216–17.

5. Hitsman, 179.

6. Ibid., 183.

7. Irving Brant, *James Madison: Commander in Chief, 1812–1836* (New York: Bobbs-Merrill, 1961), 214.

8. George F. G. Stanley, *The War of 1812: Land Operations* (Toronto: Macmillan of Canada, 1983), 246–47.

9. Ibid., 249.

10. James Wilkinson, *Memoirs of My Own Times*, vol. 3 (Philadelphia: n.p., 1816), Appendix 1.

11. Stanley, 216–18.

12. Brant, 221.

13. Ibid.

14. Stanley, 208–10.

15. Ibid., 210–12.

16. John Sugden, *Tecumseh: A Life* (New York: Henry Holt, 1997), 379.

17. Benjamin Drake, *Life of Tecumseh* (Cincinnati: E. Morgan, 1841), 202–3.

18. Ibid., 209.

19. Hitsman, 176.

20. Stanley, 214.

21. Reginald Horsman, *The War of 1812* (New York: Alfred A. Knopf, 1969), 114.

22. Hitsman, 176.

23. William Dunlop, *Tiger Dunlop's Upper Canada: Comprising Recollections of the American War 1812–1814, by a Backwoodsman* (Toronto: McClelland and Stewart, 1967), 10.

24. Berton, 218–19.

25. Stanley, 254–56.

26. Ibid., 254–59.

EIGHTEEN: UNDER GREAT DANGER

1. Irving Brant, *James Madison: Commander in Chief, 1812–1836* (New York: Bobbs-Merrill, 1961), 222.

2. Ibid., 222–23.

3. J. C. A. Stagg, *Mr. Madison's War: Politics, Diplomacy, and Warfare in the Early American Republic, 1783–1830* (Princeton, NJ: Princeton University Press, 1983), 345.

4. James Wilkinson, *Memoirs of My Own Times*, vol. 3 (Philadelphia: n.p., 1816), Appendix 24.

5. J. Mackay Hitsman, *The Incredible War of 1812: A Military History* (Toronto: Robin Brass Studio, 1999), 190–91.

6. Ibid., 191.

7. Ibid., 192.

8. George F. G. Stanley, *The War of 1812: Land Operations* (Toronto: Macmillan of Canada, 1983), 218–24.

9. James F. Hopkins, ed., *The Papers of Henry Clay: Volume 1—The Rising Statesman, 1797–1814* (Lexington: University of Kentucky Press, 1959), 839–40.

10. Stagg, 347.

11. Ibid., 362–63.

12. Count Gallatin, ed., *The Diary of James Gallatin: Secretary to Albert Gallatin—A Great Peace Maker, 1813–1827* (New York: Charles Scribner's Sons, 1920), 5.

13. Elizabeth Donnan, ed., "Papers of James A. Bayard, 1796–1815," *Annual Report of the American Historical Association for the Year 1913*, 1915: 232–36.

14. Ibid., 235.

15. Bradford Perkins, *Castlereagh and Adams: England and the United States, 1812–1823* (Los Angeles: University of California Press, 1964), 22.

16. Henry Adams, ed., *The Writings of Albert Gallatin* (New York: Antiquarian Press, 1960), 546–52.

17. Ibid., 568–69.

18. Ibid., 584–87.

19. Gallatin, 10.

20. Ibid., 12.

21. Fred L. Engelman, *The Peace of Christmas Eve* (London: Rupert Hart-Davis, 1962), 46.

22. Gallatin, 13.

NINETEEN: DESTITUTE OF MILITARY FIRE

1. Walter Lowrie et al., eds., *American State Papers: Documents, Legislative and Executive of the Congress of the United States* (Washington: n.p., 1832–1861), 621.

2. Ibid., 622–23.

3. Irving Brant, *James Madison: Commander in Chief, 1812–1836* (New York: Bobbs-Merrill, 1961), 239–41.

4. James F. Hopkins, ed., *The Papers of Henry Clay: Volume 1—The Rising Statesman, 1797–1814* (Lexington: University of Kentucky Press, 1959), 866.

5. Ibid., 869.

6. George F. G. Stanley, *The War of 1812: Land Operations* (Toronto: Macmillan of Canada, 1983), 333–34.

7. Brant, 254.

8. Francis F. Beirne, *The War of 1812* (Hamden, CT: Archon Books, 1965), 246–49.

9. J. C. A. Stagg, *Mr. Madison's War: Politics, Diplomacy, and Warfare in the Early American Republic, 1783–1830* (Princeton, NJ: Princeton University Press, 1983), 366–78.

10. Ibid., 380–86.

11. J. Mackay Hitsman, *The Incredible War of 1812: A Military History* (Toronto: Robin Brass Studio, 1999), 201.

12. Brian Jenkins, *Henry Goulburn, 1784–1856: A Political Biography* (Montreal: McGill-Queen's University Press, 1996), 81.

13. Bradford Perkins, *Castlereagh and Adams: England and the United States, 1812–1823* (Los Angeles: University of California Press, 1964), 36.

14. A. T. Mahan, *Sea Power in its Relation to the War of 1812*, vol. 2 (Boston: Little, Brown, 1905), 330–31.

15. Ibid., 331.

16. Hitsman, 238.

17. Ibid.

18. Theodore Roosevelt, *The Naval War of 1812* (Annapolis, MD: Naval Institute Press, 1882), 262.

19. Hitsman, 238.

20. Roosevelt, 263.

21. Reginald Horsman, *The War of 1812* (New York: Alfred A. Knopf, 1969), 138–40.

22. Hitsman, 219.

23. Roosevelt, 321–23.

24. Pierre Berton, *Flames Across the Border: 1813–1814* (Toronto: McClelland and Stewart, 1981), 277–78.

25. Ibid., 322.

26. Hitsman, 209–10.

27. Ibid., 211–12.

28. Brant, 257.

29. Hitsman, 216–17.

30. Brant, 266–67.

TWENTY: GREAT OBSTACLES TO ACCOMODATION

1. Count Gallatin, ed., *The Diary of James Gallatin: Secretary to Albert Gallatin—A Great Peace Maker, 1813–1827* (New York: Charles Scribner's Sons, 1920), 14.

2. Frank A. Updyke, *The Diplomacy of the War of 1812* (Gloucester, MA: Peter Smith, 1965), 187–88.

3. Henry Adams, ed., *The Writings of Albert Gallatin* (New York: Antiquarian Press, 1960), 602–3.

4. Elizabeth Donnan, ed., "Papers of James A. Bayard, 1796–1815," *Annual Report of the American Historical Association for the Year 1913*, 1915: 286.

5. Adams, 602.

6. Ibid., 612–13.

7. Gallatin, 21.

8. Adams, 605–6.

9. James F. Hopkins, ed., *The Papers of Henry Clay: Volume 1—The Rising Statesman, 1797–1814* (Lexington: University of Kentucky Press, 1959), 890–91.

10. Donnan, 306–8.

11. Worthington Chauncey Ford, ed., *Writings of John Quincy Adams: Volume V—1814–1816* (New York: Greenwood Press, 1968), 48.

12. Charles Francis Adams, ed., *Memoirs of John Quincy Adams*, vol. 2 (Freeport, NY: Books for Libraries Press, 1969), 641–44.

13. Henry Adams, 632.

14. Ibid., 627.

15. Bathurst to Prevost, Colonial Office fonds, MG 11–CO 42, vol. 23, Library and Archives Canada.

16. Leslie Stephen and Sidney Lee, eds., *The Dictionary of National Biography* (London: Oxford University Press, 1937–1938), 108.

17. Lee Bienkowski, *Admirals in the Age of Nelson* (Annapolis, MD: Naval Institute Press, 2003), 152–69.

18. Brian Jenkins, *Henry Goulburn, 1784–1856: A Political Biography* (Montreal: McGill-Queen's University Press, 1996), 80.

19. Charles Francis Adams, 652.

20. Ford, 50–51.

21. Ibid., 52–57.

22. Charles Francis Adams, 656–67.

23. Gallatin, 27.

24. Charles Francis Adams, 657.

25. Ibid., 657–58.

26. Fred L. Engelman, *The Peace of Christmas Eve* (London: Rupert Hart-Davis, 1962), 119.

27. Gallatin, 27.

28. Raymond Walters, Jr., *Albert Gallatin: Jeffersonian Financier and Diplomat* (New York: Macmillan, 1957), 274.

29. Ford, 64.

30. Ibid., 64–65.

31. Ibid., 68.

TWENTY-ONE: SUMMER OF STALEMATE

1. Irving Brant, *James Madison: Commander in Chief, 1812–1836* (New York: Bobbs-Merrill, 1961), 277.

2. Ibid., 271–72.

3. J. C. A. Stagg, *Mr. Madison's War: Politics, Diplomacy, and Warfare in the Early American Republic, 1783–1830* (Princeton, NJ: Princeton University Press, 1983), 408.

4. Brant, 272.

5. Stagg, 409–11.

6. Reginald Horsman, *The War of 1812* (New York: Alfred A. Knopf, 1969), 175–76.

7. George F. G. Stanley, *The War of 1812: Land Operations* (Toronto: Macmillan of Canada, 1983), 300.

8. Donald R. Hickey, *The War of 1812: A Forgotten Conflict* (Chicago: University of Illinois Press, 1989), 185.

9. Stanley, 311–13.

10. Horsman, 177.

11. Stanley, 315–18.

12. Ibid., 321.

13. Pierre Berton, *Flames Across the Border: 1813–1814* (Toronto: McClelland and Stewart, 1981), 340–41.

14. J. Mackay Hitsman, *The Incredible War of 1812: A Military History* (Toronto: Robin Brass Studio, 1999), 229.

15. Prevost to Bathurst, August 14, 1814, Colonial Office fonds, MG 11–CO 42, vol. 157, Library and Archives Canada, 42.

16. Stanley, 325–26.

17. William Dunlop, *Tiger Dunlop's Upper Canada: Comprising Recollections of the American War 1812–1814, by a Backwoodsman* (Toronto: McClelland and Stewart, 1967), 64–67.

18. Stanley, 326–27.

19. Ibid., 328–29.

20. Ibid., 329.

21. Horsman, 183.

22. Stanley, 331.

23. Ibid., 331–32.

24. Ibid., 343–44.

25. Ibid., 337.

26. Berton, 363–64.

27. Horsman, 156–57.

28. Ralph Ketcham, *James Madison: A Biography* (New York: Macmillan, 1971), 575.

29. Stagg, 414–15.

30. Ibid., 416.

TWENTY-TWO: A SINE QUA NON

1. Bradford Perkins, *Castlereagh and Adams: England and the United States, 1812–1823* (Los Angeles: University of California Press, 1964), 60.

2. Charles William Vane, ed., *Correspondence, Despatches and Other Papers of Viscount Castlereagh, Second Marquess of Londonderry* (London: John Murray, 1853), 68.

3. Ibid., 68–72.

4. Charles Francis Adams, ed., *Memoirs of John Quincy Adams*, vol. 3 (Freeport, NY: Books for Libraries Press, 1969), 3.

5. Fred L. Engelman, *The Peace of Christmas Eve* (London: Rupert Hart-Davis, 1962), 127.

6. Adams, 3–5.

7. James F. Hopkins, ed., *The Papers of Henry Clay: Volume 1—The Rising Statesman, 1797–1814* (Lexington: University of Kentucky Press, 1959), 953.

8. Adams, 5.

9. Perkins, 71.

10. Adams, 6.

11. Perkins, 72.

12. Adams, 6.

13. Hopkins, 954.

14. Adams, 6.

15. Count Gallatin, ed., *The Diary of James Gallatin: Secretary to Albert Gallatin—A Great Peace Maker, 1813–1827* (New York: Charles Scribner's Sons, 1920), 27–28.

16. Frank A. Updyke, *The Diplomacy of the War of 1812* (Gloucester, MA: Peter Smith, 1965), 205–6.

17. Worthington Chauncey Ford, ed., *Writings of John Quincy Adams: Volume V—1814–1816* (New York: Greenwood Press, 1968), 74.

18. "Letters from Henry Goulburn to Earl Bathurst: August 9th to December 30th, 1814," Lord Bathurst Papers, Reel H-2091, vol. Λ 8, MG 24, Library and Archives Canada, 190–95.

19. Ibid., 190–91.

20. Adams, 11–13.

21. Elizabeth Donnan, ed., "Papers of James A. Bayard, 1796–1815," *Annual Report of the American Historical Association for the Year 1913*, 1915: 316.

22. Ford, 83.

23. Perkins, 61.

24. Brian Jenkins, *Henry Goulburn, 1784–1856: A Political Biography* (Montreal: McGill-Queen's University Press, 1996), 84.

25. Ford, 83.

26. Adams, 14–15.

27. Ford, 89.

28. Vane, 86–91.

29. "Letters from Henry Goulburn to Earl Bathurst," 196–99.

TWENTY-THREE: A CAPITAL BURNED, A CAMPAIGN LOST

1. Charles Francis Adams, ed., *Memoirs of John Quincy Adams*, vol. 3 (Freeport, NY: Books for Libraries Press, 1969), 19.

2. Bradford Perkins, *Castlereagh and Adams: England and the United States, 1812–1823* (Los Angeles: University of California Press, 1964), 78.

3. Duke of Wellington, ed., *Supplementary Dispatches, Correspondence, and Memoranda of Field Marshal Arthur Duke of Wellington, K.G.*, vol. 9 (London: John Murray, 1862), 192–93.

4. Ibid.

5. Worthington Chauncey Ford, ed., *Writings of John Quincy Adams: Volume V—1814–1816* (New York: Greenwood Press, 1968), 90.

6. James F. Hopkins, ed., *The Papers of Henry Clay: Volume 1—The Rising Statesman, 1797–1814* (Lexington: University of Kentucky Press, 1959), 968.

7. Henry Adams, ed., *The Writings of Albert Gallatin* (New York: Antiquarian Press, 1960), 637–39.

8. J. Mackay Hitsman, *The Incredible War of 1812: A Military History* (Toronto: Robin Brass Studio, 1999), 241–43.

9. Harry Ammon, *James Monroe: The Quest For National Identity* (New York: McGraw-Hill, 1971), 331–33.

10. Donald R. Hickey, *The War of 1812: A Forgotten Conflict* (Chicago: University of Illinois Press, 1989), 198.

11. G. R. Gleig, *The Campaigns of the British Army at Washington and New Orleans, 1814–1815* (London: John Murray, 1827), n.p.

12. Hitsman, 243.

13. Ralph Ketcham, *James Madison: A Biography* (New York: Macmillan, 1971), 578–79.

14. J. S. Williams, *History of the Invasion and Capture of Washington* (New York: n.p., 1857), 274–75.

15. Reginald Horsman, *The War of 1812* (New York: Alfred A. Knopf, 1969), 200–201.

16. Hickey, 199–201.

17. Raymond Walters, Jr., *Albert Gallatin: Jeffersonian Financier and Diplomat* (New York: Macmillan, 1957), 262.

18. Ketcham, 581–82.

19. Irving Brant, *James Madison: Commander in Chief, 1812–1836* (New York: Bobbs-Merrill, 1961), 323.

20. Ketcham, 582–83.

21. Horsman, 203.

22. Ibid., 204.

23. Ibid., 206–7.

24. Hickey, 203–4.

25. George F. G. Stanley, *The War of 1812: Land Operations* (Toronto: Macmillan of Canada, 1983), 369.

26. Horsman, 163–64.

27. Stanley, 343–44.

28. Horsman, 189–92.

29. Stanley, 348–49.

30. Brant, 325.

TWENTY-FOUR: BREAKING POINTS

1. *State Papers, on the Negotiation and Peace with America, 1814* (London: Sherwood, Neely and Jones, 1815), 35–38.

2. Ibid., 33–35.

3. Charles Francis Adams, ed., *Memoirs of John Quincy Adams*, vol. 3 (Freeport, NY: Books for Libraries Press, 1969), 20–22.

4. "Letters from Henry Goulburn to Earl Bathurst: August 9th to December 30th, 1814," Lord Bathurst Papers, Reel H-2091, vol. A 8, MG 24, Library and Archives Canada, 200–202.

5. Adams, 20–23.

6. *State Papers, on the Negotiation and Peace with America, 1814*, 39–45.

7. "Letters from Henry Goulburn to Earl Bathurst," 203–4.

8. Charles William Vane, ed., *Correspondence, Despatches and Other Papers of Viscount Castlereagh, Second Marquess of Londonderry* (London: John Murray, 1853), 101–2.

9. Duke of Wellington, ed., *Supplementary Despatches, Correspondence, and Memoranda of Field Marshal Arthur Duke of Wellington, K.G.*, vol. 9 (London: John Murray, 1862), 214.

10. Worthington Chauncey Ford, ed., *Writings of John Quincy Adams: Volume V—1814–1816* (New York: Greenwood Press, 1968), 108.

11. "Letters from Henry Goulburn to Earl Bathurst," 206.

12. Adams, 24–30.

13. "Letters from Henry Goulburn to Earl Bathurst," 206.

14. Count Gallatin, ed., *The Diary of James Gallatin: Secretary to Albert Gallatin—A Great Peace Maker, 1813–1827* (New York: Charles Scribner's Sons, 1920), 30.

15. "Letters from Henry Goulburn to Earl Bathurst," 208.

16. *State Papers, on the Negotiation and Peace with America, 1814*, 45–50.

17. Adams, 31.

18. Ibid., 31–33.

19. *State Papers, on the Negotiation and Peace with America, 1814*, 50–57.

20. Ford, 132.

21. "1814 July–Dec, To Lord Gambier, Henry Goulburn, and William Adams from British Foreign Office," Foreign Office fonds B-2003, vol. 102, Library and Archives Canada, n.p.

22. Adams, 36.

23. "Letters from Henry Goulburn to Earl Bathurst," 213.

24. "Letters from Lord Liverpool to Earl Bathurst: August 9th to December 30th, 1814," Lord Bathurst Papers, Reel H-2091, vol. A 8, MG 24, Library and Archives Canada, 173–74.

25. Francis Bickley, ed., *Report on the Manuscripts of Earl Bathurst* (London: H. M. Stationery Office, 1923), 288–89.

TWENTY-FIVE: SHIFTING STANCES

1. "Letters from Henry Goulburn to Earl Bathurst: August 9th to December 30th, 1814," Lord Bathurst Papers, Reel H-2091, vol. A 8, MG 24, Library and Archives Canada, 209–10.

2. Reginald Horsman, *The War of 1812* (New York: Alfred A. Knopf, 1969), 225–29.

3. "Letters from Henry Goulburn to Earl Bathurst," 209.

4. Ibid., 210.

5. *State Papers, on the Negotiation and Peace with America, 1814* (London: Sherwood, Neely and Jones, 1815), 58–60.

6. Charles Francis Adams, ed., *Memoirs of John Quincy Adams*, vol. 3 (Freeport, NY: Books for Libraries Press, 1969), 36–38.

7. Count Gallatin, ed., *The Diary of James Gallatin: Secretary to Albert Gallatin—A Great Peace Maker, 1813–1827* (New York: Charles Scribner's Sons, 1920), 31–32.

8. *State Papers, on the Negotiation and Peace with America, 1814*, 61–68.

9. Fred L. Engelman, *The Peace of Christmas Eve* (London: Rupert Hart-Davis, 1962), 195–96.

10. Adams, 45.

11. Henry Adams, *The Life of Albert Gallatin* (New York: Peter Smith, 1943), 532–33.

12. Worthington Chauncey Ford, ed., *Writings of John Quincy Adams: Volume V—1814–1816* (New York: Greenwood Press, 1968), 149–51.

13. James F. Hopkins, ed., *The Papers of Henry Clay: Volume 1—The Rising Statesman, 1797–1814* (Lexington: University of Kentucky Press, 1959), 982.

14. "1814 July–Dec, To Lord Gambier, Henry Goulburn, and William Adams from British Foreign Office," Foreign Office fonds B-2003, vol. 102, Library and Archives Canada, n.p.

15. Bradford Perkins, *Castlereagh and Adams: England and the United States, 1812–1823* (Los Angeles: University of California Press, 1964), 95.

16. Duke of Wellington, ed., *Supplementary Dispatches, Correspondence, and Memoranda of Field Marshal Arthur Duke of Wellington, K.G.*, vol. 9 (London: John Murray, 1862), 290.

17. Ibid., 298.

18. "1814 July–Dec, To Lord Gambier, Henry Goulburn, and William Adams," n.p.

19. *State Papers, on the Negotiation and Peace with America, 1814*, 68–74.

20. Ibid., 74–78.

21. Charles Francis Adams, 50–53.

22. Ibid., 56.

23. Ralph Ketcham, *James Madison: A Biography* (New York: Macmillan, 1971), 591.

24. Irving Brant, *James Madison: Commander in Chief, 1812–1836* (New York: Bobbs-Merrill, 1961), 333.

25. Ibid., 335.

26. Ibid., 329–331.

27. Ketcham, 593.

28. Robert Allen Rutland, *The Presidency of James Madison* (Lawrence, KS: University Press of Kansas, 1990), 179.

29. Wellington, 367.

30. "Letters from Henry Goulburn to Earl Bathurst," 227.

31. Charles Francis Adams, 57.

32. *State Papers, on the Negotiation and Peace with America, 1814*, 81–82.

TWENTY-SIX: A GAME OF BRAG

1. Charles Francis Adams, ed., *Memoirs of John Quincy Adams*, vol. 3 (Freeport, NY: Books for Libraries Press, 1969), 60.

2. Ibid., 61–62.

3. Brian Jenkins, *Henry Goulburn, 1784–1856: A Political Biography* (Montreal: McGill-Queen's University Press, 1996), 85.

4. Duke of Wellington, ed., *Supplementary Dispatches, Correspondence, and Memoranda of Field Marshal Arthur Duke of Wellington, K.G.*, vol. 9 (London: John Murray, 1862), 404–5.

5. Adams, 60–67.

6. Wellington, 427.

7. "Letters from Henry Goulburn to Earl Bathurst: August 9th to December 30th, 1814," Lord Bathurst Papers, Reel H-2091, vol. A 8, MG 24, Library and Archives Canada, 232–35.

8. Wellington, 438.

9. "Letters from Henry Goulburn to Earl Bathurst," 236–39.

10. Adams, 70.

11. Ibid., 71–75.

12. Count Gallatin, ed., *The Diary of James Gallatin: Secretary to Albert Gallatin—A Great Peace Maker, 1813–1827* (New York: Charles Scribner's Sons, 1920), 34.

13. Adams, 76–78.

14. Frank A. Updyke, *The Diplomacy of the War of 1812* (Gloucester, MA: Peter Smith, 1965), 321.

15. Adams, 75.

16. Ibid., 79.

17. Bradford Perkins, *Castlereagh and Adams: England and the United States, 1812–1823* (Los Angeles: University of California Press, 1964), 123.

18. Adams, 89–90.

19. "Letters from Henry Goulburn to Earl Bathurst," 240–42.

20. Adams, 94–104.

21. Ibid., 105–12.

22. Updyke, 349–50.

23. "Letters from Henry Goulburn to Earl Bathurst," 249–50.

24. Adams, 119–27.

25. Henry Adams, ed., *The Writings of Albert Gallatin* (New York: Antiquarian Press, 1960), 645–47.

26. James F. Hopkins, ed., *The Papers of Henry Clay: Volume 1—The Rising Statesman, 1797–1814* (Lexington: University of Kentucky Press, 1959), 1007–8.

TWENTY-SEVEN: THE BLESSING OF PEACE

1. Bradford Perkins, *Castlereagh and Adams: England and the United States, 1812–1823* (Los Angeles: University of California Press, 1964), 129–30.

2. Worthington Chauncey Ford, ed., *Writings of John Quincy Adams: Volume V—1814–1816* (New York: Greenwood Press, 1968), 255.

3. Donald R. Hickey, *The War of 1812: A Forgotten Conflict* (Chicago: University of Illinois Press, 1989), 206.

4. A. T. Mahan, *Sea Power in its Relation to the War of 1812*, vol. 2 (Boston: Little, Brown, 1905), 389–90.

5. Reginald Horsman, *The War of 1812* (New York: Alfred A. Knopf, 1969), 238.

6. Mahan, 390.

7. Horsman, 238–39.

8. Ibid., 239–40.

9. Hickey, 207.

10. Horsman, 240–42.

11. Hickey, 210.

12. Horsman, 245.

13. Hickey, 207.

14. Horsman, 246–48.

15. Charles Francis Adams, ed., *Memoirs of John Quincy Adams*, vol. 3 (Freeport, NY: Books for Libraries Press, 1969), 138.

16. Ibid., 138–39.

17. Ford, 267.

18. Ibid., 268.

19. Adams, 144–45.

20. Theodore Roosevelt, *The Naval War of 1812* (Annapolis, MD: Naval Institute Press, 1882), 358–69.

21. Irving Brant, *James Madison: Commander in Chief, 1812–1836* (New York: Bobbs-Merrill, 1961), 360.

22. Philip S. Klein, ed., "Memoirs of a Senator from Pennsylvania: Jonathan Roberts, 1771–1854," *Pennsylvania Magazine of History and Biography*, vol. 62 (1938): 377.

23. Brant, 369.

EPILOGUE: HONOUR PRESERVED

1. "Address of Boston Federalists, February 27, 1815," *Boston Gazette* (Supplement), March 2, 1815, n.p.

2. Donald R. Hickey, *The War of 1812: A Forgotten Conflict* (Chicago: University of Illinois Press, 1989), 307.

3. Bradford Perkins, *Castlereagh and Adams: England and the United States, 1812–1823* (Los Angeles: University of California Press, 1964), 134.

4. Fred L. Engelman, *The Peace of Christmas Eve* (London: Rupert Hart-Davis, 1962), 295.

5. Henry Adams, *The Life of Albert Gallatin* (New York: Peter Smith, 1943), 678.

—

Books

Adams, Charles Francis, ed. *Memoirs of John Quincy Adams*. Freeport, NY: Books for Libraries Press, 1969.

Adams, Henry. *The Life of Albert Gallatin*. New York: Peter Smith, 1943.

———, ed. *The Writings of Albert Gallatin*. New York: Antiquarian Press, 1960.

Ammon, Harry. *James Monroe: The Quest For National Identity*. New York: McGraw-Hill, 1971.

Atcheson, Nathaniel. *Compressed View of the Points to be Discussed in Treating with the United States of America*. N.p., 1815.

Balinky, Alexander. *Albert Gallatin: Fiscal Theories and Policies*. New Brunswick, NJ: Rutgers University Press, 1958.

Bamford, Francis, and the Duke of Wellington, eds. *The Journal of Mrs. Arbuthnot, 1820–1832*. London: Macmillan, 1950.

Barnes, James. *Naval Actions of the War of 1812*. New York: Harper & Brothers Publishers, 1896.

Bartlett, C. S. *Castlereagh*. Toronto: Macmillan, 1966.

Beirne, Francis F. *The War of 1812*. Hamden, CT: Archon Books, 1965.

Bemis, Samuel Flagg. *The American Secretaries of State and their Diplomacy*. New York: Pageant Book Company, 1958.

———. *John Quincy Adams and the Foundations of American Foreign Policy*. New York: Alfred A. Knopf, 1956.

Benn, Carl. *The War of 1812*. Botley, Oxford: Osprey Publishers, 2002.

Berton, Pierre. *Flames Across the Border: 1813–1814*. Toronto: McClelland and Stewart, 1981.

———. *The Invasion of Canada: 1812–1813*. Toronto: McClelland and Stewart, 1980.

Bickley, Francis, ed. *Report on the Manuscripts of Earl Bathurst*. London: H. M. Stationery Office, 1923.

Bienkowski, Lee. *Admirals in the Age of Nelson*. Annapolis, MD: Naval Institute Press, 2003.

Bigham, Charles Clive. *The Prime Ministers of Britain, 1721–1921*. 4th ed. Freeport, NY: Books for Libraries Press, 1924.

Brant, Irving. *James Madison: Commander in Chief, 1812–1836*. New York: Bobbs-Merrill, 1961.

———. *James Madison: The President, 1809–1812*. New York: Bobbs-Merrill, 1956.

Chatterton, Lady Georgina. *Memorials, Personal and Historical of Admiral Lord Gambier, G.C.B.* London: Hurst and Blackett, 1861.

Coffin, William F. *1812—The War and the Moral: A Canadian Chronicle.* Montreal: John Lovell, 1864.

Colton, Calvin. *The Life, Correspondence, and Speeches of Henry Clay: Vol. I, Life and Times.* New York: A. S. Barnes, 1857.

———. *The Life, Correspondence, and Speeches of Henry Clay: Vol. IV, Correspondence.* New York: A. S. Barnes, 1857.

Dangerfield, George. *The Era of Good Feelings.* London: Methuen, 1953.

Derry, John W. *Castlereagh.* London: Penguin Books, 1976.

Drake, Benjamin. *Life of Tecumseh.* Cincinnati: n.p., 1841.

Dunlop, William. *Tiger Dunlop's Canada: Comprising Recollections of the American War 1812–1814, by a Backwoodsman.* Toronto: McClelland and Stewart, 1967.

Easterbrook, W. T., and Hugh G. J. Aitken. *Canadian Economic History.* Toronto: Macmillan Company of Canada, 1958.

Eaton, Clement. *Henry Clay and the Art of American Politics.* Toronto: Little, Brown, 1957.

Edmunds, R. David. *Tecumseh and the Quest for Indian Leadership.* Toronto: Little, Brown, 1984.

Engelman, Fred L. *The Peace of Christmas Eve.* London: Rupert Hart-Davis, 1962.

Ferguson, E. James, ed. *National Unity on Trial, 1781–1816.* New York: Random House, 1970.

———, ed. *Selected Writings of Albert Gallatin.* New York: Bobbs-Merrill, 1967.

Ferrell, Robert H. *American Diplomacy: A History.* 3rd ed. New York: W. W. Norton, 1975.

Fitzgibbon, Mary Agnes. *A Veteran of 1812: The Life of James Fitzgibbon.* Toronto: Prospero Books, 2000.

Ford, Worthington Chauncey. *The Treaty of Ghent, and After.* Madison, WI: State Historical Society of Wisconsin, 1915.

———, ed. *Writings of John Quincy Adams: Volume V—1814–1816.* New York: Greenwood Press, 1968.

Fryer, Mary Beacock, and Christopher Dracott. *John Graves Simcoe, 1752–1806: A Biography.* Toronto: Dundurn Press, 1998.

Gallatin, Count, ed. *The Diary of James Gallatin: Secretary to Albert Gallatin—A Great Peace Maker, 1813–1827.* New York: Charles Scribner's Sons, 1920.

Gleig, G. R. *The Campaigns of the British Army at Washington and New Orleans, 1814–1815.* London: John Murray, 1827.

Hecht, Marie B. *John Quincy Adams: A Personal History of an Independent Man.* New York: Macmillan, 1972.

Hickey, Donald R. *The War of 1812: A Forgotten Conflict.* Chicago: University of Illinois Press, 1989.

Hinde, Wendy. *Castlereagh.* London: William Collins Sons, 1981.

Hitsman, J. Mackay. *The Incredible War of 1812: A Military History.* Toronto: Robin Brass Studio, 1999.

Hopkins, James F., ed. *The Papers of Henry Clay: Volume 1—The Rising Statesman, 1797–1814.* Lexington: University of Kentucky Press, 1959.

Horsman, Reginald. *The Causes of the War of 1812.* New York: Octagon Books, 1972.

———. *The War of 1812.* New York: Alfred A. Knopf, 1969.

Jenkins, Brian. *Henry Goulburn, 1784–1856: A Political Biography.* Montreal: McGill-Queen's University Press, 1996.

Johnson, Paul. *A History of the American People*. London: Phoenix Giant, 1998.

Jones, Edgar Dewitt. *Lords of Speech: Portraits of Fifteen American Orators*. Freeport, NY: Books for Libraries Press, 1937.

Ketcham, Ralph. *James Madison: A Biography*. New York: Macmillan, 1971.

Kraus, Michael. *The United States to 1865*. Ann Arbor: University of Michigan Press, 1959.

Kuppenheimer, L. B. *Albert Gallatin's Vision of Democratic Stability: An Interpretative profile*. Westport, CT: Praeger, 1996.

Leigh, Ione. *Castlereagh*. London: Collins, 1951.

Lewis, Michael. *A Social History of the Navy, 1793–1815*. London: George Allen & Unwin, 1960.

Lossing, Benson. *The Pictorial Field Book of the War of 1812*. New York: Harper & Brothers Publishers, 1868.

Lowrie, Walter, et al., eds. *American State Papers: Documents, Legislative and Executive of the Congress of the United States*. Washington: n.p., 1832–1861.

Mahan, A. T. *Sea Power in its Relation to the War of 1812*. Boston: Little, Brown, 1905.

Mallory, Daniel, ed. *The Life and Speeches of the Hon. Henry Clay, Volume I*. New York: A. S. Barnes & Burr, 1860.

Manning, Helen Taft. *British Colonial Government After the American Revolution: 1782–1820*. Hamden, CT: Archon Books, 1966.

Manning, William R., ed. *Diplomatic Correspondence of the United States: Canadian Relations, 1784–1860*. Washington: Carnegie Endowment for International Peace, 1940.

Marriott, J. A. R. *Castlereagh: The Political Life of Robert, Second Marquess of Londonderry*. London: Methuen, 1936.

Maxwell, Sir Herbert. *A Century of Empire: 1801–1901*. London: Herbert Maxwell Edward Arnold, 1909.

———, ed. *The Creevey Papers: A Selection from the Correspondence & Diaries of the Late Thomas Creevey, M.P.* London: J. Murray, 1903.

Mayo, Bernard. *Henry Clay: Spokesman of the New West*. Boston: Archon Books, 1966.

Mooney, Booth. *Mr. Speaker: Four Men Who Shaped the United States House of Representatives*. Chicago: Follett Publishing, 1964.

Morison, S. E., ed. *John Quincy Adams and Others on the Peace of Ghent, 1814*. Boston: Old South Leaflets, 1917.

Morse, John T., Jr. *John Quincy Adams*. New York: Houghton, Mifflin, 1898.

Nagel, Paul C. *John Quincy Adams: A Public Life, a Private Life*. New York: Alfred A. Knopf, 1998.

Nevins, Allan, ed. *The Diary of John Quincy Adams, 1794–1845: American Diplomacy and Political, Social, and Intellectual Life, from Washington to Polk*. New York: Charles Scribner's Sons, 1951.

Parish, John C. *The Robert Lucas Journal of the War of 1812 During the Campaign Under General William Hull*. Iowa City: State Historical Society, 1906.

Perkins, Bradford. *Castlereagh and Adams: England and the United States, 1812–1823*. Los Angeles: University of California Press, 1964.

———, ed. *The Causes of the War of 1812: National Honor or National Interest?* New York: Holt, Rinehart and Winston, 1962.

————. *Prologue to War: England and the United States, 1805–1812.* Berkeley: University of California Press, 1961.

Petrie, Sir Charles. *Lord Liverpool and His Times.* London: James Barrie, 1954.

Plumer, William, ed. *Memorandum of Proceedings in the United States Senate, 1803–1807.* Edited by Everett Somerville Brown. New York: Macmillan, 1923.

Pratt, Julius W. *Expansionists of 1812.* New York: Macmillan, 1925.

Read, D. B. *Life and Times of Major-General Sir Isaac Brock.* Toronto: William Briggs, 1884.

Remini, Robert V. *Henry Clay: Statesman for the Union.* New York: W. W. Norton, 1991.

Richardson, John. *War of 1812.* Brockville, ON: n.p., 1842.

Roosevelt, Theodore. *The Naval War of 1812.* Annapolis, MD: Naval Institute Press, 1882.

Rutland, Robert Allen. *The Presidency of James Madison.* Lawrence, KS: University Press of Kansas, 1990.

Sargent, Epes. *The Life and Public Services of Henry Clay, down to 1848.* Edited by Horace Greeley. Philadelphia: Portland Coates, 1852.

Schurz, Carl. *Henry Clay, Vol. I.* New York: Frederick Unger Publishing, 1968.

Stagg, J. C. A. *Mr. Madison's War: Politics, Diplomacy, and Warfare in the Early American Republic, 1783–1830.* Princeton, NJ: Princeton University Press, 1983.

Stanley, George F. G. *The War of 1812: Land Operations.* Toronto: Macmillan of Canada, 1983.

State Papers, on the Negotiation and Peace with America, 1814. London: Sherwood, Neely and Jones, 1815.

Stephen, Leslie, and Sidney Lee, eds. *The Dictionary of National Biography.* London: Oxford University Press, 1937–1938.

Stevens, John Austen. *Albert Gallatin.* Boston: Houghton, Mifflin, 1972.

Strachey, Lytton, and Roger Fulford, eds. *The Greville Memoirs, 1814–1860.* London: Macmillan, 1938.

Sugden, John. *Tecumseh: A Life.* New York: Henry Holt, 1997.

Sutherland, Stuart, ed. *A Desire of Serving and Defending My Country: The War of 1812 Journals of William Hamilton Merritt.* Toronto: Iser Publications, 2001.

Tupper, Isaac, ed. *The Life and Correspondence of Major-General Sir Isaac Brock, K.B.* London: Simpkin, Marshall, 1847.

Updyke, Frank A. *The Diplomacy of the War of 1812.* Gloucester, MA: Peter Smith, 1964.

Vane, Charles William, ed. *Correspondence, Despatches and Other Papers of Viscount Castlereagh, Second Marquess of Londonderry.* London: John Murray, 1853.

Van Thal, Herbert. *The Prime Ministers, Volume the First: Sir Robert Walpole to Sir Robert Peel.* London: George Allen & Unwin, 1974.

Walters, Raymond, Jr. *Albert Gallatin: Jeffersonian Financier and Diplomat.* New York: Macmillan, 1957.

Wellington, Duke of, ed. *Supplementary Dispatches, Correspondence, and Memoranda of Field Marshal Arthur Duke of Wellington, K.G.* London: John Murray, 1862.

White, Patrick C. T., ed. *The Critical Years: American Foreign Policy, 1793–1823.* Toronto: John Wiley & Sons, 1970.

————. *A Nation on Trial: America and the War of 1812.* New York: John Wiley & Sons, 1965.

Wibley, Charles. *Political Portraits: Second Series.* London: Macmillan, 1923.

Wilkinson, James. *Memoirs of My Own Times.* Philadelphia: n.p., 1816.

Williams, J. S. *History of the Invasion and Capture of Washington*. New York: n.p., 1857.

Wood, William, ed. *Select British Documents of the Canadian War of 1812*. New York: Greenwood Press, 1968.

Woodford, Frank B. *Lewis Cass: The Last Jeffersonian*. New York: Octagon Books, 1973.

Yonge, Charles Duke. *Life and Administration of Robert Banks, Second Earl of Liverpool, K. G., Late Lord of the Treasury*. London: Macmillan, 1868.

Young, D. M. *The Colonial Office in the Early Nineteenth Century*. London: Longman's, 1961.

Zaslow, Morris, ed. *The Defended Border: Upper Canada and the War of 1812*. Toronto: Macmillan Company of Canada, 1964.

Zimmerman, James Fulton. *Impressment of American Seamen*. Port Washington, NY: Kennikat Press, 1966.

Articles & Journals

"Address of Boston Federalists, February 27, 1815," *Boston Gazette* (Supplement), March 2, 1815.

Donnan, Elizabeth, ed. "Papers of James A. Bayard, 1796–1815." *Annual Report of the American Historical Association for the Year 1913* (1915).

Klein, Philip S., ed. "Memoirs of a Senator from Pennsylvania: Jonathan Roberts, 1771–1854." *Pennsylvania Magazine of History and Biography*, vol. 62 (1938).

Sloane, William. *The Treaty of Ghent: An Address Delivered before the New York Historical Society on its One Hundredth and Tenth Anniversary, Tuesday November 17, 1914*. N.p., 1914.

Unpublished Sources

"1814 July–Dec, To Lord Gambier, Henry Goulburn, and William Adams from British Foreign Office," Foreign Office fonds B-2003, vol. 101, Library and Archives Canada.

Annals of Congress, 12th Cong., 1st sess., June 1812.

British Colonial Office Papers, Public Record Office.

Lord Bathurst Papers, MG 24, A 8, Library and Archives Canada.

Sir Isaac Brock Papers, MG 24, A 1, Library and Archives Canada.

A. Bulger Correspondence, MG 19, E 5, Library and Archives Canada.

Sir Alexander Cochrane Papers, MG 24, A 44, Library and Archives Canada.

Thomas Evans Collection, MG 24, F 70. Library and Archives Canada.

Sir George Prevost Papers, MG 24, A 9, Library and Archives Canada.

General Robinson Letter on Plattsburg, MG 24, F 21, Library and Archives Canada.

Sir John Sherbrooke Papers, MG 24, A 57, Library and Archives Canada.

Jonas Simonds, 1813–1814, MG 24, F 16. Library and Archives Canada.

INDEX

MARK ZUEHLKE is the author of many books about military history and the influence of the nation's war experiences on Canadian society including *Juno Beach*, *Holding Juno*, and *The Gothic Line*—part of a much-lauded trilogy tracing Canada's role in the World War II Italian campaign—and *The Canadian Military Atlas*. He lives in Victoria, British Columbia.